SCOTLAND:
MAPPING THE NATION

CHRISTOPHER FLEET studied Geography at the University of Durham. He is Senior Map Curator in the National Library of Scotland. In 2010, he was awarded the Fellowship of The Royal Scottish Geographical Society.

MARGARET WILKES is a Member of the Steering Committee of the Scottish Maps Forum, a Director of The Royal Scottish Geographical Society, Convenor of its Collections & Information Committee and Joint Chairman of its Edinburgh Centre.

CHARLES W.J. WITHERS is Professor of Historical Geography at the University of Edinburgh. He is a Fellow of the British Academy, the Royal Society of Edinburgh and The Royal Scottish Geographical Society.

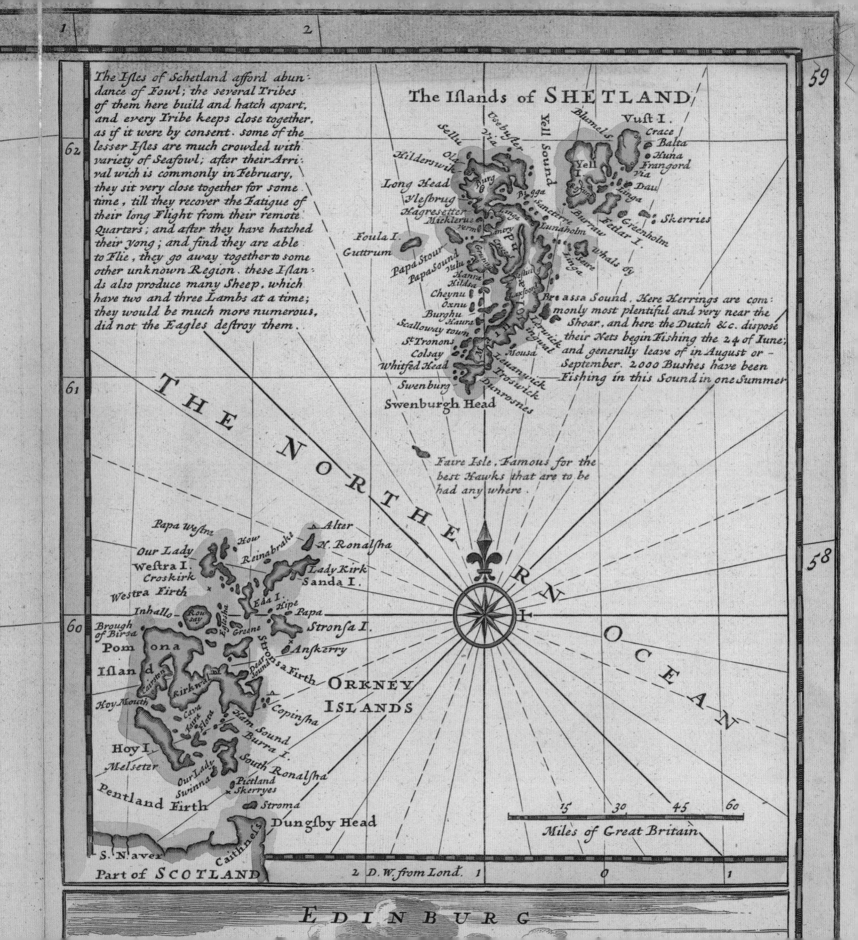

The Islands of SHETLAND

The Isles of Schetland afford abundance of Fowl; the several Tribes of them here build and hatch apart, and every Tribe keeps close together, as if it were by consent. some of the lesser Isles are much crowded with variety of Seafowl; after their Arrival wich is commonly in February, they sit very close together for some time, till they recover the Fatigue of their long Flight from their remote Quarters; and after they have hatched their yong; and find they are able to Flie, they go away together to some other unknown Region. these Islands also produce many Sheep. which have two and three Lambs at a time; they would be much more numerous, did not the Eagles destroy them.

Vust I.
Crace
Balta
Huna
Frangord
Via
Linga
Greenholm
Skerries
Fetlar I.
Whals Sy
Blumels
Voebuster
Via
Yell Sound
Sellu
Olla
Hilderswick
Long Head
Ylesbrug
Hagresetter
Micklerue
Foula I.
Guttrum
Papa Stour
PapaSound
Julu
Manza
Hildsa
Cheynu
Oxnu
Burghu
Haura
Scalloway town
St Tronons
Colsay
Whitsed Head
Swenburg
Swenburgh Head
Yell I.
Burg
Bragga
Sanctery
Lunaholm
Laxe
Linga
Nesting
Laxfoord
Lerwick
Ingual
Mousa
Lewanwick
Troswick
Dunrosnes
Dau
Zinga
Fetlar I.

Braassa Sound. Here Herrings are commonly most plentiful and very near the Shoar, and here the Dutch &c. dispose their Nets begin Fishing the 24 of Iune; and generally leave of in August or September. 2000 Bushes have been Fishing in this Sound in one Summer

THE NORTHERN OCEAN

Faire Isle. Famous for the best Hawks that are to be had any where

Papa Westra
Our Lady
Westra I.
Croskirk
Westra Firth
Inhallo
Brough of Birsa
Pomona Island
Hoy Mouth
Hoy I.
Melseter
Pentland Firth
How
Reinabrakt
Rousay
Eglisha
Greene
Eda I.
Hipe
Papa
Stronsa I.
Stronsa Firth
Anskerry
Dedrosound
Caya
Fara Flota
Ham Sound
Burra I.
South Ronalsha
Our Lady
Swinna
Pictland Skerryes
Stroma
Alter
N. Ronalsha
Lady Kirk
Sanda I.
Kirkwal
Caitnes
Copinsha

ORKNEY ISLANDS

Dungsby Head

S. N aver
Caithael's

15   30   45   60
Miles of Great Britain

2 D.W. from Lond. 1   0   1

EDINBURG

SCOTLAND:
MAPPING THE NATION

Christopher Fleet, Margaret Wilkes and Charles W.J. Withers

Birlinn *in association with the* National Library of Scotland

This edition first published in 2012 by
Birlinn Limited
West Newington House
10 Newington Road
Edinburgh
EH9 1QS

www.birlinn.co.uk

ISBN: 978 1 78027 091 3

British Library Cataloguing-in-Publication Data
A catalogue record for this book is available from the British Library

Designed and typeset by Mark Blackadder

Printed in Slovenia on behalf of Latitude Press

CONTENTS

Dunnas ness · Tofiness · How · Elnesholm
Selchfkerrie · Westnes · Clet · Holland · Overy · Everby · Oufkerrie
NORTH RANALS OY · Leny · Oren · S. Petre · STREONS OY
· SAND OY · Rodneiphead
Tungness · Myre · Spurnes · Linga
Whytmailness · Croscoy
Holm of Papa · Burness · Calf of Keth Oy
Ouquin · HETH OY
Papa · The Skyr · Green Tostes
Clafire · Redholm · Selchfkerry · Stroem holm
Akerness · Clet · Mo · SIAPINS OY · ILE
WESTRA OY · Holland · Miness
Westra · Fara · Fara · Kircbuster · Oert Sound
KNEY · holm · Roostholm · Sands · D
Tringness · Eglis Oy
Breck · Wyer · Hen of Gersa
ROOUS OY · Cors · Contreness · The Mule of D
Wasbuster · Gres Oy · The Baires of
Westnes · Dam · Kirkcwal · Kirkabuster
Athallow · Oy · A · N · COUPINS
The Brugh of Byrsa · Byrsa · Starch · Clart · Kyrth · Foubuster · Holm of Coupins
Sandwick · Stenes · Orfer · Hoom · The new work of Dee
Marwick · M · A · Clet · Rofeness
Mousland · Fara · Burra
The Comb of Hoy · S. Margeret Houp
Bow · Sandw · SOUTH RANALS
The most magnificent · S. Nicolas · Rysa · HOY · Barswick
natural Fort called Brabrugh · Rakwick · Mancole · Brughness
Sneucktourn · FLOTTA · Pentland or
Tornes · Snelster · Southa · Pichtland Skerri
PENTLAND · Souna · FYRT
Windieknap Head · Dungsby · Setre
Row Ra · Strath · Conansbey · Freswyck
Hoburn Head · Ratter · Okengill · No

FOREWORD

I have the enormous privilege of chairing the Board of Trustees of the National Library of Scotland and the pleasure here of writing a Foreword to this fascinating and beautifully produced book. *Scotland: Mapping the Nation* charts the development of maps and the mapping of and in Scotland over the past two millennia, describing the maps' changing purposes, languages and makers. It is the work of three enthusiast–experts, self-confessedly 'enthralled by maps', all with huge experience of revealing the secrets of maps to users of all kinds, and it is illustrated with an amazing range of images, mostly drawn from the collections of the National Library of Scotland. Much of the content was a real revelation to me, and I know it will be also to many other readers.

As I write this in 2010, we live in a world where developments in digital mapping technology are opening up multiple new ways of presenting maps for an ever-expanding range of users. Almost weekly, we are offered new kinds of overlays, new online maps, some of which present a series of successive images to show changes over time, or offer the ability to map variables selected by the user. But the old limitations still remain: the user is restricted to those elements of the 'real world' that the map-maker wants the map reader to see, largely within the map frameworks and range of scales that the maker has provided. Mappable information is never absolutely up to date. And, if we are to understand the result, we still need to know the symbolic conventions that are part of our own but not of other cultures: contour lines, orientation of maps with north at the top, today's colours for different kinds of roads, for example, are all comparatively recent inventions.

We can all speak from experience of working with maps. A few months ago, I was driving in broad daylight on the main road approaching the motorway outside Stirling. I did not need a map to access the motorway because I had driven this route dozens of times before. But the driver in front of me clearly did not know the road, and he was relying on his satellite navigation system to help him to understand the unknown. As he approached a new roundabout, he paused slightly as if puzzled, then followed his system's instructions and 'took the first exit' – and suddenly ground to a halt and did a rapid U-turn, as he realised he was entering the Auction Mart.

He, no doubt, cursed one perennial feature of his 'modern technology': it was 'out of date'. But had he been using a similarly out-of-date Ordnance Survey map he should have noticed that he had to cross a small river, and pass a garden centre, before reaching the motorway roundabout. His focus, and that of his rolling map, was on roads; most other details were deliberately omitted. Even if there had been a blue line on his picture, he might well not have realised its significance. His experience, compared with mine, nicely illustrates, for the modern world, some of the perennial features of maps and map use that are drawn out so wonderfully in this book. It is a work to read, with reward, and to savour.

Professor Michael Anderson, OBE, MA, PhD, Dr HC, FBA, FRSE, FRHistS, Hon FFA

PREFACE AND ACKNOWLEDGEMENTS

Maps are everywhere. On walls; hand held; as colourful city plans designed for tourists; on our TV screens as weather forecasts and location guides; in our vehicles; bound together as atlases and used in classrooms; stored and looked at in computer and satellite devices; and, even, of course, stored in our heads as mental maps, un-inscribed and almost innate ways of living in and dealing with space as we walk in our local neighbourhood or journey to work. Maps are commonplace objects, even taken-for-granted things. So are map-related metaphors: peace talks often refer to 'the road map' for the future, for example, to 'charting' the way forward.

Maps show the world, or portions of it. Even at a most basic level, however, maps do not straightforwardly correspond to the world, or even to the parts of it, that they purport to show. Things are missed out – they have to be – in order to simplify the map and make it clear to read. Those items that are included are, often, shown out of proportion – again, for the ease of the map user – but in ways that distort the real geography of places: motorways are shown on most travel maps as proportionally much larger than they are in reality. And because the geography of places may have changed since the map was made, maps can become out of date. Nor do maps always behave as we, the users, would want them to. J. M. Barrie, the Kirriemuir-born author best known for his *Peter Pan*, had clearly experienced what countless others have in working with maps when he wrote 'Shutting the map', part of his *An Auld Licht Manse and other Sketches*, in 1893. 'Prominent among the curses of civilisation', wrote Barrie, 'is the map that folds up "convenient for the pocket". There are men who can do almost anything except shut a map. It is calculated that the energy wasted yearly in denouncing these maps to their face would build the Eiffel Tower in thirteen weeks.' There will be few people who will not at one time or another have had their 'Barrie moment' with a map.

All these things are true. They are the basis to the commonplace nature of maps and in one way or another they speak, like Barrie's heartfelt complaint, to our experience of maps today. Because maps date and places change, there is a flourishing industry in making new maps, updating road atlases on paper or as electronic data. But it is also true that these are modern questions, modern experiences born of the place of the map, paper or electronic, in contemporary society. Such issues simply do not hold for the nature of maps in the past, or for the place of maps in society at different times. Today, for example, we use the commonest types of maps, road maps and route planners, most often to navigate the route from place A to place B, thinking of the geographical distance between those places either in terms of linear distance or as time. In the past, most maps were simply not used this way. There are exceptions, of course, but in general terms route maps as guides to travel were not invented until the end of the seventeenth century.

In the past, maps had different functions: these included being statements of political authority; or expressions not of accuracy and certainty regarding the shape of a nation but of symbolic representations of it. Maps, far from being commonplace and comprehensible to everyone, were relatively few in number, were the preserve of a literate minority, and, on occasion, came to be regarded as state secrets, so important and valuable was the information they contained – about such things as the location of ports and forts, the true extent of a country, or the line of a border. We now know, on the whole, how to 'read' a map and what a contour does, and that black shading is used to symbolise towns. But contour lines are modern inventions – partly by the French but also by map-makers in Scotland, towards the end of the eighteenth century – and symbols for urban places are likewise part of a rich yet complex cartographic vocabulary that has changed over time.

Simply put, maps and mapping have a history – actually, many histories. Maps have to be produced, and so we can think of a history of map-making, of technical capacity and printing styles. Maps have their uses and their users, from kings and generals to tourists and school children, so a history of maps includes elements of social history, political history and the history of education. Maps are much used in local history and in finding our way, in familiar environments and in unfamiliar ones where we trust the lines and colours shown on maps.

Maps are thus vital historical and geographical objects and sources which can help reveal how people in the past viewed their nation, or show what the countryside or town looked like at a certain moment. And because maps have a language – of lines and symbols, of scale, of colours to show different height ranges for hills for instance – map history is also a history of maps' language and of the cultural comprehension of maps, of understanding how to read them. Map history recognises that questions such as 'What is a map?' or 'How does a map work?' have neither single nor simple answers. Maps, then, are commonplace but complex objects. Precisely because they are both commonplace and complex, their interpretation requires care – and can be a source of rich reward.

This book focuses on these and other questions about maps, mapping and map history as they concern Scotland. It is the first of its kind to do so. It brings together a great many images of Scotland's maps with an interpretation of them in historical, intellectual and geographical context. This is not to say that there has not been important work done before now on Scottish maps, on the history of Scottish mapping and on Scotland's map-makers. The two volumes of *The Early Maps of Scotland*, produced by the Royal Scottish Geographical Society in 1973 and 1983 respectively, are still valuable, as, too, is *The Atlas of Scottish History*, published in 1996. As we show here, considerable work has been done on aspects of Scotland's map history, and we have drawn on such scholarship in what follows. But even the most recent of the *Early Maps* volumes is over twenty-five years old, and the *Atlas of Scottish History* is difficult to find outside of major libraries and pays no attention to the history of Scotland as a mapped object. Researchers in other subjects and countries have turned to the history of Scottish book production, for instance, to highlight the place of Scotland's first atlas in its European context, or have studied individual map-makers, map publishing forms, or simply individual maps, in ways which have greatly advanced understanding of Scotland's cartographic heritage. In the course of the last quarter of a century, the discipline of map history as a whole has undergone major change.

Technological advances now allow interrogation of the early maps of Scotland in ways not possible even a few years ago. Advances in computing and in electronic data management mean that many new maps are available online but not in conventional printed form. Computer systems and data storage programs mean that images of paper maps and maps 'born digital' can be stored and manipulated for study. In building upon this work, we want to draw together studies in the last twenty-five years or so on Scotland's map history, show how new technology can aid our understanding of maps and how it changed the nature of maps and, with reference to new ways of thinking in map history more generally, place Scotland's map history in wider context.

This book is the first to approach the study of the maps of Scotland in ways which both illuminate Scotland's geography and history and show how Scotland's maps and its map history have a history – indeed, are themselves the very 'stuff' of Scotland's history.

All books are collective enterprises. We owe a debt of gratitude to Hugh Andrew of Birlinn not just for his invitation to consider such a book but for his support and enthusiasm as we have tried to bring his vision of the project, and ours, into being. Our thanks also go to Andrew Simmons and the staff at Birlinn for their help. The book would not have been possible without the support of the National Library of Scotland, notably but not only the staff within the Map Division, who kindly facilitated access to the many images produced here. For their comments on earlier drafts, we owe a very great deal to Ian Cunningham, Jeff Stone and Bruce Gittings. We acknowledge the kind help of various institutions and individuals for their permission to reproduce figures here, without whose gracious support our discussion of the visual representation of Scotland's map history would have been the poorer: they are acknowledged individually throughout the book. We acknowledge with sincere thanks Professor Michael Anderson, Chairman of the Board of Trustees of the National Library of Scotland, for graciously providing the Foreword. And we owe a collective debt to the many people whose work on Scotland's maps, mapping and map history is incorporated here. It is our profound hope that they, and other readers, will find reward in what is intended as an accessible synthesis and interpretation of Scotland's rich and significant cartographic legacy.

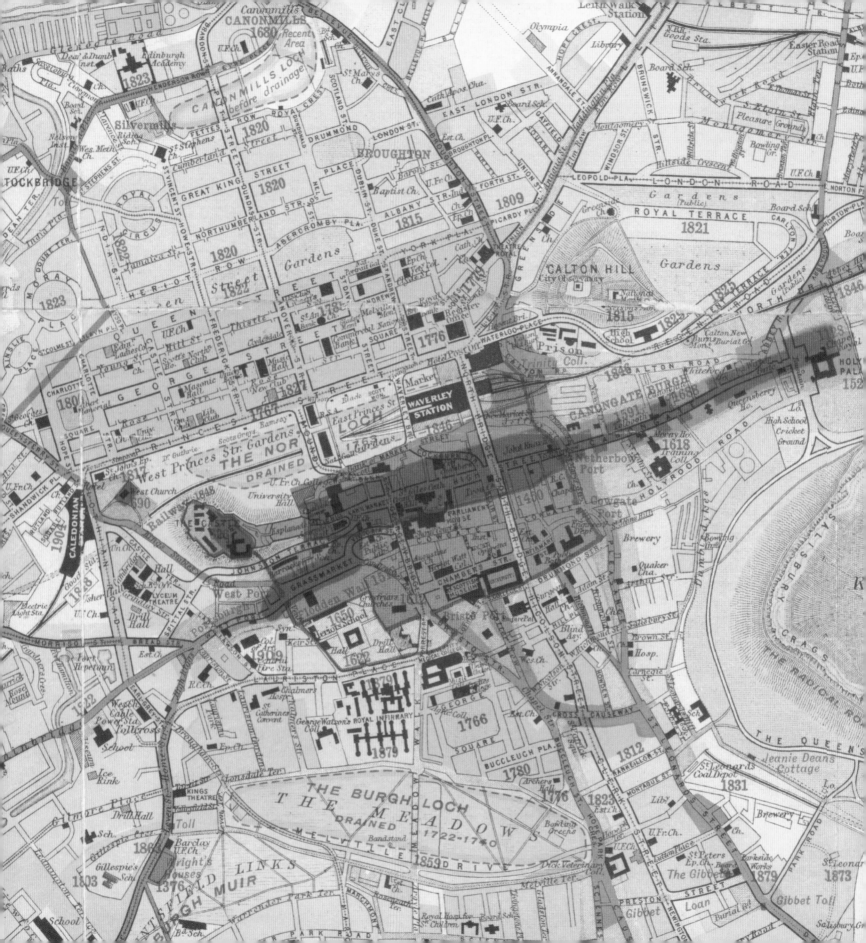

A TIMELINE OF
SCOTTISH MAP HISTORY

Landmark dates in Scotland's map history	Landmark dates in the history of cartography	Dates in Scottish and world history
c. AD150 Ptolemy's map of Scotland	*c.*150–AD160 Compilation by Ptolemy of *Geographia*	*c.*150 Polybius publishes first part of *Histories*
*c.*1250 Scotland appears on Matthew Paris's maps	1200–50 Invention of compass	*c.*1266 Seventh Crusade ends; Norway cedes Western Isles to Scotland
*c.*1360 Gough Map	*c.*1375 Catalan Atlas	*c.*1347–1354 Black Death sweeps Europe 1314 Battle of Bannockburn 1320 Declaration of Arbroath
1457 John Hardyng's map of Scotland	1472 First printed map	1455 Wars of the Roses begin 1456 Cape Verde islands discovered 1493 Lordship of the Isles abolished 1492 Columbus discovers New World; Vasco da Gama discovers sea route to India; 1507 Scotland's first printing press
1540 Scotland circumnavigated	1540 Sebastian Munster's *Geographia*	1513 Battle of Flodden 1540 Aztecs wiped out by Spanish

Landmark dates in Scotland's map history	Landmark dates in the history of cartography	Dates in Scottish and world history
1544–50 First military maps of Scotland		1544 The Rough Wooing
1566 First map to show Scotland alone	1569 Mercator's projection	1560 Reformation in Scotland
	1570 First printed 'modern' atlas, A. Ortelius's *Theatrum Orbis Terrarum*	
	1570–78 Christopher Saxton's county surveys	
1583 Nicolas de Nicolay's map of Scotland	1584 First printed sea atlas, L. J. Waghenaer's *Spieghel der Zeevaerdt*	1587 Mary Queen of Scots is beheaded 1588 Spanish Armada is defeated
	1585 Mercator's world atlas (first part)	
1596 T. Pont's only dated map	1610 John Speed publishes *Theatre of the Empire of Great Britain*	1601 First European sets foot on Australia; John Napier's logarithm tables published; 1603 Union of English and Scottish Crowns 1638 Signing of National Covenant
1647 James Gordon's bird's-eye view of Edinburgh	1645 Blaeu's England and Wales *Atlas Novus* Vol. IV	1647–49 British Civil War
1654 Publication of *Theatrum Orbis Terrarum, sive Atlas Novus* [the first 'atlas of Scotland'] Vol. V		1660 Monarchy restored in Scotland 1666 Newton discovers gravitation
1680–81 John Adair begins county mapping work	1675 J. Ogilby's *Britannia*	
1683 Modernisation of Board of Ordnance		1688–1746 Jacobite Uprisings 1692 Massacre of Glencoe 1695 Act for the Division of Commonties 1698–99 Darien scheme

Landmark dates in Scotland's map history	Landmark dates in the history of cartography	Dates in Scottish and world history
1703 J. Adair, *Description of the Sea-Coast and Islands of Scotland*		1707 Union of Parliaments of England and Scotland
1714 H. Moll, *The North Part of Great Britain called Scotland*		1722 First mineral waggonway in Scotland, Tranent to Cockenzie
		1724 General Wade appointed Commander-in-chief in North Britain
		1725 Bering Straits discovered
1734 J. Cowley, *Display of the Coasting Lines of Six Several Maps of North Britain*		
1747–55 Military Survey of Scotland under W. Roy	1744–89 Triangulation Survey of France	1746 Battle of Culloden
		1755–84 Commission for the Forfeited Annexed Estates
1750 M. Mackenzie, *Orcades*	1759 Society of Arts awards prizes for 'accurate actual surveys'	
		1768–71 First issue of *Encyclopaedia Britannica* (in Edinburgh)
		1768–90 Scotland's first Canal, the Forth & Clyde, constructed
1774 M. Mackenzie, *A Maritim Survey of Ireland and the West of Great Britain*		1775–1786 American War of Independence
		1786 Formation of British Fisheries Society
1774–76 'Schiehallion Experiment'		1789–99 French Revolution
1776 Taylor and Skinner – Scotland's first road atlas		
1791 Ordnance Survey founded		1791–99 *Statistical Account of Scotland*
1793 W. Roy, *Military Antiquities of the Romans in North Britain*		
1795 Hydrographic Office founded		
	1796 Invention of lithography	

Landmark dates in Scotland's map history	Landmark dates in the history of cartography	Dates in Scottish and world history
	1801 First Ordnance Survey Map	1801 First British Census 1803 Commission for Highland Roads and Bridges established 1803–15 Napoleonic Wars
1807 J. Arrowsmith, *Map of Scotland*		1807 First Sutherland Clearances
1808 L.A. Necker de Saussure's first geological map of Scotland		
		1811 First passenger railway (Kilmarnock & Troon) opened
1819 Ordnance Survey begins in Scotland (interrupted by 1823, not resumed until later 1830s)		
1825 W. & A. K. Johnston founded		1822 George IV visits Scotland (first visit by reigning monarch since 1651)
1826 Bartholomew company established under George Bartholomew		
1828 J. Wood, *Town Atlas of Scotland*		
1832 J. Thomson, *Atlas of Scotland*		1832 Cholera in Scotland; Great Reform Act
	1836–55 Tithe mapping of England and Wales	
	1841 HQ of Ordnance Survey established at Southampton	
1847 Ordnance Survey mapping begins		1847 Chloroform first used 1846–56 Highland potato famine 1853–56 Crimean War
1855 Ordnance Survey 1:2,500 mapping of rural areas		1856 First secret ballots in world (Tasmania) 1859 *Origin of Species* published 1870 Tramways Act

Landmark dates in Scotland's map history	Landmark dates in the history of cartography	Dates in Scottish and world history
1875–86 Bartholomew Reduced OS Half-Inch Series of Scotland		1883–84 Napier Commission 1884 Foundation of Royal Scottish Geographical Society
1889 John Bartholomew & Co. established as a private limited firm by John George Bartholomew		
1895 RSGS/Bartholomew *Atlas of Scotland* 1897–1909 Bathymetrical Survey of Scotland	1908 First photograph from an aeroplane	1901 Queen Victoria dies 1911 Amundsen first to reach South Pole 1914–18 First World War
	1928 First motorists' maps published	
1933–48 Land Utilisation Survey		1939–45 Second World War
1955–60 Five-volume Bartholomew/ Times *Atlas of the World*	1962 Re-triangulation and revision of geodetic levelling completed by Ordnance Survey	
		1969 First human on the Moon
1984 First digital map produced by Bartholomew		
1985 Bartholomew firm sold to News International		
		1988 Lockerbie disaster
1999 First *Times Comprehensive Atlas of the World* produced entirely digitally		1996 Stone of Destiny returned to Scotland; Scottish Parliament reconvenes after 272 years
2005 Geographical Information Strategy for Scotland		2004 Scottish Parliament building opens

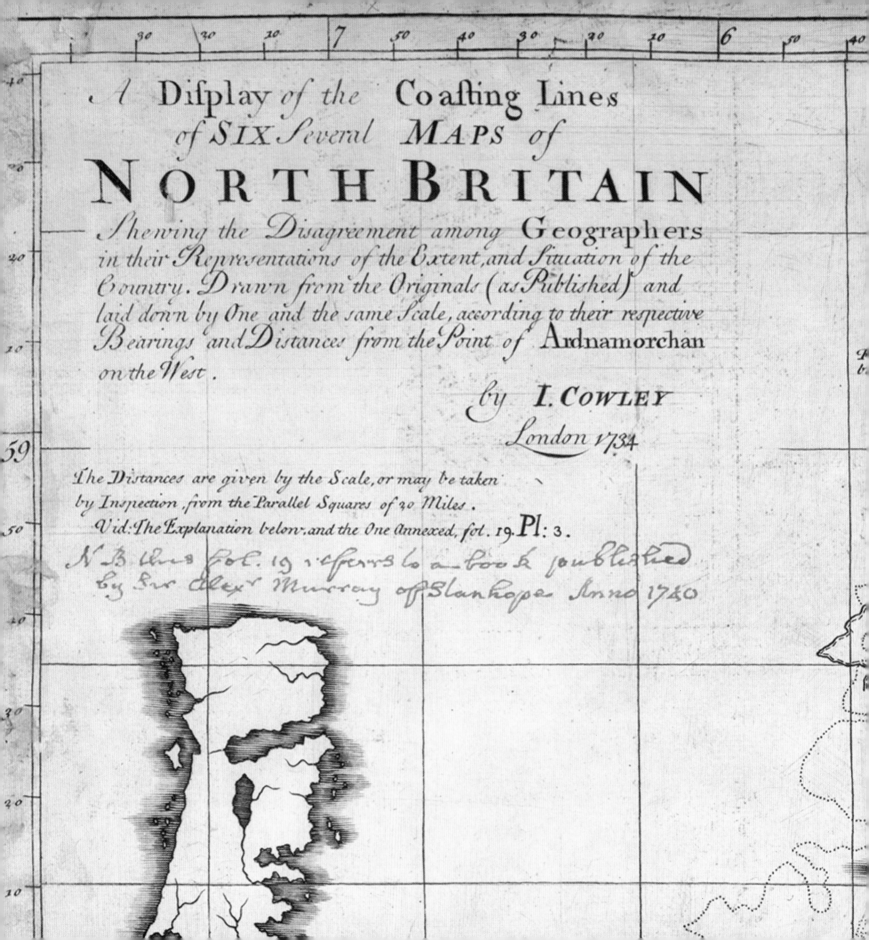

A Display of the Coasting Lines
of SIX Several MAPS of

NORTH BRITAIN

Shewing the Disagreement among Geographers
in their Representations of the Extent, and Situation of the
Country. Drawn from the Originals (as Published) and
laid down by One and the same Scale, according to their respective
Bearings and Distances from the Point of Ardnamorchan
on the West.

by I. COWLEY
London 1734

The Distances are given by the Scale, or may be taken
by Inspection, from the Parallel Squares of 20 Miles.
Vid: The Explanation below. and the One Annexed, fol. 19. Pl: 3.

N.B. this fol. 19 refers to a book published
by Sir Alexr Murray of Stanhope Anno 1740

CHAPTER I

PUTTING SCOTLAND ON THE MAP

I am told there are people who do not care for maps, and I find it hard to believe.

ROBERT LOUIS STEVENSON

Maps are commonplace and familiar objects – found at bus stops, in newspapers, as guides to walking, in atlases, on television screens and mobile phones. Most maps are understandable as simplified pictures of the world or a part of it, and are used to find a place – 'where in the world is that?' – or to make our way between places. We use maps of one form or another every day. We place our trust in them because, in one way or another, maps work.

Yet, for all their currency and utility, maps are also complex and unfamiliar things. Maps work, but not because they show a complete picture. Most of us recognise that the map is a problematic device of correspondence with the world when, as map readers and users, we encounter features that the map does not show. One reason why this happens is because, in their preparation and production of maps, map-makers leave out elements of the real world. Maps have to function at a scale of less than 1:1 – how could one produce, never mind consult and revise, a map that was at the same scale as the object it represented?

Maps do more than omit. They stylise what they do show, according to certain conventions, not according to the original objects' actual shape or real size: in everyday terms, think of churches with steeples as shown on modern Ordnance Survey maps, for example, or the symbols used for towns, or the lines and shadings employed to represent topography.

At the same time, maps, or more precisely their makers, may, and regularly do, make repeated claims to accuracy, to being 'up to date'. We buy and consult road atlases on the grounds that they are current, even to the extent of showing projected road and transport developments. But in any map there is always a time lag between its conception, production and publication. The 'up-to-dateness' of maps as records of place and space is always a matter of the gap in time between the now and the then. What is also true is that, because maps show the world selectively, and because they are always the product of someone's decision about what to show and how to show it, maps are never neutral things.

For these reasons, maps are not mirrors to the world. Maps are widespread and useful, but they are always

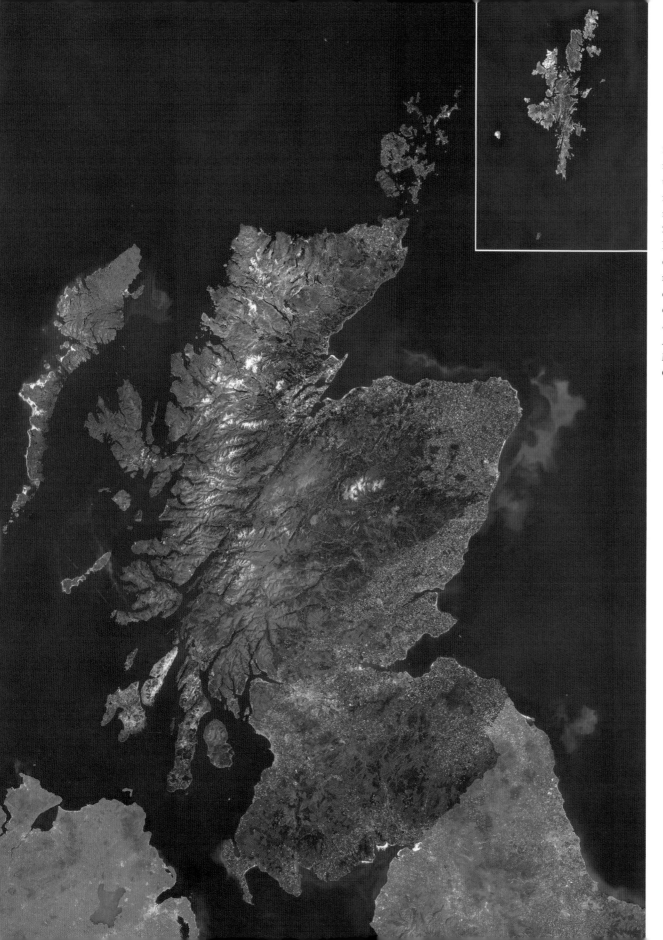

FIGURE 1.1 In this remotely sensed image of Scotland, the outline of the country is immediately recognisable: a familiar geography, made so by the many maps of Scotland that take this outline. But as other figures show – see especially fig. 1.2 – knowing and mapping Scotland's shape with certainty has been a long and distinctly uneven historical process. *Source*: *Scotland from Space: Satellite Maps/Realised by M-Sat*. Slough: M-Sat Ltd (*c.*1997). Copyright © PlanetObserver.

partial. As guides to the present and as keys to the past, maps and the processes that produce them require careful interpretation. Maps are visual sources: they can picture a nation (fig. 1.1). But they are also value-laden objects, and objects always have a history: of production, of use, of an underlying purpose.

Maps today have a common cultural currency as documents, as guides, as selective pictures of the world or parts of it. Yet this state of affairs has not always existed. Once, maps were the preserve of a literate few, precious objects written as manuscript not printed on paper, and were treated as state secrets: we shall see this of sixteenth-century maps (fig. 2.7), of military maps in the early eighteenth century (fig. 4.5) and of William Roy's military surveying in the 1750s (chapter 4). In the past, no less than today, maps would claim to be the work 'of the best authorities', or to be based on 'actual survey', or 'astronomical observations'. In such language, map-makers could assure their customers and different users of the 'modernity' of their work. Yet the world has, literally and metaphorically, changed shape throughout history. That this is true of Scotland is clear from the several 'Scotlands' outlined in fig. 1.2. Maps also need not be paper and portable to carry meaning (fig. 1.3).

Scotland's map history is a distinctive part of the world's map history. World maps produced in Europe before the 1490s did not show what came to be known as the 'New World' for the simple reason that, to European geographers and map-makers, the Americas had not been 'discovered' and so did not exist. By the late eighteenth century, uncertainty still surrounded the shape of the unknown new lands revealed in the southern oceans: Terrae Australes Incognita, from which we get Australia. As continental outlines were sketched with increasing certainty, map-makers of one sort or another – individuals

planning new estates, groups of military surveyors, institutional parties from Ordnance Survey or the Geological Survey – helped put territory and nations to order by way of maps. This is true of Scotland, as we shall see, in several ways: in the 'straightening' of the Great Glen; in the way Skye was put to shape by different map-makers (fig. 1.4, fig. 7.6). In the twentieth century, mapping was additionally undertaken using, firstly, aerial reconnaissance and, latterly, remote sensing and satellite imagery. Electronic maps now offer interactive components in representing space. At one level, any map is a technical accomplishment, and map history is a history of technical capacity.

At another level, maps always have a varied and rich content, and map history is a matter of its interpretation. Maps show things in place at a certain time. They thus reflect geographical and historical knowledge. But maps do more than reflect. They help produce such knowledge precisely because, in the absence of direct encounter with faraway lands, or the unknown nearer to home, the map becomes a powerful means of representing and imagining space, of producing geographical meaning even if the map does not conform in conventional cartographic fashion to the real world that it symbolises (fig. 1.5). Very few humans have voyaged beyond the earth's atmosphere and gravitational field to look down upon the dimensions of its continents, the course of the world's great rivers, the shape of its seas and oceans. But, with maps, we do not have to so escape our earthly bounds: we can hold an image of space in our hands. Someone, somewhere – the map-maker – has somehow reduced global dimensions to portability, turned immeasurable complexity to generalised simplicity, put lines and colours to good and effective use. In maps we trust.

All this is by way of stating that maps can show history in terms of changes in the geography of the world. They

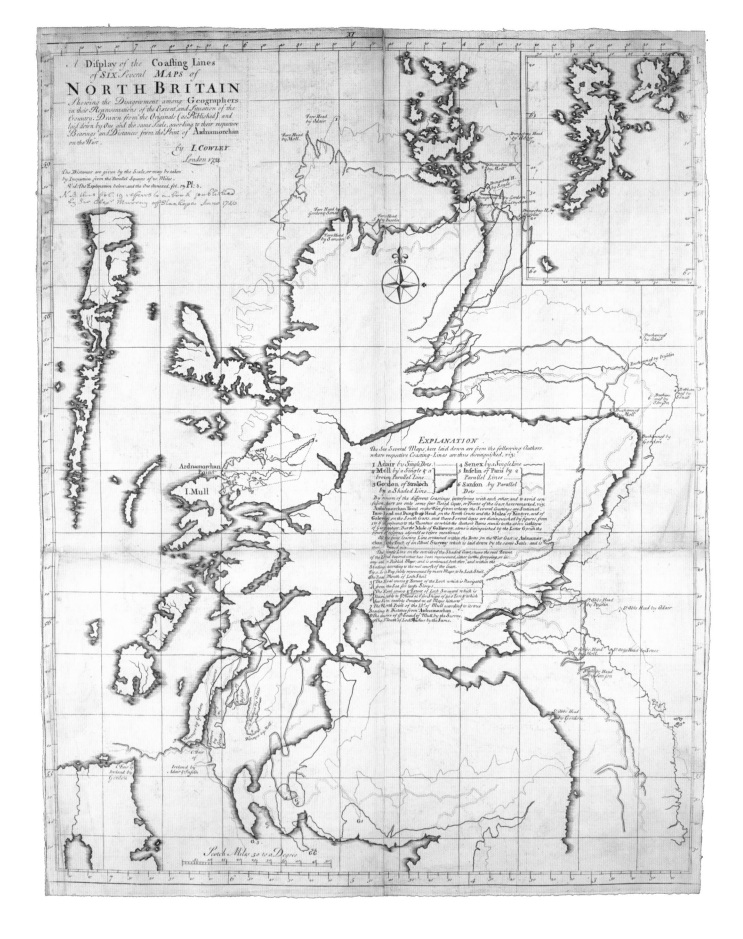

A Display of the Coasting Lines of SIX Several MAPS of
NORTH BRITAIN
Shewing the Disagreement among Geographers
in their Representations of the Extent and Situation of the
Country, Drawn from the Originals (as Published) and
laid down by One and the same Scale, according to their respective
Bearings and Distances from the Point of Ardnamorchan
on the West.

By I. COWLEY
London 1734

EXPLANATION

FIGURE 1.2 *Opposite*. This map of Scotland reveals the uncertainty of maps and of map-makers as to the exact outline of the country. Its maker, John Cowley, shows these differences by depicting the outlines of Scotland mapped by Robert Gordon of Straloch (in the Blaeu *Atlas of Scotland* of 1654), John Adair, Herman Moll, Nicolas Sanson, John Senex and Charles Inselin all on one map.
Source: John Cowley, *A Display of the Coasting Lines of Six Several Maps of North Britain* [Adair, Moll, Gordon of Straloch, Senex, Inselin, Sanson] (1733). Reproduced by permission of the Trustees of the National Library of Scotland.

FIGURE 1.3 *Above*. Maps are not just paper and portable objects. They can take unusual forms, as in this large concrete map, some 70 metres across, located just outside Eddleston, near Peebles. It was constructed in 1975 over seven weeks by a group of Poles working to the design of Kasimierz Trafas and intended as a permanent reminder of the hospitality given by Scotland to General Maczek's Polish forces during the Second World War. Bartholomew Half Inch Series maps were used to help render the outline and relief features correctly.
Source: General Stanislaw Maczek, Great Polish map of Scotland constructed in concrete (*c*.1975). Reproduced by permission of Adam Ward.

can show the changes over time in how places looked (fig. 1.6). They can depict past landscapes or features in it (fig. 1.7). Maps themselves have a history. And the study of maps and their production also has a history: the dissemination of maps in their different printed forms, for example, features within the history of print culture (fig. 1.8). In making sense of these inter-related issues, it is important that maps be read and understood on their own terms (fig. 1.9). What people called maps in the past may not be what we today understand by the term.

No less than today, maps in the past came in different types, reflecting different purposes. Thematic maps, which deliberately set out to illustrate geographical variations in a particular social or physical phenomenon, for example, and to do so according to administrative boundaries, are not the same thing as topographic maps, which set out to show a greater range of the physical or other geographical features of a place or region, often in stylised form and with established colour systems for things like height variations. The word 'cartography' – used widely if wrongly in relation to maps and map-making for all periods – did

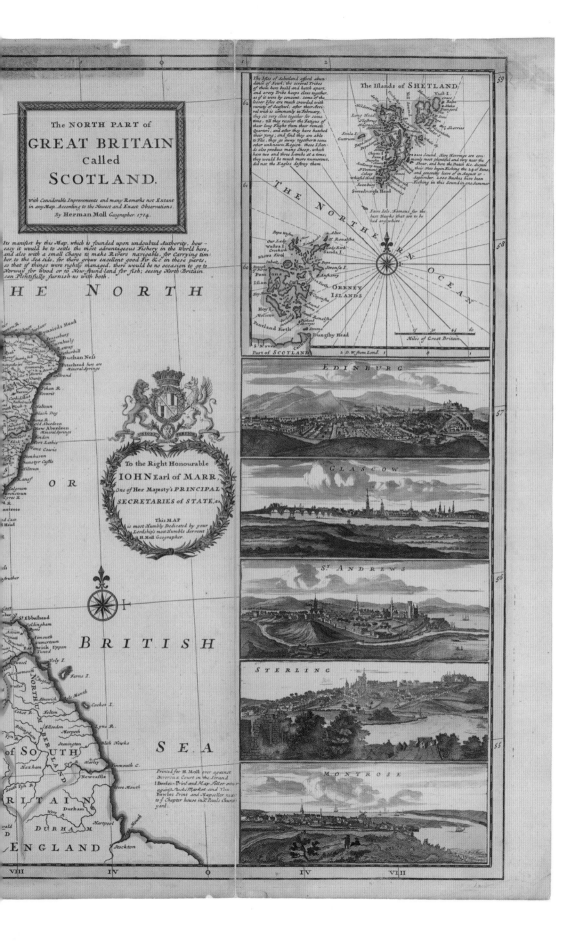

FIGURE 1.4 A map of Scotland in 1714, produced by the Dutch map-maker Herman Moll and based on the outline of the country laid down in Gerard Mercator's map of 1564. Several 'errant' features are notable – for example the 'crooked' line of the Great Glen, the blunt north end to the Island of Lewis and the orientation of Skye. Moll (like many other map-makers) based his map not upon detailed first-hand survey, which would have been expensive in time and money, but upon others' existing work, with the result that the outline of the country remained unchanged, though names and locations of places – the content of the country – were brought up to date. The depictions of the locations are taken from John Slezer's *Theatrum Scotiae* (1693)
Source: Herman Moll, *The North Part of Great Britain called Scotland* (1714). Reproduced by permission of the Trustees of the National Library of Scotland.

FIGURE 1.5 An example of cartography and caricature. The outline and the geographical content of Scotland in map form is secondary to the role played by the map as a space for the representation of symbols of Scottish identity: the kilted figure, the fisherwoman, the bagpipes and the fish, all designed carefully to fit the nation's geographical space. *Source*: John Bartholomew, *Philp's Comic Map of Scotland* (1882). Reproduced by permission of the Trustees of the National Library of Scotland.

8

FIGURE 1.6 The value of maps as comparative 'snapshots' in time is evident in these two images of the town of Coatbridge, in a period when it was at the heart of development of Scotland's principal mineral fields. Surrounded by collieries and with the huge ironworks at Gartsherrie (north of the town centre) and Dundyvan (immediately south of the town centre in the triangle of railway lines) on its outskirts, the map [A] shows the built form of this town in 1867. The *Ordnance Gazetteer* of 1885 adds a vivid description of the activity round the town: 'Fire, smoke and soot, with the roar and rattle of machinery, are its leading characteristics'. By the date of the later map, in 1904 (fig. 1.6B), the town has much expanded its suburbs to east and west, though by 1904 the dominance of the ironworks as a source of employment had passed its peak, and a chemical works is shown adjacent to Gartsherrie. *Source*: Ordnance Survey of Scotland, *One Inch to One Mile. Sheet 31, Airdrie* [A] 1867 and [B] 1904. Reproduced by permission of the Trustees of the National Library of Scotland.

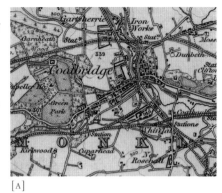

[A]

[B]

FIGURE 1.7 *Below.* Maps do not have to show the geography of their own time, but may be used to depict former geographies and relict features in the contemporary landscape. Here, the particular focus of attention is the Antonine Wall, and the general purpose is to portray Scotland as a land of antiquities and as a land once on the extreme edge of the Roman Empire. *Source*: Source: John Horsley, *A general map of Antoninus Pius's wall in Scotland* (1732). Reproduced by permission of the Trustees of the National Library of Scotland.

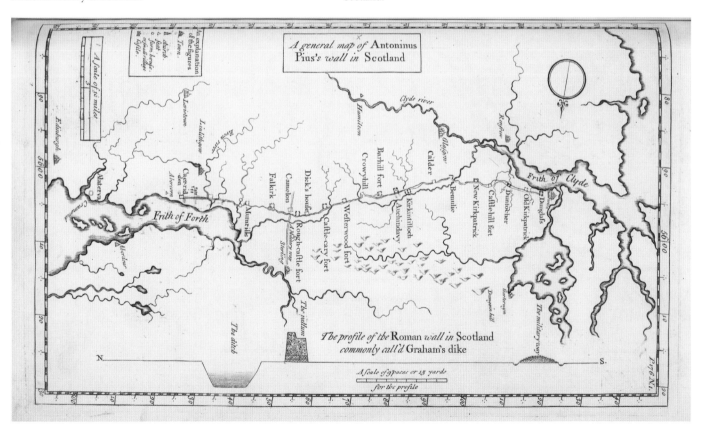

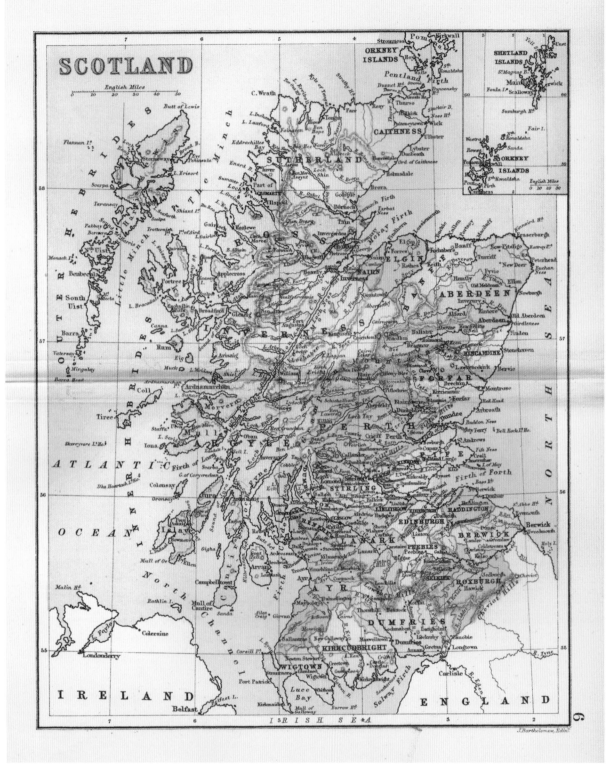

FIGURE 1.8 Books of maps – atlases – are commonplace but recent features in the history of mapping, originating in Europe mainly from the late sixteenth century. By the late eighteenth century and into the nineteenth century and beyond, atlases became widespread, providing maps drawn usually to a standard format and size, often for particular audiences such as schoolchildren. This map of Scotland is from the work of the Edinburgh-based map-maker John Bartholomew. *Source*: Bartholomew, 'Scotland', from Oliver and Boyd's *Handy Atlas of the World* (1881). Reproduced by permission of the Trustees of the National Library of Scotland.

FIGURE 1.9 *Left.* This detail from the cartouche to Ainslie's important 1789 map of Scotland illustrates the depictive and symbolic values often contained in maps. Here, cattle, sheep and a goat are shown, and they, together with the fishermen dragging their catch ashore, are intended to personify the products of those areas shown on the map itself.
Source: John Ainslie, *Scotland, Drawn and Engrav'd from a Series of Angles and Astronomical Observations . . .* (1789). Reproduced by permission of the Trustees of the National Library of Scotland.

FIGURE 1.10 *Overleaf.* In comparing the two maps of the Scottish estate of Loch Rutton, in 1774 (A) and 1815 (B), we are given a clear indication of the transformation of the Scottish farming and rural landscape. Note the characteristic representation of the open-field landscape, with the strips of land often worked by different land workers, and, in contrast, the landscape of 41 years later. In part, the sense of order and improvement apparent in the later map is a consequence of the map-makers' style, the use of more formal symbols and the portrayal of the Scottish countryside as the almost scenic locus of fruitful and efficient activity.
Source: Figure A: James Wells, *A Plan of the Barony of Lochrutton* (1774). Reproduced by permission of the Trustees of the National Library of Scotland. Figure B: William Mounsey, *A Plan of the Lochrutton Estate Comprending the Property in Loch Rutton and Urr Parishes in the Stewarty of Kirkcudbright belonging to Marmaduke Constable Maxwell . . .* (1815). Reproduced by permission of the Trustees of the National Library of Scotland.

not exist until the 1830s. Properly, the term denotes the more mathematically based production of maps from this period, given changes in the ways the natural and the social worlds were then becoming subject to detailed subject-specific scrutiny. The word 'scientist' with its modern connotations of professionalism, regulated methods of enquiry and social status appears at the same time for the same reasons. Map types, the status and terminology of maps and mapping have changed over time. We should recognise, too, that the meaning of maps and how they have been valued, their place in society, have been different in different ages.

These issues – about the production and use of maps, their commonplace nature, the fact that maps and mapping and map-makers have a history, and that maps can illuminate history and geography – lie at the heart of this book. In what follows, we show how Scotland has been depicted in maps at different times, and how Scotland has been geographically imagined through maps and mapping. Ours is an account not just of individual maps as artefacts. It is a story of the history of mapping in Scotland and of how Scotland's history and geography can be revealed through maps, be they political documents, estate plans (for example, fig. 1.10), marine charts, military sketches or tourist guides. Before we come to tell this story, however, it is helpful to address in a little more detail the history of maps, the nature of maps and their languages and forms.

[A]

[B]

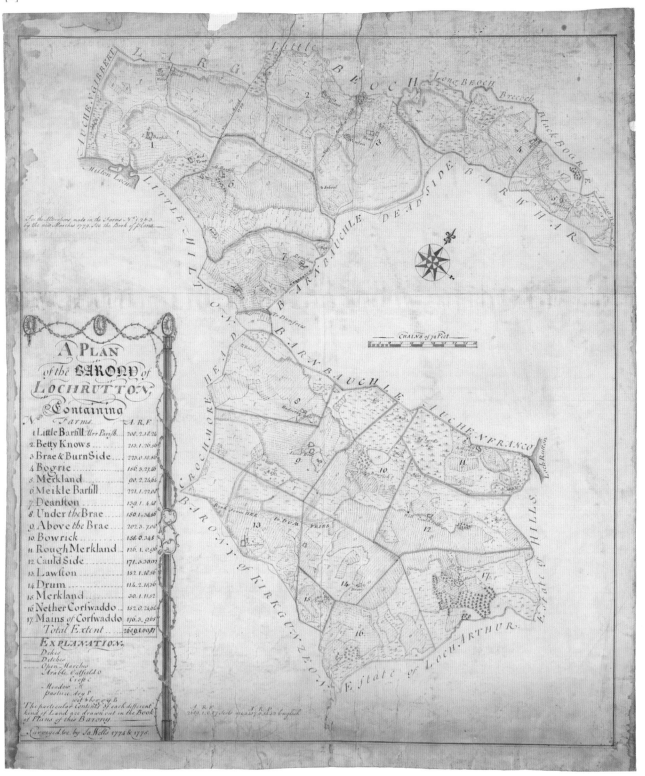

A PLAN of the BARONY of LOCHRUTTON Containing

No.	Farms	A. R. F
1	Little Barfill *Urr Parish*	208.2.18.24
2	Betty Knows	210.1.26.56
3	Brae & Burn Side	225.0.10.56
4	Bogrie	156.3.27.16
5	Merkland	90.2.24.64
6	Meikle Barfill	221.1.22.88
7	Deanston	120.1.4.48
8	Under the Brae	150.1.34.56
9	Above the Brae	202.3.7.08
10	Bowrick	156.0.34.8
11	Rough Merkland	126.1.0.96
12	Cauld Side	171.3.20.00
13	Lawston	152.1.10.56
14	Drum	114.2.16.56
15	Merkland	30.1.11.52
16	Nether Corswaddo	152.0.24.04
17	Mains of Corswaddo	176.3. 9.08
	Total Extent	2649.1.00.91

EXPLANATION.

Dikes
Ditches
Open Marches
Arable Outfield O
Croft C
Meadow M
Pasture dry P
wet & low C & B

The particular Contents of each different
kind of Land are drawn out in the Book
of Plans of this Barony.

Surveyed &c. by Ja. Wells 1774 & 1775.

CHAINS of 74 Feet

For the Alterations made in the Farms N.º 1, 2 & 3
by the new Marches 1778. See the Book of Plans.

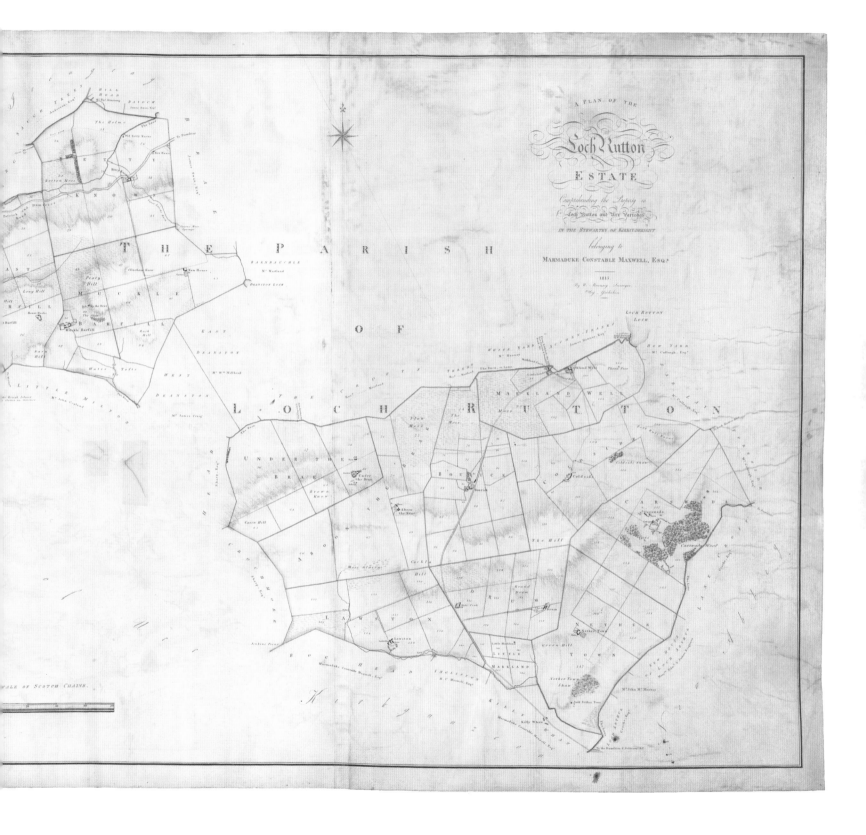

A PLAN OF THE

Loch Rutton

ESTATE

Comprehending the Property in
Loch Rutton and Urr Parishes
IN THE STEWARTRY OF KIRKCUDBRIGHT
belonging to
MARMADUKE CONSTABLE MAXWELL, ESQ.

1815

MAPS, MAPPING AND MAP HISTORY

As a form of communication, maps predate writing. What is taken to be the world's oldest known map is a town plan of a settlement in modern-day Turkey, and dates from about 6,500 years BC. Humans have been mapping for 3,000 years before they were writing. World map history is thus almost 8,500 years old, and map history begins not on paper but on plaster. Maps printed on paper were once dominant, but computer-based mapping is now common: we cannot know what forms of delivery the future holds for maps.

It is not appropriate to think of maps as having a single and simple history. Mapping traditions and practices in one country are not necessarily the same as in another. What counts as a map often results from the interests and practices of particular persons being promoted over those of others: of colonial surveyors in the Americas over indigenous peoples, for instance, or of the instrumental plotting of European explorers over their African guides' hand-drawn sketches, and so on. Understanding the history of maps importantly depends upon where you start from.

From a European perspective, in which context Scotland's maps and map history must be placed, maps were important in Classical Europe and in the intellectual and practical worlds of medieval Christendom. There, as well as in the caliphates of the Islamic world, amongst India's princely states and in the imperial courts of the Far East, maps served to delimit territory, indicate trade routes and express geographical identity.

In Europe especially, the history of the map is linked indivisibly to the power of the Christian Church and to the related rise of the nation state, including European nations' colonialist and imperial projects. That is why,

broadly speaking, many Renaissance maps and early atlases were produced in Italian city-states such as Venice with its myriad trade interests. That is why, as the world was carved in parchment and ink, the lines of Spanish and Portuguese settlement in the New World were sanctioned by Pope Alexander VI, why Iberian patrons and map-makers led the world in the sixteenth century as their navigators circumscribed the globe, extended trade routes, stretched the geographical imagination and so required that maps be drawn anew. And, as Italian and Iberian mercantile and political authority waned and that of the Low Countries grew, throughout the seventeenth century, that is why European map-making became dominated by cities like Antwerp and Amsterdam rather than Lisbon and Venice, and why mapping then became associated with the rise of the mathematical sciences promoted by men less hidebound by religious dogma. As the imperial, military and mercantile interests of the French superseded the Dutch, and, from the later eighteenth century, those of the British in turn superseded the French, so maps of the land and charts of the seas everywhere emphasised the ordering of space, the authority of map-makers and the interests of the state.

Such brevity does scant justice, of course, to complex histories, to different types of maps and to their different purposes, and it overplays the nation as the standard measuring device for the history of maps. But it serves to endorse the centrality of the map to European and other cultures and the act of mapping as an expression of political and intellectual authority – and so helps place Scotland's mapping story.

What is surprising given this millennia-long presence of maps in world culture is how recent the historical study of maps is. Maps were studied in the past because they were useful in one way or another. Map collecting was the fashionable pursuit of a few from the later seventeenth century if not earlier, at much the same time as maps and globes began to have a status as domestic adornments for the well-to-do. But the serious study of maps – map history or the history of cartography – is less than 150 years old. As with other histories, different views have been taken by map historians at one time or another over what a map is and does. The details of these differences need not concern us but the essential features are instructive.

What may be called 'traditional map history' – that range of activity undertaken before about 1990 – tended to focus on maps produced by Europeans in the period between the Renaissance, at the end of the fifteenth century, and the Enlightenment, at the end of the eighteenth century. On the whole, emphasis was placed upon map history as a story of technical improvement over time, of maps as increasingly accurate and faithful documents and of map-making as a chronological narrative of progress. Further, as mapping became more 'modern', so it shed its artistic embellishments (see fig. 1.11). Mapping embraced a language of increasing plainness: ornate decorative motifs praising kings, for example, were dispensed with in favour of simple lines, scale bars and acknowledgements to government agencies. Plainness, it was felt, endorsed the language of accuracy. Map history was a narrative of the shift from artistic inaccuracy to scientific exactitude.

Within the last twenty years, these views within map history have been profoundly challenged. New theoretical and explanatory arguments have ousted descriptive enquiries. Chronological narratives of progress have been replaced by cross-cultural viewpoints. Europe's place in

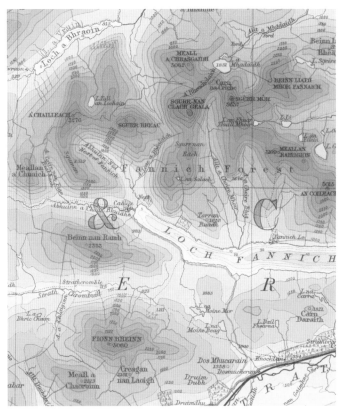

FIGURE 1.11 Topographic maps – for example, showing stylised colour-based conventions for changes in height of the land and depth of the waters – appear only from the mid-nineteenth century. This example is taken from the work of Bartholomew map-makers, who became internationally famous for perfecting the use of layer colours in depicting relief. Their half-inch to the mile series, first completed for Scotland in 1894, was used for a range of later maps, including this one in the *Survey Atlas of Scotland* of 1912.
Source: Bartholomew, Detail of Loch Fannich environs, from Bartholomew *Survey Atlas of Scotland*, plate 45 (1912). Reproduced by permission of the Trustees of the National Library of Scotland.

map history has been complemented by the study of mapping traditions elsewhere. Less attention has been devoted to the aesthetics of maps and more to their function, away from maps' 'beauty' to their 'visual form', so to speak. Perhaps more than anything, historians of maps have become attentive to the use and meaning of maps, to their social and political context. Discussion of what a map is, how maps work and what maps mean is now an interdisciplinary undertaking.

For these reasons, and from our perspective now, it is inappropriate to consider map history in terms of a language of betterment and improvement, to see mapping as simply a matter of technological advance, to see maps in the past as having utility only in terms of their accuracy to the modern reader. To do so is to read early maps from only a limited point of view and to attribute meaning and importance to them only in relation to our notions – of accuracy just as a matter of correct measurement, for example, or in terms of the location or dimensions of a selected feature. What if the map-maker's purpose in the past was not about accuracy of depiction but praise for a patron (as many were)? What if the tools and procedures were different (as they were)? What if the institutions which undertook mapping in the past were different from today's (as they were)? We cannot attribute significance to

earlier and different maps by reading them with modern eyes and by using terms like 'That's a better map than that one', or 'That map is not very accurate', without recognising that the nature and function of maps and the values contained in them have changed over time.

Because of all of this, for Scotland's and for other countries' maps and map history, it is not sensible to ask in the abstract 'What is a map?'. It is better, perhaps, to ask 'What does a map do?' 'How does a map work?' or, 'For whom does a map work?' Just like other forms of text, maps have 'authors' – map-maker was a common term in the past – publishers and 'readers'. But how do we make a map? Direct personal survey of the area of ground in question is one answer. But such was not always possible – and it is certainly not common even today where revision of maps for later editions is based on satellite imagery and inference from only a few measured locations. Maps also result from word-of-mouth information, from testimony given rather than from first-hand observation or instrumental reading. Maps may capture the lie of the land in the sense of its topography, but they often also lie about the land, by omitting things, reducing complexity to simple forms, subtle variations in the landscape to straight lines and fixed colours. Maps are powerful documents for lending false certainty.

THE POWER AND GLORY OF MAPS

Maps have a language as well as a history. Where we now understand terms like 'scale' and 'symbol', know what a contour line does, and take for granted that maps are orientated with north to the top, this has not always been the case. Each of these terms, like the word 'map' itself, has a history. The term 'orientation', for instance, derives from the fact that early medieval Christian maps of Europe centred upon Jerusalem, with the Mediterranean Sea running lengthways, top to bottom of the page so to say, which had the effect of placing East (the Orient) at the 'top' of the map – hence, to orientate the map.

Most of us are probably more familiar than most of our forebears with the map and with its languages and uses. But this may be because we are more familiar with what we think a map is than we are with the processes of mapping or with the precise language of maps and their production – a language of 'projections', 'triangulation', 'graticules' and 'prime meridian', to name only a few terms. And while computer-based maps on screens, satellite navigation systems in vehicles and remotely sensed images now supplement their paper counterparts, they often do so to the neglect of what might be taken as proper cartographic vocabulary – a north arrow, scale bars, and so on.

The idea that maps have a language – indeed, that maps *are* a kind of visual language – is one of the most important features of the modern history of mapping since the 1990s. Amongst the most important words used in the language of maps is scale. But scale, at least as it is understood today as the expression of the mathematical ratio of the size of the map to the size of that bit of the world being mapped, can be given in different ways – thus making map comparison awkward. Notions of a standard scale over time and between different countries' mapping traditions simply do not hold. Symbol is also an important mapping term. Here, too, certain conventions have become familiar to us: 'molehills' in two or three dimensions signifying hilly ground, for instance, giving way to sketched lines called 'hachures' or 'hachuring', where the closeness of the lines indicated steepness as the terrain was seen in plan view, and then to that simple, subtle yet misleading device, the contour line, whose delineation as an unbroken lines hides the fact that it is based on scattered point measurements.

A further idea to emerge from modern map history is that maps express and embody power and authority. This point about maps and power can be divided, albeit not always neatly, into two. Power is internal to any map as a depiction of the world since, in certain stylised ways, the form it takes and the visual language it employs are always the result of somebody's decision. Because they miss things out – they select and they generalise – maps also omit and silence. Power is also external to the map in the sense that, as a document or artefact, maps prompt action. Maps guide soldiers and boy scouts, tourists and travellers. But the benign power of maps has its malign parallels: maps may be deliberately deceitful, distorting relationships to make a political point.

Maps, then, have a history, a language, a content and a context. Maps and the processes of mapping are always part of wider histories – of printing, or of geographical exploration, of scientific survey, of the growth of towns and cities, of changes in the countryside and in rural life. Maps themselves are at once historical and geographical objects. In illuminating our understanding of the past, maps from an earlier time may depict a place as once it

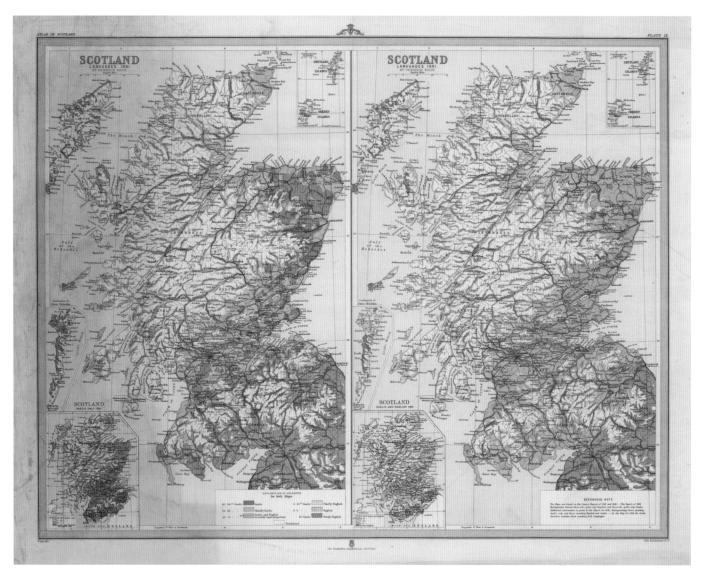

was or appeared to be. Maps are, nevertheless, essentially static pictures, even of something as dynamic as language (fig. 1.12). Maps alone seldom reveal why or precisely when that rural landscape or that city's streets, to take just two examples, changed in their form and with what consequences. In contemporary society, maps are widely used to plot the geographical patterns of certain social phenomena: 'hot spots' of urban crime, the incidence of disease, even to predict flood patterns at some point in the future. In the 1850s, this sort of thematic distribution map was a major innovation. But, at any time, such maps alone do not offer explanations of the social and natural processes determining these events and patterns.

Maps are both artistic and scientific objects. They are illustrative devices which may show, for example, the symbolic significance of a geographical or other feature

18

FIGURE 1.12 *Opposite*. These maps, showing the percentages of Gaelic speakers from the censuses of 1881 and 1891, are examples of thematic maps. Such maps are useful in depicting geographical variations in phenomena, but sometimes misleading since they may suggest that such variations alter sharply at administrative boundaries when, in reality, the variation is more subtle. *Source*: Friedrich Bosse, 'Scotland: Languages. 1881 and 1891'. Plate 9 of *The Royal Scottish Geographical Society's Atlas of Scotland by J. G. Bartholomew* (1895). Reproduced by permission of the Trustees of the National Library of Scotland.

FIGURE 1.13 *Left*. Maps can be used as part of the description and communication of scientific ideas. Here, Charles Piazzi Smyth, Regis Professor of Astronomy at the University of Edinburgh, delimits the different 'sound geographies' of the one o'clock gun sited at Edinburgh Castle: note the 1 second and 5 second time distances he plots, each as a concentric circle, from the point of explosion. In reality, these sound contours vary according to wind direction and air temperature. *Source*: W. & A. K. Johnston, *Hislop's Time-Gun Map of Edinburgh & Leith* ('Time circles each one second, number of rings distant from Gun indicate no. of seconds for sound to travel.') (1881). Reproduced by permission of the Trustees of the National Library of Scotland.

rather than its accurate delineation. Maps are one form of visual method used in ordering the world according to certain principles, such as the use of standardised measurement: think of graphs, statistical diagrams, even photography (fig. 1.13). It is not helpful to think of art and science as separate categories in maps and map history. Every map is a work of art and of science. Maps do not, then, simply reflect what is 'out there' in the world: they help frame the pictures people have of the world and help illuminate our understanding of the relationships between things and places.

In these and in other ways, maps are fascinating and vital documents and that is why they play – and have played – an intrinsic part in most people's lives.

MAPS, MAP HISTORY, MAPPING SCOTLAND

Three underlying and related themes or aims drive our concerns.

The first is with Scotland on the map. We want to show when and how Scotland has been shown on maps, at different times and in different ways. In looking at when and how Scotland was put on the map, it is our intention to record something of this changing depiction of Scotland as part of other, wider, cartographic concerns. Scotland appeared as part of maps of Britain and of Europe, for example, long before it was itself the object of a single map. Yet, by the mid-seventeenth century, Scotland was, arguably, one of the best-mapped countries in Europe. Our first aim, then, is to focus on Scotland as the subject of mapping, and to examine how and why Scotland became, and has continued to be, a mappable object.

The second aim is directed at Scotland's map history. We want to show how maps of Scotland have a history. Rather than treat maps of Scotland simply as artefacts, we want to illuminate the context to the nation's maps, to show something of why Scotland's maps look as they do at different periods and for different themes. Scotland's map history cannot be understood by reference to the maps alone (fig. 1.14). As we show, 'behind' the nation's maps lie stories of political intrigue, of kingly ambition, moments of individual enterprise and institutional success, and moments of failure, of mapping plans abandoned or unevenly effected – even, for the unfortunate William Edgar, a story of death through overwork whilst working on maps to aid the Hanoverian government in the 1740s.

Our third aim is to show how maps provide illuminating and powerful documents for understanding Scotland's history and its geography. More than just powerful: vital. Maps have been and are used in Scotland and of Scotland as political documents, as educational tools and to illustrate scientific understanding. Town maps whose initial conception was with urban sanitation now show alterations in urban form. Estate plans capture the patterns of change in Scotland's countryside as it was transformed in the eighteenth and nineteenth centuries. There are maps of battles on Scottish soil, several, to take just one example, of Culloden, the last mainland battle in Britain. But just as this highly charged event in British history has produced different views amongst later political and social historians as to its significance, so it prompted different contemporary maps, by map-makers with Jacobite sympathies and by those keen to demonstrate their loyalty to the Hanoverians. Now and in the past, maps provide a key basis to Scotland's civic and political administration, guides to recreational use and plans for city growth or developments in transport and communication. Maps show that the names we employ to record features and places are not constant (fig. 1.15). And, like everyone else, Scots carry maps in their heads, 'mental maps', and use such maps and the metaphorical language of mapping as

FIGURE 1.14 *Opposite*. This extract from Emanuel Bowen's map of 1746 is one of several in this edition to have the additional imprint 'Published Feb: 24th 1745' – that is, the old-style dating for February 1746. Bowen here adopts a convention characteristic of the time, that of promoting his 'new & accurate map' on the grounds of it being drawn from surveys, and from using other 'approved Maps & Charts'. Note, too, the hierarchy of towns in the key, the use of symbols and the text commentary which makes reference to 'astronomical observations' – that is, to the use of measurement – and the use of others' earlier maps such as 'Bryce's Survey' [of 1744] (see fig. 6.2).
Source: Emanuel Bowen, *A New & Accurate Map of Scotland or North Britain* (1746). Reproduced by permission of the Trustees of the National Library of Scotland.

A NEW MAP OF SCOTLAND OR NORTH BRITAIN

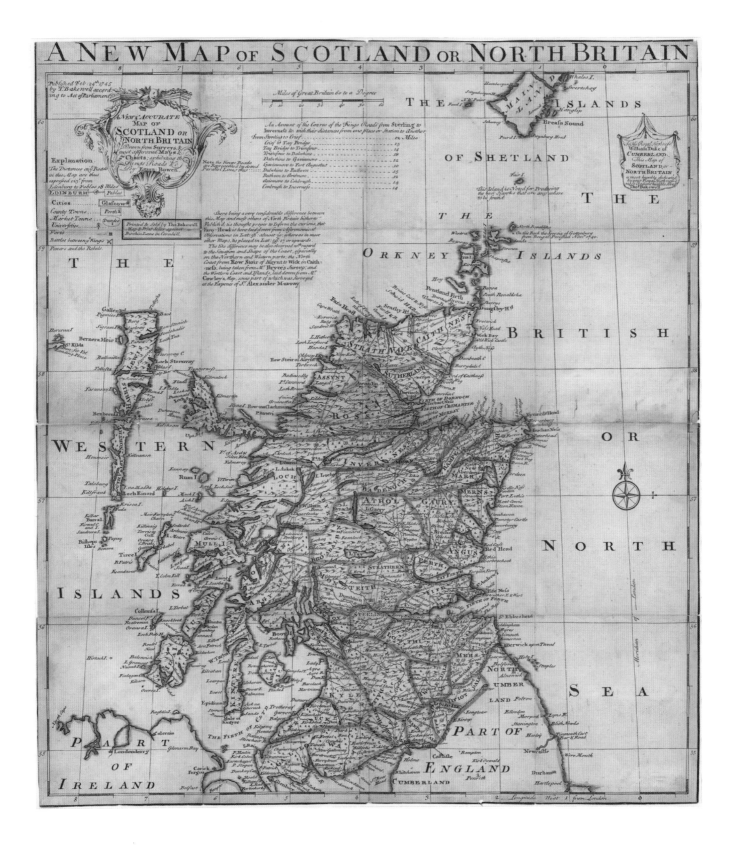

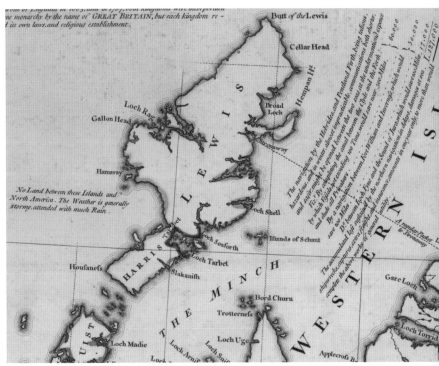

FIGURE 1.15 (a) *Opposite and detail above.* This glorious representation of Scotland by a leading Amsterdam map-maker coincided with the beginning of the joint reign in Scotland of William and Mary II. The map-maker's clever use of colour in depicting the boundaries and areas of the different provinces of Scotland, as well as the inclusion of the symbols of kingship and nationhood − lion, unicorn, crown and royal insignia with suitably gilded embellishment − add immeasurably to the grand effect of the map. But, unlike John Knox a hundred years later (see 1.15b), despite putting place names at right angles to the coastline more in the tradition of early sea charts than maps (see chapter 8), Visscher did not include 'The Minch' as a name for the sea channel between the Western Isles and mainland Scotland for the reason that the term, derived from the French 'La Manche' (a channel), was not then in common currency for this stretch of water. By the time of Knox's map of 1782, The Minch was so known.
Source: Nicolaes Visscher, *Exactissima Regni Scotiae tabula tam in septentrionalem et meriodionalem . . .* (1689). Reproduced by permission of the Trustees of the National Library of Scotland.

FIGURE 1.15 (b) Not only does John Knox include the name, 'The Minch', as the stretch of water separating the Isle of Skye and the mainland from the Western Isles, he also fills the open sea space with interesting ideas relating to the possible shortening of the sea voyage round the Scottish coasts. These ideas came to fruition within the next forty years in the Forth & Clyde, Caledonian and Crinan canals.
Source: John Knox, *A Commercial Map of Scotland* (1782). Reproduced by permission of the Trustees of the National Library of Scotland.

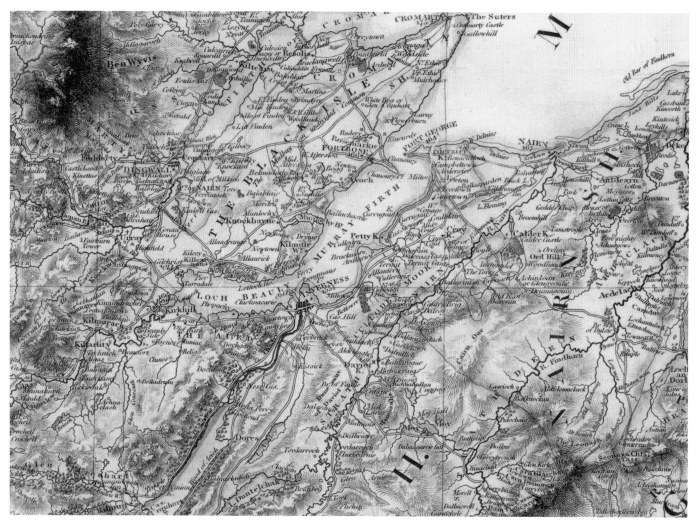

expressive forms for meaning in art, in poetry and in novels.

Our treatment of these three central aims and of the many maps and stories that illustrate them is part chronological and part thematic. Scotland's 'map coverage' ranges across more than two thousand years. It begins with the earliest known representation of the country in map form, in a map of the British Isles by Claudius Ptolemaeus, known usually as Ptolemy, who lived between about AD 90 and 168. It has no end, since we make maps all the time, and maps of Scotland are widespread and varied in modern context, but we close our enquiries here with reference to maps in contemporary popular culture.

To give structure to these concerns, chapters 2 and 3 provide a chronological overview of the depiction of Scotland in maps from Ptolemy to administrative and county maps in the mid- and late eighteenth century: here, we suggest, is how Scotland has been put on the map, how the nation has been 'shaped' over time in maps. The idea of Scotland being made through its maps is then developed, in a series of principally thematic chapters, from chapter 4 onwards, with attention being paid to key moments in the mapping of the nation (for example, figs. 1.16 and 1.17). Each chapter addresses a particular theme in Scotland's map history and does so largely chronologically within the theme in question. In this way, we illustrate the importance of maps as historical and geographical documents and show how maps were used, and for what purpose, by reference to key themes and processes which have shaped Scotland's history and geography.

We start our thematic treatment in chapter 4 by outlining something of the ways in which maps reveal the defence of Scotland and how mapping was part of Scotland's evolving relationship with its neighbour, England. From there, since defence of courtly and urban life was part of this relationship and the resultant map work, we turn in chapter 5 to the growth of towns and the utility of maps as documents of the urban scene. Chapter 6 looks at the ways maps depict life in the countryside and in rural livelihood. One feature of the scrutiny paid to Scotland by its map-makers has been the 'emergence' of its islands: always there, of course, but thanks to maps more and more evident in Scotland's geographies and sense of national identity from the later seventeenth century. Chapter 7 documents the cartography of Scotland's islands. Chapter 8 illustrates the mapping of Scotland's seas and waters: here, as in land-based mapping, Scotland was put to order in different ways by the demands of those for whom maps as trustworthy objects in use at sea meant the difference between life and death (fig. 1.18). As for terrestrial mapping, maps of Scottish waters sought to depict their content, not just their extent: to catch your fish or to restrict such catches, you must know where to find it.

In chapter 9, we highlight elements of the rich map evidence relating to travel and communication in Scotland. The role that maps have played in discovering and portraying Scotland as a scientific landscape is the focus of chapter 10. For subjects such as geology, maps are vital tools but not because they show what can be seen: in geological mapping, the map is an inferential guide to the invisible. Chapter 11 looks at the different ways in which

M E M O I R

RELATIVE TO

THE CONSTRUCTION

OF THE

M A P   O F   S C O T L A N D,

PUBLISHED BY

AARON ARROWSMITH,

IN THE YEAR

1807.

FIGURE 1.16 *Opposite.* Aaron Arrowsmith's 1807 map is a landmark work in Scottish map history. Produced in June 1807, it remained the basis to the country's mapping for the following half century. Arrowsmith based his map on an examination of others' earlier maps (including William Roy's Military Survey (see chapter 4)) by accurate surveying and attention to detail. The complex county boundary between Inverness and Nairn, for example, first appeared on Arrowsmith's map as a result of Alexander Nimmo's survey of the boundary in 1806.
Source: Aaron Arrowsmith, *Map of Scotland Constructed from Original Materials* (1807). Reproduced by permission of the Trustees of the National Library of Scotland.

FIGURE 1.17 *Above.* This is the title page to the *Memoir* which accompanied Arrowsmith's important map of 1807. The conjunction of map and memoir – a printed discussion of the sources used, the methods employed, and thus statements about the credibility of the map and of its maker – was a common feature of map-making in the eighteenth and early nineteenth centuries.
Source: Aaron Arrowsmith, *Memoir Relative to the Construction of the Map of Scotland* (1809). Reproduced by permission of the Trustees of the National Library of Scotland.

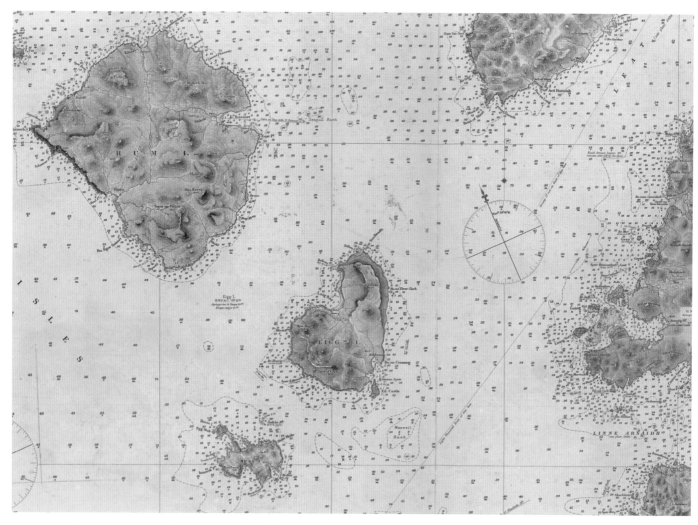

maps have been and are today important with respect to patterns of recreation and leisure. What we take for granted as map accessibility – in the twin sense of the availability of maps and in the fact that they presume access to the geography they show – is a recent phenomenon. Since maps may reflect and produce different forms of meaning, chapter 12 examines their presence and prevalence in popular culture. There is no formal conclusion, but chapter 13 returns to some of the ways in which Scotland's map history may be thought of and reiterates the connections between maps as technical and cultural objects, map history, social history and historical and geographical change (see fig. 1.19).

In being a study of the maps of Scotland and of Scotland's map history, and a study in how maps illustrate Scotland's history and geography, this book aims to illuminate and to explain Scotland's rich cartographic heritage. In doing so, we have sought not just to describe and examine this vital component of Scottish culture, past and present, but also, we hope, to stretch the reader's imagination over the idea of Scotland's 'mapness' – the nation's shaping in maps and the presence of maps in Scottish life – and to stimulate further interest in it. Full captions have been provided in order that individual maps may be understood as more than a static image and thus placed in relation to wider themes. In the guide to further reading, we indicate the main sources we have drawn upon, and the material available for more detailed study, including web addresses for online map collections and related map work.

It is possible, therefore, to read and to refer to this book in different ways. One – the most usual way in all likelihood – is to proceed from start to finish, chapter by chapter, perhaps consulting the guide to further reading, to work from text to map and back to the text. Another way might be to look only at the maps, reading their captions, and so take a 'snapshot' approach, bypassing the longer dynamic story outlined in the text. Yet further ways might be to look only at certain themes, or to explore related work using the guide to further reading before returning to the narrative.

However the book is read and used, it is worth noting that our coverage is incomplete. We have not set out to provide a complete record of all known maps of Scotland, nor to provide biographical details of every map-maker or map publisher who has been at one time or another concerned with Scotland. We are not, in any detailed way, concerned with the techniques of map production or with the volumes of output and the marketing of maps, except where such matters have particular relevance to given maps or certain themes.

As individuals enthralled by maps – in thrall to maps perhaps – and who have worked with and wondered about maps in one way or another all our scholarly lives, our concern overall is to bring to wider audiences something of the rich history embodied in Scotland's mapping. What follows is 'recognition of sorts' of Scotland's maps, mapping and map history, of one nation's map culture. It is, after a fashion, also a tribute to it. It is, certainly, written in the hope that others may become similarly enthralled by maps' seductive power and historical importance.

FIGURE 1.18 *Opposite*. The official Admiralty Chart of the Small Isles precedes the official 'land' mapping of Ordnance Survey by some twenty years and therefore fills an important information gap in terms of its depiction of the human elements of the landscape, not least in displaying the sparse settlement pattern. But, more importantly in terms of its primary function as a sea chart, it brought accurate charting of the coasts and coastal features to levels not seen before and by doing so lessened the risk of shipwreck.
Source: Hydrographic Office, *Ardnamurchan Point to Loch Bhreatal, Skye, Including the Small Isles and Sleat Sound.* Admiralty Chart 2507 (Surveyed 1852–63). Reproduced by permission of the Trustees of the National Library of Scotland.

FIGURE 1.19 *Above*. The west side of Bartholomews' Edinburgh Geographical Institute, from South Gray Street, with the larger arched Lorry Entrance to the right, and further right still, the smaller Workers' Entrance. Note the firm's delivery lorry loaded with copies of 'The Times Survey Atlas of the World' (1919).
Source: Bartholomew, 'Employees outside the side entrance of the Bartholomew Edinburgh Geographical Institute in Duncan St'. Copyright © published with permission of HarperCollins Publishers.

DEVCALEDO NI

Thyle insula

Medium insulæ

Nouantum prom: et Chersonesus

OCEA NV

Orcades insulæ triginta circiter

Rerigonius sinus

Epidium prom.

Itys fluu.

Volsas sinus

Dumna

Ocitis

Vidogara Sinus

Cernotes

Creones

Carnonacæ

Taruedrum quo

Epidij

Longus fl.

Carini

Cornabij

Viruedrum prom

Vanduara

Iolamonius sinus

Caledonia Silua

Simertæ

Logi

Gadini

Loxa flu.

Veruuium prom.

Dam—nij

Banatia

Cale—dony

Cantæ

Ripa alta

Lindum

Clota æstuarium

Tamia

Alata cast.

Varar Esluarium

Colania

Coria

Alauna

Iuesis

Victoria

Vacemagi

Curia

Bremenium

Orrea

Calnius flu.

Tuesis esluarium

Otadeni

Venni cones

Deuana

Tæzali

Tæzalum prom.

Vedra flu.

Bodiria esluarium

Alaunus flu.

Tina flu.

Tana esluarium

Diua fluuius

Saxonum insulæ tres

Dunum Sinus

um leg ictrix

Gabrantuicorum portuosus sinus

OCEANVS

CHAPTER 2

MAPS OF SCOTLAND BEFORE *c*.1595

The earliest known depiction of Scotland in map form appears as part of a map of the British Isles in the work of the Greek astronomer–mathematician Claudius Ptolemaeus, known usually as Ptolemy, who lived between *c*.AD 90 and *c*.AD 168. The earliest known map in which Scotland is the principal object in view dates from the mid 1560s. In the centuries between, Scotland figures in a variety of ways in medieval maps but never as what we might think of as the maps' main feature. For part of this period, it is, strictly speaking, inappropriate to think of nations as the territorial and political units they later became, as it is to think of maps as just or simply topographical pictures. What we have in Ptolemy's map is a depiction of Scotland before Scotland was, properly, Scotland.

Yet, by the later sixteenth century, Scotland was an established geographical and political entity, the central focus and object of mapping projects from leading figures in the Low Countries such as Gerard Mercator and Abraham Ortelius. Maps had become widely recognised across Europe as instruments of territorial and political administration. Mathematicians and ministers of state alike had become map minded. This chapter examines the reasons for these changes and considers how in its early maps Scotland was imagined and cartographically shaped, before and after it became a nation.

The words 'earliest known' are important in considering the mapped representation of Scotland. What we have in the early and medieval map images of Scotland may not have been all there ever was. It is very hard to know, however, what may once have existed but now does not survive. Before the invention in Germany of mechanical printing and movable type in the 1450s, maps were either hand-drawn or woodcut images, and maps were not reprinted but hand-copied. Intellectual culture largely centred upon monasteries. Maps helped serve and promote Christian authority. While we know clerics and other learned men produced and worked with maps, it is possible that the utility of maps depended to a greater degree than in later periods upon explanation by word of mouth. Fragile and ephemeral, most maps were not thought of as enduring historical records. If they did survive, they were often lost to sight or remained as unique items within private libraries or the scriptoria of religious houses.

Knowledge of Ptolemaic geography and mathematics reached a few people in the Christian West by the end of the twelfth century, and Arab scholars had advanced geographical knowledge in ways not known to Christian commentators. But Ptolemy's maps and books and much else of classical geographical knowledge were effectively unknown until their rediscovery in the Renaissance. Printed versions of Ptolemy's *Geographia* only began to appear, in Italy, from the fifteenth century. In contrast to later periods, medieval and early modern Europe had no state institutions for map production. Kings, clerics and courtiers ruled the land, not cartographers. Maps were understood and used as topographic records. We know that there were such things as medieval estate maps – although not if they were known as such, and none survive for Scotland from this period – and that mapping was associated with displays of property, possibly even used in legal disputation over boundaries and so on. Maps were certainly vital to navigation and trade by sea. And medieval mapping also had significant symbolic purposes – for churchmen and for kings – a fact which helps explain the particular, even peculiar, forms they sometimes took.

Between Ptolemy and Mercator, ideas of what a map was and what maps did changed dramatically. We can talk, by the end of the sixteenth century, of an emergent map culture in Europe which understood the value of maps in trade, in politics and in depicting territory: Scotland, in contrast to its marginal position in medieval maps, would be at the centre of things in early modern European map culture.

SCOTLAND APPEARS ON THE MAP: PTOLEMY'S SCOTLAND

The first known map depicting Scotland is remarkable (fig. 2.1). Instead of running more or less north–south, the country is shown turned on its side, its west coast shown at the top in a 'northern' position, its east coast shown at the foot in a 'southern' position. What we know as the Hebrides and the northern isles are only hinted at, shown as a scattering of shapes. Within this bent geography and on its margins, only a very few features can be made out, and coverage is uneven: the east coast is recognisable; some native settlements and Roman forts are shown; there is even a stylised suggestion of the Caledonian Forest. How and why should Scotland be drawn like this, shown almost at right angles from its 'usual' position whilst England is, more or less, depicted as usual? To answer this question, we need to understand something of how maps were made at this time and who could be relied upon as a credible authority.

The Ptolemaic map of Scotland appears as part of a map of Britain in Ptolemy's eight-book *Geographia*. As a scholar working in the library at Alexandria, Ptolemy was a sedentary synthesiser of others' work, not a first-hand observer. Few people were first-hand observers, at least not in any modern sense. Classical map-makers and geographers – often termed 'cosmographers' because of their engagement with astronomical measurements and their concerns to study the earth in relation to other heavenly bodies – were mainly based in and around the towns and cities of the Mediterranean and so knew that world well. For knowledge of other parts of Europe, they were dependent upon other, earlier, authors and upon travellers' and traders' accounts.

Ptolemy was heavily reliant upon the works of four

people for his *Geographia*. The first was Pytheas of Massilia, what is today Marseilles, who in around 325 BC undertook a trading trip to Britain. During his journey, Pytheas undertook astronomical observations with a view to fixing latitude. The second, at one time librarian at Alexandria, was Eratosthenes of Cyrene (*c.*276–*c.*195 BC). For his work on earth measurement and astronomy, Eratosthenes is often regarded as the founder of geogra–

FIGURE 2.1 Scotland as depicted by Claudius Ptolemaeus – Ptolemy. This map is taken from the Blaeu *Atlas* of Scotland published in 1654. Maps such as this, derived from Ptolemy, and from other Classical geographical writers, continued to be produced even in the face of advances in mathematics and astronomy and the results of numerous voyages of exploration, in part because of a growing interest in ancient geography for its own sake.

Source: Joan Blaeu, 'Insulae Albion et Hibernia', from *Atlas Novus* (1654). Reproduced by permission of the Trustees of the National Library of Scotland.

phy. The third, another Greek, Strabo (*c*.63/64 BC–AD 24), wrote a work entitled *Geographica* in which he drew upon the work of Eratosthenes and others, but in which he supplemented the claims of earlier writers with more up-to-date knowledge based on traders' and other accounts. The fourth, a Roman scholar, was Marinus (sometimes Marinos) of Tyre (*c*.AD 70–130) who, apart from coining the word 'Antarctic' as the theoretical polar opposite to Arctic, was a leading figure in developing ideas of latitude and longitude. In addition, Ptolemy drew upon Roman historians and military sources for knowledge of the land that was to become Britain – knowledge which was very limited in the case of Scotland.

Leading figures though they were, these men did not have standard ways to proceed, nor did they agree upon the size of the linear units to use in measuring the size of the earth or the size of a degree of longitude (east–west measurements). Longitudinal variations were particularly great in their work. As a result, linear distances were regularly foreshortened, so places on the map were not where they actually were in the world. Eratosthenes produced a map of Europe showing what we now know as the British Isles, but because he, Strabo and others conceived of the known earth, the *oikumene* as it was called, as shaped like a rectangle, not a circle or sphere, these geographical features were the wrong shape, the wrong size and in the wrong position. Furthermore, there was then no separate geographical word for Scotland, the term 'Brettanike' being used for England and Scotland.

For these men, geographical information, however arrived at, had to fit a pre-conceived idea of the shape of the known world. This is not to say that they thought their facts wrong: what they took to be facts, in their terms accurately arrived at, had to be made to agree with established conceptions. To top it all, Marinus, for all his interest in the geometry of the earth, was also a copyist – and copyists make mistakes. And where Roman soldiers could and did bring back information from their occupation of Britain, most of such material as Marinus could draw upon concerned southern Britain. Such knowledge of Scotland as could have been useful – such as Tacitus's report in about AD 98 that 'Caledonia stretches a vast length of way towards the north' – seems not to have been used by Marinus.

What Ptolemy shows us for what we know as Scotland reflects practices of geographical enquiry and map-making at that time – sedentary collection rather more than active in-the-field work. His map is, strictly speaking, not really his. It bears the stamp of several men working over decades who, because they could not see things for themselves or work in standard ways, had to accept the authority of the sources upon which their knowledge depended. We should not blame Ptolemy for his depiction of a wrongly aligned Scotland, not least since the country did not exist under that name. The distortion is due not to anything he did but notably to errors in latitude, in distance and in alignment already in place in the work of Eratosthenes and Pytheas. Marinus, upon whom Ptolemy in particular based much of his own writings, had no reliable means to correct others' figures and texts. Marinus could and did draw upon information about the Romans in England and amended others' earlier work accordingly. But the Romans' limited presence in Scotland provided only scanty information and no means to re-position the bent northern part of 'Brettanike', and so Scotland stands, misshapen and uncorrected, until his work was rediscovered and amended centuries later.

SCOTLAND ON MEDIEVAL WORLD MAPS

In the eleven centuries between the end of the Roman empire and what we can think of as the 'mapping revolution' of the mid-sixteenth century, there is almost no evidence at all of Scottish map-making, and very limited evidence of Scotland on maps.

Sometime around AD 686, the Iona-based Scottish cleric Adomnán, author of an account of the life of Columba, produced plans of four sites in the Holy Land, based on on-the-spot measurements taken by a French bishop, Arculf. These are as much architectural drawings, schematic representations of church buildings in plan view, as they are maps.

Scotland is shown in early Christian world maps – the centuries between Ptolemy and Mercator are far from 'blank' – but, where it is shown, it is indistinct and always marginal. From the early fourteenth century, Scotland figures in medieval portolan charts – maps designed as navigational tools for trade by sea, showing sailing directions by compass bearings and, usually, with coastal outlines (see chapter 8) – but not as the object of such mapping until much later. The reason for this limited coverage is not that people were not map minded (evidence from other countries shows that estate maps and property plans existed and were used), but because of the poor survivability of maps, and because Scotland was geographically peripheral within the known Christian world.

Scotland does figure – clearly, if not accurately in terms of topography – in one significant type of medieval map, the *mappa mundi* (fig. 2.2). The *mappa mundi* is a particular, even rather peculiar, type of map. In it, the medieval imagination incorporated elements of Christian history, often shown figuratively, with depictions of events

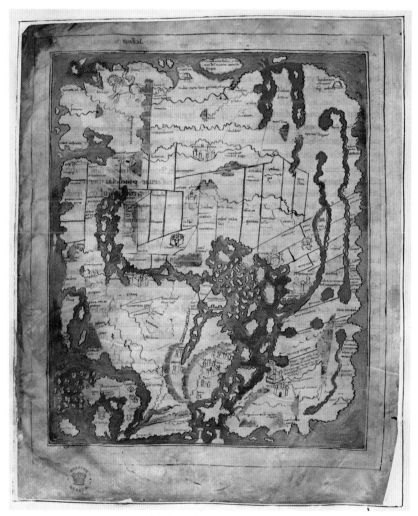

FIGURE 2.2 In this early eleventh-century Anglo-Saxon map of the world, the British Isles appear in the bottom left-hand corner of the map, corresponding to their marginal place when – in early medieval mapping – the world was shown centred on the Mediterranean. Scotland is shown as part mainland, part a collection of scattered islands, all imprecisely delineated. *Source:* Anon., Anglo-Saxon map of the world (eleventh century). Reproduced by permission of the British Library.

in time having precedence over accurate depictions of place. Sometimes, features such as the Garden of Eden were shown in the margins, beyond the terrestrial limits of the human world, but a vital part of Christian history nevertheless. There is no grid scheme, no apparent criteria for inclusion. In general, *mappae mundi* appear from the early twelfth century in association with the authority of monastic and scholarly learning. Scotland is incorporated because several of those few maps that survive were undertaken in England. It is not known whether there was ever a Scottish-based *mappa mundi*. Plan-view maps of landscapes showing field boundaries and roads were in use by the medieval period and would have been more common in daily life than the larger, coloured and symbolic *mappae mundi* which, for all their glory and rich symbolic content, were not public map artefacts except, perhaps, as altar pieces.

The picture that emerges of Scotland in, for example, the different maps of Britain undertaken by the St Albans-based Matthew Paris in the late 1250s, is barely recognizable in terms of shape and is less detailed than the picture of England (fig. 2.3). We know little about Paris, even less of his methods. It is likely that his maps were designed to accompany or perhaps even to represent an itinerary, as route maps for travel. Places are shown, but topography is

absent. For Scotland, certain features are named – 'Ros', 'Cathnes' and 'Scocia' as a whole – and the more elaborate of the maps suggests that Paris was revising his maps over time, but we do not know on whose information. The fact that north-west Scotland is shown as curved in this figure has been taken to suggest that Paris was working from an earlier, circular, map.

Scotland is again less clearly shown than England in the Gough map of about 1360 (fig. 2.4). Virtually nothing is known of the maker, purpose or use of this map: even the name is taken from its later discoverer, Richard Gough, an eighteenth-century antiquarian and topographical writer. It is possible that this map was prepared for Edward I to assist in his armed interventions into Scotland in the early fourteenth century: several Scottish place names on the Gough Map are listed in surviving itineraries of the English king's Scottish journeys, and virtually nothing is shown north of the Moray Firth, the farthest reach of Edward's travels. Scotland appears as almost an afterthought, nevertheless, with a rather extended mainland having only a few embayments to suggest the firths and lochs, and with its islands skirting both sides.

Military intentions certainly underlie John Hardyng's map of Scotland, produced in 1457 (fig. 2.5). This was undertaken as part of his *Chronicle* of England, originally

FIGURE 2.3 *Opposite*. Very little is known of Matthew Paris, author of this map of Britain (and of a further three similar maps), but it is supposed that his identification of places in England was the result of an itinerary from south to north, though whether by Paris himself is not known. Scotland is geographically 'empty' by comparison with England: in Paris's first map (not shown), only a handful of names are given and the lochs of the Great Glen are much truncated. In the more elaborate map of the two (here shown), Scotland is more fully named: note, too, the stylised lines of ramparts signalling Hadrian's Wall and the Antonine Wall.
Source: Matthew Paris, Map of Great Britain (*c.*1250). Reproduced by permission of the British Library.

FIGURE 2.4 *Overleaf*. In the Gough Map of *c.*1360, the map is – in the original meaning of the term – properly oriented, that is, with east to the top. Scotland is again a poor cartographic relation to England, with no roads shown, fewer settlements than were known to be in existence and a very rough topographical outline for the coasts, especially with respect to the west coast and the outlying islands.
Source: Anon., Gough Map of Great Britain (fourteenth century). Reproduced by permission of the Bodleian Library, Oxford.

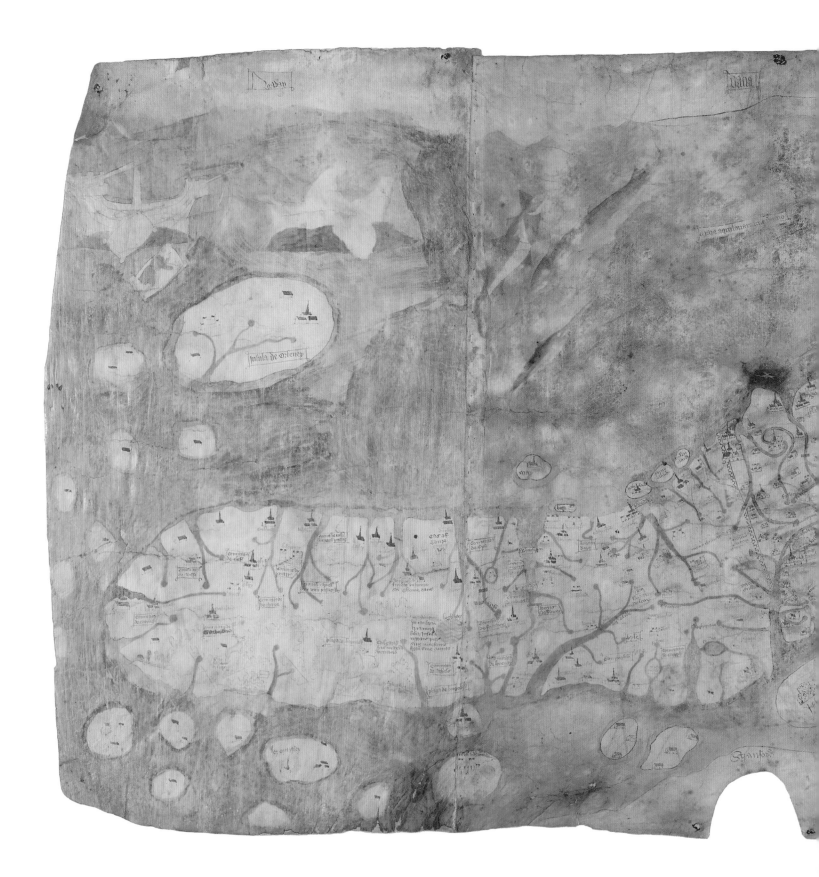

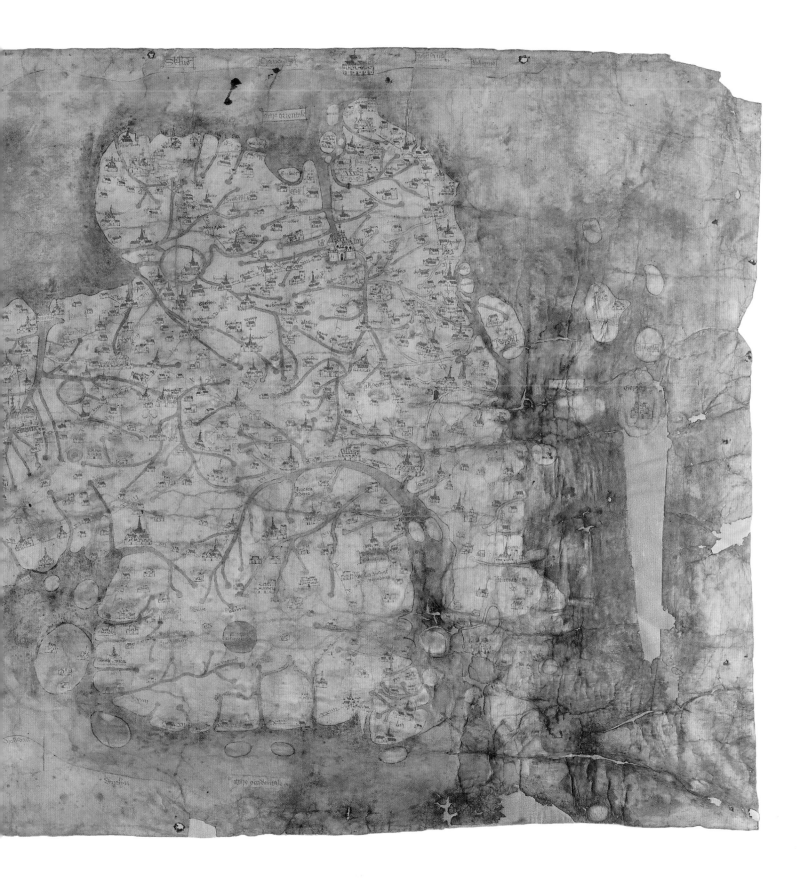

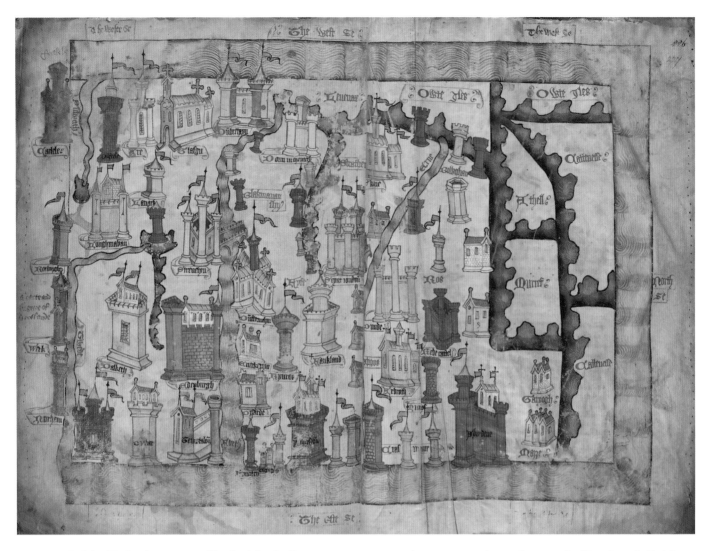

FIGURE 2.5 In John Hardyng's 1457 map of Scotland, Scotland's towns and churches appear almost as images of property, as they do today in estate agents' publicity: beckoning, highlighting an opportunity, laying out a future potential.

Source: John Hardyng, Map of Scotland, from the *Chronicle of John Hardyng* (1457). Reproduced by permission of the British Library.

prepared for the English king Henry VI. Hardyng, an English courtier, used his *Chronicle* to try to persuade Henry of England's sovereign rights over Scotland. There are no coasts to Hardyng's map of Scotland, or at least none that bear any relation to the country's geography. Hardyng also got the orientation wrong by modern conventions – west is to the north. Regional divisions within the body of the nation are stylised, separated from one another by imaginary bodies of water. Settlements are shown almost as bird's-eye view models. But accuracy of location, shape and symbol were secondary to Hardyng's concerns. His map is designed as a piece of visual propaganda: a map to lead a king to war. That is why the towns are shown high-walled and the churches grandly steepled: look at Edinburgh and at Aberdeen in this respect. Here, Hardyng is saying, is a land worth having. Stylised it may be, this is Scotland mapped as military opportunity.

SCOTLAND TAKES SHAPE, 1546–1595

The first printed map that shows Scotland alone dates from about 1566 (fig. 2.6). It is thought to be the work of Paolo Forlani, a Veronese map-maker active in Venice. It is based on a map of 1546 by an English divine, George Lily, who, whilst in Rome, undertook geographical research as part of a description of Britain published in 1548. Lily's sources seem to have included the Gough Map, at least for the names of places, but in other respects his map is a new departure and was probably based on information to which Lily, a Catholic, had access whilst a religious exile.

Half a century later, Scotland in the form of the 'Scotia Regnum' map (Scotland the Kingdom), appears in the 1595 edition of the *Atlas* of Gerard Mercator, then the world's leading map-maker. By then, Scotland had also been circumnavigated, although the resultant map, of 1583, was based on information from the 1540s (a story we develop in chapter 8). The nature of these maps and the location of their creation is instructive. In this half century, the world of map-making was moving away from places like Rome and Venice towards Antwerp and Amsterdam. Scotland's mapping reflects this shift in the geography of European cartography.

Others were at work producing maps of Scotland in

FIGURE 2.6 *Scotia: Regno di Scotia*, from around 1566 and perhaps as early as 1561, is based on George Lily's 1546 printed map of the British Isles. But it is carelessly based: the copyist, probably Paolo Forlani, has placed Arbroath north of Montrose and omitted several place and regional names such as Lothian and Clyde, which appear on Lily's original.
Source: Paolo Forlani/George Lily, *Scotia. Regno di Scotia* (*c.*1561). Reproduced by permission of the Trustees of the National Library of Scotland.

these fifty years. Amongst them was a Highland-born priest, John Elder, probably a spy for the English crown, who has left us notes about a map, now lost, which he prepared for Henry VIII of England in 1543. Elder's map was a 'plotte' as he describes it; the term 'plot' as an area of land then had close connotations with the idea of the map 'plate' (the metal plate on which it was inscribed) as a depiction of territory. He meant too that this was to illuminate a political plot – a plan to unite the kingdoms of Scotland and England. In part at least, the map's making was based on first-hand experience. 'I was born in Caithnes', Elder tells us, 'which is the northe part of the said plotte; . . . educatt, and brought up, not onely in the West yles of the same plotte, named the Sky and the Lewys, where I have bene often tymes with my frendis, in ther longe galeis, arriving to dyvers and syndrie places in Scotland, wher they had a do; but also, beinge a scholar and a student in the southe parts of it, called Sancandrois, Abirdene and Glasgow, for the space of XIIthe yeares, wher I have travailed, as well by see as by land, dyvers time'. Only a few years later the Scottish bishop John Leslie, who also spent much time in Rome, incorporated a map in his 1578 *History of Scotland*. The Flemish man of maps Abraham Ortelius produced a map of Scotland in 1573, basing it on a map of 1564 by Gerard Mercator. And the English man of action Laurence Nowell, involved like Elder in courtly intrigue, produced two manuscript maps of Scotland sometime between 1561 and 1566 (fig. 2.7).

Maps prepared by Catholic priests in religious exile, kingly plots, lost maps, Flemish mathematicians working from one another's maps, maps in history books: how are we to make sense of all of these? Explanation for this heightened activity concerning maps, and the move to the recognisable shape of Scotland that maps reveal by

FIGURE 2.7 Laurence Nowell's map of Scotland was produced sometime between 1561 and 1566. Nowell, a graduate of Cambridge and Oxford universities, fled to Germany as a Protestant exile following the accession of Queen Mary, returning to England in the reign of Elizabeth I. Nowell's map has about 600 place names, and is particularly accurate in terms of its delineation of the coastline. It is possible there is some connection with the 1583 Nicolay map of Scotland derived from the circumnavigation of 1540: see fig. 2.11.
Source: Laurence Nowell, Map of Scotland (1561–66). Reproduced by permission of the British Library.

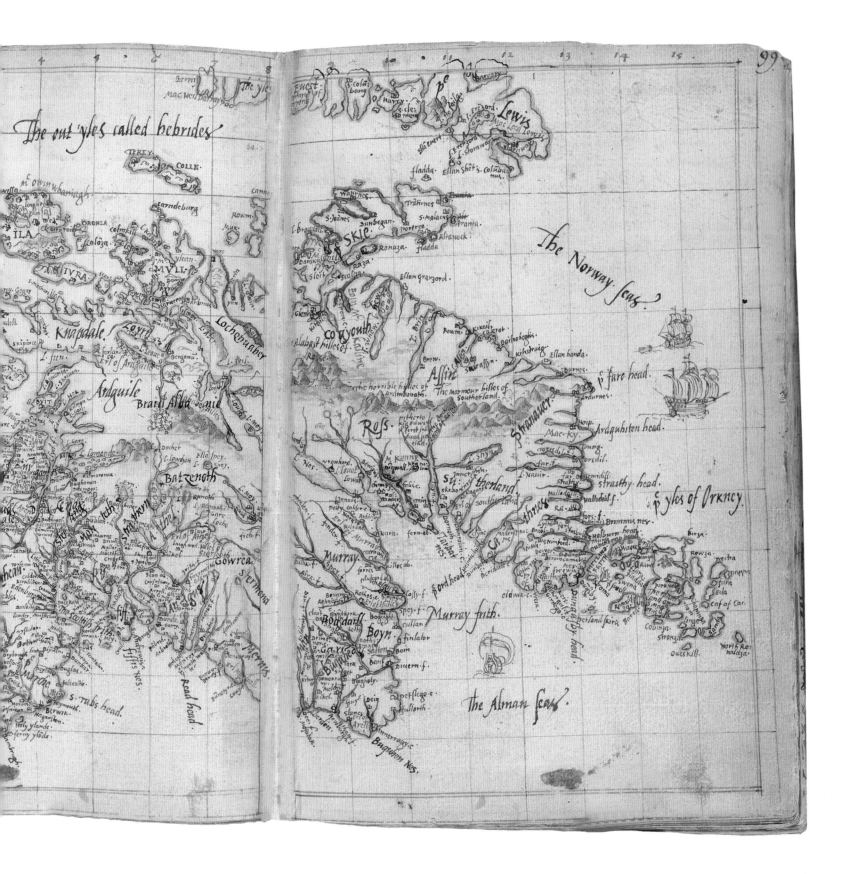

1595, rests in a combination of things. For convenience, let us bracket them under three related headings: geographical and associated intellectual activity; military and commercial needs; and questions of national identity and political governance.

To Europeans, the discovery by Columbus in 1492 of the Americas and the West Indies, and the voyages of the Italians, Spanish and Portuguese to the East Indies in the following decades, radically transformed the contemporary geographical consciousness. The world was now bigger and more varied. Scriptural reasoning was tested. Conceptions of social order, of human origins and cultural difference all had to be re-cast. New souls required saving. The world had to be re-imagined; maps had to be re-thought.

In the same year as Columbus encountered what he took to be the Orient, Martin of Behaim, a German navigator and geographer to the king of Portugal, produced the world's first globe. The works of Ptolemy, by then available in printed translation, revealed a legacy of geographical enquiry even as the new discoveries showed much classical learning to be erroneous. In 1533, the Friesland-born mathematician Gemma Frisius was the first to describe triangulation as a method of measurement and survey. In doing so, he provided an earthly parallel to the heavenly enquiries of Nicolaus Copernicus, whose 1543 *De Revolutionibus Orbium Coelestium* (*On the Revolutions of the Heavenly Spheres*) showed that the earth and other planets moved around the sun – and that the earth was not the centre of the cosmos as the Church had taught. Copernicus's work transformed the earth's place in the cosmic order, alarmed clerics, and, with Frisius and others, helped establish mathematics as the language by which to understand nature, correct the ancients, and measure terrestrial and celestial space. In

1569, Gerard Mercator invented the map projection which bears his name, a projection designed for navigation at sea, based on lines representing a constant course, or loxodromes as they are properly known. Here were changing geographies, fresh ideas and new tools: firsthand discovery and refined methods for accurate measurement. The dissemination of printing allowed these ideas and technologies to spread.

Traders and merchants always require a knowledge of routes, by land and by sea, and of faraway places: to them, travel distance means time, and time means money. The portolan charts of the fourteenth century and later were designed as enhanced navigational tools, for use with the magnetic compass. Alongside the demands of commerce, ever more global in reach after 1500, changes in military technologies reinforced the cultures of maps and mapmaking. For soldiers, knowing where your enemy is, and what his strength is, always matters. Historians have debated the nature and timing of the 'military revolution' in early modern Europe, to no single conclusion. It is generally agreed, however, that from the early 1500s new battle tactics and the development of artillery and siege warfare required a new knowledge of terrain, new designs for fortifications and almost a new type of soldier – the military engineer. Plans of forts, and maps laying out the terrain, were as invaluable to military commanders as charts of safe passage in trade routes were to ships' captains.

The sixteenth century also witnessed a growth in what, to use a modern term, we might think of as civic or national identity: the idea of 'the realm' and of the constitutional sovereignty of a monarch over the people, and a strengthening association, at least in Europe, between people and territory. Building upon the earlier rediscovery of perspective in art and architecture, maps

FIGURE 2.8 This image, and the related two figures following (figs. 2.9 and 2.10), illustrate other ways in which maps and plans were produced in the early modern period. Here, Edinburgh is shown in bird's-eye view with the houses, streets and open spaces not quite in plan perspective. Taken from Georg Braun and Franz Hogenberg's *Civitates Orbis Terrarum*, published in six volumes between 1572 and 1617, the Edinburgh image dates from about 1582.
Source: Georg Braun and Franz Hogenberg, *Edenburgum, Scotiae Metropolis.* (1583). Reproduced by permission of the Trustees of the National Library of Scotland.

of towns adopted a topographic or 'bird's-eye' form as well as plan views (figs. 2.8, 2.9). Mapping of towns could also take symbolic form (fig. 2.10). Where merchants relied on maps for trade, historians and geographers helped fashion narratives of national origin, legitimising one nation's place in the world, and often its authority (real or imagined) over others.

To kings and those who were charged with governing territories, at home and overseas, maps were documents of authority: on paper, one can view and plan space. For clerics, caught in the swirling currents of the Reformation and Counter-Reformation, maps could help delimit the reach of the established Church, Catholic or Protestant. For men like Ortelius and Mercator, and for their patrons, map-making had powerful political as well as intellectual consequences. As a profession and as an intellectual practice, as a way of picturing the world and

marketing the world, mapping in sixteenth-century Europe profoundly changed the world.

These matters to do with geography, politics, empire, religion, the history of ideas, the dissemination of print culture and the globalisation of trade did not happen all at once, nor had they the same effect everywhere. But in combination, and over time, they acted to produce new levels of map mindedness and to instil in literate circles widespread recognition of the value of maps. What followed was the emergence of more distinctively separate types of map: topographical maps, which outlined the shape and content of nations; town plans; battle plans and military maps; sea charts for coastal and oceanic navigation.

Lily's map of 1546, the basis to Forlani's copy of 1566, was undertaken whilst Lily was in religious exile, as we have seen. But for some of his geographical information

S. ANDRE. SIVE ANDREAPOLIS
Scotiæ Vniuersitas Metropolitana.

collegium S. Saluatoris

Arx Episcopi.

Ecclesia S Saluatoris

Franciscanorum
ædes.

Domus
vrbis

Dominicanorum
ædes.

Ecclesia Perochiæ
ciuitatis.

collegium D. Mariani

Collegium
D. Leonardi

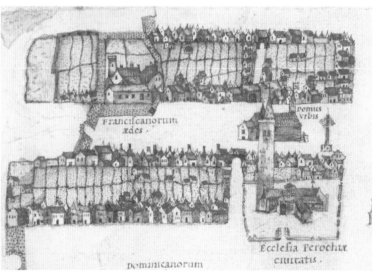

Franciscanorum ædes.

Domus Vrbis.

Dominicanorum.

Ecclesia Perochiæ ciuitatis.

FIGURE 2.9 St Andrews is here portrayed in an almost plan view perspective by Geddie around 1580. But note, too, the stylised representation of some the principal civic buildings, in the style of Braun and Hogenberg's picture of Edinburgh (fig. 2.8).

Source: John Geddie [?], *S. Andre sive Andreapolis* (*c.* 1580). Reproduced by permission of the Trustees of the National Library of Scotland.

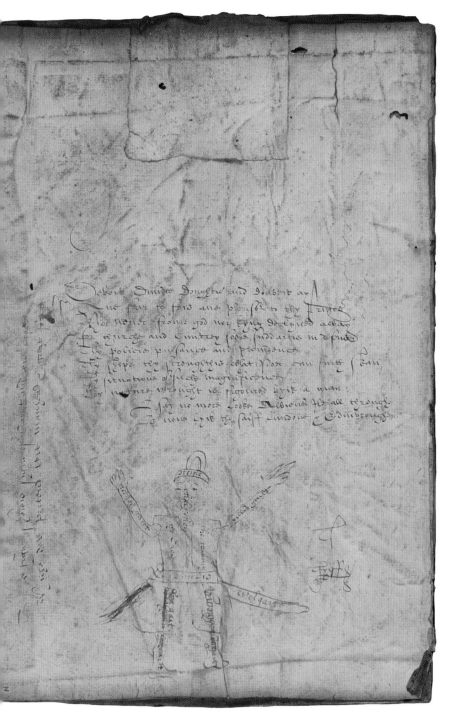

Lily also drew upon the work of two Scottish historians, John Mair's *History of Great Britain* (1526) and Hector Boece's *History of Scotland* (1521). Lily, and others, would have found these books to be powerful arguments about Scottish nationhood. Elder's lost map of 1543 – intended as part of a plan to unite Scotland and England – may have been used as part of the English invasion of Scotland between 1544 and 1551, the so-called 'Rough Wooing', whose mapping we examine in chapter 4.

The Lily and Elder maps from the 1540s were about knowing Scotland's political and religious content – the nation 'from the inside', so to speak. The 1583 map published by the French cosmographer Nicolas de Nicolay, but the result of a navigation of Scotland in the 1540s and the work of 'the excellent Scottish pilot and hydrographer' Alexander Lindsay (sometimes Lyndsay), was based on knowing Scotland's bounds 'from the outside' (fig. 2.11). Here, too, as we discuss in chapter 6, we may note connections between the map as image and the printed word, and between the map and politics. The

FIGURE 2.10 Here is Dundee, shown in symbolic form as a figure and drawn by an unknown author in the later sixteenth century. This sort of anthropomorphic map image was not uncommon in an age when kings (and queens) were often held to embody the nation in question. *Source:* Anon., Sketch of Dundee from Protocol Book of Alexander Wedderburn (1589–92). Reproduced by permission of Dundee City Archives.

FIGURE 2.11 Nicolas de Nicolay's fine chart of Scotland in 1583 is based on the work of a Scottish hydrographer, Alexander Lindsay (see chapter 8 and figs. 8.2 and 8.3). It was copied closely and published some hundred years later by Scottish map-maker John Adair – with due acknowledge-ment to Nicolay – because Adair felt unable to produce his own general chart of Scotland before completing his survey of the Scottish coastline: sadly, this did not come to fruition. *Source:* John Adair, *A true and exact Hydrographical description of the Sea Coast and Isle of Scotland* (1688). Reproduced by permission of the Trustees of the National Library of Scotland.

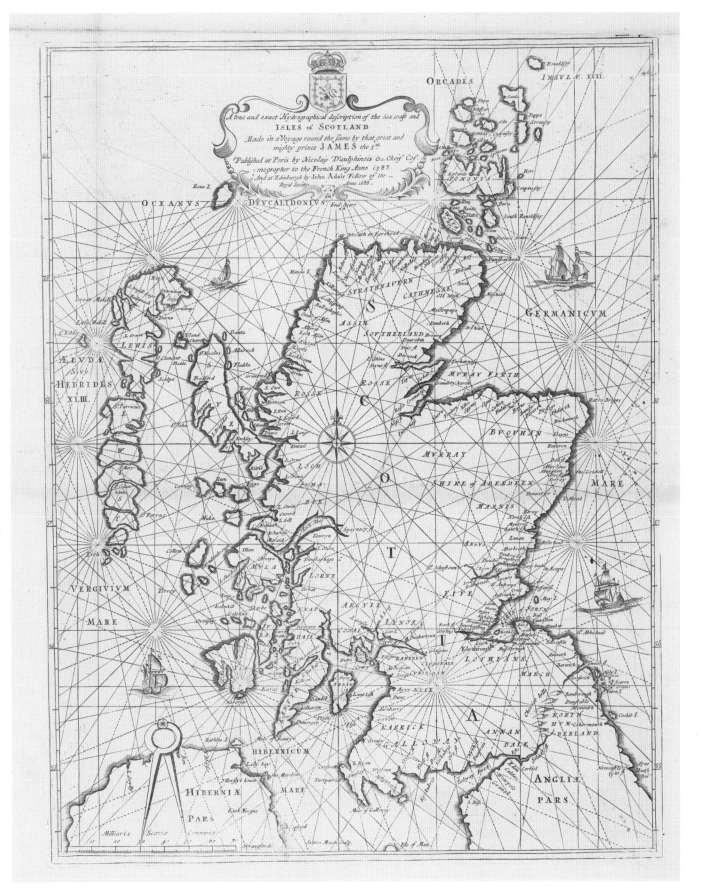

map was part of a rutter (a manual of sailing directions), a form of maritime knowledge important in expanding commerce. The principal purpose of King James V in navigating Scotland lay in homeland security. Between the forfeiture of the Lordship of the Isles in 1493 and about 1550, several attempts were made to re-establish the power of the Highland lords along Scotland's north and west coasts. Maps as a form of state surveillance help locate your enemies, whether they are across the Tweed or in Ross and Lochaber.

The representation of Scotland by the Low Countries' map-makers Abraham Ortelius and Gerard Mercator in several maps from 1564 until Mercator's first map of Scotland alone in 1595 (fig. 2.12) reflects the leading position of these men and of those countries as map-making nations. But because maps and the engraved metal plates on which they were inscribed could be expensive, maps from one maker would often be copied by later publishers, or amended only slightly in later editions. The map which appears in Bishop Leslie's 1578 *History*, for example, is a modified version of Ortelius' 1573 'Scotiae Tabula' map, which is itself based on Mercator's 1564 map.

All these facts serve to remind us that Scotland's mapping and map history, certainly in the fifty years from 1546 if less evidently in the 1,100 years from the death of Ptolemy, were bound up with wider changes affecting Europe. Scotland was marginal on Europe's early maps, but it moved to a more and more central position in European map culture. Noting this, we should also observe that, with the exceptions of the lost 1543 map of John Elder and the work of Alexander Lindsay, Scotland's mapping before the end of the sixteenth century was undertaken by everyone but Scots. From the 1580s and 1590s, this would change.

FIGURE 2.12 Produced in 1595 at a scale of about 25 miles to the inch by the Flanders-based map-maker Gerard Mercator, the outline of the map is likely to have been based on the Nicolay map of 1583 (fig. 2.11) and, for parts of his map, on that of Nowell in the 1560s (fig. 2.7). But Mercator also took many of the place names from his own 1564 map of Scotland. This 1595 map became the basis for maps of Scotland until the mid-seventeenth century when the work of Pont, Blaeu and Gordon provided the basis for its amendment (see chapter 3).
Source: Gerard Mercator, *Scotia, Regnum* [Scotland the Kingdom] (1595). Reproduced by permission of the Trustees of the National Library of Scotland.

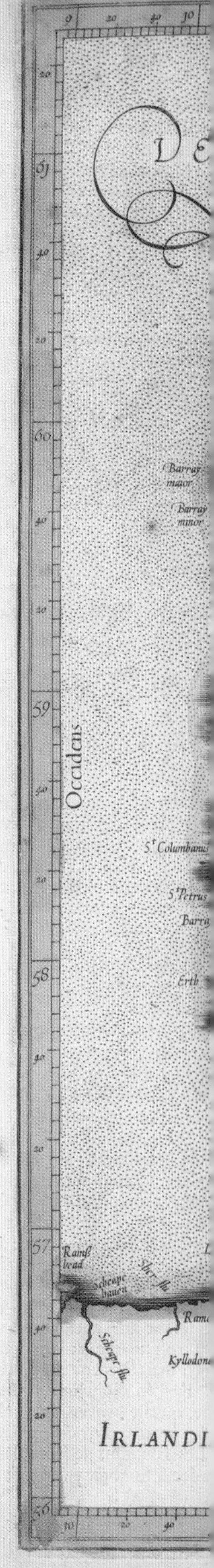

SCOTIA, Regnum.

Per Gerardum Mercatorem
Cum Priuilegio

A MAPP of SCOTLAND.

made by R. Gordon Author of Bleau's Atlas of Scotland, Corrected and Improved by Rob. Morden. To which is Added Alphabetical Tables For the Ready finding out any Place in the Mapp, Sold by Rob. Walton at the Globe and Compaßes in St Pauls Church-yard, and by Rob. Morden at the Atlas in Cornhill LONDON.

Tollsta
Back
Stenish
Eggenes
Souleshadyr
Yl. Adam
Yl. an Nuan
Knok
Yl. Huilme
Laxa
Harror
Lewis
Steornway
C.

nibeg
Borg
Chader
rvas

Cher
Cun
L. Lusponf
Ch
S
Ynnaboll
Tralhgurst
Achan
Alsi

CHAPTER 3

A KINGDOM AND A
NATION DEPICTED *c.*1583–1700

In 1654, Scotland was put on the map as never before. In his *Theatrum Orbis Terrarum, sive Atlas Novus* – known usually as *Atlas Novus* – the Dutch map-maker Joan Blaeu brought together forty-nine maps of Scotland, 154 pages of descriptive text concerning the country, and six maps of Ireland (fig. 3.1). Published in Amsterdam, these maps and written geographical descriptions form volume V of an ambitious world atlas publishing project by the Blaeu family firm. Modern scholars claim with some justification that with its publication Scotland became one of the best-mapped countries of the seventeenth-century world. For contemporaries, the *Atlas Novus* presented a striking vision of the kingdom and nation: 'Look at Scotland', wrote Blaeu, 'and enjoy a feast for the eyes'. And so we can, for in its combination of word and map, the *Atlas Novus* presents a uniquely important picture of Scotland and represents, too, part of a major European publishing achievement.

But Blaeu's *Atlas Novus* is not straightforwardly a work of the mid-seventeenth century. Nor is the *Atlas Novus* the work solely of this leading European publisher. The *Atlas Novus* – the first comprehensive presentation of Scotland in maps and texts – is in large part the printed

end result of mapping work begun nearly seventy years earlier by Timothy Pont, a Scottish clergyman. Sometime between about 1583, the year he is taken to have graduated from the University of St Andrews, and 1614, by which year his parish, Dunnet, in Caithness, had a different minister, Pont mapped Scotland, and compiled written descriptions of parts of the country as part of that work. Pont's maps were added to and amended after his death by other Scottish map-makers, notably by Robert Gordon and his son, James. On both sides of the North Sea, politicians, publishers and Church ministers played an active part in bringing forward the maps and the geographical descriptions for publication.

The Pont–Gordon–Blaeu mapping work is a major achievement. It is significant, too, for what it signals about who was mapping Scotland. Previously there had been map-makers working in and on Scotland, but, without diminishing the earlier work of John Elder and Alexander Lindsay in the 1540s, most map-makers were based outwith Scotland. Here were native Scots for the first time charting their country's bounds and its geographical features. The surviving results – seventy-eight manuscript maps on thirty-eight sheets – reflect this remarkable

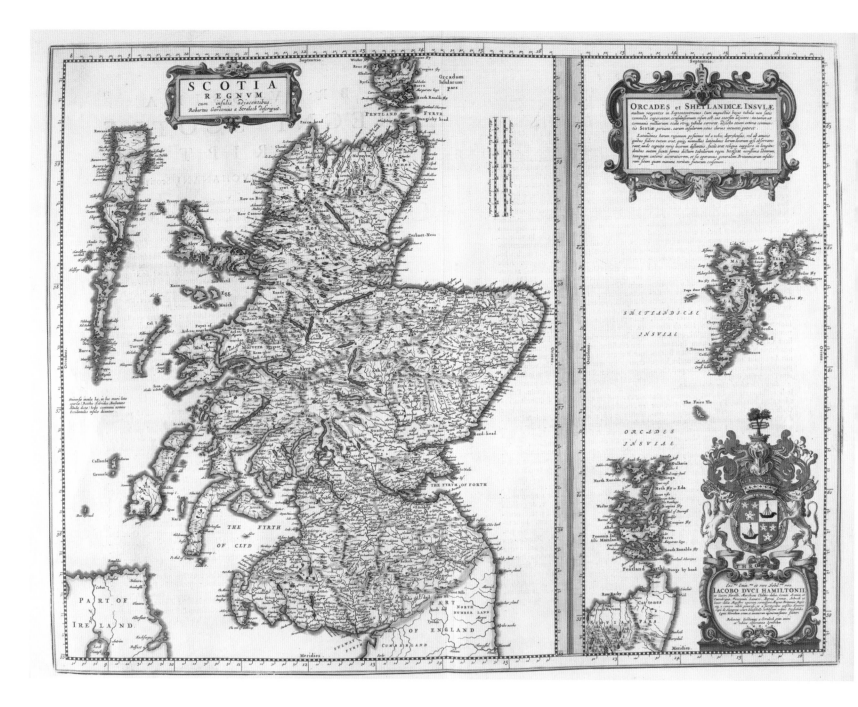

SCOTIA REGNVM cum insulis adjacentibus. Robertus Gordonius a Straloch Descripsit.

ORCADES et SHETLANDICÆ INSVLÆ

PART OF IRELAND

THE FYRTH OF CLYD

PART OF ENGLAND

NORTHUMBERLAND

CUMBERLAND

SHETLANDICÆ INSVLÆ

ORCADES INSVLÆ

IACOBO DVCI HAMILTONII

undertaking. They are one of Scotland's – and early modern Europe's – greatest cartographic treasures.

As remarkable as the story of their undertaking, however, is the related story of how these maps undertaken by a St Andrews-educated cleric in the late sixteenth century came, with others' work, to be the basis decades later for Scotland's first atlas. This chapter lays out the tale of Pont's mapping, its study and amendment by others, and the delay in its publication. It is a story of kings and geographers, Dutch publishers, Scots poets, politicians and men of God, of war, bookworms and neglectful children.

FIGURE 3.1 Robert Gordon of Straloch's *Scotia Regnum* [Scotland the Kingdom] was the principal map of Scotland to appear in Blaeu's *Atlas Novus* of 1654. The fact that his outline is less accurate than several earlier maps of Scotland – for instance in the alignment of Skye and of the lochs in the Great Glen as well as the 'squashed' northern tip of Lewis – is regarded as the result of Robert Gordon's misinterpretation of Timothy Pont's earlier manuscript maps.
Source: Robert Gordon, *Scotia Regnum* (1654). Reproduced by permission of the Trustees of the National Library of Scotland.

TIMOTHY PONT AND THE MAPPING OF SCOTLAND, *c.*1583–1614

The story must begin with Pont, although the facts are sparse. So far as is known, Timothy Pont was born in the mid-1560s, possibly in 1565 or 1566, the second son of Robert Pont, who had inherited the lands of Shiresmill, north of Culross, in 1550. His father was a learned clergyman, friend to John Knox, and an advisor to King James VI. Amongst the many offices Robert Pont held was Church Commissioner for Moray, Inverness and Banff, and between 1571 and 1585 he was Provost of Trinity College, Edinburgh. We know that in 1574 the Master of Trinity College granted Timothy Pont lands in Strathmartin, income from which was to be used to pay for his education. We can be certain about Timothy matriculating at St Leonard's College in St Andrews for the academic year 1580–81, but although he paid his graduation fee in November 1583 we cannot be entirely sure of his graduation date. We know that in 1592 John Lindsay, Master of the Mines in Scotland, appointed Pont to undertake a survey of minerals and metals in Orkney and in Shetland (a commission he may have owed to his father's influence). In 1601, Pont was appointed to the Caithness parish of Dunnet.

It is possible that Timothy Pont's mapping work was complete by then, although it is conceivable too that he was, in effect, an absentee minister, using his time and the Church's money to carry on mapping into the seventeenth century. Pont's only dated map is that of Clydesdale, in 1596 (fig. 3.2). His written description of Cunningham district in south-west Scotland dates from about 1604 to 1608. We know that Pont tried, unsuccessfully, to secure new lands being settled by Scots in Ulster

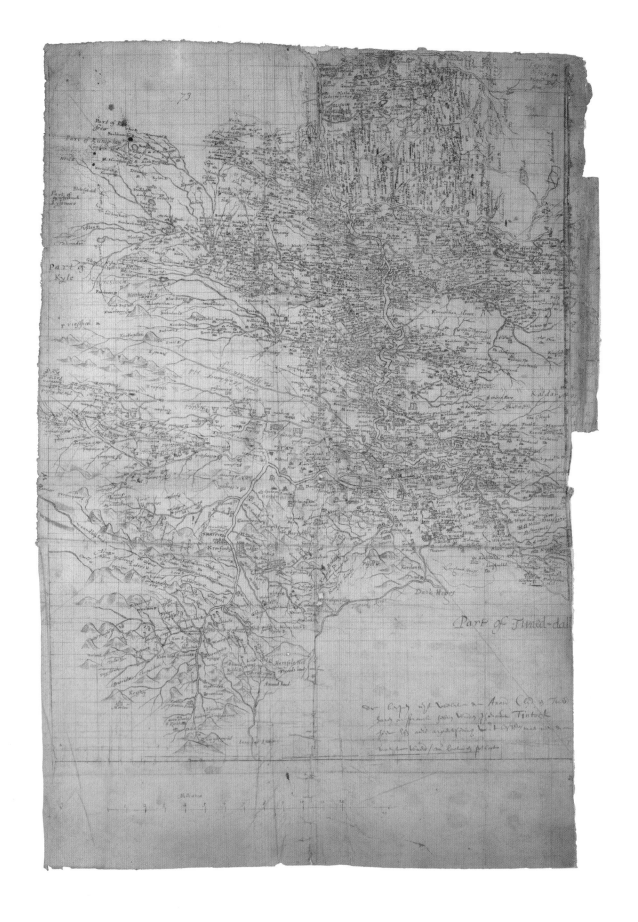

in 1609. In 1611, he was in Edinburgh, but we do not know how long he had been there, or for how long he stayed. By 1615, Pont was dead: his wife, Isobel, is that year recorded as a widow.

These are the few facts as to who Pont was. More pressing questions follow: 'What did Pont do?' 'How did he do it?' And, perhaps most interestingly, 'Why, and for whom?' These questions are all the more compelling given the age in which Pont was at work mapping Scotland: in the turbulent years of the Counter-Reformation; at a time when map-making was becoming a state concern; when the centre of gravity for map and atlas publishing in Europe was shifting away from Italy towards the Low Countries.

The surviving manuscript maps show that Pont mapped large parts of Scotland but that his coverage was incomplete (fig. 3.3). Whether he ever covered the whole country including the western and northern isles is unknown – we know that not all his manuscripts survive. His maps identify over 9,500 named places, mainly of human habitation. His maps show not just locations of features, but also stylised 'pictures', in two dimensions, of hills and mountains (fig. 3.4), and, for many of the more notable individual buildings, front or side views (fig. 3.5). For Scotland's towns, Pont commonly uses a stylised and figurative representation of a 'huddle' of buildings, seen in front rather than plan view, and often with the most prominent landmarks of the town in question: St John's

Church and the buildings along the west side of the River Tay in Perth, for example (fig. 3.6), or the distinctive cathedral in Elgin (fig. 3.7). In doing so, Pont is using map symbols – notably for settlements and for features such as mills and some churches – but he does so inconsistently. Similarly for natural features: rivers, lochs and

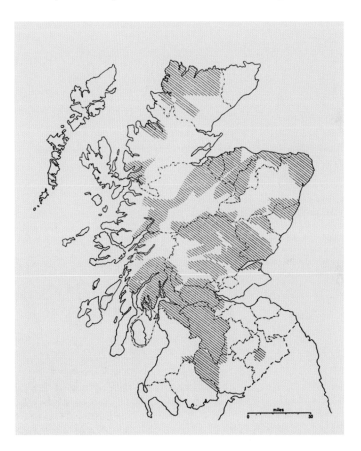

FIGURE 3.2 *Opposite.* This map of Clydesdale provides the only date on any of Pont's maps – '.../Sept et/ Octob:/1596 Descri/ pta' [top right of the image]. Although it has different alignments to its constituent parts, it is a well-finished draft from which Joan Blaeu was able to engrave the map for his *Atlas Novus* of 1654.
Source: Timothy Pont, Clydesdale, Pont 34 (*c*.1593–1614).
Reproduced by permission of the Trustees of the National Library of Scotland.

FIGURE 3.3 *Above.* We will never know for sure if Timothy Pont mapped the whole of Scotland, its outer islands included. The surviving manuscript maps show good coverage of Scotland south and east of the Great Glen, less complete coverage north and west of that divide, but large parts of south-west Scotland and of the eastern Borders were without known coverage.
Source: Timothy Pont, Index map of Scotland showing coverage of Pont's manuscript maps (*c*.2005). Reproduced by permission of Dr Jeffrey Stone.

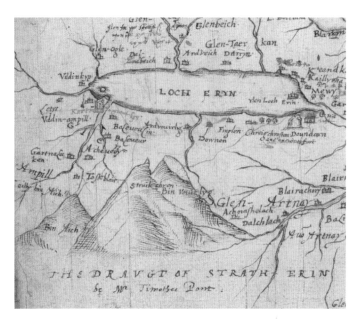

FIGURE 3.4 Pont's stylised depiction of topographical features – here of Stuic a'Chroin and 'Bin Vouirlyg' [Ben Vorlich], south of 'Loch Eryn' [Loch Earn] – lends a pictorial elegance to his maps: the hills are not drawn to scale, but as prominent and visible features in the landscape.
Source: Timothy Pont, Stuic a' Chroin and Ben Vorlich, Loch Earn, from Pont 21 (*c.*1583–1614). Reproduced by permission of the Trustees of the National Library of Scotland.

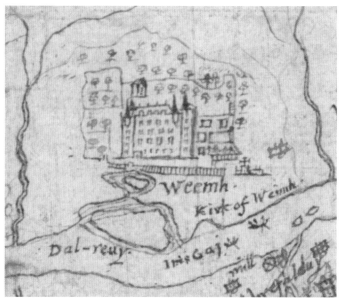

FIGURE 3.5 In this depiction of Castle Menzies at Weem, Perthshire, Pont mixes his lines of sight: a front view of the castle is accompanied by a plan view of its grounds: note, too, the stylised symbols for the chapel and for the trees.
Source: Timothy Pont, Castle Menzies, from Pont 23 (*c.*1583–1614). Reproduced by permission of the Trustees of the National Library of Scotland.

FIGURE 3.6 Timothy Pont's depiction of Perth shows St John's Church, the buildings of the city to the north and south of the High Street along the west bank of the River Tay (but no other street alignments), and, in a rather curious projection – drawn this way to make clear that it was a bridge – the bridge over the Tay that made Perth's position so strategically and commercially vital. The city's walls are also shown, as a two-ringed enclosure, to the west of the built-up area.
Source: Timothy Pont, Detail of Perth, from Pont 26 (*c.*1583–1614). Reproduced by permission of the Trustees of the National Library of Scotland.

FIGURE 3.7 In this fine Timothy Pont / Robert Gordon view of Elgin, many distinctive features of the town can be seen: its elevated castle (left), kirk (centre) and cathedral (right), surrounded by walls with ports (gateways) controlling access. The use of the cross within a circle – mid-left of the image – to signify a mill on the River Lossie, is characteristic of Pont's symbolisation.
Source: Timothy Pont, Elgin, from [Gordon 23] (*c.*1583–1614). Reproduced by permission of the Trustees of the National Library of Scotland.

the topographical 'lie of the land' are shown, but not in standardised ways.

Some parts of Scotland are identified rather generally – he describes part of Sutherland as 'extreem wildernes' for instance – yet for other regions the wealth of detail is great. Such variations are suggestive of the differing levels of geographical content to be recorded – then, as now, human settlement was concentrated in the south and east of Scotland – and, perhaps, of his spending longer in certain parts of the country than others, or because he may not even have visited all parts of Scotland. The names of the owners of many of the larger properties are given. Woodland is shown as one form of land cover, and Pont's maps have three woodland symbols. This may point to the fact that he was trying to differentiate between woodland of different type or age, although it is perhaps more likely that later hands added to or amended his symbolisation in this and in other respects. He shows woodland cover both as a general land feature and, in places, within parkland or the bounds of estates (fig. 3.8).

Short descriptions of the produce of areas are noted: Loch Tay, for instance, is remarkable for its 'fair salmonds trouts eeles and pearle' (fig. 3.9), and lands around Durness and Tongue are described as 'Gallant country of corn'. Several of his maps also have written notes in which historical sources are cited for the geographical information included. The fullest piece of textual description is Pont's account of Cunningham district, for which he lists, amongst other things, the 'Faiers and Mercats', notable towns and the region's soil types.

What Pont gives us is a unique picture of Scotland at the end of the sixteenth century: a still largely rural country, of fermtouns, great houses and country mills. He does so in an inconsistent cartographic language that

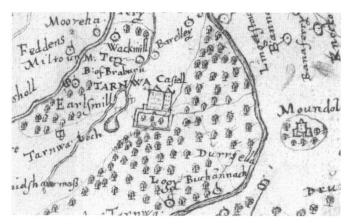

FIGURE 3.8 The detail shown here from Pont's map is of the woodlands round Darnaway, a few miles south-west of Forres. Darnaway Castle is shown as 'Tarnwa'. Note, too, the boundaries marking the extent of the 'Parck of Tarnwa' in contrast to the unenclosed woodland that is Mekil Wood to the south and east of the River Findhorn.
Source: Timothy Pont, Detail of Darnaway Castle, Moray, from Pont 8 (*c*.1583–1614). Reproduced by permission of the Trustees of the National Library of Scotland.

is wholly consistent with the period: stylised front-view drawings for prominent buildings, for towns and cities, and different symbols for woodland and the smaller settlements. He shows much of the topography of Scotland and its river systems.

Was this really the work of just one man? The answer to this must be 'yes', given the absence of evidence to the contrary, but with qualifications. One later letter noted that 'he [Pont] undertook all that work completely on his own'. But it is likely that Pont had guides to secure his safe passage through parts of the country which he cannot have known or been familiar enough with to make his way whilst writing things down or sketching. We are told of one 'Ewin Camro', Ewan Cameron, as an informant regarding details on one map. Pont, who probably did not speak Gaelic and so would have needed

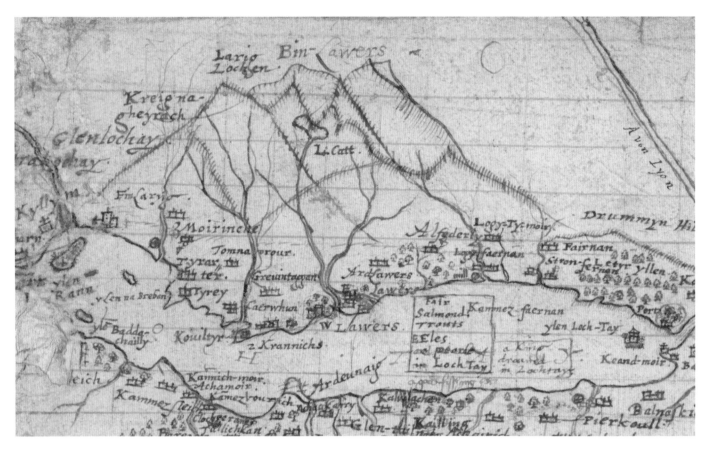

FIGURE 3.9 Timothy Pont's map of Ben Lawers and Loch Tay is illustrative of many of the features that make his maps so vital a source for the mapped representation of Scotland's topography and its economic and populated landscapes – and also so problematic. Pont shows settlements, woodland, and hints at previous crannog dwellings (ancient and early medieval lake houses, set on piles in the loch) with his mention of 'Krannichs' near the north shore. But his depiction of Ben Lawers is not accurate and cannot be presumed to be from the opposite bank of Loch Tay: the lochan shown here – 'L.Catt' [Lochan nan Catt] – on the mountain's slopes, is not visible from the far side. It is likely that Pont drew upon the knowledge of local informants.

Source: Timothy Pont, Detail of Ben Lawers and Loch Tay, from Pont 18 (*c.*1583–1614). Reproduced by permission of the Trustees of the National Library of Scotland.

linguistic as well as cartographic assistance, must have had more than one such guide for his labours. We have evidence of his secretary hand and his italic hand: both were common forms of writing style by this period. Pont seems to have used his secretary hand for all notes and his italic hand style for all place names (fig. 3.10). And, as we shall see, others later worked on his maps in preparing them for publication: Pont's is not the only handwriting on view (fig. 3.11).

How did he do all this? Answers to this question are less clear. The methods of triangulation were known by this time, but there is no evidence he used them. There are compass bearings given on eight of the maps. About

[A]

FIGURE 3.10 [A] Pont's use of italics (especially for place names) is clear in this figure, as is his use of abbreviations (including the colon to indicate the word is truncated), and his use of symbols for the smaller settlements. *Source:* Timothy Pont, Pont's italic hand from [Gordon 20] (*c.*1583–1614). Reproduced by permission of the Trustees of the National Library of Scotland.

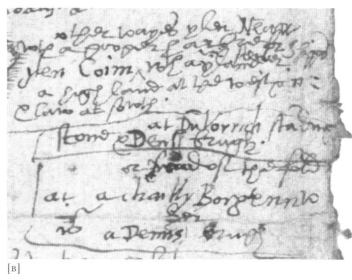

[B]

FIGURE 3.10 [B] This figure shows Pont's secretary hand, a common form of handwriting in daily use in this period, and used by Pont for all textual notes. *Source:* Timothy Pont, Secretary hand, from Pont 2 (*c.*1583–1614). Reproduced by permission of the Trustees of the National Library of Scotland.

one-third overall have notes on linear distances between places. From the evidence of the handwriting, however, and from the inks used, it is likely that these were added by Robert Gordon. There is no standard scale and little evidence to suggest that Pont used instruments in the field to fix the position of places. Planimetrically (the physical extent of a feature shown in plan view), many features are inaccurate.

There are, nevertheless, clues to his methods. Many features are shown as sketches, in outline or two-dimensional form, almost as if he had gained vantage points in the countryside in order to depict them. Two-thirds or so of his manuscript maps are bounded on their inland edges by rivers or by a watershed: it may even be that such catchment areas – Glen Isla, Strath Carron or Glen Almond, for example – provide the basic 'unit' of Pont's mapping. Pont probably followed the lines of rivers and river valleys, piecing together smaller 'mosaic' pictures to make larger correct composite maps, almost certainly drawing by eye rather than measuring by chain or rule.

How should we understand what Pont has done? His is not in any proper sense a topographic survey, born of detailed measurement. His coverage is incomplete, his symbolisation inconsistent. He uses textual description to elaborate upon place-based information. It is inappropriate to think in terms of 'map accuracy', if by that term

FIGURE 3.11 In this image, we see not only the difference between the handwriting of Timothy Pont and Robert Gordon – Gordon's handwriting dominates the left-hand side of the map – but the later 'overlay', in red ink of the grid of lines, probably by Robert Gordon to aid in the later engraving and printing of the map.

Source: Timothy Pont / Robert Gordon, Handwriting comparison between Pont and Gordon, from Pont 32 (*c.*1583–1614). Reproduced by permission of the Trustees of the National Library of Scotland.

we mean locational exactitude, scaled representation, the delineation of natural and human features in standard ways. His remarks often concern the quality of places, the lineage of families – the content of the nation rather than its dimensions. What Pont gives us is not a geographical or topographical survey underpinned by a concern for representational accuracy, but rather an essentially qualitative, even impressionistic, account in text and image of the nature of the nation. Contemporaries knew this as chorography.

Chorography was the most widely practised form of geographical enquiry throughout Europe in this period. Unlike cosmography, which dealt with the earth in relation to other heavenly bodies, and geography, which dealt with the description of the whole earth, chorography aimed at the delineation, in maps and text, of local areas, or parts of the globe. Chorography was essentially concerned with the qualities and characters of places and areas rather than with their accurate location or measurement. We would know it now as 'regional geography'. Chorography then was a widespread form of political 'land writing' – of knowing which landed families were where, where mines and forests lay, where towns were located and, roughly, their size, what the produce of a region was, and so on – as well as a geographical method.

Knowing that what he undertook was a chorography and that chorography was commonplace helps greatly in understanding what Pont did. But it only partly explains why. Although we still do not know his motivations, far less how he did what he did, several reasons may be advanced for his undertaking this mapping work.

The use of chorography as a form of state political and geographical survey has its origins in Renaissance Italy. But it was later revived and strengthened in Europe more generally by Abraham Ortelius, author of *Theatrum Orbis Terrarum* (1570), arguably the world's first modern atlas, and, in the same year, of *Parergon*, a collection of maps illustrating mainland Europe's Roman legacy. In England, chorography found expression from the 1530s in the work of John Leland, who aimed to serve 'king and country' through the textual art of regional description, and in a 1576 survey of Kent. It reached a high point there in the publication in 1586 of William Camden's *Britannia*. Ortelius's *Parergon* and Camden's *Britannia* were major works of chorography, but, perhaps because they were innovative, they were also incomplete. *Parergon* had no maps of Britain, and Camden's *Britannia* had no maps of Scotland until its second edition of 1607, which included Mercator's map of 1595.

Was Pont's work an attempt to fill the gaps in these European geographical projects? There is, unfortunately, no evidence to confirm this. We know his father moved in learned and courtly circles in Scotland and that at least one element of Timothy Pont's career, the time he spent as an inspector of mines and minerals, was directly consistent with the aims of state surveillance and chorographical enquiry. We can surmise that, in the years when he was a St Andrews undergraduate, he would have encountered William Welwood, professor at St Salvator's College who taught arithmetic, geometry, geography and astronomy and, significantly, 'the making of the cartes [charts, that is maps] universall and particular'.

Or was the need for mapping as statecraft greater at home? King James VI faced considerable unrest in the Highlands and Islands in the 1580s and 1590s. His *Basilicon Doron* (1599) was a manual of kingship and civil administration to deal with the 'Highland problem'. The king's concern for civic order in the Highlands reached a high point with the passing of the Statutes of Iona in 1609: English was to be the language of civilisation; burghs were to be established to promote commerce; all aimed at bringing 'the Hielandis and Iles to civilitie'. Even if these statutes were honoured more in the breach than the observance, the political intent was clear. Recall, too, that Nicolay's maritime map of 1583 had delineated the kingdom's margins. Was Pont – employed as a mineral surveyor in the early 1590s, on the move as a chorographer, an author on Cunningham district – filling in the nation's terrestrial content?

Might his work have been part of a yet bigger

geographical need – to understand that new political entity 'Great Britain'? With the ascension of James VI of Scotland as James I of England in 1603, knowing one's realm through maps assumed great importance for the new united kingdom. That is certainly why Pont's near contemporary, John Speed, produced his 1611 *Theatre of the Empire of Great Britaine*, Britain's first atlas, to help integrate the 'empire' that was the newly established Great Britain from the handful of its constituent kingdoms.

And, no less than kings, churchmen and civil authorities also need to know their areas of jurisdiction – particularly, as in Pont's time, where the writ of God and government was being ignored for lack of ministers and parish officers, or, for some far worse, where Catholicism lingered in a post-Reformation Scotland. From 1588, Robert Pont had been appointed to a commission whose brief was to visit northern Scotland with a view to 'planting' ministers there, that is, filling the Church vacancies or the new positions with churchmen loyal to the new faith. Was Timothy Pont's task actually ecclesiastical, even specifically Presbyterian – to map the location of churches and nobles' houses and thus plot the bounds of religious and political loyalty? It is hard to imagine that Pont was not exposed to something of his father's and others' concerns to populate Scotland with right-minded men or to know where they might be found.

Although we shall probably never know for sure what prompted his work, we should not be in any doubt over Pont's manuscript maps and textual descriptions. They are a crucial record of Scotland's geography and history, and a vivid demonstration of the importance of mapping in national self-recognition. It took others, however, to bring Pont to print. And, as they did so, they added to Pont's work in the process.

THE PUBLICATION HISTORY OF BLAEU'S 1654 *ATLAS NOVUS*

Pont's heirs neglected his maps. By the 1620s, the maps were reported as being 'worm and moth-eaten', 'becoming illegible even to careful eyes'. But where his family failed to understand their significance, others did. In 1628, they were acquired by one of Scotland's leading government officers, Sir James Balfour of Denmilne, then

FIGURE 3.12 Portrait of Joan Blaeu (*c.*1650).
Source: Copyright © National Maritime Museum, Amsterdam.

Lord Lyon. The following year, King Charles I – recognising his father James VI and I's earlier unfulfilled intention to support Pont in his mapping – provided Balfour with £100 (Scots) to assist with their publication. Balfour, meantime, had passed the maps to a fellow civil servant, Sir John Scot of Scotstarvit, Director of Chancery, Lord of Session and a Privy Councillor. More than any other single figure, Sir John Scot is the link that connects Pont to Blaeu (fig. 3.12).

FIGURE 3.13 Portrait of Robert Gordon of Straloch (*c.*1640).
Source: Reproduced by permission of the Trustees of the National Library of Scotland.

Intellectually and economically, Scotland was closely bound to the Low Countries in the seventeenth century. Amsterdam was by then the world centre of geographical publishing, the Blaeu firm, under the guidance of Willem Janszoon Blaeu and his son Joan, its leading map publishing house. Scot had been in correspondence since the 1620s with the Blaeus over the publication of a volume of poetry. Like Balfour of Denmilne, who wrote (but never published) 'Topographical descriptions relating to Scotland', Scot was active in geographical authorship as well as politics. The Blaeus were engaged in their world atlas project. For Scot, and for the Blaeus, albeit for different reasons, the mapping work in his charge was a chance to place Scotland – and themselves – at the heart of European publishing.

By 1631, Scot had passed Pont's maps to the Blaeu firm. By 1642, Joan Blaeu had completed the engraving of about thirty-five or thirty-six maps directly from Pont's work. But the maps forwarded by Scot were insufficient, either lacking in coverage or illegible, so Joan Blaeu, in order to complete the atlas, pulled together a list of the areas for which more complete maps were still needed. Sometime before 1636, Blaeu passed back to Robert Gordon those of Pont's original maps on which he required further assistance. Seven more maps were then compiled by Robert Gordon using Pont manuscripts with no addition or revision. Three smaller-scale maps were also compiled by Robert Gordon (fig. 3.13) to cover remaining blanks in the atlas and incorporating new information. One map was drafted by James Gordon.

The result of these cartographic exchanges was, essentially, twofold: the Gordons provided seven drafts based exclusively on Pont's observations, as well as four new maps for what would become the 1654 *Atlas*, including

FIGURE 3.14 *Above*. This map of part of Strathcarron
in Easter Ross is from a Robert Gordon map, based
on a now-lost (or perhaps never undertaken) map by
Timothy Pont.
Source: Robert Gordon, Detail from Strathcarron,
Easter Ross from Gordon 19 (*c.*1636–52). Reproduced
by permission of the Trustees of the National Library
of Scotland.

FIGURE 3.15 *Opposite*. This map of Lauderdale –
'Lauderdalia' – from Blaeu's 1654 *Atlas Novus* – shows
many of the features typical of the work as a whole:
a hierarchy of settlement size suggested by the use of
different symbols; woodland; stylised topography; and,
to the bottom left, acknowledgement in the words
'Auct. Tim. Pont' of the man with whom it all began.
Blaeu's acknowledgement in the colourful cartouche
is to John Maitland, Earl of Lauderdale, and astutely
reflects the patronage networks through which the
work was brought to fruition.
Source: Joan Blaeu, 'Laudelia sive Lauderdalia' from
Atlas Novus (1654). Reproduced by permission of
the Trustees of the National Library of Scotland.

James Gordon's map of Fife, which was undertaken in
1642, and, importantly, Robert Gordon transcribed many
of Pont's written notes and embellished and annotated
many of Pont's original maps. Thus Blaeu worked with
Pont's original materials, supplemented by Robert
Gordon's drafts – even some poetry from writers like
David Buchanan and Arthur Johnston – and new work
from the Gordons. For some parts of Scotland, this additional work is now all we have: the work of the Gordons
on maps based on Pont has survived, but the original
Pont manuscript has not (fig. 3.14).

What Sir John Scot and others recognised is that, for
chorography to work, maps – even ones added to by later
authors – are better if accompanied by up-to-date textual
descriptions. During the 1640s, Sir John Scot petitioned
the General Assembly of the Church of Scotland for its
ministers to provide topographical information to
accompany the map. Scotland's churchmen discussed the
Atlas project six times at their General Assembly between
1641 and 1649. Whilst the idea was sensible in conception
– for who else but parish clergy could be relied upon for
detailed knowledge of their parishes and presbyteries? –
it was impossible to realise, given the religious and political conflict then sweeping Scotland, and also because
population movement was restricted on account of
outbreaks of bubonic plague and smallpox. So Blaeu
turned for his *Atlas* not to current testimony but to
William Camden's 1607 *Britannia* for many of the
regional accounts and to George Buchanan's 1582 *History
of Scotland* for the geographical overview: there was
almost nothing else currently available.

By 1649 Blaeu was ready to begin printing volume V
of his *Atlas Novus*. But, again, events beyond his control
conspired to stay his hand – King Charles I was executed;
Cromwell's armies occupied Scotland; and Scotstarvit

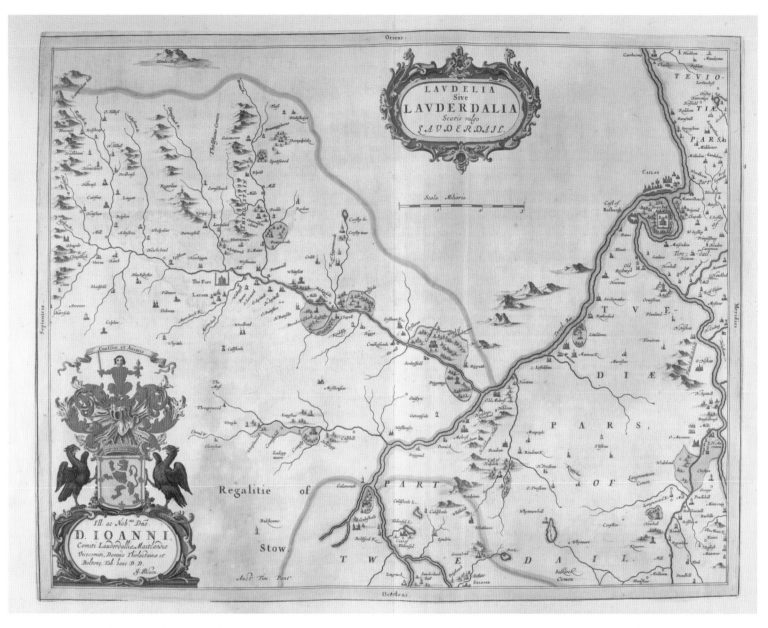

was later fined and stripped of his official posts by Cromwell. Disease and crop failure were again making life hazardous. The Anglo-Dutch War of 1652–54 had halted cultural and economic exchange.

In June 1654, however, in the wake of war, after its constituent parts had several times crossed the North Sea, having being rescued from neglect, written upon by others, and supplemented by yet others' textual descrip-

tions, Pont's manuscript maps became the basis of an Amsterdam-published *Atlas* – part of a world series of mapping – in which Scotland stands centre stage. 'Now at last', wrote Robert Gordon, 'after many labours endured, the loss of much time and troubles, such as the mind shudders to recall, our Scotland is put on view'. The maps, presented by region or county, illustrate and illuminate Scotland as never before (fig. 3.15).

THE AFTERLIFE OF *ATLAS NOVUS*: PONT AND BLAEU'S LEGACY AND LATER MAPPING

We should be in no doubt that volume V of Blaeu's *Atlas*, based on Pont's chorographical work and others' maps and words, is a hugely important work in the history of Scottish mapping and European publishing. Yet, for the reasons outlined, we must be cautious about seeing it as the work of a single 'author' map-maker, and in treating its maps and descriptions as a single 'time window' on Scotland's past. The maps were produced at different moments by different people. The texts are uneven in length, content and accuracy. Not everyone could or would read it. It was first published in Latin, the language of the literate, not of daily conversation. Although Dutch, French and German editions followed the 1654 printing, and a Spanish edition appeared in 1659 – there never was an English language edition – the *Atlas Novus*, as with other works by Blaeu, would have been a valued possession, even a status object, rather more than a work on open access to the public, affordable and available to all.

It is appropriate, then, in placing this work in the longer history of Scotland's mapping to distinguish between its contemporary or near-contemporary reception, and later changing judgement of it, and of Pont and his work over the longer term. People have been studying Pont's maps for over 400 years, Blaeu's *Atlas* for over 350 years – but not necessarily to agree. Where, now, Pont is understood as a chorographer, he was once a 'surveyor', even Scotland's 'first topographer'. We have no idea what he called himself. Historians have at one time or another differently attributed the maps, and the handwriting on them, as Pont's or Robert Gordon's: only recently has the advent of new technology allowed clear distinction to be made between them.

Expanded textual descriptions of parts of Scotland and some textual corrections appeared in a 1662 edition of the *Atlas*. Later in the seventeenth century, Scotland's Geographer Royal, Sir Robert Sibbald, planned to update Blaeu's work. Sibbald engaged in a great variety of geographical work and he recognised that, in part, his credibility as geographer to the king and the state depended upon doing new work or, at least, in exposing the flaws in the old. In his *An Account of the Scotish Atlas* (1683) Sibbald complained about Blaeu's use of Camden and 'the bulk' of Blaeu's published '*Theater of Scotland*' as he termed it. But mainly Sibbald stressed that new mapping work was needed because the geography of the country had changed in the interim: 'There are many Islands around this ancient Kingdom of *Scotland* . . . which ought to be exactly described for the security of Trade. And because the face of the country, by the peace and quiet we enjoy under his *Majestie's* happy Government, is quite changed from what it was of old . . . , therefore a new and full description was much desired by all ingenious persons.'

This was true of course. But Sibbald was too busy to do the work himself and although he gathered materials for a new geography of Scotland – at one time he had possession of Pont's papers – the work of mapping Scotland from the 1680s fell mainly to another man, John Adair, who partly worked in association with Sibbald (before the two argued over funding), but mainly on his own.

John Adair – 'Mathematician and skilful Mechanick' as Sibbald described him before they fell out – undertook county-based mapping of the east of Scotland in the early 1680s (fig. 3.16), before gradually making his way north-

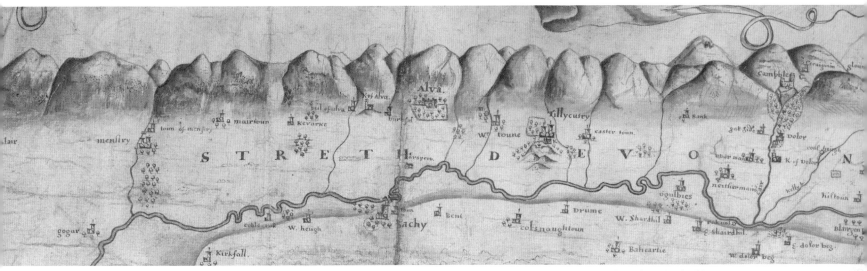

FIGURE 3.16 In May of 1681, the map-maker John Adair had been given 'incouragement and assistance' from the Privy Council 'to take a Survey of the whole Shires in the Kingdom, and to make up Mapps thereof'. One of those which survives is an original manuscript version of his map of Clackmannanshire with its striking rendering of the 'wall-like' Ochil Hills as background, rather like a theatre stage backcloth.
Source: John Adair, *A Mapp of Clakmanan Shire* (*c.*1681). Reproduced by permission of the Trustees of the National Library of Scotland.

wards to produce sea charts of the Western Isles and other maps. Adair's work matters not just because, with others, he was seeking to delineate Scotland in more up-to-date maps than Blaeu's *Atlas*. He is significant because, with the possible exception of Sibbald who owed his status more to royal than civil patronage, Adair was funded as a map-maker by the Scottish purse. He is recognition that mapping mattered to the nation's economy. In June 1686, an act was passed 'In Favours of John Adair, Geographer, for Surveying the Kingdom of Scotland, and Navigating the Coasts and Isles thereof', with the money coming from a tonnage levy applied to Scottish and foreign ships.

But it was never sufficient. Adair's work, like others since, was undercut by lack of finance even as mapping was recognised as vital.

By the late seventeenth century, Scotland's mapping was evident in several ways. The Pont–Gordon–Blaeu work still had a central place. One reason for this is that mapping as a form of geographical representation and national identity, and its publication, was expensive, as Adair knew only too well. Because it is, many later map-makers – despite using terms such as 'new' and 'accurate' in promotion of their work – often used older outlines, denying their own claims to currency and novelty in

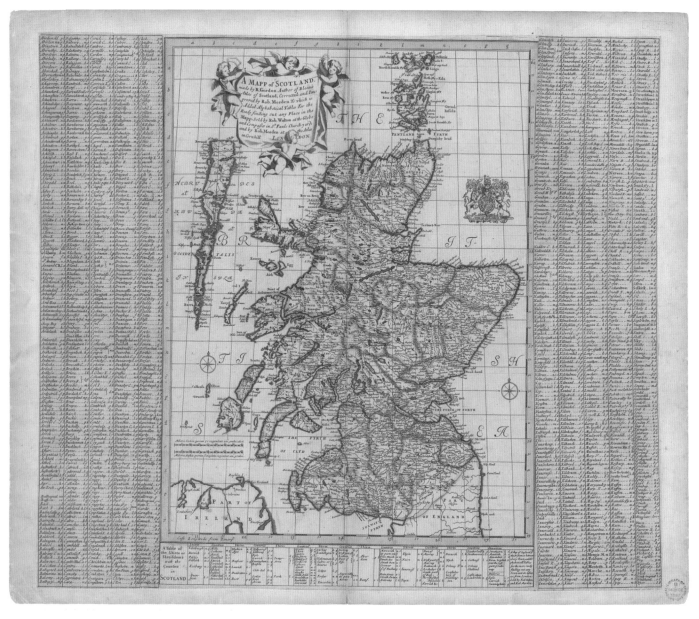

FIGURE 3.17 The English map-maker Robert Morden entitled his
1687 map, 'A Mapp of Scotland: made by R.[obert] Gordon, Author of
Bleau's [sic] Atlas of Scotland, corrected and Improved by Rob.
Morden' – see the vignette on page 50. Yet Morden has done little to
justify this title other than to add a grid-square and the alphabetical
tables: the shape of Skye, of the lochs in the Great Glen and of the Butt
of Lewis are all taken, without correction or improvement, from Blaeu.
Source: Robert Morden, *A Mapp of Scotland: Made by R. Gordon . . .
Corrected and Improved by Rob. Morden.* (1687). Reproduced by
permission of the Trustees of the National Library of Scotland.

doing so (fig. 3.17). Blaeu's outline of Scotland continued
to frame some map-makers' depiction of Scotland until
the late eighteenth century (fig. 3.18).

Timothy Pont cannot have dreamed his work would
have been so important, its publication so complicated,
his legacy so enduring. At the same time, map-makers
within Scotland, like Adair, and from other countries,
turned to Scotland, either as the object of their mapping

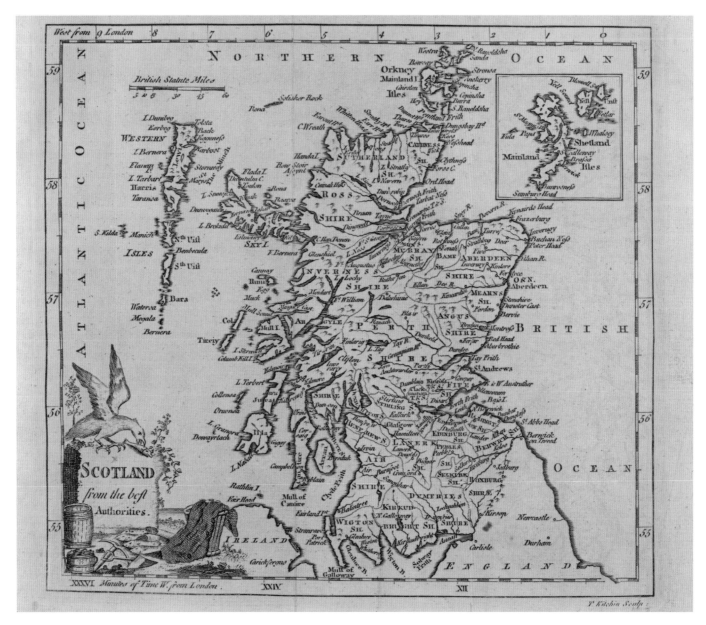

or as part of geographical works and atlases, and increasingly with a sense of the power of maps as visual documents (fig. 3.19). By the early eighteenth century, different sorts of maps were becoming more common, and maps were being used in different walks of life. It is to these types of maps and to the ways that maps illustrate themes in the history and geography of the nation that we now turn.

FIGURE 3.18 Thomas Kitchin's 1771 map 'Scotland from the best Authorities' claims in its title an authority and novelty that its content belies: it is based on Joan Blaeu's work of nearly 120 years earlier! *Source:* Thomas Kitchin, *Scotland from the Best Authorities* (1771). Reproduced by permission of the Trustees of the National Library of Scotland.

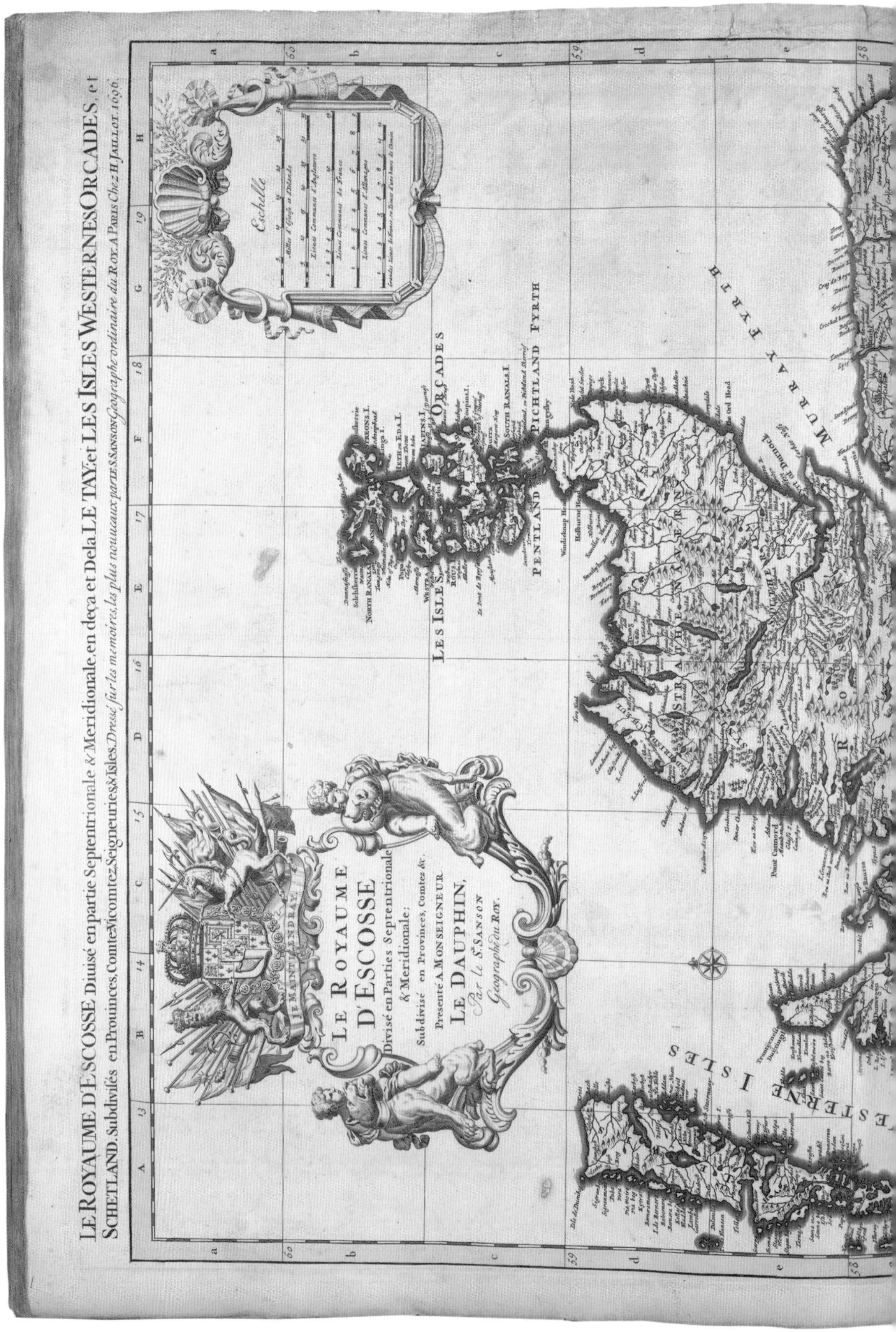

FIGURE 3.19 This map of Scotland by the
leading French geographer Nicolas Sanson
appeared as part of the *Atlas Nouveau Contenant
toutes les parties du Monde* in 1696, published by
Hubert Jaillot in Paris.
Source: Nicolas Sanson, *Le Royaume d'Escosse
Divisé en parties Septentrionale* (1696).
Reproduced by permission of the Trustees of
the National Library of Scotland.

CHAPTER 4

SCOTLAND OCCUPIED
AND DEFENDED

In May 1544, English armies under the command of the Earl of Hertford swept through south-east Scotland. In the events that followed, that quarter of the Lowlands was laid waste. Castles were demolished, towns were garrisoned, and thousands of people lost their lives. In two raids on Edinburgh, one-third of the men on the burgh's muster roll were killed, whilst at the Battle of Pinkie (1547), near Inveresk, over 15,000 Scots were slain and a further 1,500 captured. In the second stage of what has become known as the 'Rough Wooing' – part of that attempt by England's King Henry VIII to force the betrothal of the young Princess Mary to his infant son Edward – over twenty fortresses were constructed at vast expense along the main passes and routes through the Borders and along Scotland's east coast. Most survived long after a shaky peace was officially declared between Scotland and England in June 1551.

The Rough Wooing – part of that long history of bitter conflict between Scotland and England – is significant in Scotland's map history. The events of the period exposed the need for new and different sorts of maps. In this period we get Scotland's first battle maps. Some of the earliest detailed maps of places in Scotland drawn from first-hand evidence date from this time: a bird's-eye view of Edinburgh (1544), for example, or the 'Platte of Milkcastle' in Dumfries-shire (1547). As well as maps of battles and of towns, maps of forts were drawn up (fig. 4.1).

These different map types illustrate the close links between warfare and cartography, and offer unique insights into the military campaigns themselves. These military maps from the mid-sixteenth century also stand at the beginning of a long and rich chapter in Scotland's mapping which extends to the present day. By far the best-funded and the most comprehensive mapping of the country has been for military purposes – one notable result of Scotland's turbulent history of warfare and conflict, particularly with England.

Scotland is not alone in this respect. Many of the most important innovations in surveying technologies and in cartographic techniques throughout Europe had a military origin, and were introduced into Scotland through the work of foreign military engineers. Those Italian

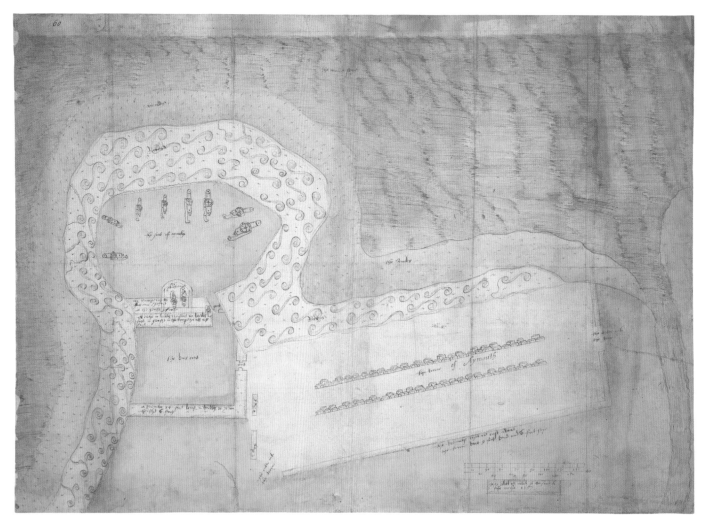

military engineers, for example, who accompanied the Earl of Hertford into Scotland not only introduced the *trace italienne* (star fort), but are also credited with introducing scale maps into Britain, maps which showed their chosen area of ground with precision and in mathematical proportion. Such maps – and such techniques – spoke to the need for equivalent precision in warfare, to the plotting and building of forts and lines of national defence. Even so, such maps for Scotland presented only a partial view of the country for conquering forces: lines of communication, the nature of the defences to be faced. New maps were needed for conquest and defence but these images were also often tools of propaganda for

external aggressors (as we have seen of Hardyng's map: fig. 2.5). Indeed, they represent something of a paradox. As this chapter illustrates, some of the most strikingly attractive maps of Scotland arose out of violence and bloodshed and were made by outsiders intending to conquer and subdue the country.

Although Scotland's military mapping dates from the 1540s, its maps and their makers belong to a much older tradition. We know, for example, that the Romans employed surveyors (*agrimensores*) to create a wide range of maps useful for imperial conquest. These were often for practical purposes – for planning roads, camps and defensive structures, as well as for commemorating battles

FIGURE 4.1 *Opposite*. Sir Richard Lee, knighted by Henry VIII of England for his role in the attack on Edinburgh in 1544, designed this simple fortress at Eyemouth in 1547 with its Italianate angle bastions – the first *trace italienne* fortification in Britain. The plan is distinctive both for its cartography and for what it reveals of innovations in military engineering. The scale and dividers serve to illustrate this early example in Britain of a map drawn to scale. Lee went on to design the impressive fortifications at Berwick-upon-Tweed along similar principles.
Source: Eyemouth – *A Plan of Aymouth, or Eyemouth, [Berwickshire] Taken in 1557, in Which Year it was Fortified by Henri Clutin, Sieur d'Oysell et de Ville Parisis* (1557). Reproduced by permission of the British Library.

and conquest. Although no original Roman maps of Scotland survive today, there is evidence from elsewhere in Europe that the Roman conquests of Scotland would have involved surveyors laying out encampments and roads and working with graphical representations of territory.

The millennium after the fall of Rome has left no evidence of military cartography in Scotland. So far as we know, most conquest relied upon oral or verbal information, and even in unusual cases when topographic information was recorded by later medieval scribes it was often in textual rather than graphic form. As we showed in chapter 2, the remarkable Gough Map (fig. 2.4) is an early topographic map with military connections, given its link to the itineraries of Edward I and to Scotland's Wars of Independence between 1297 and 1328. Although the purpose of this map and its precise association with Edward I are uncertain, the features selected for inclusion may well have had military value: many of the place names on it relate directly to routes taken by the English armies. Nevertheless, there is no evidence that this map served a practical role in planning conquest, in laying out lines of advance or in depicting defensive strongholds, all features found on such maps in later periods.

MAPPING AND THE MILITARY REVOLUTION

Between 1500 and 1700, throughout Europe, armies dramatically expanded in their size and complexity. Standing armies became the norm. There was a significant increase in the killing power of artillery in particular. This 'military revolution' prompted the design and building of new types of defence to try to withstand this heightened capacity to destroy from distance. There is compelling evidence of the importance of maps as instruments of warfare and of related changes in maps and map production to suit this purpose.

In many countries, these changes also resulted in the development of specialist corps of military engineers, trained in military academies. These men, skilled in mathematics, in geometry, in ballistics, in such things as 'the theory of fortifications' and, not least, in the ability to read the land from a military perspective and to put such a reading down in map form, created maps, at a range of scales, as practical tools for these new forms of warfare. In turn, over time, and although the combatants and the locations of warfare changed, military maps began to share distinctive features and to develop, particularly from the eighteenth century, a specific military map language: drafted in pen and watercolour, they had prescribed military colour schemes and scale. Mapping in these ways developed its own standards, but it did not reach wider audiences. Such mapping was made for restricted military audiences, commanders in the field or for queens, kings and emperors who sheltered behind the lines.

At certain moments – not least during the Rough Wooing of the 1540s, but also during the Cromwellian Protectorate of the 1650s, and in the peak years of Jacobite insurrection in 1708, 1715–16, and 1745–46 – Scot-

FIGURE 4.2 Cromwellian military might is well symbolised in this plan. The fortress at Ayr was designed by Hans Ewart Tessin and constructed on hitherto undeveloped ground to the south of the river estuary as a hexagonal structure with ramparts and bastions.
Source: Thomas Walker, *A Plan of the Town and Citadell of Air* (1650s). Reproduced by permission of the British Library.

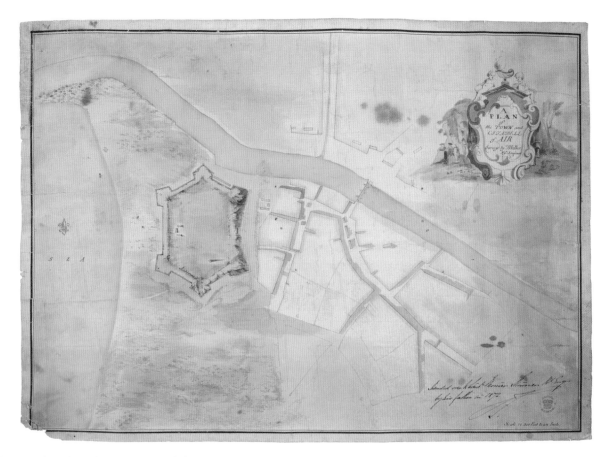

land was the theatre for the playing out of these new military technologies and the distinctive forms of cartographic depiction which accompanied them.

Relatively few maps survive from the Cromwellian period and the rule of General Monck in Scotland. The few which do chiefly illustrate the imposing citadels, situated in Ayr, Inverness, Leith and Perth, that were begun in the early 1650s (fig. 4.2). These citadels formed part of a wider system of garrisoned forts and were a familiar solution to the problem of subjugating an alien and hostile population in Scotland with limited resources and where lines of supply stretched over distance. These were impressive and expensive buildings – one contemporary

estimated that the construction of each citadel cost over £100,000 pounds – and they were doubtless effective in symbolising the might of the Lord Protector. It is important to note, however, that most of these forts were never fully completed, and most were substantially demolished soon after the Restoration of King Charles II in 1660. The maps of them that survive are thus important as unique cartographic records of military intent rather more than as depictions of enduring features in the landscape. From the later seventeenth century, most of the military maps and the military engineering that was done in Scotland were undertaken through the Board of Ordnance.

THE BOARD OF ORDNANCE MAPS OF SCOTLAND

The Board of Ordnance was first established in the four-teenth century and is not to be confused with Ordnance Survey, begun in 1791, which was also, as we shall see, heavily involved in mapping from a military point of view. In 1683, the Board of Ordnance was modernised and re-structured as an agency of government whose central purpose was to provide technical assistance in matters to do with artillery and military engineering. Mapping was a crucial part of its work, alongside respon-sibility for munitions and, as the Board was custodian of forts and castles, the defence of the realm. As a result, its activities were predominantly focused on maps of fortifi-cations, but the Board's engineers were also employed in making maps of roads, battles and even the wider coun-tryside from a military point of view.

The Board of Ordnance military maps of Scotland were drafted with a clear understanding of military purpose and context. As with many of their European counterparts, they adopted a conventional map language in their use of colour and symbol, although some of their images mixed plan views of buildings with topographic views of the surrounding landscape, or, to use a then contemporary term, the 'scenography' of the countryside (fig. 4.3).

This work and mapping depended upon a sound understanding of mathematics and geometry. The responsibilities of the chief engineer as laid down at the modernising of the Board in 1683 stated, for example, that he was 'to be well-skilled in all the parts of the Math-ematicks, more particularly in Stereometry, Altemetry, and Geodoesia'. He was, furthermore, 'To [be able to] take Distances, Heights, Depths, Surveys of Land, Measure of solid Bodies; . . . to draw and design the situ-ation of any place, in their due Prospects, Uprights, and Perspective; . . . To keep perfect draughts of . . . the Forti-fications . . . of our Kingdoms, their situation, figure and profile'. Such language echoes what we saw in chapter 3 of the instructions to John Adair at much the same time. It does so because of the emphasis then being placed by bodies such as the Royal Society upon mathematical precision and 'plainness in speech' as advanced methods in natural philosophy – what would later come to be known as science. From the 1720s, engineer cadets were given formal instruction in these subjects and military draughtsmanship in the Drawing Room of the Tower of London, and, from 1741, the Royal Military Academy at Woolwich provided more formal training.

This growing military and cartographic expertise is beautifully illustrated in over 800 surviving military maps of Scotland made by the Board of Ordnance between 1689 and 1814. These maps and plans show what we might think of as Scotland the Militarised Landscape: some document the repair and redevelopment of medieval castles (such as Dumbarton, Edinburgh, Stirling and Inverness), for instance, whilst others show the plan-ning and construction of wholly new forts (such as Inversnaid, Ruthven, Bernera, Kiliwhimen and Fort George at Ardersier) (fig. 4.4).

The earliest surviving town plans of Inverness and Perth were drafted by Board of Ordnance engineer Lewis Petit in 1716, immediately following the towns' recapture from the Jacobites (fig. 4.5). Lewis Petit was a French Huguenot, who escaped religious persecution in France after the revocation of the Edict of Nantes in 1685 by joining the Board of Ordnance. He saw active and distinguished service in mainland Europe in the War of

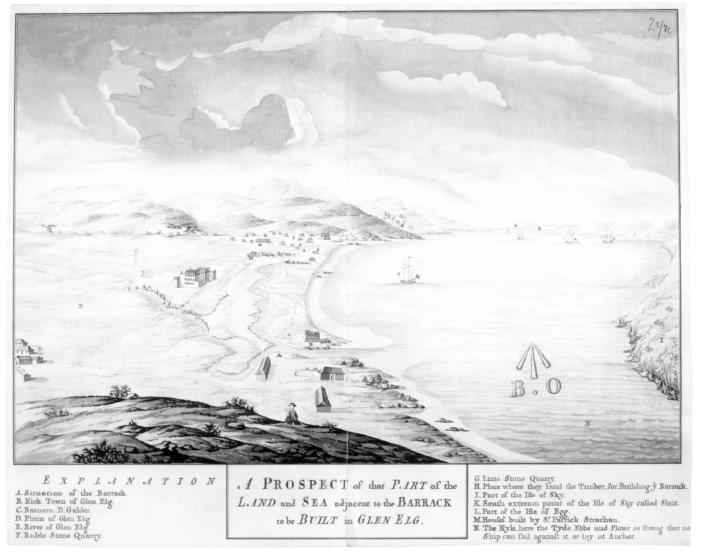

EXPLANATION

A. Situation of the Barrack.
B. Kirk Town of Glen Elg.
C. Barnera. D. Galder.
D. Plain of Glen Elg.
E. River of Glen Elg.
F. Ruble Stone Quarry.

A PROSPECT of that PART of the
LAND and SEA adjacent to the BARRACK
to be BUILT in GLEN ELG.

G. Lime Stone Quarry.
H. Place where they land the Timber, for Building ŷ Barrack.
I. Part of the Isle of Sky.
K. South extream point of the Isle of Sky called Slait.
L. Part of the Isle of Egg.
M. Houses built by Sr Patrick Strachan.
N. The Kyle, here the Tyde Ebbs and Flows so throug that no
    Ship can sail against it, or lay at Anchor.

FIGURE 4.3 The depiction of the barracks at Bernera, near Glenelg in Wester Ross, shows several of the features typical of Board of Ordnance mapping: a topographic portrayal of landscape and the layout of the buildings. Bernera was constructed from the 1720s as a defensible barracks with accommodation for 200 men, to control the crossing to Skye. Note the engineer at work in the foreground.
Source: [John Henry Bastide], *A Prospect of that Part of the Land and Sea adjacent to the Barrack . . . in Glen Elg* (1720). Reproduced by permission of the Trustees of the National Library of Scotland.

the Spanish Succession, and was chiefly responsible for the capture of Minorca from the French in 1708. In 1714 he was sent to Scotland to report on the dilapidated state of defences at Fort William and outlying forts. Plans by him and by others survive of Castle Tioram (fig. 4.6), Duart Castle, Invergarry Castle and Eilean Donan Castle. In the following year, the Duke of Argyll appointed Petit Chief Engineer, and it was in this capacity that he was first at the scene following the recapture of Perth from the Jacobites in January 1716.

Following General George Wade's commission

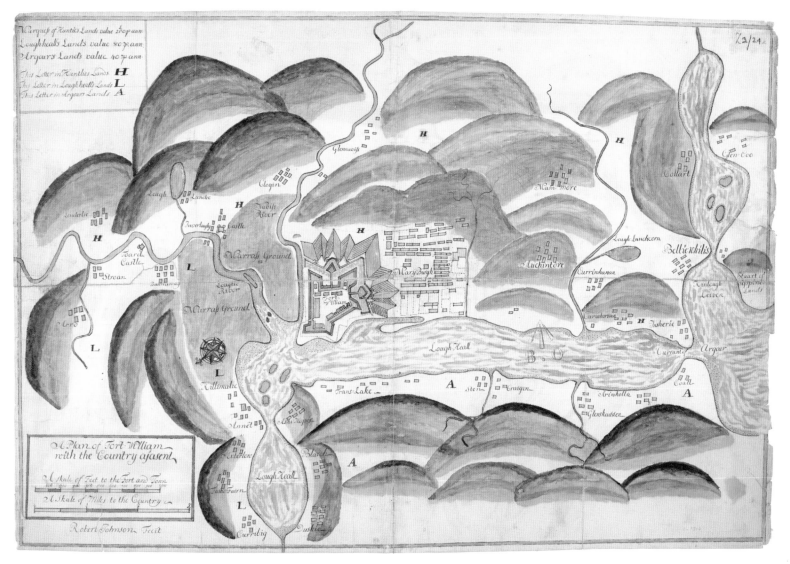

between 1724 and 1740 as Commander-in-Chief of His Majesty's forces in North Britain, maps were drawn up to plan and construct over 250 miles of military roads to link the emerging network of new forts and garrisons. Buildings were shown in detail, as were such things as barracks, officers' quarters, gunpowder stores: this was mapping to know the capacity of the state to wage war (fig. 4.7). In part, too, and in keeping with the Cromwellian period, some Board of Ordnance plans were just that – plans of projected military schemes and of an imagined military landscape, never realised owing

FIGURE 4.4 Fort William was the first of a new generation of forts in Scotland, hastily constructed from timber in 1689, and able to be supplied by sea. It retained its prominence throughout the eighteenth century, not least because of its situation at the south-western end of the Great Glen in the heart of Jacobite Lochaber. Robert Johnson was overseer of the fort during the Jacobite risings of 1708 and 1715. His plan of the environs of Fort William in 1710 emphasises the commanding mountains, perhaps underlining something of the fort's vulnerability to hostile forces in doing so.
Source: Robert Johnson, *A Plan of Fort William with the Country ajasent* [*sic*] (1710). Reproduced by permission of the Trustees of the National Library of Scotland.

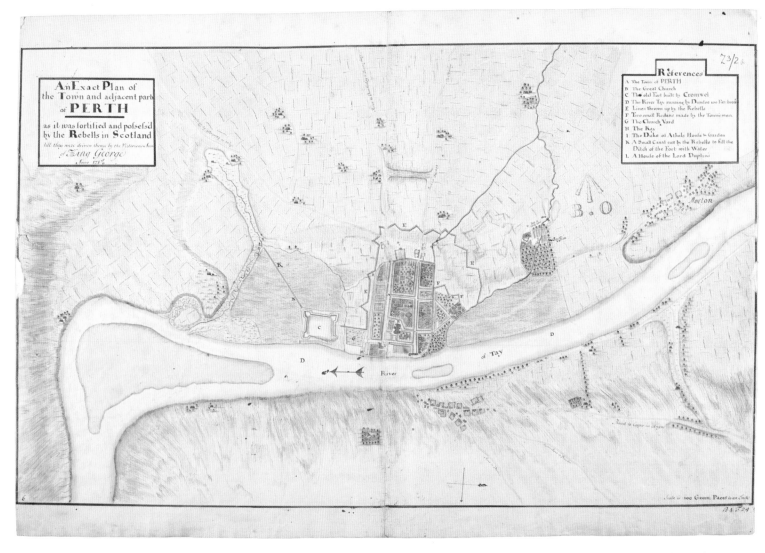

FIGURE 4.5 Lewis Petit's plan, 'as it was Fortified and Possess'd by the Rebells in Scotland' (1716), shows the recapture of Perth from the Jacobites after the 1715 rising. The plan illustrates the emergence of new European military mapping styles and content in Scotland and focuses on the essential topographic features of military importance, as well as showing the main shape and extent of the town with its principal streets. The plan is coloured according to established convention: red for masonry and buildings; blue for water; different shades of green to distinguish marshy ground, enclosed formal grounds and arable fields. Shaded slopes indicate higher ground. Detailed features of military interest are shown, including the V-shaped revetments or redans rapidly assembled by Jacobite forces during their occupation. The Old Cromwellian citadel built in 1652 on South Inch with its earthen ramparts and deep moat is also shown. The King's Lade or Town Lade that supplied the fosse around the city walls appears as an important barrier, bridged only opposite the ports or gateways, with the old quay at the end of Canal Street also shown, presumably for its possible military value.

Source: Lewis Petit, *An Exact Plan of the Town and adjacent parts of Perth as it was fortified and possess'd by the Rebells in Scotland* (1716). Reproduced by permission of the Trustees of the National Library of Scotland.

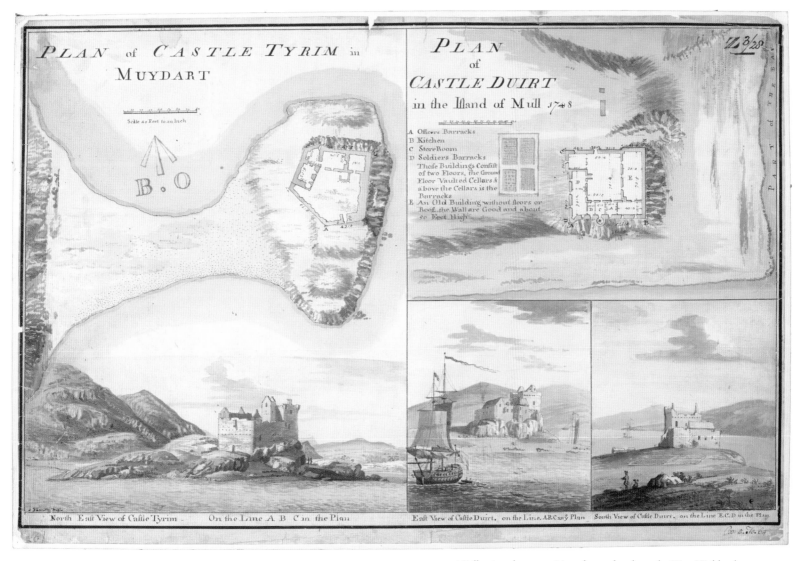

FIGURE 4.6 Following the 1745 rising, the castles along the West Highland coast were investigated with a view to their possible refortification. This attractive plan and view of Castle Tioram in 1747 is by Paul Sandby (1725–1809), later to become a well-known watercolourist, who was then the chief draughtsman on the Military Survey of Scotland.
Source: Paul Sandby, *Plan of Castle Tyrim in Muydart / Plan of Castle Duirt in the Island of Mull* (1748). Reproduced by permission of the Trustees of the National Library of Scotland.

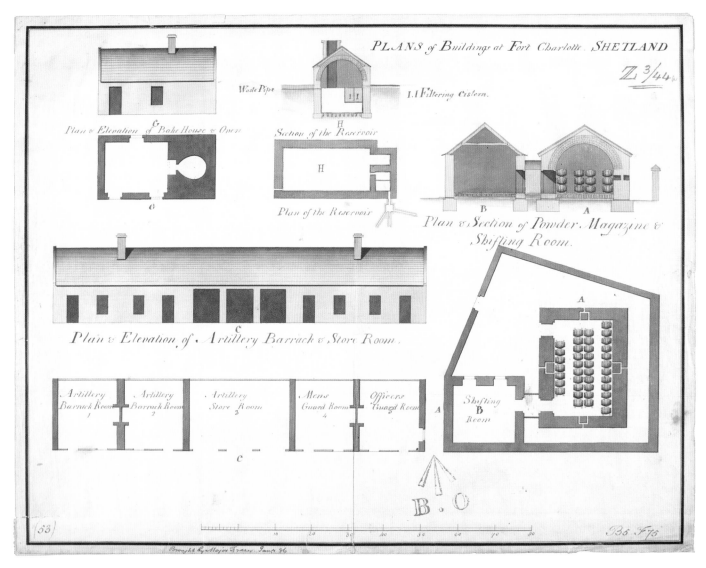

to lack of funds (fig. 4.8). The Board also produced a handful of battle plans: for Sheriffmuir (1715), Glenshiel (1719) – see fig. 4.9 – and the battles of the '45, including Prestonpans (1745), Falkirk (1746) and Culloden (1746).

Military information, just like other mappable information, can take time to gather, and, once gathered, to be translated into map form. At first glance, for example, the distinctive 1731 map produced by Clement Lemprière, a French draughtsman working for the Board, simply shows the main Jacobite forces who mustered against the British Crown in the Rebellion of 1715 (fig.

4.10). Over 20,000 Jacobites fought in the 1715 Rebellion, but of much greater concern to the British Crown was the knowledge that those hostile forces outnumbered the Hanoverian supporters, as the accompanying explanation in Lemprière's map makes alarmingly clear. How long would it be before these men, in such numbers, would rise again? The map indicates the clan territories by name, with the number of men each clan contributed to the 1715 Rising written in red.

Behind this surface impression, the map affords several revealing insights into the perceptions of the Jacobite

FIGURE 4.7 *Opposite*. Fort Charlotte (named after the wife of King George III) was developed from 1781 in Lerwick, Shetland. Andrew Frazer's portrayal shows the plans and sections of the bake house, reservoir, gunpowder magazine, and the artillery barracks.
Source: Andrew Frazer, *Plans of Buildings at Fort Charlotte, Shetland* (1781). Reproduced by permission of the Trustees of the National Library of Scotland.

FIGURE 4.8 *Left*. During the 1745 Jacobite Rebellion, the original castle of Fort George in the centre of Inverness was irreparably damaged. The Board of Ordnance engineer, Lewis Marcell, worked out costed plans for a new fort to the north of the town. As shown here, this pentagonal bastioned trace, along the lines of the original Cromwellian fortress of a century earlier, would be encircled by a moat of water, drawn from the River Ness. However, Marcell's plan was never constructed, a decision made instead to construct a more elaborate and imposing fortress at Ardersier point (see fig. 4.11).
Source: Lewis Marcell, *A Plan of a New Fort design'd for Inverness, Done Exactly upon the Old Lines of Olivers Fort . . .* (1746). Reproduced by permission of the Trustees of the National Library of Scotland.

threat by Hanoverians, and how they intended to conquer and control Scotland. It also indicates what we might think of as an uneven ignorance regarding the shape and content of the geography of the Highlands. In its outline, the map is largely based on the outlines of Scotland published in the Blaeu *Atlas Novus* of 1654 (chapter 3). Yet Lemprière's map is one of the earli correctly show the Great Glen as a straight first-hand surveying only easily possible for diate area around castles and towns, cartograp

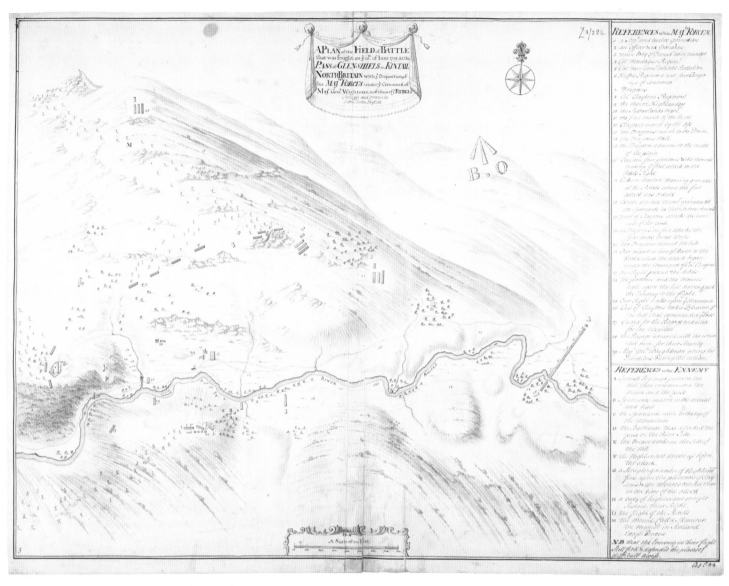

FIGURE 4.9 In 1719 the Jacobites joined forces with the
Spanish Duke of Ormonde, who brought his troops by sea into
the north-west Highlands. The combined force was confronted
by Hanoverian forces led by General Wightman at the pass of
Glenshiel. Bastide's plan of the field of battle offers an animated
view of the action. His depiction combines vertical and bird's-
eye perspectives to portray the impressive relief of Glenshiel, as
well as a flattering portrayal of General Wightman − shown on
horseback − leading his forces from the front.
Source: John Henry Bastide, *A Plan of the Field of Battle . . . at the
Pass of Glenshiels . . .* (1719). Reproduced by permission of the
Trustees of the National Library of Scotland.

FIGURE 4.10 Clement Lemprière's superb map is one of the first to record the new military roads being constructed under George Wade, Commander-in-Chief of North Britain from 1724 to 1740. These include the Fort William to Inverness road (1725–27), the roads from Crieff and Dunkeld north to Inverness (1728–30), and the route over the Corrieyairack Pass from Dalwhinnie to Fort Augustus (1731). The roads were undertaken to link a network of new fortified barracks: Inversnaid by Loch Lomond, Ruthven in Strathspey, Fort Augustus by Loch Ness, and Bernera facing Skye (see fig. 4.3). There are echoes of Roman influence and parallels in this military strategy: why else might one choose to show the Roman camp at Ardoch, and the Antonine Wall (Grahams Dike)?
Source: Clement Lemprière, *A Description of the Highlands of Scotland* (*c.*1731). Reproduced by permission of the Trustees of the National Library of Scotland.

edge of the wider country was always limited, despite the activities of the Board's engineers and surveyors. Indeed, despite the Board's mapping work – even, to some degree, because of it in the sense that the Board exposed how little was known of the extent and geography of the country from a military point of view – the 1745 Jacobite Rebellion in particular brought home to Britain's military commanders how vital maps were. It was, for some, an acute embarrassment given the 'want of a proper survey of the country' (fig. 4.11). And so, soon after the

defeat of the Jacobites at Culloden on 16 April 1746 (fig. 4.12), King George II was petitioned to support the idea of a Military Survey of Scotland. Initially encharged to Lt.-Colonel David Watson, the primary practical responsibility for this was delegated to the then Assistant Quartermaster in the Board of Ordnance in Scotland, William Roy. He was to be responsible for one of the most significant military mapping projects in Scottish, and British, map history.

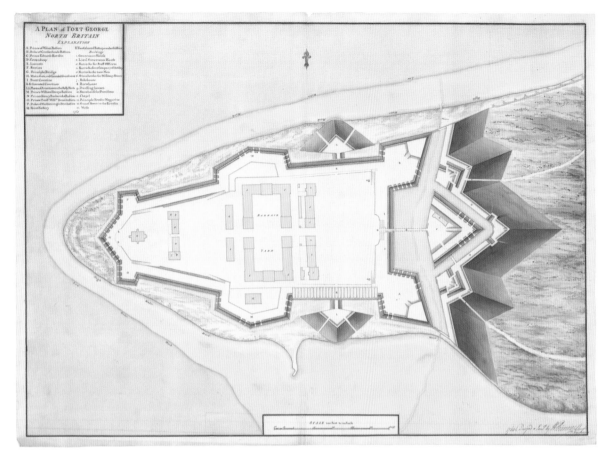

FIGURE 4.11 *Above.* The British army's embarrassment over how quickly some of their forts had fallen during the 1745 Rebellion was a key factor behind the construction of Fort George at Ardersier Point. This massive fort was planned on 42 hectares of land, 9 miles north-east of Inverness, and took over twenty-three years to complete. It is a superb artillery fortification, planned geometrically, with huge and thick low walls, extensive outer defensive works, and was designed to allow convergent lines of fire from the ramparts. On the map, and on the ground, it is the best illustration in Scotland of eighteenth-century European expertise in military engineering. When complete, it was the largest barracks in Britain, able to house 1,600 men, or two whole infantry divisions. Fort George is a mighty – and mightily impressive – military and political statement. William Skinner, the Board of Ordnance's chief military engineer, was responsible for its design and execution, a project that cost over £200,000 (twice his original estimate). Skinner became the first governor of the fort. His plan shows the fort in 1763, and is one of an extensive set of plans showing its construction.

Source: William Skinner, *A Plan of Fort George North Britain / by W. Skinner, Chief Engineer.* (1763). Reproduced by permission of the Trustees of the National Library of Scotland.

FIGURE 4.12 *Right.* This is a rare surviving military map drawn from a Jacobite perspective. John Finlayson was a mathematical instrument maker, and served as Prince Charles Edward Stuart's engineer and commissar. His plan of the Battle of Culloden and the adjacent country is acknowledged as one of the most detailed and useful depictions of the battle. The cartouche is replete with sad symbols indicating the end of the Jacobite dream: a snuffed-out candle, a broken unicorn horn, a chained lion and broken thistles.

Source: John Finlayson, *A Plan of the Battle of Culloden, and the Adjacent Country, Shewing the Incampment of the English Army at Nairn, and the March of the Highlanders in Order to Attack them by Night* (1746). Reproduced by permission of the Trustees of the National Library of Scotland.

A
BATTLE of
Culloden
the Adjacent
CNTRI
Incampment of the
SH ARMY
AIRN
March of
landers in
to Attack

W — E
S

NAIRN

The Encampment of the English Army at Nairn

NAIRN River

The Shipping and Transports that supplyed

and attended the Dukes Army.

Culraick

to Culloden

The High Road from INVERNESS to NAIRN

Culraick

to Culloden

Return from

Culraick

Culloden

The Highlanders

The Highlanders

The Highlanders March in Order to Surprise the

the Field of Battle

to Culloden

Culraick

A

Duke in his Camp

F

C

b

c

d

i

f

k

p

q

g

h

o

B

D

Highlanders

March from his Camp

The Duke of Cumberlands

A

References
to the
ENGLISH ARMY.

First Line commanded by L.d Albemarle
and B.r Sempel.
a. Pultney,   e. S.t Fuziliers.
b. Royal,   f. Monro.
c. Cholmondeley,   g. Barrel,
d. Price
Second Line commanded by M. Gen. Huske
h. Howard.   l. Sempil.
i. Fleming.   m. Ligonier.
k. Bligh.   n. Wolfe.
Third Line commanded by B.r Mordaunt.
o. Battereau.   p. Blackney.
Horse commanded by L. Gen. Hawley,
and M. Gen. Bland.
q. Squ.n Cobhams Drag.n r. Kingstons Horse.
s. L.d Markhers and   t. Guard of the Baggage.
Cobhams Dragoons.   u. Campbells.

HIGHLAND ARMY.
First Line commanded by L.d G. Murray, L.d J. Drummond,
and the Duke of Perth.
1. Athol Men   8. M.c Leans.
2. Camerons.   9. M.c Leods.
3. Stewarts of Apin. 10. Chisholms.
4. Stewarts under John Roy. 11. Clanronald.
5. Frasers.   12. Keppoch.
6. M.c Intoshes.   13. Glen Garry.
7. Farquharsons.   14. Duke of Perths.
Second Line commanded by B.r Stapleton.
15. The Highland Horse. 20. Irish Piquets.
16. Benerman of Elsick. 21. L.d Lewis Gordons.
17. Henbuket   22. Fitz James's Horse.
18. French Royal Scots 23. The Pr.
19. Kilmarnock.   24. L.d Ogilvies Reserve.

By a return of the Officers and Men, the day
of Battle, the 13 Battalions were just 6411 which
with the Dragoons, Kingstons Horse, the Artilery, Lord
Loudens, and the Argyleshire Highlanders, made the Dukes
Army always reckoned about 10000 Men.
The Highlanders that Day in the Field, by their own
Muster Rolls would not have exceeded 6000, had the
different Corps been compleat.

WILLIAM ROY AND THE MILITARY SURVEY OF SCOTLAND 1747–1756

In contrast to men like Petit, Lemprière and other military map men at work in Scotland, Roy was a native. He was born at Miltonbridge, near Carluke, the son of an estate factor. Roy was only in his early twenties when he was placed in superintendence of the Military Survey, what became known to his contemporaries as the 'Great Map', the most comprehensive, detailed mapping of mainland Scotland at any time prior to the work of Ordnance Survey. Looking back on his endeavours thirty or so years later, Roy was clear why and where it all began: 'The rise and progress of the rebellion which broke out in the Highlands of Scotland in 1745, and which was finally suppressed … at the battle of Culloden in the following year, convinced Government of what infinite importance it would be to the State, that a country, so very inaccessible by nature, should be thoroughly explored and laid open, by establishing military posts in its inmost recesses, and carrying roads of communication to its remotest parts.'

The survey was conducted in two parts, first the Highlands from 1747 to 1752 (but not the islands), and then the Lowlands in the years to 1755, before the outbreak of the Seven Years' War in Europe in 1756 led to engineers being recalled from Scotland. Survey parties consisted of an engineer with a non-commissioned officer and six soldiers. The theodolites (circumferentors or surveying compasses for measuring angles) were fairly simple, 7 inches in diameter and with simple narrow slits for sights rather than telescopes, whilst the chains for measuring distance were 45–50 feet long. Only selected landscape features (roads, rivers and lochs) were surveyed in this manner using trigonometry, with other landscape features (towns and settlements, enclosures and wood-land, as well as relief), sketched in by eye or copied from existing maps (fig. 4.13).

Despite its title, the work was one of rapid reconnaissance rather than a measured topographic survey. Features of interest to an army commander, such as roads, rivers, the positions of villages and hamlets, as well as general land-cover and terrain, are depicted clearly. The designed landscape around some of the larger country houses and estates is also particularly impressive in its delineation. But for other features in the landscape, notably those of less or no military or political value, there are inconsistencies and omissions. In contrast to the many maps of estate re-organisation in this period (see chapter 6), the delineation of arable ground is inaccurate, and many field boundaries are merely conventionalised symbols, not reflections of real patterns on the ground. There is no indication of property ownership, or of the detailed form of larger settlements and hamlets. The numbers of red dots do not necessarily equal the number of buildings, and there are quite wide variations in the recording of smaller hamlets and farms, with many missing. Place names are often quite variable, sometimes reflecting local pronunciation, recorded by surveyors who were unfamiliar with Gaelic and Scots. The map includes several planned constructions, such as Fort George at Ardersier, many years before they were actually built.

The reasons for all this lie partly in the limited availability of men, especially when compared with the work of Ordnance Survey a century later. But they are also to be explained by the need for speed of coverage, not accuracy of depiction. Further, the Survey was based not upon triangulation, but rather upon a set of measured traverses along important features using theodolites and chains.

The surveyors' field measurements and sketches (the original sketch books and records of measurement are lost) were worked up in the Board of Ordnance's Drawing Room in Edinburgh Castle during the winter months into what was called an 'original protraction' at a scale of 1 inch to 1,000 yards.

For all these reasons, Roy described the resultant map as rather a 'magnificent military sketch, than a very accurate map of the country'. As he also remarked, 'no geometrical exactness is to be expected, the sole object in view being, to shew remarkable things, or such as constitute the great outlines of the Country'. Roy's use of the word 'sketch' is not without significance: the Survey does have a vibrant aesthetic quality. One of its chief draughtsmen was Paul Sandby, who went on to become a celebrated watercolour artist. The wonderful three-dimensional depiction of relief is usually accredited to him. Yet, for all its flaws, the Military Survey is a remarkable achievement. It made Roy's name, helped establish Ordnance Survey in 1791 and was used as a reference source by later Scottish map-makers.

After Culloden, the Jacobite threat rapidly receded, but new threats to Hanoverian rule led to continuing work by the Board of Ordnance in Scotland. In the 1780s, concern over the intrusions of American privateers led to a decision to re-establish Fort Charlotte (named after George III's Queen) at Lerwick in Shetland. The construction of this fort had begun over a century earlier in the 1660s, primarily to counter Dutch threats – later versions of the events which, as we saw in chapter 3, delayed the production of the 1654 *Atlas Novus* – but the fort was not completed then. Fort Charlotte was constructed with a barracks for 270 men, officers' lodg-ings, a powder magazine and extensive ramparts, but it was occupied only relatively briefly and was never the subject of attack.

In the 1790s, growing concerns over a possible Napoleonic invasion resulted in a string of defences – often hastily planned, mapped and erected – being constructed at coastal locations including Dunbar, Leith, Montrose, Aberdeen, Peterhead, Banff, Campbeltown and Greenock. As the threat of invasion waned, so in time the Board of Ordnance ceased to have a clear function. Military work to such purpose, including military mapping, was not undertaken again until the 1940s.

FIGURE 4.13 *Overleaf.* The Military Survey of Scotland, (1747–55) known to its contemporaries as the 'Great Map', is one of the most famous maps of Scotland. A landmark of cartography, it exemplifies emerging standards in military surveying and map-making in Britain, with its striking portrayal of landscape relief. This depiction of the area near Kenmore, at the eastern end of Loch Tay, illustrates this well through its expert use of colour, line styles and symbols. It was a major influence on the early work of Ordnance Survey. Of military value and aesthetically rich, it can also be regarded as a symbolic show of cartographic power, allowing Scotland to be brought to order and controlled from a distance. *Source:* William Roy, Military Survey of Scotland. Reproduced by permission of the British Library.

O

Culdars

GlenLyons house *Drenacharys*

☐ New Kirk of Fortingaul

Roman Fort

The Fearnan

N

Bla

Stron

Y

Port Kenachragan

Kenmore

Kenloc

Craignachape

Taymou

Balnafiberf

Coltachanbeg

Lurichlouman

Craigmartickmor

Tomagrou

Aucharin

MILITARY MAPPING FROM THE NINETEENTH CENTURY

During the nineteenth century, particularly through the work of Ordnance Survey, mapping for military purposes was increasingly undertaken as part of broader civilian projects. That is not to say that military mapping was no longer undertaken: simply, military cartography was incorporated in the work of Ordnance Survey or, until the 1860s, was under the direction of the War Office. Perhaps paradoxically, two features were characteristic of military mapping in this period. Given changes in printing technology, many of the maps of Ordnance Survey, which had responsibility for depiction of military features in its work, were available in much larger numbers than before and so, with copying and usage by other map-makers, they could reach larger audiences than their earlier counterparts. Yet such maps were not always militarily accurate. What many showed was selective cartographic silence: for reasons of state security, the features of certain buildings such as prisons, castles, docks and other military installations were not always shown in detail.

During the twentieth century, warfare and cartography were again transformed in association with the development of new destructive military technologies. This had the effect of superseding previous defensive capacities, in Scotland and elsewhere: cartography may provide the locations of military features, but it cannot show their state of military preparedness (fig. 4.14). The aeroplane has been one of the most transformative technologies behind innovations in map-making and in map use. During the Second World War, millions of aerial photographs of Scotland were taken by the Luftwaffe and the Royal Air Force (fig. 4.15). Aerial photography and air warfare allows what earth-bound map-makers can only symbolise: views of the ground from above. The value of maps for military

FIGURE 4.14 *Opposite and detail above.* Found hidden in the 1980s in an attic of a sea-front house in east Scotland, this detailed German chart of the coastline round the important east coast port of Peterhead was originally published by the German Oberkommando der Kriegsmarine in Berlin in 1904. Closely resembling the British Admiralty chart for the same area, and obviously copied from it, thirty-nine years later it was re-printed with small corrections during the height of the Second World War. Note the swastika incorporated in the cartouche.
Source: Oberkommando der Kriegsmarine, Nordsee Schottland, Ostküste, Peterhead Bucht. Chart 231. Scale 1:10,000 (originally published 1904, reprinted with amendments 1943). Reproduced by permission of the Trustees of the National Library of Scotland.

reconnaissance and topographic surveying was proved beyond all doubt from the 1940s onwards, and in the post-war era aerial survey has been an essential part of Ordnance Survey's data capture methods as it has for other mapping organisations (fig. 4.16).

During the second half of the twentieth century, new types of aerial mapping became possible, chiefly because

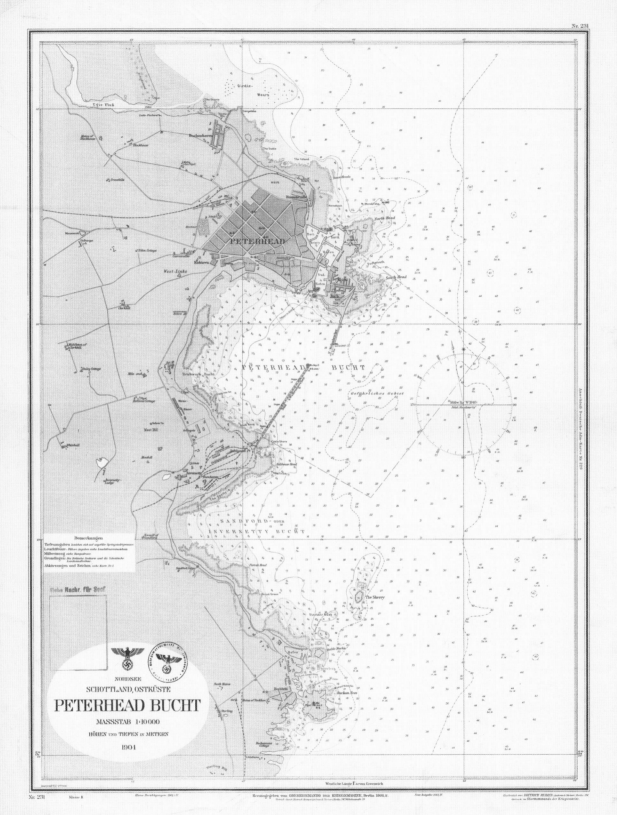

NORDSEE

SCHOTTLAND, OSTKÜSTE

PETERHEAD BUCHT

MASSSTAB 1:10000

HÖHEN UND TIEFEN IN METERN

1904

PETERHEAD

PETERHEAD BUCHT

SANDFORD- ODER
INVERNETTY BUCHT

Bemerkungen

Siehe Nachr. für Seef.

Nr. 231   Blatte 8   Kleine Berichtigungen 1941 VI.   Herausgegeben vom OBERKOMMANDO DER KRIEGSMARINE, Berlin 1904. II.   Neue Ausgabe 1941 IV.   Gedruckt von DIETRICH REIMER (Andrews & Steiner), Berlin SW.   Vertrieb im Oberkommando der Kriegsmarine.

Westliche Länge von Greenwich

FIGURE 4.15 This German bombing map of Edinburgh from 1941 provides chilling insight into the military technologies of the Second World War. Based on a standard Ordnance Survey map of Edinburgh, the map has been overprinted with a range of colour-coded information, with text and a legend in German, to assist the potential aerial bombardment of the city by the Luftwaffe. Similar maps printed by the German Army survive for other British cities. A much larger number of maps for bombing purposes was made by Britain and its Allies, colour-coded for cities in Germany and elsewhere.
Source: German Army – Generalstab des Heeres, German bombing map of Edinburgh – *Stadtplan von Edinburgh mit Mil.-Geo.-Eintragungen* (1941). Reproduced by permission of the Trustees of the National Library of Scotland.

three related technical developments revolutionised the possibilities for recording military phenomena above, on and even below the landscape: improvements in the quality and range of satellite sensors; the ability to capture multiple visible and invisible wavelengths and so to differentiate types of land-cover; and, increasingly, the use of computers to process and integrate the imagery.

Different national military organisations exploited these developments differently. In the 1990s, for example, the release of staggeringly impressive Soviet mapping for numerous countries around the world illustrated only too well the power of others' maps as military devices (fig. 4.17). Such Cold War mapping is a salutary reminder of the secrecy intrinsic to military maps, of topographic information not available to any public. These Soviet maps were simply not known about in the West. Their form is greatly different, and their language is literally and symbolically not the same as earlier counterparts. But, in their function and underlying political purpose, such maps would have been understood by the Earl of Hertford, Oliver Cromwell, Lewis Petit and William Roy. For Scotland's would-be occupiers and her defenders, the technologies of military mapping have changed dramatically over time, but the importance of maps as documents of security and secrecy remains.

Stadtplan von Edinburgh
mit Mil.-Geo.-Eintragungen

Sonderausgabe VII. 1941
Nur für den Dienstgebrauch!

EDINBURGH

CITY PARISH OF EDINBURGH

LEITH

FISHERROW SANDS

MUSSELBURGH SANDS

MUSSELBURGH

Mil.-Geo.-Zeichen mit Erklärung

Kaserne
Krankenhaus
Großgarage
Kunstsammlung, Kulturdenkmal
Eisenbahnwerkstätten, Güterbahnhof, Gleisanlagen
Postamt
Futterspeicher, Getreidesilo
Gebäude, für die kein besonderes Zeichen besteht
Docks, Hafenanlagen
Steinkohlenbergbau
Kohlenlager
Brikettfabrik
Gaswerk
Zementwerk
Steinbruch
Glasfabrik
Eisenwerk
Eisenhütte
Eisengießerei
Maschinenfabrik
Autofabrik
Werft, Trockendock
Chemische Fabrik
Öl- u. Farbwerke
Tankanlage
Ölmühle
Farbenfabrik

Wachsfabrik
Dynamomaschinenfabrik
Großkraftwerk
Seil- u. Segeltuchfabrik
Weberei, Strumpffabrik
Segeltuchfabrik
Papiermühle
Buchdruckerei
Gerberei
Kautschukwerk
Biskuitwerk
Getreidemühle
Destillerie
Brauerei, Mälzerei
Molkerei
Sägewerk
Wasserwerk
Wasserbehälter
Schlachthof
Kläranlage
Werke, für die kein besonderes Zeichen besteht
Eisenbahnbrücke
Straßenbrücke
Tunnel
Hauptdurchführtstraßen

Maßstab 1 : 15000

Die Höhen sind in englischen Fuß angegeben

Gezeichnet des Heeres, Abt. f. Kriegskarten und Vermessungswesen (IV. Mil.-Geo.)

Planzeiger für England.

Planzeiger 1 : 15000

[A]

[B]

FIGURE 4.16 Aerial photography, even that undertaken in peacetime, was prompted by military need and so was heavily censored. Ordnance Survey published these images from aerial photography flown by the Royal Air Force between 1944 and 1951. These photo mosaics, as they are called, were intended as a rapid reconnaissance exercise to aid post-Second World War reconstruction as shown in map [A] featuring the important Prestwick Airport (mid-left of image). Following security concerns that the mosaics might fall into the wrong hands, amended sheets were re-issued for what were deemed to be sensitive locations, including airfields and military installations. In image [B], a false landscape of fields and hedgerows, as shown here for Prestwick, was carefully drawn in following erasure of the airfield from the photo mosaic.

Source: Ordnance Survey / Royal Air Force, 1:10,560 Air photo mosaics of Prestwick showing erased airfield, NS32NE (1946 and 1950). Reproduced by permission of the Trustees of the National Library of Scotland.

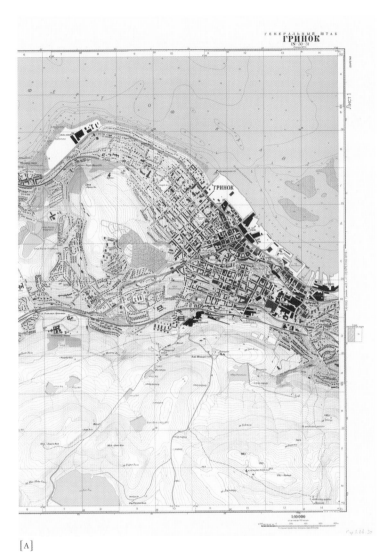

[A]

[B]

FIGURE 4.17 From 1919 to the early 1990s the Soviet Army gathered and produced the most comprehensive and detailed mapping of the world. The Soviet's military mapping was by far the largest cartographic enterprise undertaken by one state mapping organisation. It has been estimated that over 35,000 staff were employed in its cartographic work, and that over one million separate maps were produced. What is more surprising is how much more information they show, here of Greenock, than the official mapping of Britain by Ordnance Survey. Widths and heights of bridges, and widths and depths of rivers are given. Buildings are colour-coded; military establishments are coloured green, administrative buildings purple and industrial plants black. Contours are shown at closer intervals than on Ordnance Survey maps: every 2.5 or 5 metres. Here was all the information one needed to mount a successful invasion.

Source: Soviet Army Topographic Mapping, 1:10,000, Grinok [Greenock], Sheet N-30-3 (1979)

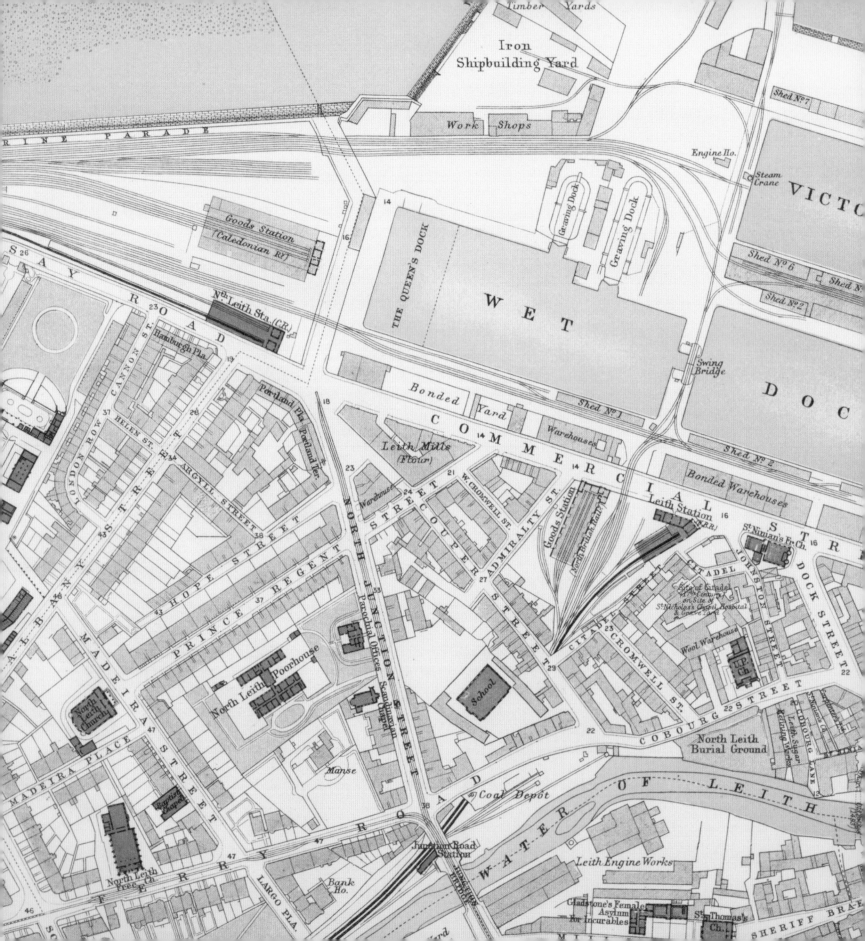

CHAPTER 5

TOWNS AND URBAN LIFE

In 1919, the world-famous Scottish cartographer and Edinburgh-based publisher John George Bartholomew published his *Chronological Map of Edinburgh showing Expansion of the City from Earliest Days to the Present* (fig. 5.1). This novel and spectacularly coloured plan attempted to map the history of Bartholomew's home town by employing tints of colour to represent periods of time: 'isochronic colouring' as he termed it. What now seems standard for us, a perhaps-to-be-expected feature of certain sorts of town map, was then much less so: Bartholomew's colourful and innovative technique in this and other maps helped make the firm internationally renowned.

Bartholomew's map of Edinburgh employs another technique. In a way, the map draws together all previous maps of the city into one image: previous delineations of the city's historical development are all transferred as it were into a single document – and so are hidden by it. Bartholomew's map has an arresting and immediate visual impact. It is also a utilitarian device. But its value depends upon obscuring other evidence. This sort of map is vital, of course, to the urban historian and geographer, to anyone interested in capturing at a glance the changing extent over time of a city's space. But it obscures the processes driving the changes in city form, and offers little explanation as to why the city should have expanded when and where it did. Beneath the surface of any such depiction of urban form lie social, economic and political processes which give towns and cities their life, not just their shape. This chapter considers the ways in which maps reveal and obscure Scotland's cities and towns and their urban experience.

The mapping of Scotland's towns is never the simple matter of depicting urban areas at one instant, or showing urban areas over different periods of time. Maps at two moments in time can allow us to compare urban form. But there are also distinct differences over time in how towns and cities have been shown, and why. The symbolic and figurative portrayal of Edinburgh or St Andrews in the late sixteenth century (see figs. 2.8, 2.9) was about the civic display of these places, centres of learning and culture as they were, in European context.

Cities, no less than countries, had to be displayed for audiences who knew neither where a place was nor what it looked like.

Such urban mapping bears little resemblance to the maps produced for reasons of sanitary or infrastructural improvement in the nineteenth century. Similarly, the military maps of Perth, Stirling or Inverness in the first half of eighteenth century are strikingly different from the maps of those self-same towns half a century later produced by private land surveyors for public use. And as Scotland's cities expanded in size and function, particularly in the nineteenth century, new maps were required for a range of new uses and audiences: for feuing land for new streets and houses, for constructing docks and routes for trams and railways, for mapping the expanding urban franchise and boundaries, and for planning new civic and industrial land uses within a city's bounds.

It is true that urban maps are valuable records of real-world features, for the historian and the modern commuter alike, albeit in different ways. Yet if it is helpful, as we suggest here, to think of urban maps and urban mapping as practices of civic display, then we may also see maps as instruments of social and moral enquiry, especially for the nineteenth century. For, as Scotland's cities became too large to be easily manageable, yet had to be governed, kept clean and free of disease, urban mapping was an essential route to civic health, to knowing where social problems lay and so might be planned for. And, in the twentieth century, maps of urban places were associated with the as-yet-unrealised visions of a better and brighter future Scotland.

Distinctive aspects of Scotland's history and geography are thus reflected differently at different times in its urban maps. It is also possible to observe over time an emerging social and public recognition of the value of maps in an

FIGURE 5.1 John George Bartholomew's map of Edinburgh showing the expansion of the city is an impressive aesthetic and conceptual achievement. With its use of colour lithography to illustrate the date of building construction, and a standard early twentieth-century Bartholomew street map as its base, it formed part of a special issue on Edinburgh in the *Scottish Geographical Magazine* (1919).
Source: J. G. Bartholomew, *Chronological Map of Edinburgh showing Expansion of the City from Earliest Times to the Present* (1919). Reproduced by permission of the Trustees of the National Library of Scotland.

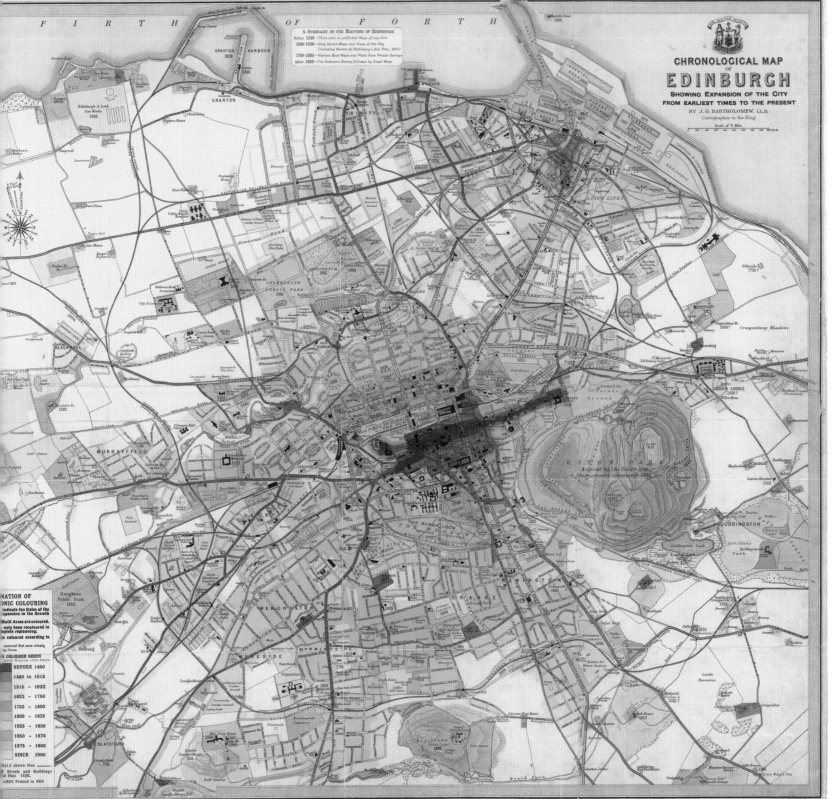

CHRONOLOGICAL MAP
OF
EDINBURGH
SHOWING EXPANSION OF THE CITY
FROM EARLIEST TIMES TO THE PRESENT
BY J. G. BARTHOLOMEW, LL.D.
Cartographer to the King

A SUMMARY OF THE MAPPING OF EDINBURGH

Before 1540 — There were no published Maps of any kind
1540-1700 — Only Sketch-Maps and Views of the City
(including Gordon of Rothiemay's fine Plan, 1647)
1700-1850 — Various Good Maps and Plans from Private Surveys
After 1850 — The Ordnance Survey followed by Exact Maps

EXPLANATION OF
CHRONIC COLOURING

BEFORE 1450
1450 to 1515
1515 — 1622
1622 — 1750
1750 — 1800
1800 — 1825
1825 — 1850
1850 — 1875
1875 — 1900
SINCE 1900

urban context – in the use of maps in trades directories from the later eighteenth century, for example, which brought together map and text as lists of tradesmen or prominent citizens, as a form of urban 'enquire-within'. Allied to this social awareness, and in part driving it, came practical changes in the technologies of map production – from manuscript, pen and ink to engraved copper plates, to the use of lithographic stones, to photographic work in mapping. All of this not only helped to establish a different aesthetic to urban maps but, in association with the rise in literacy, helped to create new, largely urban, markets for maps, and new sorts of maps altogether.

URBAN SCOTLAND IN MAPS BEFORE *c.*1700

In the earliest maps of Scotland such as those by Matthew Paris (fig. 2.3) or in the fourteenth-century Gough Map (fig. 2.4), the country's towns simply appear either as rather roughly done symbols or, as in Hardyng's figurative portrayal, almost as icons of prosperity (fig. 2.5). Over time, however, there is an evident trend from the use of symbols to the use of pictures, to plan-view surveys in the depiction of towns, within Europe as well as Scotland. This is apparent in the more detailed representation of towns in some of the earliest surviving plans: in the illustration of Edinburgh that appears in the sixteenth-

FIGURE 5.2 Sebastian Münster's *Cosmographia* was the earliest German description of the world, and one of the most successful and popular books of the sixteenth century. It included over 500 woodcut illustrations by various artists, following the illustrative tradition of Hartmann Schedel's *Nuremberg Chronicle* of the 1490s. This view of Edinburgh from the north picks out distinctive features and buildings – including Arthur's Seat, Holyrood, the Castle and Nor-Loch – but as part of a very stylised and part-imaginary townscape. *Source:* Sebastian Münster, Plan of Edinburgh from *Cosmographia* (from 1544). Reproduced by permission of the Trustees of the National Library of Scotland.

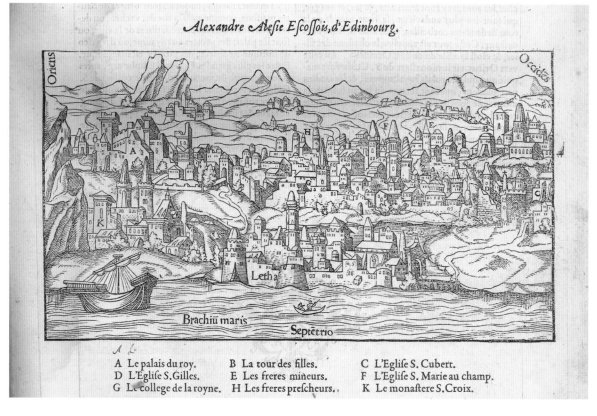

A Le palais du roy. B La tour des filles. C L'Eglise S. Cubert.
D L'Eglise S. Gilles. E Les freres mineurs. F L'Eglise S. Marie au champ.
G Le college de la royne. H Les freres prescheurs. K Le monastere S. Croix.

century book *Cosmographia*, for example, the work of the German geographer Sebastian Münster offers a stylised representation with little that might be said to be distinctive of that city (fig. 5.2). Within a century, however, notably in Georg Braun's *Civitates Orbis Terrarum*, with maps engraved by Franz Hogenberg, there is a more consistent style to the depiction of urban places and an attempt made to show the individuality of towns.

The *Civitates* is an impressive achievement of sixteenth-century urban cartography. From its first volume in 1572, it grew by 1617 to become a five-volume work with 550 illustrative views of Europe's towns. It shares similarities with the near contemporary work of Abraham Ortelius, who in 1570 had brought together small-scale maps in what was effectively the world's first modern atlas, the *Theatrum Orbis Terrarum*. Ortelius drew together maps from a variety of sources, but, uniquely for the time, produced them to a uniform size and scale and bound them together in a single volume; similarly Braun and Hogenburg drafted or copied pictures from far and wide for inclusion in the *Civitates*. A total of eighteen British towns, including Edinburgh, were engraved (see fig. 2.8). It is possible that the bird's-eye view of St Andrews produced in the 1580s (see fig. 2.9) was drafted for possible inclusion in the *Civitates*.

The manuscript maps of Timothy Pont, discussed in chapter 3, are vital for viewing Scotland's urban past. Pont's maps provide the earliest depiction in map form of many of Scotland's towns. There are particularly clear depictions of Arbroath, Dumfries, Dundee, Elgin (see fig. 3.7), Falkirk, Forfar, Fraserburgh, Glasgow, Hamilton, Inverkeithing, Inverness, Lanark, Linlithgow, Paisley, Perth (see fig. 3.6), Rutherglen, Stirling and Tain. The shape and relative size of towns is shown, and in some cases the internal layout of streets, houses and burgage plots is care-

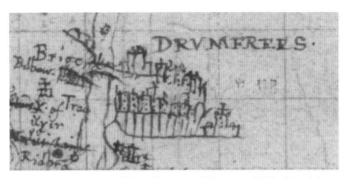

FIGURE 5.3 Pont's view of Dumfries, part of his map of Nithsdale, picks out several useful details, including the old bridge over the Nith, the large tolbooth building (upper left) and market cross – an excellent depiction of burgage plots, still open spaces at this time – extending behind the frontages of buildings on either side of the High Street, and St Michael's Kirk (lower right) at the bottom of the High Street.
Source: Timothy Pont, Pont's view of Dumfries from his map of Nithsdale, Pont 35 (*c.*1583–1614). Reproduced by permission of the Trustees of the National Library of Scotland.

fully depicted. For some towns, distinctive larger buildings including parish kirks, cathedrals, abbeys, castles, palaces and tolbooths, as well as market crosses, trons (public weighbeams), bridges, town walls and gates all feature (fig. 5.3). Pont – and his contemporaries – knew that towns served their local areas. To indicate their central place in the local area as well as their own individual form and importance, Pont used distinctive capital letters to reflect a burgh's status and its privileges. In word and in symbol, what he shows is a simple relative urban hierarchy as well as a location and a pictorial view.

As we have seen, Pont's maps were worked upon and revised by others after his death. This correction and revision of Pont's work in the 1640s provided the impetus for arguably the finest of all of the bird's-eye views of Scotland's towns. James Gordon surveyed the county of Fife in 1642 for Blaeu's 1654 *Atlas Novus* and included in his work detailed hand-drawn views of St Andrews and of the market town of Cupar. In size, content and artistic accomplishment, however, these maps are overtaken by his splendid bird's-eye views of Edinburgh in 1647 (fig. 5.4) and of Aberdeen in 1661 (fig. 5.5). These maps

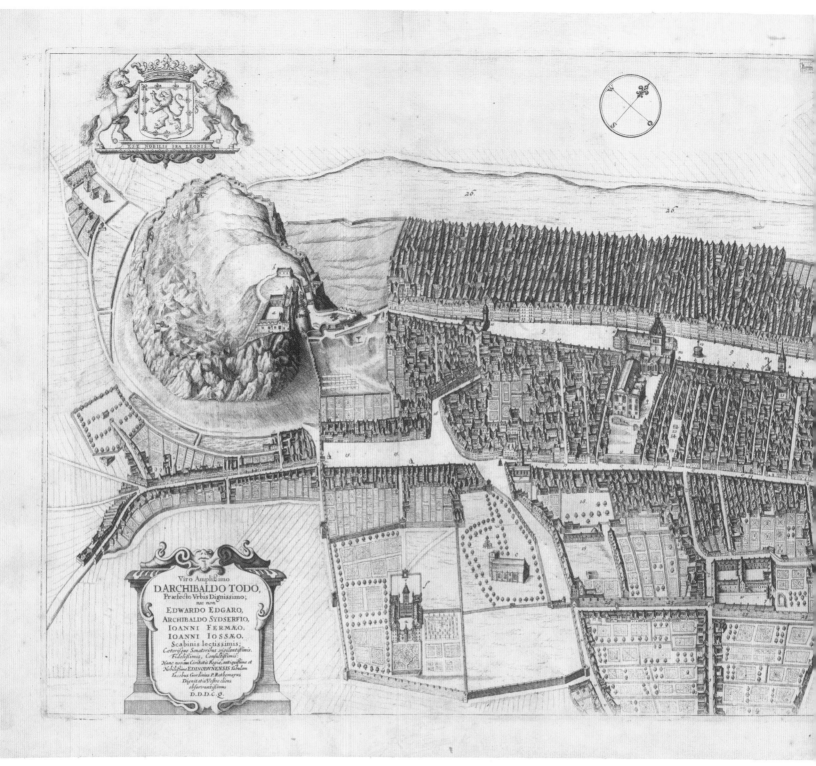

FIGURE 5.4 This stunning depiction – in bird's-eye format – of Edinburgh from the south was drafted by James Gordon in 1647 and commissioned by Edinburgh Town Council. Gordon manages to combine multiple perspectives and a deliberate distortion of scale to portray the town and its buildings, whilst retaining an accuracy of ground detail that few maps of the city achieved until the nineteenth century. The Town Council was delighted: they paid Gordon 500 merks and elected him a burgess and guild brother. The plan was intended for inclusion in Blaeu's 1654 *Atlas Novus*, but this did not happen, and it appeared only later in various Dutch and English topographic publications.

Source: James Gordon, Bird's-eye view of Edinburgh (1647). Reproduced by permission of the Trustees of the National Library of Scotland.

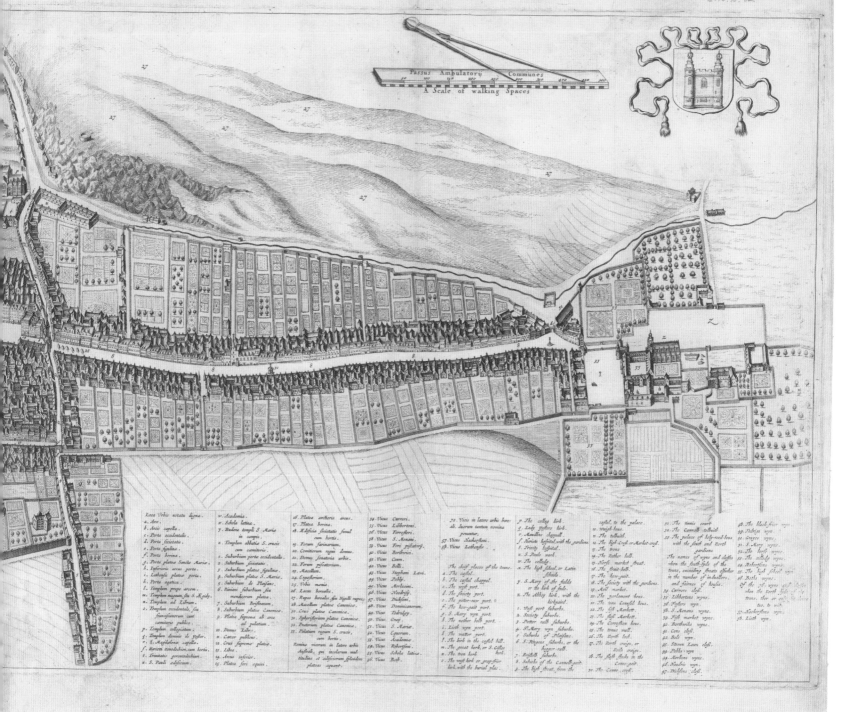

Passus Ambulatory Communes

A Scale of walking Spaces

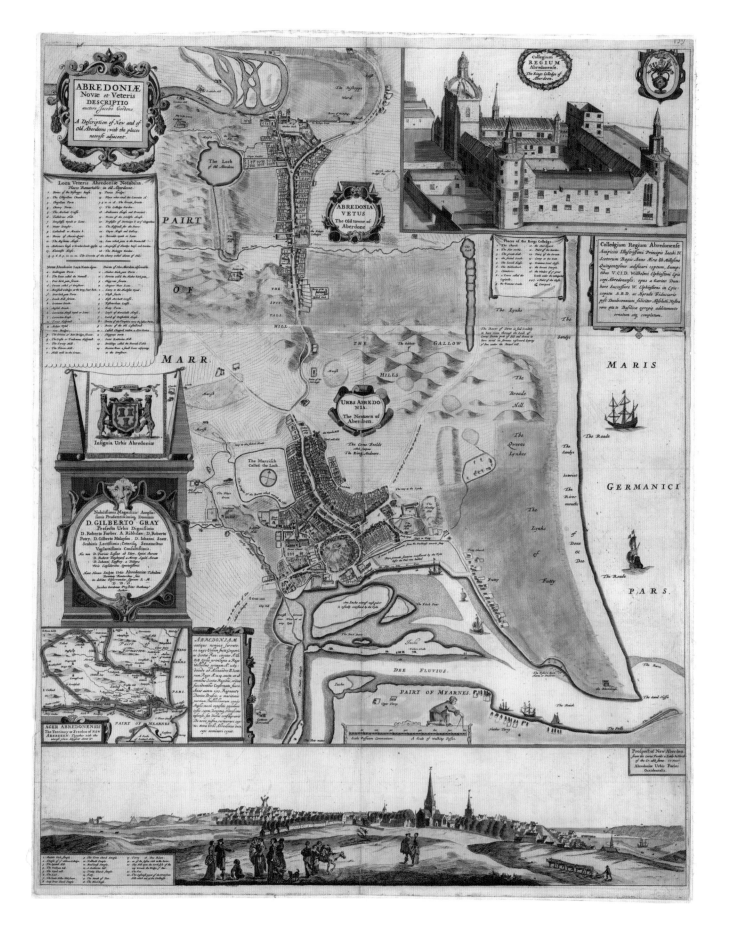

emphasise the symbolic and political importance of the towns in question, just as those of Braun and Hogenberg did a century earlier. This is cartography that means more than it is able to show. It is the cartography of early modern civic marketing: both maps were financed and promoted by their respective town councils.

FIGURE 5.5 *Opposite and details above:* This striking and uniquely informative plan and view of the old and new towns of Aberdeen is effectively its earliest detailed map. James Gordon, parson of Rothiemay parish in Aberdeenshire, was commissioned to draft this map by Aberdeen Town Council, who were delighted with the result, giving him 'a silver piece or cup of twenty ounces of silver, ane silk hat for his own use, and ane silk gown for his bedfellow'. With its unrivalled topographic detail of the town itself, and vignettes of the King's College and a view of the town from south of the river, this cartographic flattery and promotion of Aberdeen can still be appreciated today, and is a superlative illustration of James Gordon's skills as an artist, surveyor and draftsman.
Source: James Gordon, *Abredoniae Novae et Veteris Descriptio* (1661). Reproduced by permission of the Trustees of the National Library of Scotland.

URBAN MAPPING IN AN AGE OF ENLIGHTENMENT

Although John Adair included a few views of towns within his county maps drawn up from the 1680s, the next significant impetus for the mapping of Scottish towns owed more to the military concerns outlined in chapter 4 than to any need to see urban mapping as a major part of county or administrative mapping. That is the reason for the existence of detailed and accurate plans of Edinburgh, Stirling, Dumbarton, Perth (see fig. 4.5), Inverness, Fort Augustus and Fort William from the early eighteenth century. Because their purpose was military, these maps show a characteristic aesthetic. But in addition to showing a handful of Scotland's towns as militarised spaces, some of these plans, such as those for Perth and Inverness, are also important in being the earliest scale plans of the towns drafted from an overhead perspective (fig. 5.6).

Maps and plans of Scottish towns do not appear in any significant numbers until the second half of the eighteenth century and into the early nineteenth century. Between 1764 and 1865, some eighty-seven detailed town plans of Glasgow were produced. Most of them were printed and accompanied history books, almanacks or directories. Over fifteen plans of Edinburgh survive for the period from 1759 to 1800. But over 120 separate maps of Edinburgh are recorded for the first half of the nineteenth century. This increase in numbers of urban maps from the mid-eighteenth century is to be explained not by military or defensive needs but by civic demands. Cities were increasingly seen as places of civility, moral order and social refinement. This is evident, for instance, in James Craig's plan of Edinburgh's New Town (1767), with its neat geometry and symmetry providing an

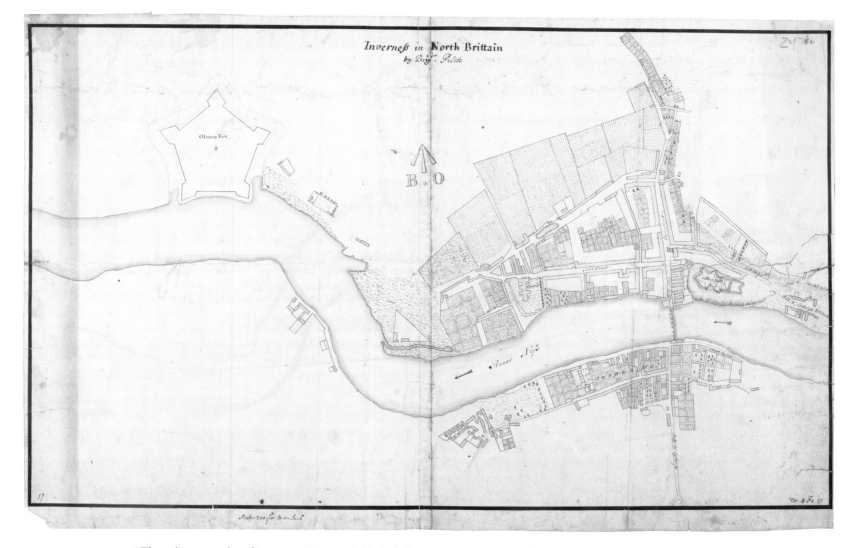

FIGURE 5.6 The earliest town plan of Inverness, this was probably drafted at the beginning of 1716, in the wake of the city's recent attack and occupation by Jacobite forces. Displaying only features of military interest, in style and in purpose it resembles Lewis Petit's Perth plan (fig. 4.5) for it is plain with generalised outlines and very few names, though with more detail given to enclosed gardens and fields. For all the singularity of purpose, it is valuable in showing the clear size and shape of the town, situated then largely on the right bank of the River Ness and forming an acute-angled triangle. Oliver's Fort or Citadel, built between 1652 and 1657, is clearly shown as a regular pentagon, with its moat originally surrounded at high tide with water. The seven-arch bridge, erected in 1685–89, is also shown as is the Old Town Hall – a plain building dating from 1708 (a site later occupied by the County Hall, built in the 1870s) *Source:* Lewis Petit, *Inverness in North Brittain* (1716). Reproduced by permission of the Trustees of the National Library of Scotland.

impressive cartographic embodiment of those principles of reason and order characteristic of a peaceful post-Jacobite North Britain (fig. 5.7). Enlightenment and civic improvement, in Scotland as elsewhere, was more and more apparent in print and in the activities of literate public audiences.

In eighteenth-century Scotland, cities provided markets for a developing print culture in periodicals, books and maps. Students, the book-buying public and members of learned societies all had need of maps: in their books of natural science and geography, to illustrate travel accounts, to see what their towns and cities looked

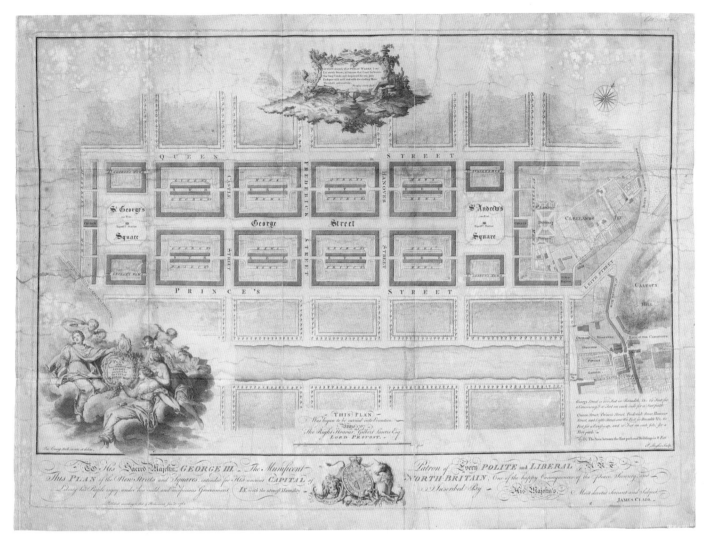

like, and to travel between them and throughout the country. From the 1750s, newspapers carried maps to illustrate the events of the day. Public lectures and private academies brought the world's affairs to discerning publics: classes in geography, for example, included instruction in surveying; new discoveries – Australia, parts of North America, Africa's rivers – extended the contemporary imagination; map sellers sold maps which visualised these new geographies, at home and abroad. Instrument makers turned their hands to globes. Land surveyors, several of whom drafted estate and county maps, drew up town plans. Many were financed by civic

FIGURE 5.7 James Craig (1744–1795) famously won the competition to plan Edinburgh's New Town when only twenty-three years old in 1767. His original design had been for a diagonal layout, echoing the design of the Union Flag in a patriotic display of Hanoverian British loyalty. The revised design – shown here – while simpler, reflected this spirit in the names of its streets and civic spaces, based on an axial grid with a principal thoroughfare along the ridge linking two garden squares. Although development was slow, the New Town gradually began to absorb the professional classes from the now less respectable Old Town, and the streets and buildings shown here were largely complete by 1800. *Source:* James Craig, *To His Sacred Majesty George III . . . This Plan of the New Streets and Squares, intended for His ancient Capital of North-Britain* (1768). Reproduced by permission of the Trustees of the National Library of Scotland.

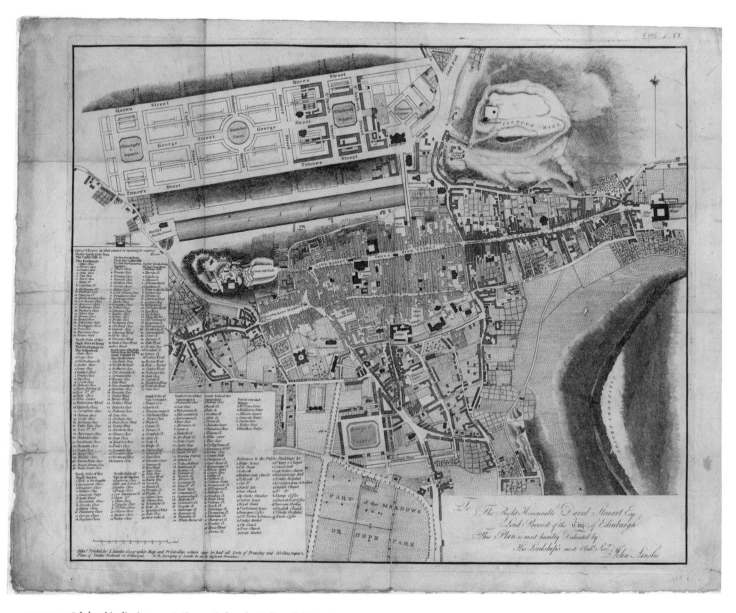

FIGURE 5.8 John Ainslie (1745–1828) married at the Tolbooth Church in Edinburgh in 1778, and by 1780 was living in Parliament Square, advertising his services on this map as a paper, map and print seller, as well as land surveyor. Ainslie worked hard to secure patronage to finance his cartographic work, and this map was dedicated to David Stewart, Lord Provost of the City. As with all of Ainslie's maps, it is clear and attractive, with a useful detailed list (with numbers given on the map) of all the closes in the Old Town. It also shows the early development of the New Town around St Andrews Square.
Source: John Ainslie, [Map of Edinburgh] (1780). Reproduced by permission of the Trustees of the National Library of Scotland.

and other patrons, and by subscribers and buyers within these emerging urban markets.

John Ainslie was one of the most successful and accomplished of Scotland's land surveyors. As well as publishing an important manual, *A Comprehensive Treatise on Land Survey* in 1812, he drafted and engraved maps of the country as a whole, maps of different counties and towns, as well as maps of coasts, canals, roads and estates. He is indicative of that new breed of map-maker then starting to appear, in Scotland as elsewhere: the professional map-maker working to commission. Ainslie trained under Thomas Jefferys, the renowned map-maker, publisher and Geographer to King George III. Ainslie produced several town plans including one of Jedburgh, his home town, in or about 1771, and he undertook several of Edinburgh, in 1780, 1801 and 1804 (fig. 5.8).

Similar circumstances were at work in Glasgow (fig. 5.9). Glasgow Burgh Council funded James Barrie, and later his assistant John Gardiner, as 'town surveyor', as well as financing other survey work. Such map work did not always pay its way: many town surveyors and map-makers necessarily had to earn their income through other activities, even as urban Scots and others became more map minded, as lawyers turned to maps to help solve disputes in law, and as landowners drew new lines on estate plans to delineate the changing social orders in the countryside. James Watt, for example, and his one-time apprentice John Gardiner, who went on to assist James Barrie, were mathematical instrument makers. The Edinburgh printer and stationer Alexander Kincaid, who prepared one of the most detailed plans of Edinburgh in 1784, illustrates well these general trends. Amongst other maps and books, he was the author in 1787 of a *History of Edinburgh*, and a *New Universal and Portable Atlas* (1798). Here was a man who knew that maps and publishing could educate and enlighten – and make money. He was one of many such men in Scotland's cities taking advantage of growing markets. Especially from the early nineteenth century, further developments in the technology of map-making, especially new lithographic printing, allowed cheaper publications to reach these expanding audiences, and from this period we can see a heightened commerce in cartography.

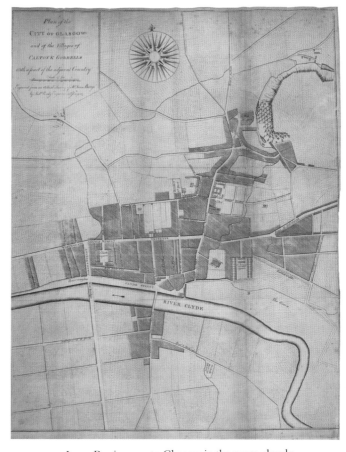

FIGURE 5.9 James Barrie came to Glasgow in the 1730s, already experienced as a land surveyor, and from the 1760s to 1780s was commissioned to undertake a large number of surveying projects by Glasgow Town Council, as well as for merchants and private speculators. On 29 March 1773, he became 'surveyor and measurer for the city of Glasgow', which involved him laying out new streets and roads, in levelling work, planning new bridges and confirming boundaries. The plan illustrated here resulted from a specially commissioned survey of the royalty of the city boundary in 1776 and an inspection and perambulation of the boundary. At a time of growing prosperity and expansion, the town council was keen to retain financial and administrative control over its burgh jurisdiction through maps such as this.
Source: James Barrie, *Plan of the City of Glasgow and of the Villages of Calton & Gorbells with a part of the adjacent Country / Engraved from an Actual Survey of Mr. James Barry's by Andw. Ready* (1777). Reproduced by permission of the Trustees of the National Library of Scotland.

MAPPING URBANISATION IN THE NINETEENTH CENTURY

The most significant private surveyor of Scottish towns in the early nineteenth century, in terms of the quality of his work and the number of maps he produced, was John Wood. Wood published fifty plans of Scottish towns between 1818 and 1826. A few of these plans (Edinburgh, Leith, Glasgow and Dundee) were based on recent town plans by other surveyors, but many were based on original surveys completed by Wood himself (fig. 5.10). These maps were published separately, but he brought together forty-eight of his plans in his *Town Atlas of Scotland* (1828). This atlas was accompanied by Wood's *Descriptive Account of the Principal Towns in Scotland*, published as a separate volume in the same year. For many smaller Scottish towns, these are the earliest plans created. In addition to showing the town at a very large scale, they often also name land and property owners. Wood was resident in Edinburgh from 1813, but he spent long periods surveying English and Welsh towns in the later 1820s and 1830s. He returned to Edinburgh in the 1840s, producing maps of Kirkcudbright, Stranraer and Airdrie before his death in 1847.

Towns appear as insets to county maps in the late eighteenth and early nineteenth centuries, and urban mapping in general at that time was part of larger, more diverse map projects, as in John Thomson's *Atlas of Scotland* (1832). This work combined existing maps with the results of new surveys. For individual map-makers such as Thomson, the rate of geographical change in the country, the increased demand for maps and the costs of undertaking in-the-field survey and back-at-home engraving all meant that he had to work with and from others' maps rather than always undertake new maps from scratch. The result, in his 1832 *Atlas* – which is mainly of county maps – is that the six town plans he includes are 'current' to

differing degrees. His depiction of Linlithgow, Stirling and Peebles, for example, is relatively up-to-date. Berwick-upon-Tweed, Haddington and Lanark, by contrast, show the state of the town some twenty years earlier than the publication date shown on the map.

Such was the pace of social change in the nineteenth century that we must, as later map users, recognise the problems faced by men like John Thomson. But we must also recognise the opportunities for map-makers that such change ushered in for urban-based mapping as a career, and that urban mapping became a theme within developing worlds of cartographic expertise. For example, Alexander Johnston, with his brother William, who was subsequently knighted and became Lord Provost of Edinburgh, founded the cartographic firm of W. & A. K. Johnston in 1825. Along with other family firms such as John Bartholomew and Son Ltd, the company was established at a time when Scotland's cities required different types of maps and plans, and when exploration overseas likewise demanded new maps. New developments in science and in the representation of scientific understanding from this period also required new types of map (chapter 10): in 1835, the Johnston firm was the first to produce, in English, a physical globe of the world incorporating new work in the natural sciences.

From the 1830s and 1840s, however, as towns were increasingly the mapped objects in focus and as they appeared on maps of different purpose, there was an important additional perspective behind the nature and purpose of urban mapping. By that period, and not just in Scotland, cities had become places of dreadful danger as well as of earthly delight, with a size and social mix not seen before. Voracious 'consumers' of people and resources, cities drew in the dispossessed rural poor, were hotbeds of disease and immorality, and, in their size and particularly in terms of housing – with the associated needs of light, clean water and adequate sanitation – they could not always cope. Scotland's civil authorities, alarmed by what they saw of urban life – and more by what they could not see – employed various devices to explore their cities. Parliamentary committees and philanthropic bodies were established: on the Poor Law; on housing; on disease prevention; on the best ways to extend moral assistance to the urban poor; on the Church's role in providing urban missionaries to explore the darkest recesses of urban Scotland much as their counterparts were doing in Africa. That new device of the 1840s and 1850s, the camera, was brought to focus on the problem: Thomas Annan's *The Old Closes and Streets of Glasgow*, produced between 1868 and 1871 at the request of the city's Improvements Trust, reflects this use of photography as a form of civic documentation and public enquiry. And so, too, urban mapping became a social and political instrument: as developments in photography also came to allow, mapping at larger scales changed the picture of the problem, got closer to the reality of Scotland's cities and helped disclose the social costs behind the urban experience.

The need for new parliamentary boundaries for implementing the Reform Act of 1832 led, for example, to new surveys and plans of seventy-five towns in Scotland (fig. 5.11). The First, or 'Great', Reform Act of that year granted extra seats in the House of Commons to those larger towns and cities whose population had expanded during the Industrial Revolution. It took away parliamentary seats from those towns with a small or declining population – the so-called 'rotten boroughs'. In Scotland, the Act expanded the electorate from 4,239

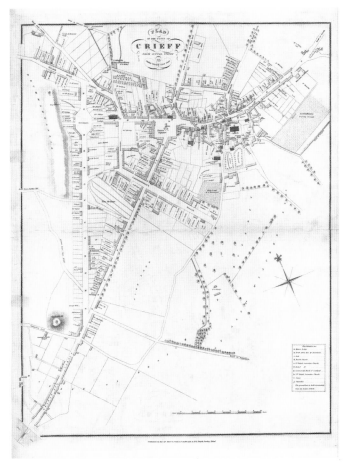

FIGURE 5.10 John Wood hailed from Yorkshire, but married in Edinburgh in 1811, and lived in the city intermittently until his death in Portobello in 1847. He is chiefly remembered today for surveying and publishing over fifty detailed plans of Scottish towns, forty-eight of which were brought together in his *Town Atlas of Scotland* (1828). His 'Plan of the Town of Crieff' captures the town at a time of transition, after the droving trysts had moved on to Falkirk, but before its development as a Victorian spa town. The Coldwell Distillery in the north, tannery in the east and Weavers' Hall on Commissioner Street to the south reflect something of the town's development after the '45 as a textile and industrial centre. The central St James Square, with the Drummond Arms Inn, along with its well (and later fountain) can still be seen today.
Source: John Wood, *Plan of the Town of Crieff from Actual Survey by John Wood* (1822). Reproduced by permission of the Trustees of the National Library of Scotland.

eligible voters in the 1820s to over 65,000 after 1832. The passage of the Act was welcomed by those seeking a fairer franchise, and, in Edinburgh, resulted in a celebratory procession of over 15,000 people through the capital's streets. Although the Act was criticised for only enfranchising 'the respectable classes', it nonetheless represented an important shift of power from aristocratic and landed interests towards the growing urban middle classes.

Seventy-five plans of towns were published in the parliamentary *Reports upon the Boundaries of the several Cities, Burghs, and Towns in Scotland in respect to the Election of Members to serve in Parliament*. The Report contains information on trade, manufactures and the general circumstances of the individual burgh, its population and number of residential houses, its assessed taxes, together with a detailed description of the proposed new boundary. Each burgh was visited by two commissioners, Mr William Murray and Captain J.W. Pringle of the Royal Engineers, and, under their direction, plans were drawn up to illustrate the verbal descriptions of the new bound-

FIGURE 5.11 Given their primary purpose, the Reform Act plans show relatively general detail for the central urban area, with buildings clumped together as shaded blocks. Major streets, public buildings, industrial units, tolls, canals, bridges and quarries are shown. The only colour on the plans is the proposed boundary in red, and water in blue. These plans form the most significant body of maps drawn specifically to illustrate urban boundaries in Scotland. Only a few examples exist of earlier mapping to this end, including Tain in 1750 and a map of the extended royalty of Glasgow in the 1820s. The Scottish plans were all executed at the scale of 6 inches to the mile, in contrast to the Reform Act plans for England and Wales in 1831–32, which were drawn at a range of smaller scales. By the time of later Reform Acts in 1868 and 1884, state-funded centralised mapping by Ordnance Survey was largely available for the purposes of illustrating parliamentary boundaries, and so there was no repeat of the 1831–32 mapping. *Source:* Great Reform Act, *Stirling* (1832). Reproduced by permission of the Trustees of the National Library of Scotland.

aries. According to their report, 'all the burghs were visited twice, some of them oftener', between November 1831 and February 1832. In this work, the urban map based on first-hand information was used to highlight the political geography of Scotland's cities.

From the 1840s, mapping undertaken by Ordnance Survey and prompted by growing concerns over sanitary conditions in towns encouraged the most detailed set of town plans ever undertaken in Scotland: this was mapping to reveal a contemporary social geography.

Ordnance Survey was officially founded in 1791. Its officers and surveyors began their work in rural Kent. From this time and place, Britain was mapped, more or less, from its bottom right-hand corner to its top left-hand corner. In the early nineteenth century, Ordnance Survey was engaged primarily in mapping southern England at a scale of 1 inch to the mile (1:63,360) before it was diverted in its operations from the 1820s to map Ireland at a scale of 6 inch to the mile (1:10,560). Survey work begun in Scotland in 1819 and renewed there and in northern England in the 1840s was coincident with heightened awareness of the power of maps to document urban form and social conditions. Increased concerns about public health and sanitary conditions in towns led to a growing opinion, encouraged by such bodies as the Poor Law Commissioners, that cartography could serve the needs of the state. And so it could, but perhaps not so effectively at the same scale of resolution as in the countryside. These and other promptings from concerned civic bodies were nevertheless soon acted upon, with over eleven English town surveys begun in 1846–47, and a further twenty-eight completed between 1848 and 1852.

In Scotland, Ordnance Survey began its work at larger scales in the south-west of the country from the 1840s, proceeding generally in a northerly direction, county by county. Fifty-nine towns were mapped between 1847 (Stranraer) and 1874 (Wick) as part of the initial county map surveys (fig. 5.12). From 1855, a different scale was adopted: that of 1:500. At that scale, essentially any feature over 6 inches in size could be shown. Many towns and cities were revealed to be places of noxious industry, the cramped conditions of employment often making worse the effects of unsanitary housing (fig. 5.13). Later, revisions were made for fourteen larger towns, along with two additional towns that were included as part of the revision of Ordnance Survey county maps in the 1890s. These revisions allow useful chronological comparisons to be made. A few towns were also surveyed at their own expense (for example, Aberdeen in 1899–1900, Dundee in 1900–01).

For virtually all of Scotland's towns, and principally because of the expense involved, there were no more detailed urban maps created at this sort of scale after this Ordnance Survey work in the nineteenth century. What the Survey had pioneered helped open a window on Scotland's urban populations, and became an opportunity for others. Commercial or municipal map-makers used these impressively detailed maps for a range of other purposes. Publishers of trade and post office directories often included a map and, for Scotland's largest towns, these were revised annually throughout the nineteenth and twentieth centuries. Commercial map-makers, like the Bartholomew and Johnston firms, exploited new opportunities for urban maps: for tourist visitors; for international exhibitions; to advertise company premises; to show railways, tramways and buses; and even to caution about social excess (fig. 5.14). More specialist maps also appeared, such as those developed from the later nineteenth century by Charles Goad & Son to illustrate fire insurance risk (fig. 5.15). Maps were even silent witnesses to the crimes committed in Scotland's streets (fig. 5.16).

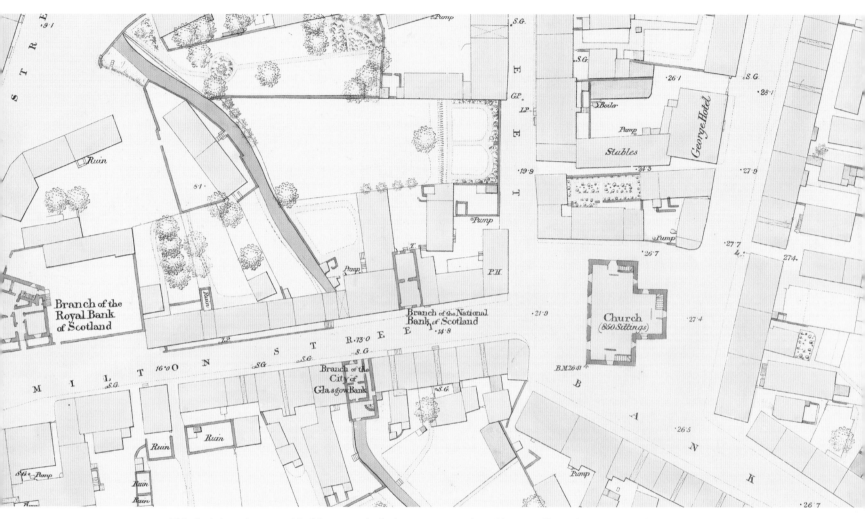

FIGURE 5.12 This depiction of streets and buildings near the harbour in Girvan in 1857 shows unrivalled detail. As a result of the 1:500 scale adopted from 1855, many small features could be shown: street bollards, lamp-posts, pavements, trees, steps and garden paths are all shown 'true-to-scale'. And, because of the maps' value in improving urban sanitation, many features relating to gas, water supply, sewerage and drainage are detailed – each S.G. shown here was a Sewer Grate – as well as accurate spot-heights and benchmarks. The maps show the divisions between buildings, including tenements, as well as the wynds and vennels so distinctive a feature of Scottish towns, but which are rarely visible on smaller-scale maps. Many domestic and commercial premises are shown, including the George Hotel and its stables; for public buildings, such as the banks and churches, their internal room layout is also indicated. Over half of these town plans have coloured sheets, as shown here, most using carmine for stone or brick buildings, grey for wooden or metal buildings, sienna for roads, and blue for water.
Source: Ordnance Survey, 1:500. *Girvan, Sheet LV.4.17*, Surveyed 1857. Reproduced by permission of the Trustees of the National Library of Scotland.

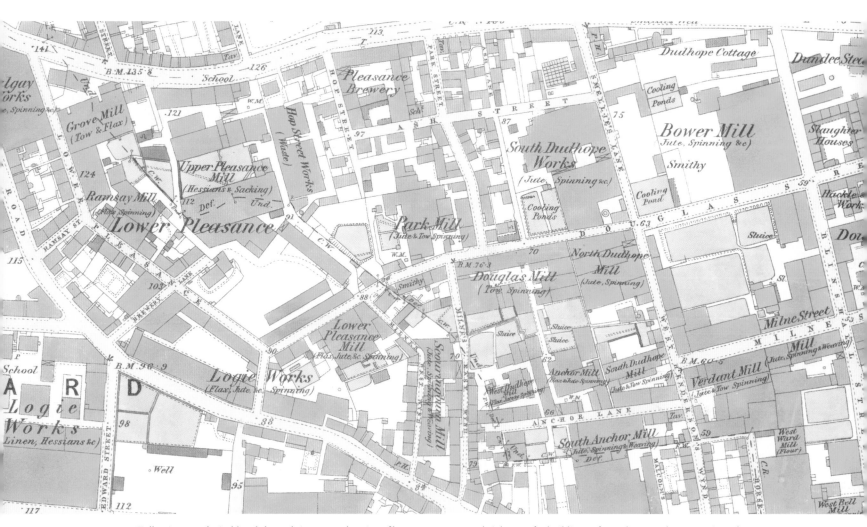

FIGURE 5.13 Following a technical breakthrough in 1833, when jute fibre was first spun mechanically in Dundee, the jute industry expanded across Western Europe with Dundee as its main centre. At its peak in the 1860s and 1870s, the jute processing industry in Dundee employed some 50,000 people in over sixty factories scattered across the city. The first Ordnance Survey 25 inch to the mile maps for Dundee, as shown here, record this mass of factories well. Their colour scheme, with red for buildings of masonry or brick, grey for buildings of wood or metal construction, along with the extensive blue cooling ponds of water, capture an industrial heartland in a blaze of colour and detail.

Source: Ordnance Survey, 25 inch to the mile. *Forfarshire Sheet LIV.5,* surveyed 1872 (published 1874). Reproduced by permission of the Trustees of the National Library of Scotland.

FIGURE 5.14 *Opposite:* The Bartholomew firm published a number of urban maps in support of the temperance movement in the late nineteenth and early twentieth centuries. This map presents a mass of red danger in the form of numerous public houses and licensed grocers, barely checked by the scattering of churches and branches of the Glasgow United Young Men's Christian Association. An accompanying statistical table reinforces the moral and cartographic message: in 1884, Glasgow had 1,485 public houses and 263 licensed grocers. In that year alone, there were 22,364 cases of assault and 14,366 people were arrested for being drunk and incapable.

Source: John Bartholomew, *New Plan of Glasgow with Suburbs by John Bartholomew, F.R.G.S., Issued by the Glasgow United Young Men's Christian Association, Showing the Distribution of Public Houses, Licensed Grocers, Churches, and Branches of the 'G.U.Y.M.C.A.'* (1884). Reproduced by permission of the Trustees of the National Library of Scotland.

FIGURE 5.15 *Below:* Charles Goad published Fire Insurance plans of selected larger Scottish towns – Dundee, Glasgow, Edinburgh, Leith, Paisley, Greenock and Campbeltown – in the 1880s and 1890s. More detailed than Ordnance Survey's large-scale town plans, they focused on information used by the insurance assessor to determine fire risk and the potential for damage. This detail of the Benmore and Highland Distillery neighbouring premises in Campbeltown illustrates this well, with details of grain stores, malt barns, wash houses, kilns, still houses and spirit stores. Unlike Ordnance Survey maps of this time, the use and ownership of property, street widths, names and property numbers are also all shown. Different line styles, and colours (red for brick buildings; yellow for wooden buildings; light blue for low-level skylights) provide an indication of internal and external building materials and exit points.

Source: Charles E. Goad, *Insurance Plan of Cambeltown, Argyllshire* (1898). Reproduced by permission of the Trustees of the National Library of Scotland.

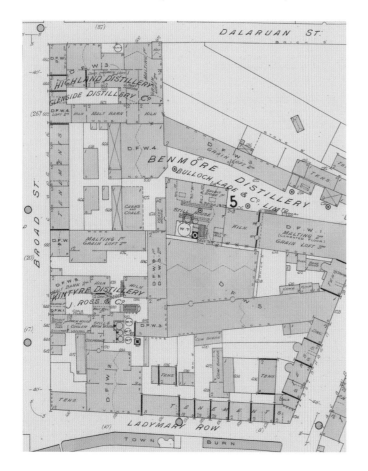

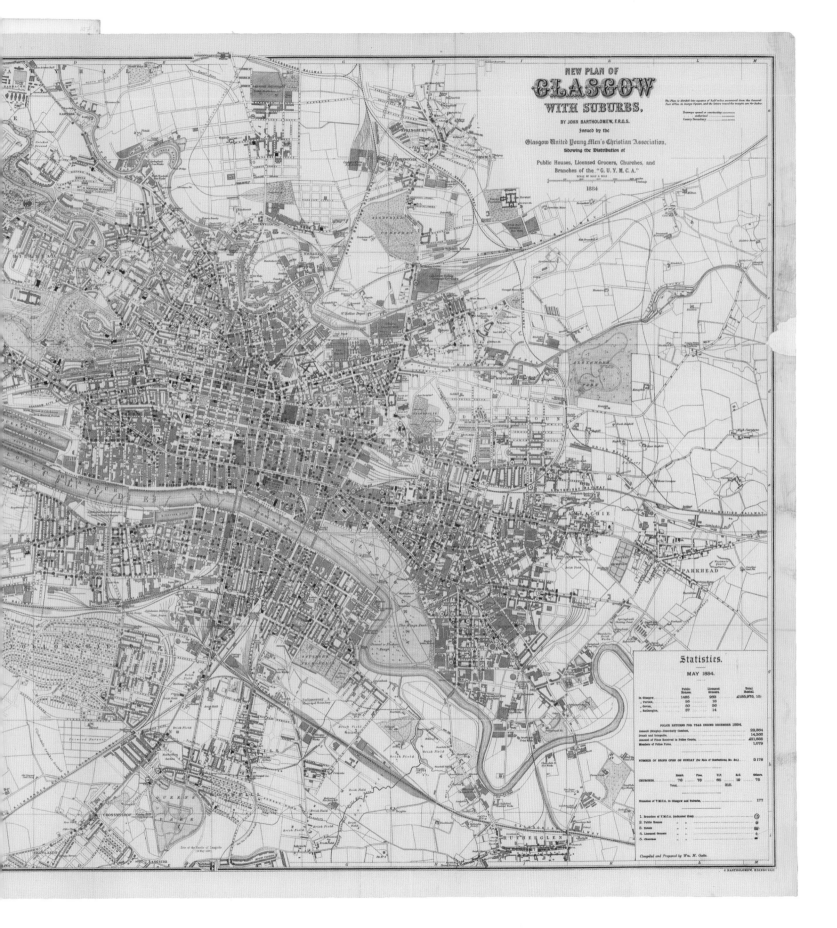

NEW PLAN OF
GLASGOW
WITH SUBURBS,

BY JOHN BARTHOLOMEW, F.R.G.S.

Issued by the

Glasgow United Young Men's Christian Association,

Showing the Distribution of

Public Houses, Licensed Grocers, Churches, and
Branches of the "G.U.Y.M.C.A."

SCALE OF HALF A MILE

1884

Statistics.

MAY 1884.

	Public Houses	Licensed Grocers	Total Rental
In Glasgow,	1485	283	£185,976, 10
„ Partick,	56	18	
„ Govan,	50	26	
„ Rutherglen,	57	14	

POLICE RETURNS FOR YEAR ENDING DECEMBER 1884.

Assault (Simple)—Disorderly Conduct,	22,904
Drunk and Incapable,	14,335
Amount of Fines Received in Police Courts,	£31,865
Members of Police Force,	1,079

NUMBER OF SHOPS OPEN ON SUNDAY (for Sale of Confections, &c. &c.) | 2,178

	Estab.	Free.	U.P.	R.C.	Others.
CHURCHES,	76	79	65	19	76
Total,			315		

Branches of Y.M.C.A. in Glasgow and Suburbs, | 177

1. Branches of Y.M.C.A. (indicated thus)
2. Public Houses „ „
3. Hotels „ „
4. Licensed Grocers „ „
5. Churches „ „

Compiled and Prepared by Wm. M. Oatts.

J. BARTHOLOMEW, EDINBURGH.

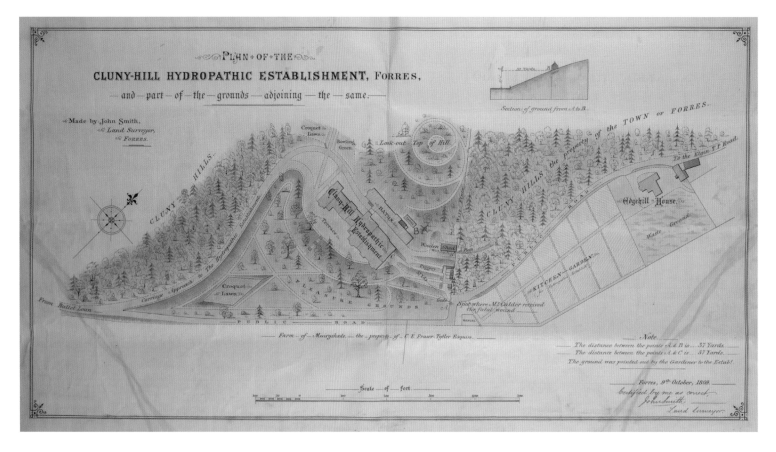

FIGURE 5.16 There are over 1,500 surviving nineteenth-century locus of crime maps for Scotland. They can provide information on the locus of crime itself, particularly in High Court cases involving crimes such as assault, murder, rape, fire-raising or neglect of duty, and give useful information about the past layout of the town in question, its streets, railway lines or even buildings – and, occasionally, facts about their owners. This plan of the Cluny-Hill Hydropathic Establishment, Forres, by John Smith (1869) related to the trial of George Norman, a former merchant, who had recklessly discharged a firearm, fatally wounding Mr James Calder, manager of the Cluny-Hill Hydropathic Establishment. Norman was found guilty of culpable homicide and sentenced to one month's imprisonment in Elgin.
Source: John Smith, *Plan of the Cluny-Hill Hydropathic Establishment, Forres* (1869). Reproduced by permission of the National Records of Scotland.

MAPPING MODERNITY

Maps of urban places have always had, at least in part, the function of display, of civic presentation: in this sense, for all the differences in angle of view and in context, there is an element of common purpose linking the pictorial representation of Edinburgh in Braun and Hogenberg's work of the 1570s (fig. 2.8) with James Craig's view of the New Town in the 1760s (fig. 5.7). And there is a connection between Craig's work and the many maps of the twentieth century and later which sought to lay out a view of the future.

In the twentieth century especially, maps of urban places were increasingly used in city and town planning. Maps were a vital device for depicting not what was, but what might be. Consider, as one example, the case of

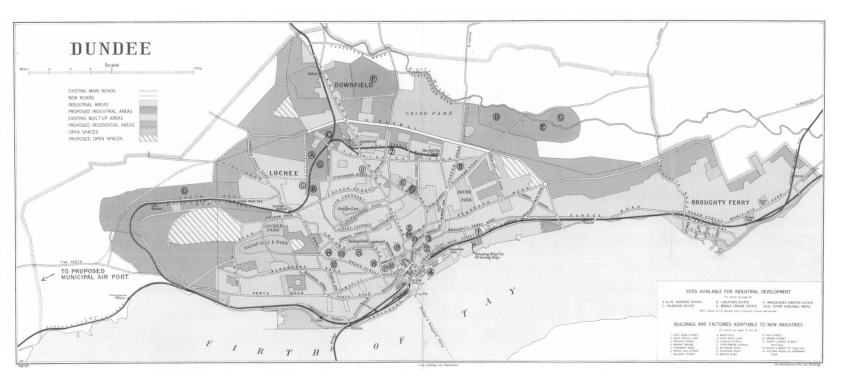

Dundee in the early 1930s (fig. 5.17). This plan of the city
bears the stamp of James Hannay Thomson, the Dundee
Harbour Trust General Manager and Engineer, who had
successfully encouraged a transition away from Dundee's
failing textile industries towards new manufacturing at
this time. Thomson, with others, looked to the future: he
recognised the future importance of transportation of
raw materials by roads, and not just by sea, even although
this was a difficult issue to 'sell' to developers, given
historical investment in the harbour and its immense
value as a source of income and employment. But this
was also a new Dundee to live in, as well as to work in.

In 1911, over 60% of households in Dundee lived in
one- or two-roomed houses. Slum clearance and better
housing was a key priority, as it was for many places in
Scotland. Between 1919 and 1939, over 8,100 local

FIGURE 5.18 Glenrothes was designated in 1948 under the New Towns (Scotland) Act 1946 as Scotland's second post-war new town (East Kilbride was designated in 1947). The first town masterplan shown here sub-divided the designated area into self-contained residential precincts or areas with their own primary schools, local shops and community facilities, based on Ebenezer Howard's Garden City principles. This was a deliberate contrast to the unplanned and polluted industrial towns and cities of the previous centuries where cramped housing and dirty industry were built adjacent to one another. In practice, several unforeseen factors – the closure of the Rothes Colliery by 1961 that had originally been intended to be the towns' largest employer, increased levels of car ownership, and a much larger residential growth than anticipated – forced the Glenrothes Development Corporation to create several revised plans in the following decades.
Source: Peter Tinto, Glenrothes Development Corporation. *Outline Plan Report* (1951). Reproduced by permission of Fife Council.

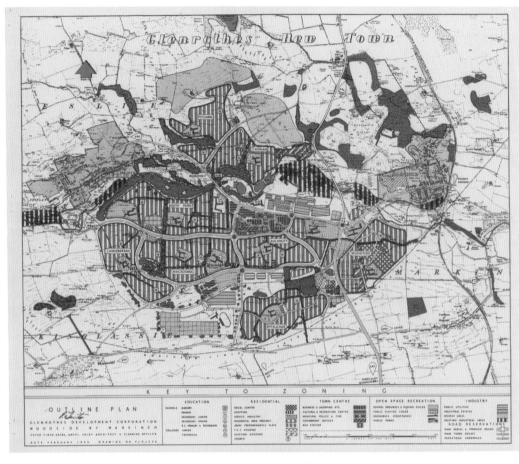

authority houses were built, many in new suburban districts such as Logie, Beechwood and Craigiebank, or Craigie Garden Suburb. Thomson's map is in many ways a social blueprint for post-war Dundee, encouraging the residential and industrial expansion north of the Kingsway ring road, and even anticipating the city's airport (albeit some three decades before its eventual opening in 1962) – he termed it the 'Proposed Municipal Airport'. Although they took time to locate in Dundee, multinational companies such as Dayco, Holochrome, National Cash Register, Timex and Michelin provided much needed post-war employment.

War damage offered city authorities a chance to rebuild Scotland's urban fabric and to look to the future. And, where Scotland's old towns could not be developed, the new towns of the 1960s had first to be imagined, mapped in the mind as well as on paper, before they were brought into being (fig. 5.18). In truth, albeit at different rates of change and with variable social consequences, Scotland's towns and cities have always been places of dynamic change (fig. 5.19): maps have always provided a key way of presenting, enquiring into and managing them.

Since the 1990s, electronic street mapping on desktop

[A]   [B]

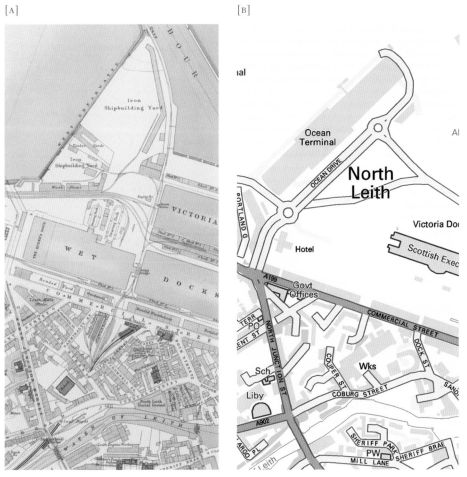

FIGURE 5.19 In this image, the power of urban maps to highlight changes in the urban environment is apparent in these two depictions of part of Leith: inset A, from the Bartholomew map of 1891, shows shipbuilding and timber yards, wet docks and bonded warehouses. Today, as is evident from inset B, the area has been physically transformed, with the Ocean Terminal shopping centre, Holiday Inn and Scottish Government Victoria Quay building. *Source:* [A] John G Bartholomew, *Bartholomew's Plan of the City of Edinburgh with Leith & Suburbs* (1891). Reproduced by permission of the Trustees of the National Library of Scotland; Ordnance Survey Street View® (2011). [B] Contains Ordnance Survey data © Crown copyright and database right, 2011.

computers, mobile devices or dashboards has provided a new and different presentation of towns on maps. This mapping changes rapidly – in content, perspective and quality – and, as an application, it can be integrated with a potentially infinite range of other information and presented as new maps. Although this may seem to offer a radically different way of representing urban spaces, it has close links with all the maps reviewed in this chapter: the bundling together of symbols, pictures and surveys, and the need to offer multiple-perspective views on urban space are still as relevant. The largest providers of this instantly available mapping – Google, Microsoft and

Yahoo – provide map content primarily built on detailed street network mapping that forms the backbone of route-planning technologies. Compared with all the maps reviewed in this chapter, such maps show a restricted range of urban features. This homogenised, global rendering of urban spaces – in what it chooses to show and omit, in its aesthetics, in the large corporations that create, control and sustain it, and in its ability to be 'mashed up' with an infinite array of other geo-referenced information content – is very much a twenty-first-century perspective. It illustrates as much about our current values as the towns we may look at and live in.

A
Plan *of* y^e Garden
& Plantation of *DRUMLANGRIG*
in SCOTLAND, *The Seat of his*
Grace y^e *Duke of* QUEENSBURRY.
To the most noble Prince CHARLES.
Duke of QUEENSBURRY & DOVER &c.
This Plan is most humbly
Inscrib'd by his Graces most
humble Servant
J: Rocque

CHAPTER 6

THE CHANGING COUNTRYSIDE

Between 1700 and 1850, the Scottish rural landscape was almost completely transformed. The predominantly open-field system and a populous countryside of scattered fermtouns, surrounded by extensive communal land – often a mixture of moorland, scattered trees and upland grazing – was replaced by an ordered, geometrical, fenced, walled and wooded landscape, with neat and more compact farms, roads and new rural employments. Under a prevailing spirit of improvement, the countryside – using that term to mean agriculture mainly but also aspects of rural industry – became more productive, efficient and lucrative (for some people), with new crops and livestock, new rotations and tools. Waste and drained land was brought into productive use, and a new infrastructure of roads and bridges facilitated movement of commodities and people.

Whether or not this was Scotland's 'Agricultural Revolution' depends both upon definitions of the term 'revolution' and when and where the changes occurred. But, more or less everywhere, these processes over time also involved immense social dislocation and hardship,

with many cottars and other land workers and tenants forced to leave the land – and often Scotland altogether – while, for those remaining, rural life was often harder and economically less secure.

Maps, and the land surveyors who created them, were key agents in this transformation, especially from the mid-eighteenth century. Agricultural revolution or not, it was, certainly in estate mapping, a 'cartographic revolution'. Land surveyors brought together a range of abilities to very definite practical outcomes: to measure land using scientific instruments, to triangulate and quantify the results, to draw maps suggesting improvements to bring out the potential of the land, and most importantly to fix rents so as to maximise long-term returns for the land-owner without bankrupting the tenant. The increased emphasis on profit and prosperity – landowners' and the nation's alike – was everywhere rooted in the idea and ideals of improvement, in an intended new look for the country. No device better illustrates this eighteenth-century emphasis on prospect – the term then meant both a look forward in time and a look outward over space and land – than the estate map. Over 50,000 plans of Scottish estates survive today, most drawn over the century or so after about 1760. They are attractive, detailed and immensely informative documents for understanding the rural landscape, but they also reflect the imposition of new values. These maps encapsulate ideas of progress, rationality and order.

This chapter pays particular attention to the estate maps of Scotland's age of improvement. But that is not its only concern. Mapping the country, mapping the countryside that is, began in Scotland as elsewhere in the smaller-scale and smaller-in-scale mapping projects of sixteenth-century chorographers and others. Estate mapping and county mapping at larger scales are particularly associated with the mid-eighteenth century and later. From the mid-nineteenth century, the work of mapping rurality was mainly undertaken by Ordnance Survey and other larger institutions, including private companies. It is striking how different these presentations of the countryside are. To an extent, these reflect differences in purpose – who commissioned the maps and why – and, of course, changes in surveying and map-making technologies. This is particularly a shift from manuscript map to printed map. Still more importantly, these maps reflect great social changes in the perception of the countryside and its perceived value over time by map-makers and map users. This can be seen in both the unintentional as well as the deliberate decisions to select and show certain features at the expense of others. These different maps of the countryside additionally reflect the growing cultural commerce of cartography in society as a whole. Yet the story of estate mapping in particular, and of countryside mapping in general, is overwhelmingly one of property and ownership and of prospects of improvement and of power.

THE COUNTRYSIDE IN MAPS BEFORE 1700

Nearly all the detailed maps of rural Scotland before about 1700 are derived from the work of three main map-makers whose work and importance we have already seen (chapter 3): Timothy Pont in the late sixteenth century, Robert Gordon in the mid-seventeenth century, and John Adair in the late seventeenth century.

Pont's manuscript maps, and the maps engraved by Joan Blaeu based on Pont's work, provide the earliest graphic portrayal of the Scottish countryside. The countryside is full in Pont's work. Perhaps as many as 20,000 place names are shown on the Pont/Blaeu maps and, despite wide regional variations, more than three-quarters of these names represent human settlements. In some cases, the density of rural settlements is staggering: in Pont's map of Clydesdale, for example, over 1,000 human settlements are shown and named. Pont also provides many other important details of the larger milltouns and fermtouns, the location and extent of woodland, of mills and bridges, the position of parish kirks, tower houses and the castles of the larger landowners. His maps and accompanying notes describe land quality, crops and other economic resources as well as unproductive land – mosses, moors and mountains. But his work does not, commonly, descend to field boundaries, to the acreage of different land-use types or to the detail of individual cropping patterns. There was no need to do so when arable agriculture was open field with few boundaries.

When James and Robert Gordon copied the work of Pont, and when they surveyed Fife (as James Gordon did in 1641) and the north-east (Aberdeenshire, Banffshire and Moray), they took the opportunity to include new

[A]

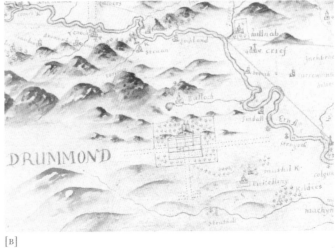

[B]

FIGURE 6.1 [A] These two details of the environs around Drummond Castle in Strathearn, by Timothy Pont in the late sixteenth century and a hundred years later by John Adair in the late seventeenth century, illustrate the considerable changes on the ground. Note in particular the disappearance of Boirlands, Drumsachy, and Drumgaurak, as well as the drainage of the loch to north of the castle.
Source: Timothy Pont, from Pont 21 (*c.*1583–1614) Drummond Castle environs. Reproduced by permission of the Trustees of the National Library of Scotland.

[FIGURE 6.1 [B]
Source: John Adair, *The Mappe of Straithern, Stormont & Cars of Gaurie . . .* (1683). Reproduced by permission of the Trustees of the National Library of Scotland.

information. Comparison between places on the different maps can be instructive: even then, the rural landscape was changing (fig. 6.1).

In his new surveys and drafts of Scottish counties from the 1680s, John Adair was perhaps the first Scottish map-maker to use triangulation. Twelve manuscript maps survive from his work at this time. They cover particularly the Lothians, Stirling, Fife, Kinross and southern Perthshire. There, and in parts of Angus, rural Aberdeenshire and Fife, the glimmerings of a new countryside and a new mentality were apparent as he worked: Sir Robert Sibbald was penning essays on agriculture and national advance; an enclosure act of 1661 was renewed in 1685; and in 1695 the 'Act Anent lands Lying in Run-rig' – that system of open-field land management, with individual holdings often scattered throughout the farm or holding – considered the system 'highly prejudicial to the improvement of the nation'. The run of disastrous harvests and outbreaks of disease between 1696 and 1703 or so – the so-called 'Seven Ill-Years' – only heightened awareness of the need for an effective agrarian economy that could help feed the nation. The political writing on the wall, so to speak, would soon enough be evident as writing on maps and as new lines on the ground.

COUNTY AND ESTATE MAPPING, *c.* 1760–*c.*1840

There are county maps in atlases and on maps from the first half of the eighteenth century – in the work of Hermann Moll (1725) and Thomas Kitchin (1749), for example. But the age of the county map really begins in Scotland in the 1760s, when a number of land surveyors created new, detailed maps of all the counties of Scotland. Several related factors motivated these new mapping initiatives: agricultural development, notably the enclosure of common land, political stability and economic prosperity.

From 1759 the Society for the Encouragement of Arts, Manufactures and Commerce encouraged county mapping by offering premiums and awards of up to £105 for maps based on original surveys, triangulation and accurate measurements for latitude and longitude, and at a scale of 1 inch to the mile or larger. Although the Glasgow estate surveyor Stephen McDougall remarked to the Society in 1760 that he thought the premium 'too little for a man to execute the survey', others disagreed and several surveyors published excellent new county maps. Andrew and Mostyn Armstrong were awarded fifty guineas for their map of Northumberland in 1768 and, encouraged by this, went on to produce county maps of Berwickshire (1771), the Lothians (1773) and Ayrshire (1775). Several years earlier, the Philosophical Society, begun in Edinburgh in 1731, commissioned a map of the north coast of Britain, partly, it is thought, from attempts to help measure latitudinal variations in northernmost Scotland in order to contribute to current debates on the shape of the earth, and partly from a concern to know the nature of the land and the geography of the coast, including the whereabouts of those coves and inlets being used, it was suspected, for smug-gling (fig. 6.2). The Society of Antiquaries, established in 1780, also supported mapping projects: one of its goals at foundation was study of 'Geography, Hydrography and Topography of the Country'. This was mapping as a civic and economic good.

Mapping the countryside had military, legal and political undertones in places. Estate owners often found themselves in dispute over boundaries, and maps were commonly drawn up and used in the settlement of such matters. County mapping was undertaken and advanced by surveyors working for the Commission for the Forfeited Annexed Estates, which, between 1755 and 1784, administered thirteen of the largest previously pro-Jacobite estates in Scotland (fig. 6.3). Like Roy's 'Great Map' (see chapter 4), many of these maps show the countryside not just as agricultural but as industrious: with forestry, weaving, bleaching and other small-scale employments being pursued to advance the economy (fig. 6.4).

In 1784, the Commission contributed to the developing commerce in map use by purchasing twenty-five copies of each of John Ainslie's county maps of Selkirk (1773), Fife (1775), Wigtown (1782) and Edinburgh environs (1779). As was the case for the Commission's own activities, several of these county maps were accompanied by geographical memoirs, printed texts describing the history and construction of the map, and often making claims (sometimes well-founded, oft-times not) as to its accuracy and validity. Andrew and Mostyn Armstrong published a *Companion to their map of the Three Lothians* (1773), with lists of towns, villages, landowners' residences and subscribers, linking county mapping, status and the new literate ranks in society.

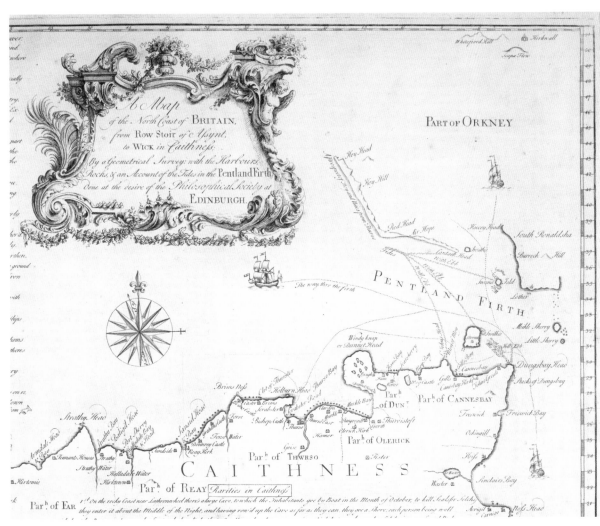

FIGURE 6.2 The Reverend Alexander Bryce, Minister in Thurso, accompanied by three assistants, made this famous survey of the northern coastline of Scotland at the request of the Philosophical Society of Edinburgh. This was the first time the coast had been surveyed using triangulation, and the resulting map, published in 1744, amongst other things confirmed for the first time that Cape Wrath and Faraid Head, regularly confused together on all earlier maps of Scotland, were indeed separate headlands. *Source:* Alexander Bryce, *A Map of the North Coast of Britain, from Row Stoir of Assynt, to Wick in Caithness* (1744). Reproduced by permission of the Trustees of the National Library of Scotland.

Subscriptions from the well-to-do, and support from wealthy and aristocratic patrons, helped pay for many of these county surveys. James Stobie used the influence and connections of the fourth Duke of Atholl (his employer) and the Duke's brother in law, Thomas Graham of Balgowan, to finance his magnificent county map of Perthshire and Clackmannanshire in 1783 (fig. 6.5). Stobie's map was not only a useful basis for his own career as an estate factor in Atholl. It was also an exemplary illustration of the values that guided such surveying, and of his own and others' views of his prospects. In significant contrast to earlier maps of the county, it was based on a trigonometrical survey, and its margins were precisely graduated with degrees for latitude and longitude. This quantifying spirit was carried through not just for the heights of the principal hills, but with facts and figures for a great range of phenomena. His accompanying description or memoir of the county is a model of Enlightenment optimism and

FIGURE 6.3 Following the Annexing Act of 1752, thirteen of the most pro-Jacobite estates in Scotland were forfeited and administered by the Commission for the Forfeited Annexed Estates. Detailed surveys were ordered and suggestions carried into effect for improvement: new agricultural methods and longer leases; new roads and bridges; more forestry in moorland areas; dyke building; rural industries (such as brickmaking, and the production of paper, soap, hemp and thread); new schools, churches and prisons; as well as the encouragement of English speaking and the banishment of Highland dress. There is a close military connection to this mapping: Lt Col. David Watson, who was centrally involved in the funding and promotion of the Military Survey of Scotland, later made famous in the work of William Roy (see chapter 4), instructed surveyors and was an influential Commissioner from the outset. The forfeited estates were often pioneers of agricultural improvement, and the maps of them illustrate a rural landscape about to experience dramatic changes. More than twenty of Scotland's leading landed proprietors were Commissioners: it is likely, then, that the Commission's mapping work had wider influence. *Source:* William Morrison, *A Plan of the Estate of Ardsheall Lying in the Parish of Appin and County of Argyll* (1773). Reproduced by permission of the National Records of Scotland.

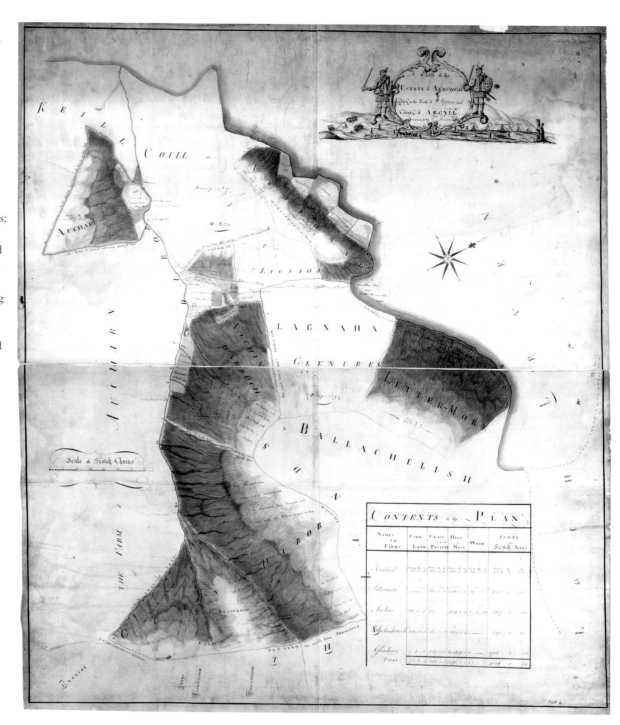

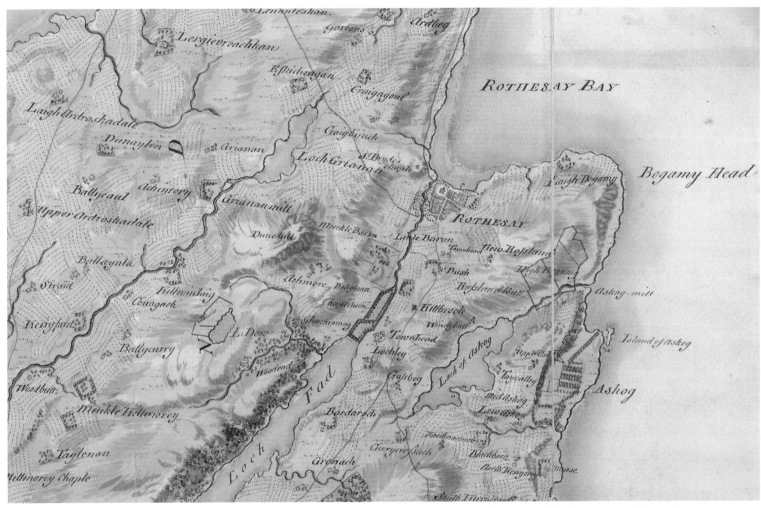

FIGURE 6.4 Although Roy's Military Survey of Scotland excluded the Northern and Western Isles, some islands close to the mainland, such as Bute, were included. This extract around Rothesay shows several features of great interest to agricultural and landscape history, including the general terrain, enclosed and unenclosed land, the shape and extent of woodland, and the 'heid dykes' surrounding many estates, such as Ascog Lodge on the right. The built environment is also well shown, with buildings and walls in red, and roads of military value as brown lines radiating from Rothesay.

Source: William Roy, Military Survey of Scotland (1747–55). Reproduced by permission of the British Library.

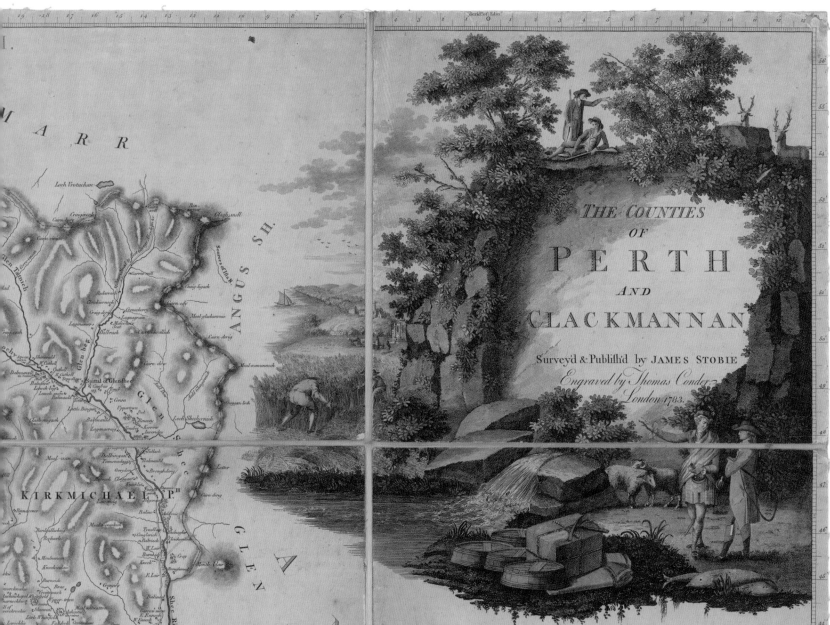

THE COUNTIES

OF

PERTH

AND

CLACKMANNAN

Surveyd & Publish'd by JAMES STOBIE

Engraved by Thomas Conder
London, 1783.

This Map

is most humbly dedicated

To the Nobility & Gentry

of the Two Counties,

by their

most obedient

and most humble Servant

ATHOLL HOUSE.
A Seat of his grace the DUKE of ATHOLL.

FIGURE 6.5 *Opposite and detail above.* James Stobie's *Counties of Perth and Clackmannan* (1783) is perhaps the most magnificent of all the county maps of Scotland. Stobie relied on an extensive network of patronage to support the map, which is hinted at by its dedication to Thomas Graham of Balgowan, Lord Lynedoch. Many owners of the larger residences who had supported Stobie's work and belonged to Graham's social circle are also shown adorning the perimeter of the map. Belmont Castle, for example, was the home of James Stewart (Lord Privy Seal of Scotland), who had also assisted John Ainslie in his map of Edinburgh and environs of 1778. Thomas Graham's sister-in-law, Louisa, married the 7th Lord Stormont, who was to inherit the earldom of Mansfield in 1793, and his father-in-law was Charles, 9th Lord Cathcart, who lived at Schaw Park by Alloa. In turn, Thomas Graham's brother-in-law, the 4th Duke of Atholl, had employed Stobie from 1780 to create new and detailed maps of his estates and, given the huge extent of the Atholl estates, covering over a tenth of Perthshire at this time, there is no doubt that this earlier estate work proved helpful in the production of the 1783 county map.
Source: James Stobie, *The Counties of Perth and Clackmannan* (1783). Reproduced by permission of the Trustees of the National Library of Scotland.

economic potential: 'The county abounds with game, has populous and fertile valleys, and produces cattle, sheep, goats, horses, butter, cheese, charcoal and oak bark.' He omitted to mention, however, that the most serious famine in eighteenth-century Scotland had happened only ten years earlier in 1772–73, and that there had been riots in Perth by angry mobs trying to stop the export of grain to England. Reduced versions of his map at one-third of the scale were issued in 1787 and 1805, and John Thomson's map of the county in 1828 was based on Stobie's original.

For Lowland counties there were new maps from updated surveys issued approximately every twenty or thirty years from the mid-1700s. In some cases, plans were laid and intentions were advertised, but the map never materialised or was limited for one reason or another: such was the case for George Mark's plan 'For publishing by subscription, An accurate map or geometrical survey of the shires of Lothian, Tweddale, and Clydsdale'. By the close of the eighteenth century, all Scottish Lowland counties had been surveyed in detail. The level of activity surpassed anything that had happened before then, and the detail of the many maps that were produced improved for the first time upon the surveys of Timothy Pont two cent-uries earlier.

From 1818 to 1830, the Edinburgh-based map publisher John Thomson began work on his monumental *Atlas of Scotland*, which, when completed in 1832, included fifty-eight detailed county maps. Most of his maps were engraved from existing maps and were, like John Wood's work at much the same time, only partially updated, but he also commissioned new surveys of several counties. Many people were employed in this project, and because he knew that local people, especially figures of authority, were likely to be both purchasers of the work and credible sources for its updating, Thomson got respected local people to attest to the accuracy of the maps. The work was engraved in Edinburgh and in London. For map producers publishing in a competitive market, accuracy and completeness can come at a cost: Thomson's *Atlas* project bankrupted him by 1830. Yet his maps – many at large scales of 1 or 2 miles to the inch – provide the most detailed county mapping of Scotland prior to Ordnance Survey.

At the larger scale of fields and farms, most estate maps in this period share distinctive characteristics: they often have boundary lines indicating ownership; frequently they are accompanied by a written terrier (a ledger or account book), or by mathematical tables quantifying areas; they are large in scale and so are detailed; and they are usually the work of private surveyors. The landscape they portray is often through the eyes of an improver, proposing new prospects of improvement. These maps promoted and enhanced the landscape for a variety of property owners through a mix of aesthetic quality, choice of content, map size and careful depiction of chosen detail (fig. 6.6).

There are, even so, important geographical differences between the local rural worlds that such maps portray and, since they are essentially static images, differences in the fast-changing social processes which maps cannot easily portray. In the south-eastern Lowlands – partly from proximity to the market that was Edinburgh and its environs – agrarian change was evident in an expansion of cereal cultivation, advances in crop rotation, fertilisation and new forms of agrarian technology and, generally, larger farms and a strict hierarchy of tenants. Here, the 'ploo-man' became king. In the south-west of Scotland, by contrast, agrarian changes from the 1720s onwards produced a region of cattle-rearing, early enclo-

FIGURE 6.6 *Opposite.* John Rocque's beautiful and detailed plan of the gardens around Drumlanrig flatters and promotes the castle and gardens as an impressive statement of aristocratic wealth and power. Rocque was a French Huguenot who was well established in London by this time as a surveyor and map-maker. Dedicated to Prince Charles, the 3rd Duke of Queensberry, Rocque's plan captures the magnificent gardens in a state of transition from a more formal French layout with parterres towards a more natural landscape style that was to become common later in the eighteenth century. It shows the water cascade (upper left), constructed by the 2nd Duke, with fountains in stone and lead. The cascade required a 2-mile long aqueduct to supply it with water, and yet could only be used briefly in summertime to avoid flooding. The plan was originally issued as plates 45 and 46 in Volume IV of *Vitruvius Britannicus*, published by Thomas Badeslade.
Source: John Rocque, *A Plan of ye Garden Plantation of Drumlangrig* [sic] *in Scotland, The Seat of ye Grace the Duke of Queensburry* (1739). Reproduced by permission of the Trustees of the National Library of Scotland.

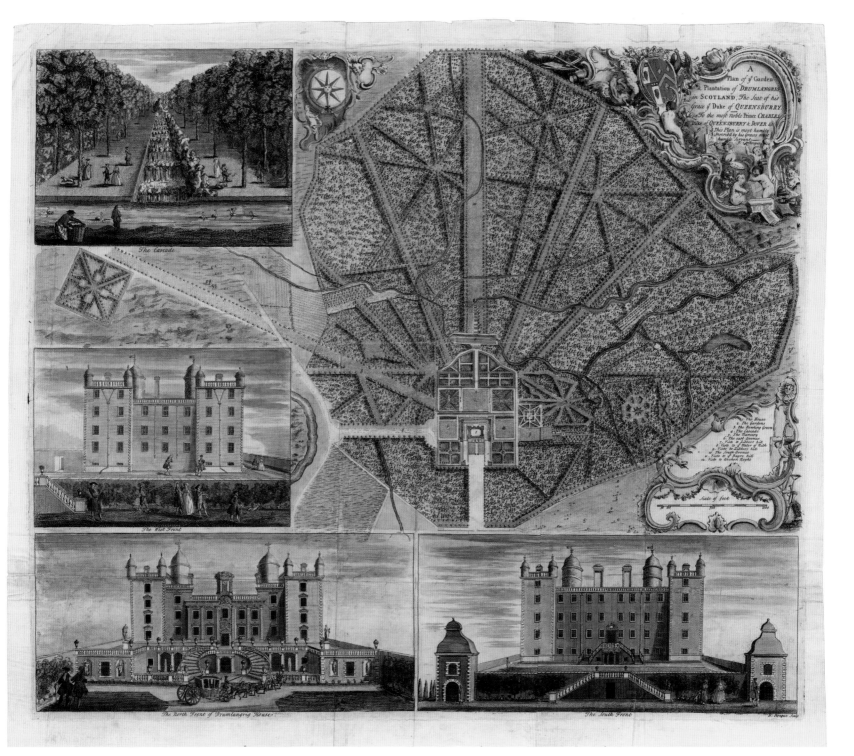

A Plan of ye Garden & Plantation of DRUMLANGRIG in SCOTLAND, The Seat of his Grace ye Duke of QUEENSBURRY. To the most Noble Prince CHARLES Duke of QUEENSBURRY & DOVER &c. This Plan is most humbly Inscribed by his Grace's most humble Servant J. Lawrence

The Cascade

The West Front

The North Front of Drumlangrig House

The South Front

Scale of feet

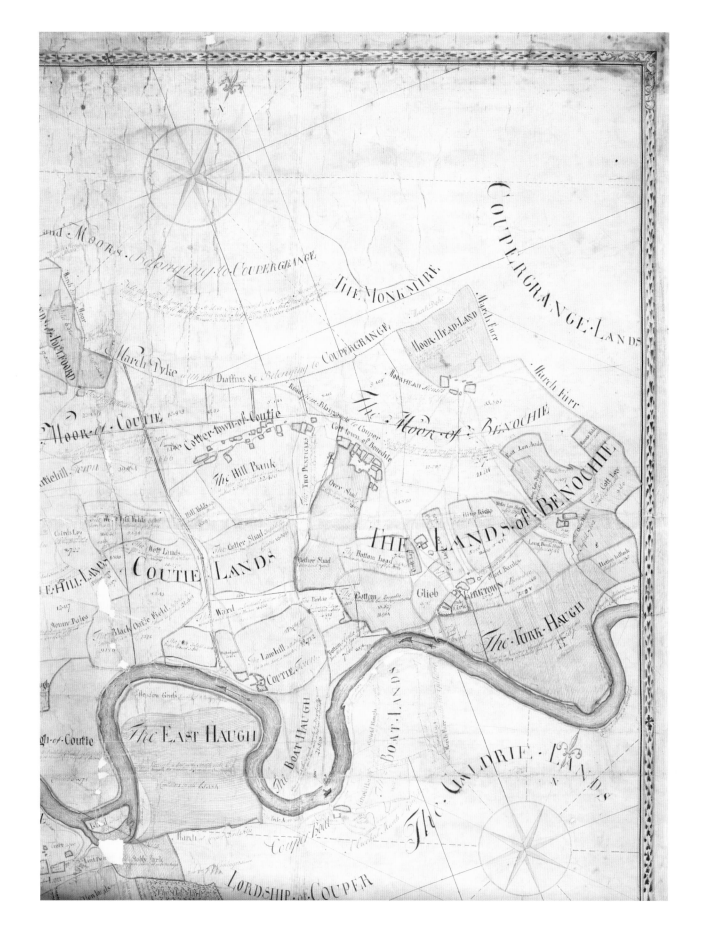

sure and farming often centred upon the family unit, with an economic orientation towards the centres of population of urban west central Scotland. In the north-east, in Aberdeen, Banff and Kincardine, and even parts of north-east Perthshire and Angus, many small one-plough farms and small crofts appeared on the marginal lands. Larger farms there, with a mixed economy and the bothy system of communal labour, appeared on the better-drained soils and nearer urban markets (compare figs. 6.7, 6.8, 6.9).

Across Scotland, planned villages were established offering new housing and industries for the dispossessed rural worker (fig. 6.10). Most of the nearly 400 such villages throughout Scotland date from about 1770 to about 1820. The many plans of them that survive depict new features in the Scottish rural landscape in a carto-graphic language of assured lines and clear symbolisation. Symbolic is what they were of course – of a new ordered countryside laid out for the future. Harbours were re-modelled (fig. 6.11), and in places such as Tobermory and Pulteneytown new settlements geared to fishing were established after the foundation of the British Fisheries Society in 1786.

In the Highlands, things were different still. Strictly, it is as inappropriate to think of 'the Highlands' as one region as it is to do so for 'the Lowlands'. And differences exist within and between the mainland – Highlands or otherwise – and Scotland's islands (chapter 7). Before the mid eighteenth century, Highland social structure was dominated by the clan system, loyalty to kin, and tenancy secured on the basis of military service. While attachment to land was through notions of recognised property and ownership in the sense of clan lands, it was also strongly moral, encapsulated in the Gaelic word *duthchas*, which embraces notions of home, heredity and belonging and was seldom enshrined in law. From the later eighteenth century, Highland tenantry was everywhere faced with the pressures of a subsistence agriculture being drawn more and more into the circuits of capital and commer-cialisation. Population pressure heightened as potato cultivation allowed plots to be sub-divided. But when the potato crop failed, as it often did and disastrously so from the later 1840s, or as sheep farms replaced small-holdings, new systems of land holding were required.

The Highland rural economy was transformed between *c.*1780 and 1850. To the north and west of the Great Glen and in the Outer Isles, crofting was dominant, a particular solution to the processes of land clearance, with a mixed economy of agricultural smallholdings, fishing and employments such as weaving and spinning.

FIGURE 6.7 *Opposite.* The estates of Kethick and Benochie lie to the north and west of Coupar Angus, in Perthshire, and this plan is significant in displaying both the contemporary landscape with irregular fields and fermtouns, and, superimposed upon it, the proposed 'new and improved' landscape with larger and more ordered fields and detached farms. By the mid eighteenth century, most land surveyors combined surveying and cartographic skills with land factoring. They frequently had extensive knowledge of land management and agricultural improvement, and acted as advisers to estate owners who were keen to undertake new scientific methods in improving and enclosing their land. The notes around the map reveal the sort of advice that was given. Kethick, for example, 'would inclose best with hedge & ditch', while the outfields were 'a very gravelly barren sand and in their present state not worth labour'. To improve the soil, Winter advised bringing in 'marle from the Monkmire' to the north, carried in carts to Benochie Kirk, then floated down the River Isla in a flat-bottomed boat. Caddam, to the south, was proposed as a seat for a new mansion (which later maps suggest was built as Kethick House), and the plan shows a proposed avenue of trees leading to it.
Source: Thomas Winter, *A Plan of the Estates of Kethick and Benochie . . . the Property of James Mackenzie of Rosehaugh* (1751). Reproduced by permission of the Trustees of the National Library of Scotland.

FIGURE 6.8 *Right.* The zeal that underlay agricultural improvement, with the reclamation of moss, the planning of new villages and roads, the enclosure of arable lands and the introduction of new techniques, is apparent in this impressive volume for the Grahams of Gartmore by the land surveyor Charles Ross. For the first time the precise quantification of land extent and ownership is shown, a very clear contrast to the military mapping with which this is contemporary.
Source: Charles Ross, 'Gartmore Inclosur's' from *Book of Maps of the Estate of Gartmore belonging to Robert Graham Esqr.* (1781). Reproduced by permission of the Trustees of the National Library of Scotland.

FIGURE 6.9 *Opposite.* Commonties − lands held and managed in common − were formerly a vital part of subsistence agriculture for grazing, fuel, building materials and reserve land to cope with population growth. Following several acts of Parliament from the later seventeenth century, commonties were divided as their land was increasingly regarded as economically useful for landlords. It has been estimated that half a million acres of commonty were divided between 1695 and 1900. The commonty of Methven Muir was divided in 1793, and comprised over 1,000 acres of land north-west of Methven village. Following a 1788 court summons by David Smythe, the laird of Methven Castle, against Thomas Graham of Balgowan and others, the surveyor, Henry Buist, who was later to be estate factor to the Earl of Haddington, was commissioned to survey the commonty in 1792 and to draw this plan.
Source: Henry Buist, *Plan of the Common Muir of Methven* (1793). Reproduced by permission of the Trustees of the National Library of Scotland.

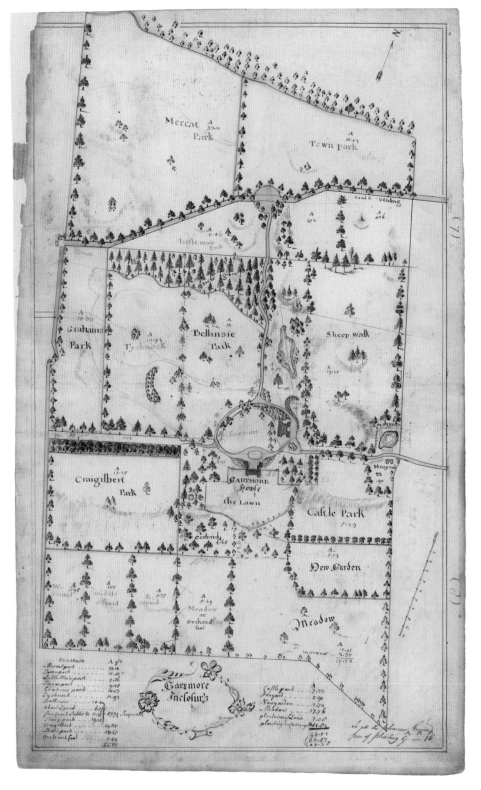

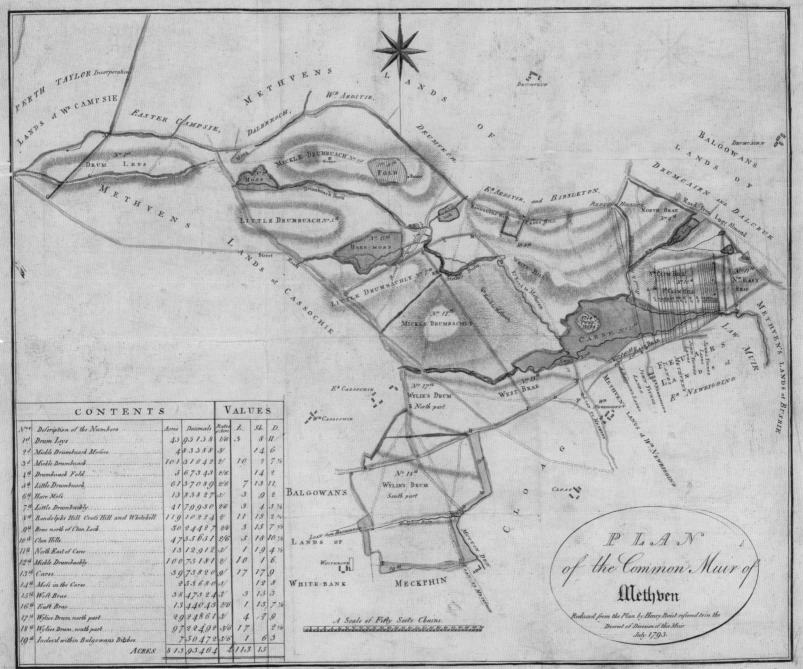

PLAN of the Common Muir of Methven

To the south and east of this divide, mixed farming was dominant, with the emphasis on sheep and cattle farming or arable farming reflecting soil type, proximity to market and the degree to which old systems of land working had been swept away.

Estate maps capture the countryside of parts of the Highlands on the eve of change and they depict the solutions that were proposed. Take the case of Sutherland, for example. In Assynt parish, the rural economy was under strain even by the 1770s. The problems of over-population and recurring famine could not easily be alleviated, even although temporary migration and emigration was encouraged by the tacksmen, the chief's principal tenants and effectively his estate factors or land managers. At this time, however, the Sutherland Estates were opposed to emigration: keeping the population, not clearing it, was vital to prosperity. John Home's *Survey of Assynt* was undertaken to check the power of the tacksmen, and to reorganise the parish into a larger number of conjointly owned farms (fig. 6.12). The 1775 rents increased slightly, but as they were based on a fairer, more precisely deter-

FIGURE 6.10 *Left*. Between 1720 and 1850, nearly five hundred planned villages, characterised by a regular layout of streets, building plots and adjacent fields, were founded on estates throughout Scotland. For the planned village of New Aberdour, a newspaper notice in the *Aberdeen Journal* of 1797–98 invited interested persons to a roup on the site of the new village to bid for lotted lands. The village was feued quite swiftly, and the previous irregular kirkton was replaced with a regular plan of buildings along a central street as shown here in the Ordnance Survey map of 1871. *Source:* Ordnance Survey, 25 inch to the mile, *Aberdeenshire, Sheet 1.16, Aberdour Parish* (surveyed 1871, published 1874). Reproduced by permission of the Trustees of the National Library of Scotland.

FIGURE 6.11 *Opposite*. Peterhead had a harbour from the late sixteenth century, but saw significant development from the 1760s. This Board of Ordnance military plan by John Jaffray also underlines the shared military and commercial interests in Peterhead and its harbour, and proposes (in yellow) various new breakwaters and sea defences. In the 1770s, John Smeaton's new developments realigning the south and west piers to widen the entrance for shipping were carried through, whilst, in the 1790s, concerns over the Napoleonic navy led to further mapping and new defensive gun batteries around the harbour. With the dramatic growth of fishing, the nineteenth century saw even greater changes, including the new canal linking through to an expanded north harbour (see fig. 4.14) *Source:* John Jaffray / Richard Cooper, *This Draught of the Town & Sea Coast About Peterhead . . .* (1739). Reproduced by permission of the Trustees of the National Library of Scotland.

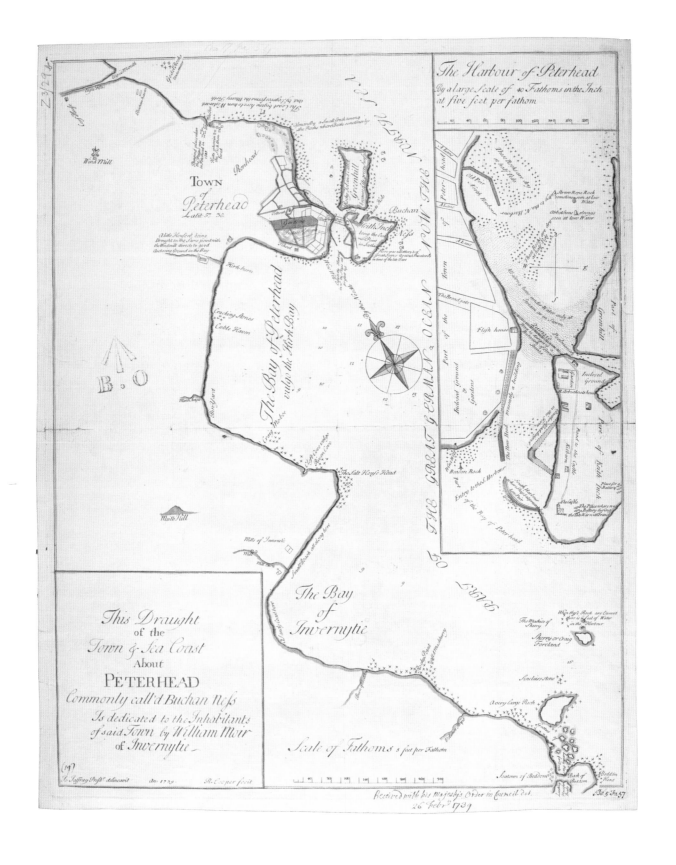

The Harbour of Peterhead
By a large Scale of 40 Fathoms in the Inch
at five feet per fathom

TOWN
of
Peterhead
Latit: 57. 30.

The Bay of Peterhead
vulgs: the Kirk Bay

The Bay
of
Invernytie

This Draught
of the
Town & Sea Coast
About
PETERHEAD
Commonly call'd Buchan Ness

Is dedicated to the Inhabitants
of said Town by William Moir
of Invernytie

Scale of Fathoms 5 feet per Fathom

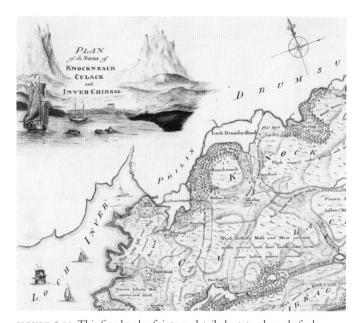

FIGURE 6.12 This fine book of sixteen detailed estate plans, drafted in pen and colour wash by John Home in his *Survey of Assynt* in 1774, is a particularly good illustration of estate mapping in a Highland context before the events of the later eighteenth and nineteenth centuries transformed the landscape. As well as being the earliest detailed, comprehensive mapping of this parish, it was also the most expensive survey made in the eighteenth century on behalf of the Sutherland Estates. The plans are accompanied by detailed descriptions covering agricultural practices and their future potential, and accurate measurements of land under crops or used for pasturing of livestock. John Home surveyed Assynt between June and September 1774, assisted by 'four lads from Dunrobin' and two apprentices, William Crawford and John Anderson, who would later became surveyors and map-makers in their own right. He worked on foot, recruiting local men to lead with the measuring chain and to point out the boundaries between farms. His accounts reveal the necessity of strong liquor 'for the use of self and assistants who led the chain to enable them to endure the fatigue of wading through lochs and mosses from morning till late at night'. These spirits were also necessary to bribe the 'tenants for showing their marches as they could not be prevail with to do so without it'.
Source: John Home, 'The Farms of Knockneach, Culach and Inverchirkag' from *Survey of Assynt* (1774). Copyright © Countess of Sutherland.

mined distribution of land and on recognition of its potential, they were reportedly well-received by the tenants.

But by the early nineteenth century the attitude of the Duke of Sutherland and his estate managers had changed to one involving the clearance, not the retention, of his tenantry. The Sutherland Clearances between the 1810s and the later 1840s were far from unusual, but they were extreme in their manner and, as with many of the clearances in Skye and the Outer Isles between the 1880s and the 1930s, are recalled still within Highland memory. The forced relocation of the Sutherland tenants from inland farms to the coast to make way for large sheep farms is reflected in several maps and plans (fig. 6.13). Throughout the Highlands, the moves to larger estate farming, and to land management for hunting, shooting or forestry, transformed the face of the land and are evident in the maps which both drove and reflected these changes (fig. 6.14).

The activities of land surveyors, at county or estate level, were thus driven by economic factors, by the demands of the Napoleonic Wars, which threatened blockade and so prompted a move to extend the areas of cultivable land, by ideas of improvement and, in certain parts of Scotland, by profound changes in attitudes to land, its ownership and the social responsibilities enshrined in large-scale land management. Conversely, as counties became more fully mapped, as estates were rationalised, and as Ordnance Survey undertook its projects of state-financed mapping from the second quarter or so of the nineteenth century, landlords could make use of a cheaper cartographic base in managing their estates. The work of land surveyors and estate mapping did not cease, of course, but after 1850 it never rivalled the impact of the previous century.

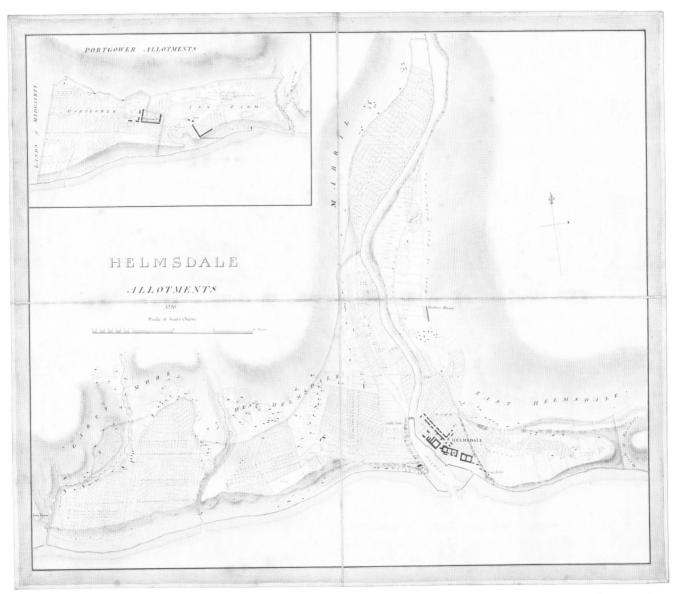

FIGURE 6.13 The model fishing village established at Helmsdale was one of several new initiatives encouraged by the Duke of Sutherland and his agents. These included a new coal pit and salt pans at Brora, and a new flax manufactory. In spite of significant capital investment, many of the projects were unsuccessful, and only Helmsdale had long-term viability. The large coloured plan of the ground allotted to fishermen at Helmsdale (1817) was a practical cartographic proposal towards a new social order for Highland rural society, and was largely implemented on the ground and accompanied by a detailed table of names of people, their land holdings and new rents.

Source: Sutherland Estates, *Helmsdale Allotments* (1817).

Copyright © Countess of Sutherland.

FIGURE 6.14 This map, part of a set of four depicting the detached estates of the Marquis of Huntly for sale, was drafted in 1840 by G. Campbell Smith 'from a partial survey and adjustment of old plans'. It is accompanied by detailed abstracts of the context and rental, and has an attractive vignette of Invergarry Castle.

Source: G. Campbell Smith, *Map of the Lands of Glengarry Lying in the County of Inverness . . . Part of the Estate of the Marquis of Huntly for Sale* (1840). Reproduced by permission of the Trustees of the National Library of Scotland.

THE WORK OF ORDNANCE SURVEY IN THE NINETEENTH CENTURY

From the beginning of their large-scale survey work in Scotland in 1843, and especially from 1855 following the decision to map all cultivated rural areas at the large 25 inch to the mile scale, Ordnance Survey maps became standard tools of rural land-use management – for registration and conveyancing, valuation, planning fields, roads, buildings, woodland, mineral exploitation and drainage. In addition, the accompanying 'Books of Reference' to the 25 inch mapping recorded acreages and land use of every piece of ground, continuing the tradition of the estate terrier as a statistical and written accompaniment to the maps.

Landowning interests were vocal from the 1830s onwards in demanding not just that Ordnance Survey speed up its work in Scotland, but also that such mapping should be done at all, and, when done, that landowners be the first to benefit. Learned societies were involved in these pleas to the Survey: the progress of science depended strongly, it was argued, on the progress of scientific mapping (chapter 10). So anxious was Sir James Matheson, proprietor of Lewis, that Ordnance Survey mapping should help rationalise his estates that he agreed to pay the Survey £1,200 and purchase 100 copies of the maps at their publication price in order that his lands in Lewis be surveyed between 1846 and 1853, effectively two decades in advance of the other Western Isles (fig. 6.15).

Ordnance Survey mapping became, in effect, the representative medium of the Scottish countryside from the 1840s to the present, and has effectively absorbed the cadastral and landowning purposes behind rural mapping. We may reasonably question whether Ordnance Survey's

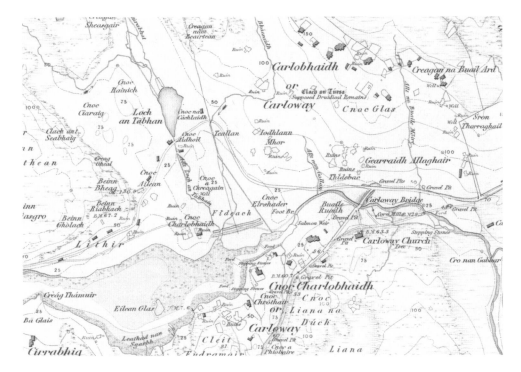

FIGURE 6.15 Carloway, a remote village on the north-west coast of Lewis, is today most famous for its iron age broch and other early remains such as standing stones (including Clach an Tursa, named here). The 6 inch to the mile map of 1850–52 is the earliest and most detailed Ordnance Survey map of the area, as well as the first map to show contours, and illustrates a variety of natural and man-made features. *Source:* Ordnance Survey, Six-Inch to the mile, *Isle of Lewis, Ross-shire, Sheet 12.* (surveyed 1850–52, published 1853). Reproduced by permission of the Trustees of the National Library of Scotland

maps were then, and are now, entirely 'a full face portrait of the country', as claimed by Thomas Larcom, one of its principal surveyors, but they offered a standard form of presentation of the landscape. The Survey's maps importantly depend upon a prior written record of notable features in the parish or, on occasion, records of folklore or historical events which were pulled together in what were called the 'Original Object Name Books'. These books often provided variants on the 'correct' name employed on the map for names of places and other geographical features. The Survey's decisions on what was 'insignificant detail', its relative blindness to antiquities, variant spellings and place names, and to archaeological phenomena before the 1920s, are all elements within its selective depiction of the countryside. And, to cut costs, and focus on more densely populated parts of Great Britain where geographical change has been greater, most

Highland counties were not mapped at basic scales between the early 1900s and the 1970s: in some cases, significant features in the rural landscape – railways, roads, plantations and buildings – have been constructed and removed without ever appearing on the map.

Nevertheless, Ordnance Survey was and remains the most detailed, accurate, and nationally consistent set of rural mapping we have available. Its cartographic style, colours and line work are familiar to us as users. Its importance has also been enhanced because its maps have been used, directly or indirectly, for other purposes and by other cartographers. Most institutional thematic mapping in the twentieth century – of geology, soils, land use, botany, forestry, and so on – has used Survey maps as its base: as we show in chapter 10, it is a style of map which has important scientific origins.

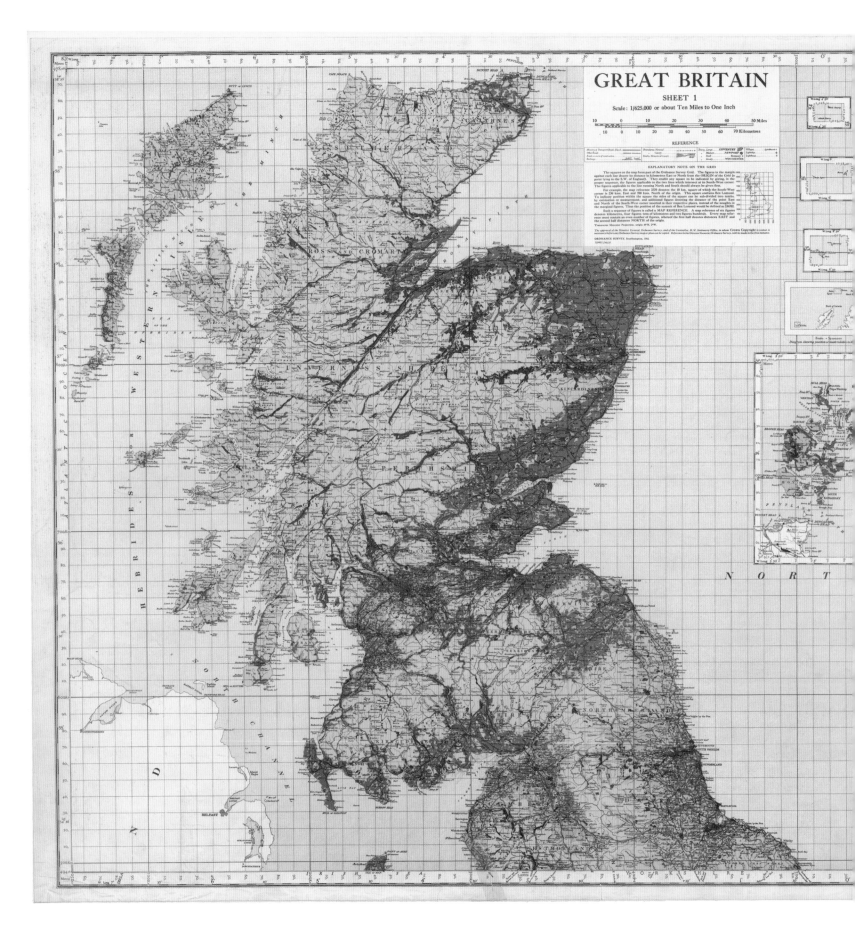

GREAT BRITAIN

SHEET 1

Scale: 1/625,000 or about Ten Miles to One Inch

REFERENCE

EXPLANATORY NOTE ON THE GRID

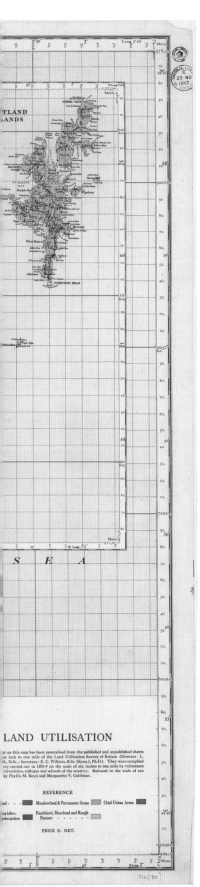

FIGURE 6.16 This map summarises at a national scale the first comprehensive land-use survey of the British Isles, instigated by Lawrence Dudley Stamp, reader and later professor of geography at the London School of Economics. By comparison with later surveys, particularly the Second Land Use Survey organised by Professor Alice Coleman, the classification employed relatively few categories. The base-map was overprinted with a wash of six basic colours to indicate broad land-use categories: yellow (moorland and heath), light green (grassland), dark green (woodland), brown (arable), purple ('gardens etc') and red (agriculturally unproductive). The key subdivided each of these by reference to the detail already present in the base-map: for example, woodland into coniferous, deciduous, mixed and new plantations. Built-up areas show essentially only two categories of urban (red) and suburban (purple) land. The suburban and urban categories in combination with the base-map detail allowed the key to subdivide suburbs into 'houses with gardens sufficiently large to be productive of fruit, vegetables, flowers, etc' and 'new housing areas, nurseries and allotments'. Urban areas were subdivided into 'land so closely covered with houses and other buildings as to be agriculturally unproductive' and 'yards, cemeteries, pits, quarries, tip heaps, new industrial works, etc'.
Source: Ordnance Survey, *Great Britain, Ten Miles to One Inch (1:625,000) Sheet 1. Land Utilisation* (1942). Reproduced by permission of the Trustees of the National Library of Scotland.

MODERN LAND-USE SURVEYS

In the twentieth century, Scotland's countryside was mapped as part of several national land-use surveys of Britain. The first, undertaken in the 1930s, was under the direction of L. Dudley Stamp. Stamp drew upon the voluntary resources of some 250,000 school children from over ten thousand schools across Britain. The land-use evidence they reported was recorded at a scale of 6 inches to the mile (1:10,560) using 6-inch field maps. The maps were published at a scale of 1 inch to the mile (1:63,360) using the Ordnance Survey One-inch to the mile 'Popular Edition' as the base. Publication of maps and reports began in 1933 and, following interruption in the Second World War, was completed in 1948. Only part of Scotland was covered in the printed sheets (fig. 6.16).

Land use mapping is now a consistent feature in Scotland's mapping, as it is more broadly, whether for the purposes of estate management (fig. 6.17) or for recreation (fig. 6.18) or other purposes such as the representation of areas of land for conservation in assessing historic land-use characteristics as the basis to future planning. Maps of the rural past are vital records of our past landscapes. The particularities of the Scottish rural scene – runrig, lazybeds, crofts, shielings, cleared landscapes or planned villages, drove roads and deer forests – are well illustrated on its maps. Maps of the countryside stand both as evidence of major change in the country and, in their different forms and in their history, as social and political documents, as part of that change.

The mapping of rural Scotland, especially in and of the Highlands, has been very much undertaken by outsiders on behalf of outsiders. Whether used by agricultural improvers, estate factors, English or Scots sappers struggling with Gaelic, deer stalkers, foresters, tour guides,

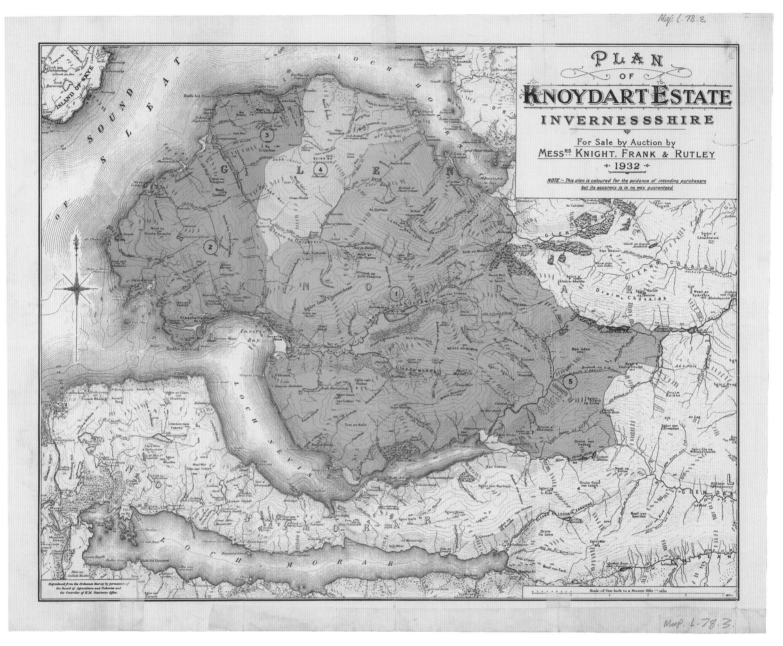

FIGURE 6.17 Rugged, beautiful, and remote, Knoydart had been part of the ancestral lands of Clan Donald, but from the nineteenth century it regularly changed hands. At the time of this map in the 1930s, the Conservative MP and Nazi sympathizer Alan Ronald Nall–Cain, later Lord Brocket, purchased it. Plans such as this, accompanying sale particulars for large landed estates, with particular deer forests highlighted in colour, were common at this time across Scotland, the map attempting to sell the land to new moneyed owners. After the war, in 1948, the Seven Men of Knoydart launched a land raid in an attempt to live independently from the landlord system. Although the raid was unsuccessful, Lord Brocket sold the Knoydart Estate soon afterwards. *Source:* Knight, Frank & Rutley, *Plan of Knoydart Estate, Invernessshire* (1932). Reproduced by permission of the Trustees of the National Library of Scotland.

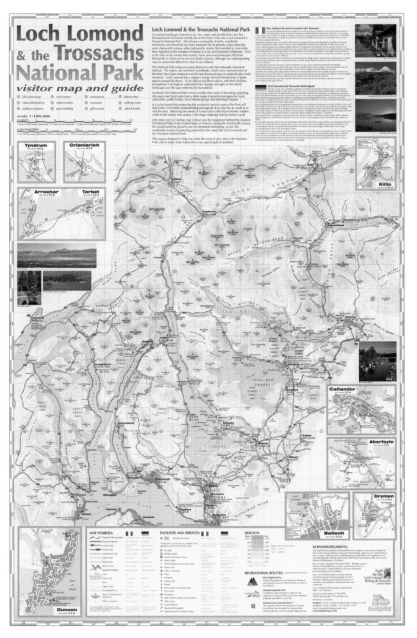

FIGURE 6.18 *Loch Lomond & the Trossachs National Park* (2002), part of Stirling Surveys' Footprint Series, represents Scotland's first national park for the modern-day tourist. It illustrates many of the useful features found on maps of the countryside over the previous four centuries – symbols, vignettes and views, layer colouring for relief, and supporting text. But it also specifically promotes the attractions of the countryside for contemporary recreation, particularly by the motor car, and ways of seeing it that would have seemed very odd in previous centuries. As well as promoting the park as an attractive and inviting place for leisure, it also necessarily advertises itself (in a competitive market place) as a broad-ranging and detailed guide, with far more to offer than just cartography. The map includes a comprehensive gazetteer of places to visit and things to do, and notes on the history, geology and wildlife of the area. It also uses colour codes to signify places of interest in green and facilities in brown.
Source: Stirling Surveys, *Loch Lomond & the Trossachs National Park* (2002). Copyright © Footprint Maps.

mountaineers, or wind farm engineers, maps of the countryside have never been neutral, objective representations of reality. Scotland's rural maps have often been drawn up to be used as part of the transformation of the landscape – in some cases a quite violent and destructive transformation – and so must always be understood in relation to wider political and economic forces. As paper documents, such maps cannot themselves always capture the weightier matters of poverty, emigration, economic downturn, power generation and mass tourism that lie behind them, but they illuminate, often very powerfully, the consequences of these broader and fundamental dynamics within the changing countryside.

Lake Grimſeter

Iſfurt

I. Siant

St Maries

erno
cks

Troda I.

Flada

Round Table

Ieſkar

Duntulm Caſtle

Erin

Altvig

Flada

Kilmartin

Dun Taviſon

D untulm

St Marys

L. Uge

Cudrich

Friſhwater
Lake

L. Snifort

Kingſbury

Vatirnes Pt

L. Fallort

Dunvegan H.

Diurines

L. Arniſort

Dunvegan C.

Rig

S K

CI E

L. Brokidil

L. Einord

Rum I.

Canna

Heiſker

Minginis

Kilmiry

Kilmor

Muck

Egg I.

Karnborg

Gometra

Ard Pt

Priest I.

L. Brine

Awan E

L. Garloch

R o

Rona

Raarſa I.

Cl ackan C.

Croulin

Scalpa

Do na

L. Car

Strath

Kil C.

Sleat

Oronſay

Ar mdil

Pt Sleat

Do

L.

Ber

L. N

L. Storn

CHAPTER 7

ISLANDS AND ISLAND LIFE

Itself part of an island, Scotland is a country of islands. Some of them are populated, others not, still others once peopled are now deserted, of humans anyway, their silent working landscapes a stark reminder of geographies lost. There are about 800 islands – if we include in that total those parts of the country surrounded by its seas – and if we include the larger freshwater islands the total rises by a further dozen. Offshore or freshwater, peopled or not, many of Scotland's islands have an enduring emotive pull as well as an economic and cultural importance – think of Staffa, or Iona, or Eriskay, Skye, the Outer Isles as a whole perhaps. Some act as familiar way markers (fig. 7.1). Many have been subject, to a much greater degree than elsewhere, to those processes of social and economic change that have shaped the nation as a whole.

Islands, in a sense, have been laboratories for Scotland's geography and history. They have been 'test sites' for policies of economic development, as in Islay, Tiree, Mull, Lewis and Rum, literally so in the case of Gruinard off Wester Ross, which was used for experiments in chemical warfare in the Second World War, or in the Uists,

where Cold War rocket ranges were established. In the early 1850s North Rona, about 60 miles north of the Butt of Lewis and more remote than St Kilda, was even thought of as the site for a possible penal colony. Scottish islands provide 'best sites' of European archaeology before Scotland was Scotland, as in the many important remains of human settlement throughout Orkney and Shetland.

Scotland's islands, perhaps particularly those off its north and west coasts, show in their place names and in the everyday language of their inhabitants the shifts in influence of Norse, Gaelic and English-speaking peoples. For some people, islands are also a place of retreat to the margins, where you 'get away from it all'. For others, islands are home. Taransay, for example, last permanently inhabited in 1942, then briefly re-populated in the 1960s before again being deserted, was in 2000 the site of marooned outsiders on a 'reality' television programme, a testing ground for remote living on the margins.

This chapter discusses several of the ways in which Scotland's islands have appeared on maps. It will be clear that the country's islands illustrate well many of the other

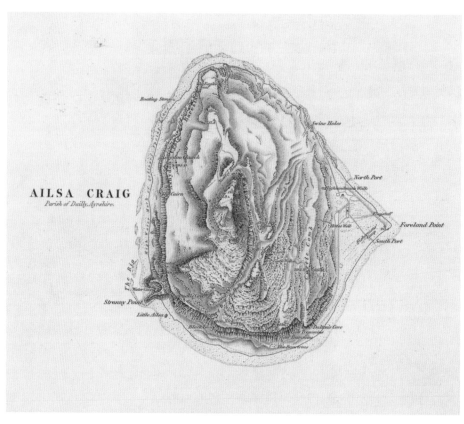

FIGURE 7.1 In the mid-nineteenth century, Glasgow and satellite ports along the inner reaches of the Firth of Clyde were renowned for shipbuilding and trade, with ships from all over the world entering and leaving these waters. Visible for miles in good weather and with a conical, arresting shape, returning sailors nearing the Ayrshire coast would keep a watch for 'Paddy's Milestone', more properly Ailsa Craig, as a first sign that they were nearing port. *Source:* Ordnance Survey, Six-Inch to the mile *Ayrshire, Sheet XLIX* (Surveyed 1856, published 1859).
Reproduced by permission of the Trustees of the National Library of Scotland.

themes addressed in this book: the more recent military landscapes of South Uist, Benbecula and St Kilda, for example, being part of that longer military mapping story discussed in chapter 4; landscape change and the economic development of the Hebrides part of that transformation of rural life noted in chapter 6. And it should be clear too that, with over 800 islands to choose from, an element of selection has been necessary. Such selection is in fact quite easy for not all Scotland's islands or island groups have always appeared on its maps.

One feature of Scotland's map history has been what we might think of as the slow and uneven appearance over time of the country's islands in cartographic form. Partly this reflects the difficulty of checking on the ground and charting from the seas – the mapping of islands is intimately connected with the mapping of Scotland's seas and waters (the subject of chapter 8). Uncertainty as to their position, shape and numbers was often one reason to omit islands altogether. The sketchy appearance of Scotland on medieval maps, which we illustrated in chapter 2, was because people did not know what shape it was – the islands, like the 'mainland', were suggestive, not definitive (see fig. 2.2 for example).

Scotland's islands, just like any other island geography, present a problem of selection and generalisation: knowledge of their existence, even of their exact shape and number, does not mean that the map-maker has to include them. And, even when an island was selected for inclusion, some are so small in acreage that mapping techniques cannot show them true to the selected scale: islands, geographically 'marginal' but central in economic or political terms, may thus be shown – if shown at all – in place but out of proportion. Perhaps nowhere better highlights this cartographic problem and this element of Scotland's map history than the final example we look at here – Rockall.

KNOWING WHAT'S WHERE AND PUTTING IT TO SHAPE: SCOTLAND'S ISLANDS BEFORE *c.* 1700

The cartographic 'coming into view' of Scotland as a nation and a national shape, even in the maps of Matthew Paris and in the Gough Map, and particularly during the sixteenth century (chapter 2), applies equally evidently to its islands as it does to the mainland as a whole. If we take the earliest known depiction of Scotland as a whole, the 'Scotia, Regno di Scotia' map of *c.*1566 (fig. 2.6), the grouping of islands known today as the Hebrides (Inner and Outer), is shown, and some are even named – Mull, 'Ila' [Islay], Cumbra, Schia Levissa [Lewis] – but far from all are identified. Most are not drawn with the correct shape or depicted in anything like the correct position one to another (fig. 7.2). For the Orkneys, too, a few settlements are symbolised. St Kilda is shown as much larger (relatively) than the other Hebridean islands. These features are echoed in other European maps at this time (fig. 7.3).

We must be cautious about terming such mapping either 'inaccurate' or 'primitive' or explaining it simply as the result of non-Scots mapping Scotland. Early map-makers tended more to recycle than to revise, until such time as new information could be established from which to change the content and shape of maps. In the absence of new knowledge, informants on the ground and direct survey or mathematical information from astronomical measurement and latitudinal positioning, this was all that anyone could do. Sailors worked from lines of sight at sea rather more than from truthful maps: what mattered was observation at first hand, not triangulation from distance. Map engravers had no ready way

FIGURE 7.2 Although the coastal waters and outlines of the islands in the inner Hebrides were known to those who lived there or who had cause to sail through them, the map-maker Paolo Forlani was in contrast based in Venice and had almost certainly never visited the Hebrides. His rendering is based on hearsay rather than on fact. It is copied rather loosely from that on an earlier map of 1546 produced in Rome. The almost random shape of each island is therefore largely invention by the map-maker.
Source: Paolo Forlani, *Scotia. Regno di Scotia* (*c.*1561). Reproduced by permission of the Trustees of the National Library of Scotland.

153

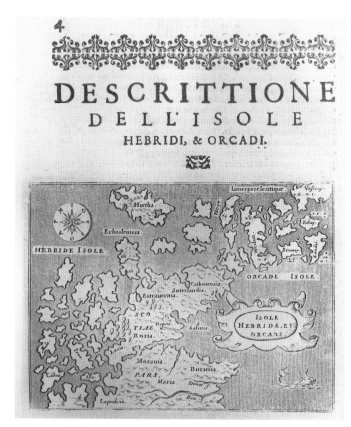

FIGURE 7.3 With its origins in fifteenth- and sixteenth-century Mediterranean map-making, the 'Isolario' or island atlas focused on the depiction and description of islands, initially those in the Mediterranean Sea itself, for such archipelagos were often less well represented – in terms of the scale at which they were drawn – on contemporary nautical charts. This somewhat primitive rendition of the island archipelagos of the Hebrides and Orkney, including the northern half of mainland Scotland, reflects that they were almost certainly at the extreme limits of Porcacchi's geographical knowledge and based on whatever map or chart sources and travellers' accounts he had access to during his information gathering. As such they included a considerable degree of generalisation, if not sheer imagination, in their rendering.
Source: Tommaso Porcacchi, 'Isole Hebride et Orcade' from *L'isole piu famose del Mondo* (originally published 1572, this edition published 1620). Reproduced by permission of the Trustees of the National Library of Scotland.

of adding new outlines. When they couldn't see things for themselves, chorographers, Scots-born or foreign, could work only from what they were told or what they read.

That is why Timothy Pont's mapping of South Uist is so important and, like much to do with Pont's work, also so intriguing and frustrating (fig. 7.4). The surviving manuscripts that made up Blaeu's 1654 *Atlas Novus* are almost entirely of the mainland – with the exception of this evidence from Pont. Pont actually provides two manuscript maps of South Uist on the same side of one sheet of paper, and, in true chorographic style, there is some accompanying text. Pont had considerable interest in islands, and his manuscript maps show other islands, to say nothing of the outlines he gives us of crannogs (artificial man-made islands) and natural islands in several freshwater lochs (see fig. 3.9 for example). Pont records sixteen islands in Loch Maree, for example, in greater detail than any later map-maker, including Ordnance Survey. Four island names are not recorded in any other written source, but are confirmed by oral testimony. Settlements are shown and named on South Uist, but rather variably: the west coast is inscribed more completely than the east on one map, for example, and it is clear that the names of settlements have been transcribed by a non-Gaelic speaker. But we do not know by whom, or when, this was done and there is no way of knowing if the blank spaces on the map are just that – and so document an un-peopled landscape – or if, and to varying degrees, Pont's map of the island is incomplete. The printed map of the island is more detailed in what it shows (fig. 7.5): it is almost certain that Pont produced a more detailed manuscript map, now lost, as the basis to the printed one that appears in Blaeu's *Atlas*, and that what has survived was a working first-draft. There is more

FIGURE 7.4 *Source:* Timothy Pont, South Uist, from Pont [36] (*c.*1583–1614). Reproduced by permission of the Trustees of the National Library of Scotland.

detail on 'Uistus Insula' than on the extant Pont manuscripts. Blaeu's source must have been using a more detailed map (by Pont, as Blaeu acknowledges). Like so many of Pont's more legible drafts, it did not come back to Scotland after it had been copied by Blaeu.

It is possible to trace, on the one hand, a continuing yet evolving representation of Scotland's island geographies in maps from the 1560s until late in the seventeenth century and even into the eighteenth century. Compare, for instance, the various depictions of the islands off the north and west coast in maps from the mid-sixteenth century (fig. 7.2) with maps a century or so later and with Arrowsmith's map of 1807, which was the result of

his careful scrutiny of other maps, field survey and astronomical measurement (fig. 7.6). On the other hand, we must be careful about thinking of the early maps of Scotland's islands as consistently wrong in shape, a sort of 'squint' offshore Scotland that simply gets 'better' over time. The different types and purposes of maps and what was possible to do in terms of accurate mapping must be borne in mind.

Scotland's islands start to take a more correct shape on maps from the later seventeenth century. They do so as a result of the emphasis then being placed upon accuracy in mapping and upon mapping as a national good (see chapter 3). John Adair's work is important in this

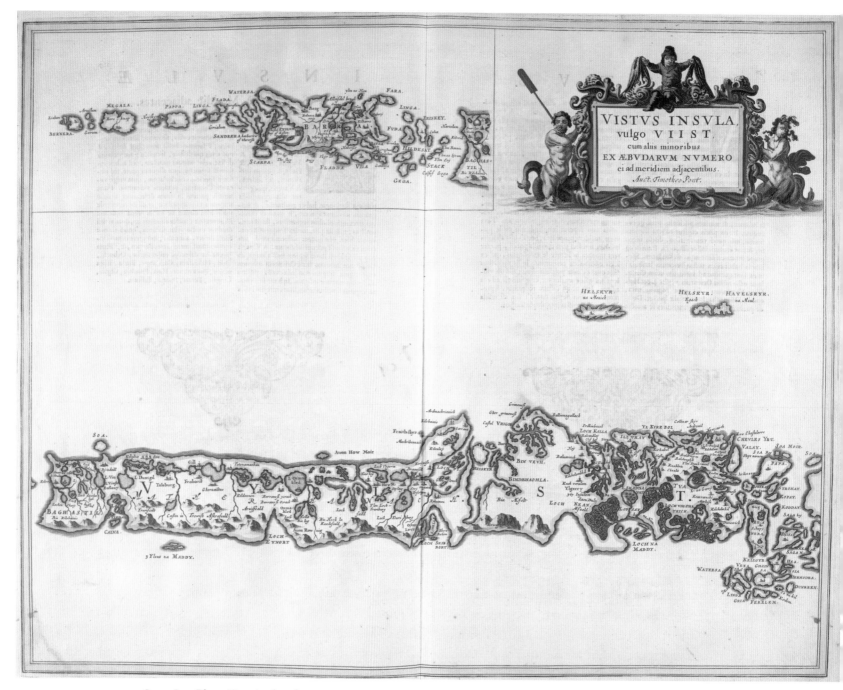

FIGURE 7.5 *Source:* Joan Blaeu, *Vistus insula, vulgo*
Viist, cum aliis minoribus ex Aebudarum numero . . .
(1654). Reproduced by permission of the
Trustees of the National Library of Scotland.

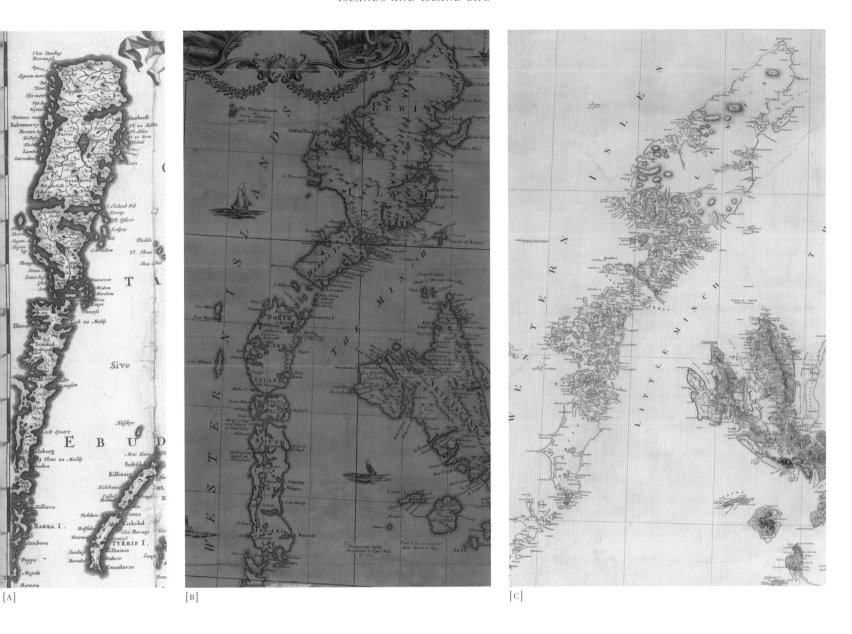

[A]　　　[B]　　　[C]

FIGURE 7.6 These three sections of maps from 1680, 1773 and 1807 by three very different map-makers illustrate well the differing levels of knowledge and interpretation of part of the Western Isles over some 150 years. In the 1807 map [C], Aaron Arrowsmith includes considerable topographic and place name detail on some of the islands (Harris, North Uist and Benbecula) but leaves major blanks in such information for Barra, South Uist and Lewis. This reflects the state of detailed survey on the ground in the islands and whether Arrowsmith had access to those

surveys made before 1807 when his map was published. North Uist was surveyed in 1799, Harris in 1804–05 and Benbecula and South Uist in 1805, so Arrowsmith included the results of these surveys, except for South Uist for some reason. But as Lewis was not surveyed on the ground until 1807–09 and Barra not until 1820–21 the information they obtained was of course too late to be included on Arrowsmith's map.
Source: Frederik De Wit, *Scotia Regnum divisum in partem septentrionalem et meridionalem . . . (c.*1680). Reproduced by

permission of the Trustees of the National Library of Scotland.

FIGURE 7.6 [B] *Source:* Thomas Kitchin, *A New and Complete Map of Scotland and Islands thereto Belonging* (*c.*1773).

FIGURE 7.6 [C] *Source:* Aaron Arrowsmith, *Map of Scotland Constructed from Original Materials* (1807).

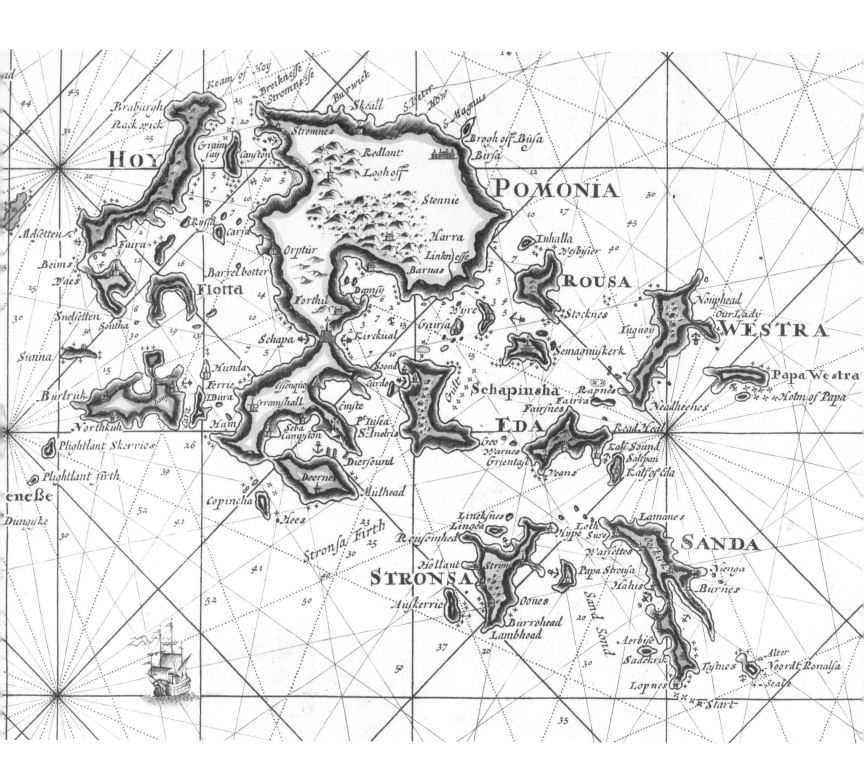

respect. Several of the maps of islands that he incorporated in his *Description of the Sea-Coast and Islands of Scotland* (1703) were a direct result of his in-the-field and on-the-sea survey and attention to accurate measurement. Map-makers began to look directly at islands and to use techniques of measurement and survey as they brought islands into view.

Of course, points of view can differ. Looked at from the perspective of seamen and merchants setting out from mainland Europe, for example, Scotland's island archipelagos might look – did look – different from, say, the view of them presented in a conventional north–south cartographic orientation (fig. 7.7). Shetland has long suffered in this respect. As an island group, Shetland is commonly either left off the map of Scotland, or marginalised, presented in its own latitudinal box as an inset to the nation: on modern Anglocentric weather maps, Shetland may hardly feature at all.

FIGURE 7.7 *Opposite.* This attractive chart was first published around 1695 and represents the Orcades (Orkney) as if viewed from the Continent where the map originated, rather than with north at the top in the more usual way. Seamen from the Low Countries had detailed knowledge of the waters surrounding these islands, as is indicated by the plethora of soundings, the indications of the best anchorages (with an anchor symbol) and the representation of the tombolo (sand/shingle spit) joining Deerness to the 'Mainland' of Orkney. The map also contains series of straight lines, known as loxodromes or lines of constant bearing, along which a navigator could set his course. *Source:* Claes Janszoon Vooght, *Nieuwe paskaart van de Orcades Eylanden door Vooght geometra* (c.1695). Reproduced by permission of the Trustees of the National Library of Scotland.

WINDOWS ON PAST LIFE

Scotland's islands also began to 'fill out' cartographically from the later seventeenth century because their inhabitants and their way of life were increasingly of interest to people elsewhere. To most Scots, and certainly for the natural philosophers of London's Royal Society – virtually the only scientific body in seventeenth-century Britain – the Hebrides were as little known as the Pacific islands: here lay 'novelty' and the unknown on Scotland's and Britain's doorstep. During his mapping of Scotland's north and west coast and islands in the late 1690s, John Adair twice encountered the Skye-born Martin Martin, who was travelling there on behalf of London's enquiring philosophers and others. Martin wrote two books, *A Late Voyage to St Kilda* (1698) and *A Description of the Western Isles of Scotland* (1703), both of which helped bring the Hebrides to the attention of the wider world, not just to anxious collectors in the Royal Society. The two men even sailed together, one commentator at the time expecting them to return 'freighted with a Large Cargoe of Natural Curiosities' for the attention of natural philosophers in London and elsewhere. Martin's map of the region was not, however, the work of Adair (fig. 7.8).

As islands came into view, so the content and the particularities of island life could be shown on maps (fig. 7.9). In its details, this map of Orkney from 1769 illustrates how maps had an almost ethnographic function as well as a topographic one: the Orkney plough is shown, and other features distinctive of that island group. By contrast, Preston's 1781 map of Shetland is without such information, being almost wholly a chart of the islands' shapes and waters (fig. 7.10). At much the same time, Scotland's islands and the nature of the seas between them came to be the object of renewed attention from

FIGURE 7.8 A native of Skye, Martin Martin included a map in his *A Description of the Western Islands of Scotland* and on the book's title page described it as 'a New MAP of the whole, describing the Harbours, Anchoring Places, and dangerous Rocks, for the benefit of Sailors'. Engraved in small letters under the map title is the information that it was drawn by H. Moll, that is, Herman Moll, the Dutch cartographer whose map of Scotland in 1714 (fig. 1.4) was to be a new and important representation of the country, although it was produced from several information sources and not the result of a detailed ground survey.
Source: Martin Martin, *A New Map of the Western Isles of Scotland (c.1695).* Reproduced by permission of the Trustees of the National Library of Scotland.

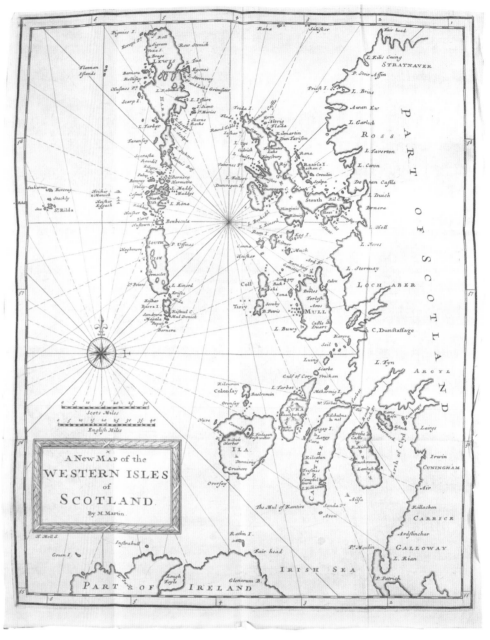

foreign map-makers, often working on behalf of their governments. Islands needed to be located and circumnavigated. Their position and content was always valuable to know: lives could depend on it. But, at times of war, islands are an easy point on which to land opposing forces in secrecy – Prince Charles Edward Stuart began that campaign which ended so bloodily at Culloden (fig. 4.12) by being landed from a French ship on Eriskay – and the French were later active in seeing Scotland's islands as the subject of cartographic study (fig. 7.11).

Land surveyors were active in the Outer Hebrides from the early nineteenth century, their concerns there as elsewhere to rationalise estates, delineate property boundaries and help settle disputes over land ownership.

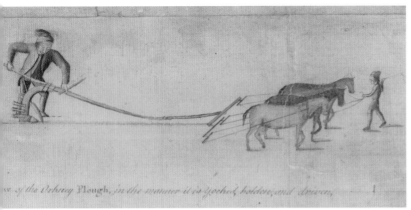

FIGURE 7.9 This remarkable representation of the Orkney Islands by the surveyor William Aberdeen combines elements of both map and chart, and also adds a fascinating picture of island life in the form of extra sketches and notes in all the available spaces. These include statistical details of the division of land, notes on the local husbandry and agriculture, as well as drawings of the Stones of Stenness, the Palace of Birsay, St Magnus Cathedral and the Earl and Bishop's Palaces. Aberdeen was employed to survey the islands by Sir Laurence Dundas, who gained most of his wealth through army contracts and had recently purchased the earldom of Orkney estate from the Earl of Morton together with further lands from the Earl of Galloway.
Source: William Aberdeen, *A Chart of the Orkney Islands in which are Pointed out the Lands . . . belonging to the Right Honourable Sr Laurence Dundas, Baronet (c.*1769). Reproduced by permission of the Trustees of the National Library of Scotland.

On Harris, for example, the picture we are afforded of settlement distribution in a map from the early nineteenth century is of a string of settlements on the coasts, with pockets of nearby arable land predominantly on the drier and sandier machair soils of the west, and, inland, common grazing and scatterings of deer forest (fig. 7.12).

This geography did not last long. Bald's map of Harris

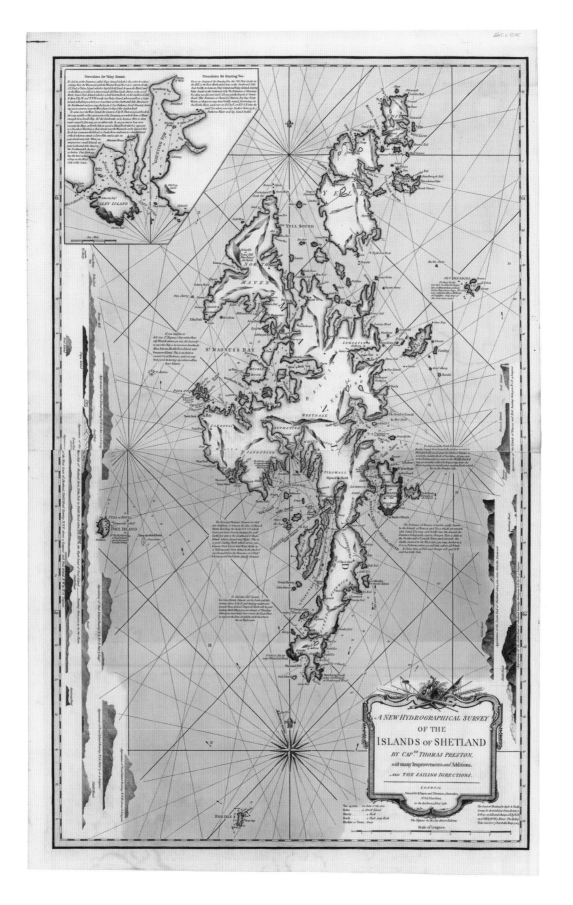

A NEW HYDROGRAPHICAL SURVEY
OF THE
ISLANDS OF SHETLAND
BY CAP.TN THOMAS PRESTON,
with many Improvements and Additions,
AND THE SAILING DIRECTIONS.

LONDON,

Scale of Leagues.

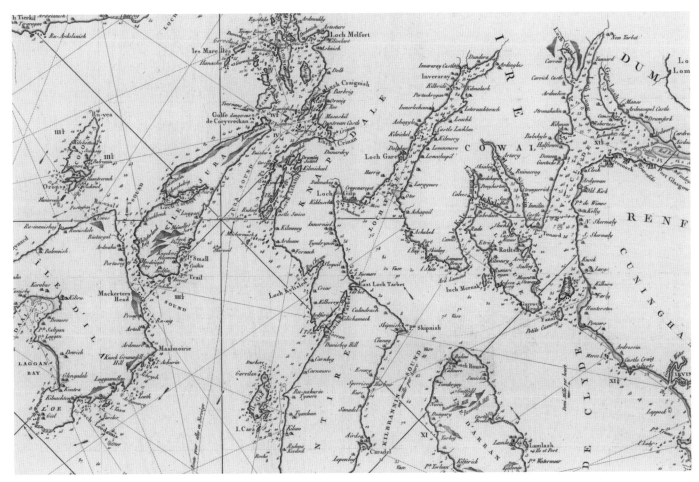

FIGURE 7.10 *Opposite.* Captain Thomas Preston had good reason to compile a chart of Shetland for he had been shipwrecked off its treacherous coast in 1743 and thereafter confined to the islands for some months. Forty years later he produced this detailed sea chart of the islands, which though inaccurate by modern standards – for instance in the shapes of Yell, Unst and Bressay as well as the position of Foula in relation to the Shetland mainland – contains detailed textual directions of how best to sail into the main sounds and voes safely. Fine line drawings of the appearance of the islands from the sea appear on nearly all the island outlines and round the edges of the chart as an aid to the navigator. It was not until 1838 that the Hydrographic Office of the Admiralty published a much more accurate chart of the islands surveyed by George Thomas.
Source: Thomas Preston, *A New Hydrographical Survey of the Islands of Shetland* (1781). Reproduced by permission of the Trustees of the National Library of Scotland.

FIGURE 7.11 *Above.* Scottish waters as charted by foreign powers, particularly at times of hostility, can be very interesting in terms of what they contain and where they derived their information content. Produced in 1803 (l'An XII) by France's then equivalent of the UK Hydrographic Office, and in the same year Britain declared war on France and a French army prepared to invade England, this chart shows the kind of detailed coastal information available to the French Napoleonic navy in planning any forays or landings on the west coast of Scotland or its islands. Though based on British chart sources, some of the place names have been 'Frenchified', as for instance 'Golfe de Coryvreckan', described on the map as 'dangereux', as indeed it is. A year later monarchy returned to France after a gap of eleven years when Napoleon Bonaparte crowned himself Emperor in Notre Dame, Paris. The threat of French invasion remained for some years.
Source: Dépôt Générale de la Marine, Paris, *Carte particulière de la côte occidentale d'Ecosse, depuis la Pointe d'Ardnamurchan jusqu'au Mull de Galloway* (1803). Reproduced by permission of the Trustees of the National Library of Scotland.

FIGURE 7.12 William Bald, a Scottish apprentice surveyor, completed a survey of the island of Harris for its owner, Alexander Hume Macleod, between 1804 and 1805 when he was aged just sixteen. In common with owners of other Highland and island estates, Macleod was intent on changes to its land use in order to increase profitability. His plans also led to dispersal of the people from the more fertile land to the coasts where they were forced to eke out a living as best they could. Bald, later to rise to eminence as a civil engineer and a Fellow of the Royal Society, was apprenticed to the then sixty-year-old John Ainslie, one of Scotland's most eminent and versatile map 'entrepreneurs'. The original manuscript map from which this later printed version was made is presumed lost.

Source: William Bald, *Plan of the Island of Harris, the property of Alexander Hume Esqr.* (surveyed 1804–5, published 1829). Reproduced by permission of the Trustees of the National Library of Scotland.

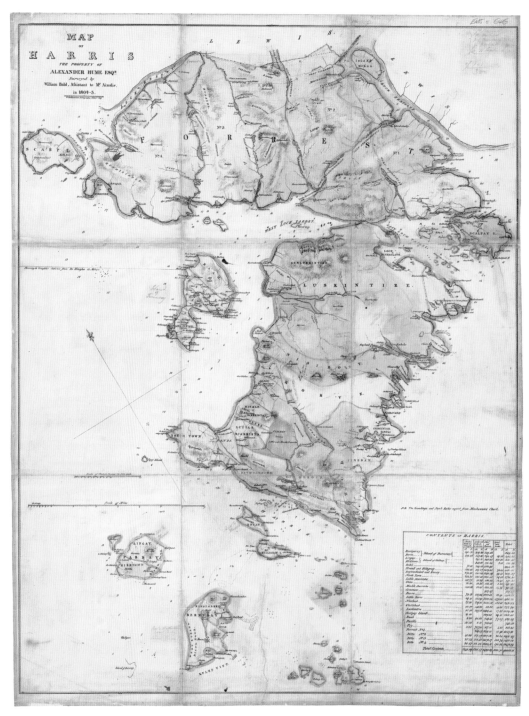

[A]

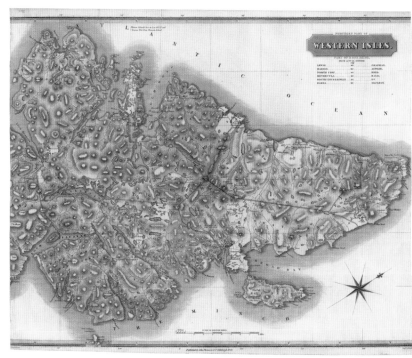

[B]

is of importance because it depicts, broadly, a 'pre-Clearance' landscape: before the smaller-scale farming communities on the west coast were moved to the less fertile east coast, before sheep farming replaced mixed farming and before cultivated land everywhere shrank from the advance of deer forests, from the 1830s. On Lewis (fig. 7.13), and on smaller islands in the Inner Hebrides (fig. 7.14), the story is much the same. Maps in general allow us glimpses of a Scotland No More, one whose histories and past geographies remain as bitter memories, deserted house plots and vestigial field boundaries. This is testimony to the importance of maps as documents which reveal individual island landscapes before – and often after – they became laboratory sites for experiments in offshore capitalism.

FIGURE 7.13 John Thomson's *Atlas of Scotland* of 1832 curiously includes two images of the island of Lewis. Fig. 7.13 [A] is an inset in the plate covering Ross & Cromarty Shires and clearly included there to put Lewis into its correct administrative context within Ross Shire. Because of the restricted space available, a smaller scale had to be used and hence there is far less detail than when Lewis is portrayed in fig. 7.13 [B], where it occupies one sheet of a triptych of plates covering the Western Isles and therefore stressing its geographical entity rather than its then local government allegiance. Interestingly, the Shiant Islands, 5 miles off the south-east coast of Lewis, are not included on the inset map, but just scrape into the Western Isles plate by breaking into its margin.
Source: William Johnson, *Ross & Cromarty Shires. Southern part. Inset: Lewis. Part of Ross Shire* (1820). Reproduced by permission of the Trustees of the National Library of Scotland.

FIGURE 7.13 [B] *Source:* William Johnson, *Western Isles* (1820 and 1822). Reproduced by permission of the Trustees of the National Library of Scotland.

FIGURE 7.14 In 1806, at the request of its owner, Reginald George MacDonald of Clanranald, Eigg was mapped like Harris (fig. 7.11) by William Bald, later to achieve fame as a surveyor, map-maker and civil engineer. The mapping came at a difficult time for the island: the previously profitable kelp industry had collapsed, there was a large population which was at the mercy of crop failures, and Clanranald was in deep financial straits. Clanranald sold his estates on Eigg in 1828 fetching £15,000. This later map by the surveyor and map-maker Thomas Leslie is dated 1824 but shows the same details as Bald's 1806 survey with regard to acreages, land use (5,580 acres over ten townships) and settlements. It is thought to have been produced in readiness for the sale of the island and, unlike the earlier, much larger manuscript map produced by Bald, was reproduced by the lithographic process in Edinburgh which allowed cheap multiple copies to be made.

Source: Thomas Leslie, *Island of Eigg* (surveyed 1806, published 1824). Reproduced by permission of the Trustees of the National Library of Scotland.

ST KILDA – MAPPING ON THE MARGINS

If it appears at all cartographically, St Kilda is nearly always on the edge of maps. The island of that name is actually no such thing – and there never was a saint of that name – but St Kilda is the name commonly given to a group of islands, the main ones being Hirta, the largest of the archipelago and the only habitable island, Soay and Boreray. The fourteenth-century Scottish chronicler John of Fordun referred to Hirta, 'Irte' as he had it, as 'on the margins of the world', and the islands were memorialised in film in 1937 in *The Edge of the World* (with Foula, one of the Shetland isles, doubling as St Kilda). But when the islands first appeared in any detail on the map, they were a central part of the economy of the Macleods of Harris.

Maps can do this: St Kilda's marginality is a cartographic consequence, not a reflection of its cultural importance. It is now home to two distinct endemic subspecies (of wren and field mouse), is a major nature reserve, and is the UK's only dual world heritage site. Yet, apart from military and civilian personnel and parties of visiting conservationists, archaeologists and ecologists, it has been uninhabited since 1930. Shown variously as a massive island on sixteenth-century Italian maps and then only as indeterminate dots in the Atlantic on mid-seventeenth-century Dutch maps, the St Kilda island group is first brought into fuller view by Martin Martin in words in his 1698 book, and in maps in his 1703 *A Description of the Western Isles of Scotland* (fig. 7.15): his description and naming of the islands as 'St Kilda' was influential in promoting that name. Martin spent time on the islands in 1697. For distant natural philosophers, Martin was, as we have noted, their field agent, collecting things and making notes on the inhabitants and their livelihood. He was also there as an assistant to the local parish minister

and on behalf of the chief of the Macleods, to whom the St Kildans owed an annual rent.

Martin's detailed written descriptions of the islands' economy and way of life – he tells us how the arable land was 'very nicely parted into ten divisions', that there were about ninety cows, about eighteen horses and perhaps as many as 2,000 sheep, and documents the locals' reliance upon sea fowl, as flesh and eggs – are not echoed in the sketchy map he has left us. As with the map of the Hebrides in his 1703 volume (fig. 7.8), it is the work not of Martin himself but of the leading Dutch map-maker Herman Moll, then active in London and, like Martin,

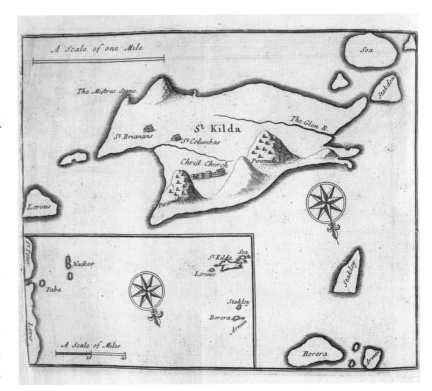

FIGURE 7.15 *Source:* Martin Martin, St Kilda (1698). Reproduced by permission of the Trustees of the National Library of Scotland.

FIGURE 7.16 A World Heritage site since 1986, the St Kilda group of islands was mapped fifty-eight years earlier at the large scale of 6 inches to 1 mile by a retired Ordnance Survey surveyor, John Mathieson, a Fellow of the Royal Scottish Geographical Society, and his assistant. Although not strictly an official Ordnance Survey map, it was printed and published by Ordnance Survey at Southampton, two years before the remaining islanders asked to be evacuated to mainland Scotland, and presents a very detailed picture of the geography of the islands and their coastal features immediately prior to evacuation. Contours are at intervals of 100 feet. An inset shows the village settlement and associated buildings and remains. *Source:* John Mathieson, assisted by A. M. Cockburn, *Map of St Kilda or Hirta and Adjacent Islands & Stacs* (1928). Reproduced by permission of the Trustees of the National Library of Scotland.

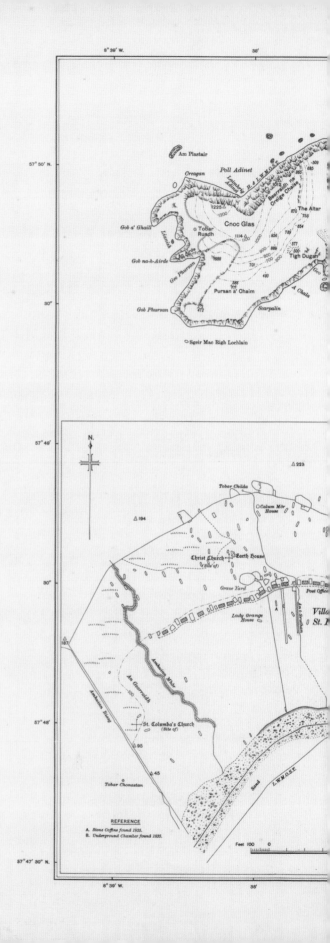

seeking patronage there for his work. We do not know whether Martin either sketched a draft to pass to him, or described the islands sufficiently clearly for Moll to draw the map. Martin's 1698 book was published a month or so before he sailed with Adair in the Outer Hebrides; whether Martin requested maps of Adair, or if such were ever drawn up, is not known. Their joint surveying voyage did not go well: their ship ran aground and was abandoned.

The attention paid to St Kilda's history since the late seventeenth century belies that 'marginality' that follows its cartographic representation. It is only marginal on the necessarily small-scale maps of the Hebrides. The population fluctuated in response to food shortages and disease. As the island was gradually incorporated into the world beyond, its products – feathers, tweed, seabirds, wool – were not always sufficient to meet the financial demands placed upon the islanders. Infant mortality was always high. Many young men left the island after the First World War. By the late 1920s, the population was only a few dozen. In August 1930, the remaining thirty-six persons making up the island's population were evacuated at their own request. Near contemporary maps (fig. 7.16) show a detail we might have wished for in the Martin–Moll depiction, when the island was functioning as a local economy and culture – that is, before marginality and modernity exacted their toll.

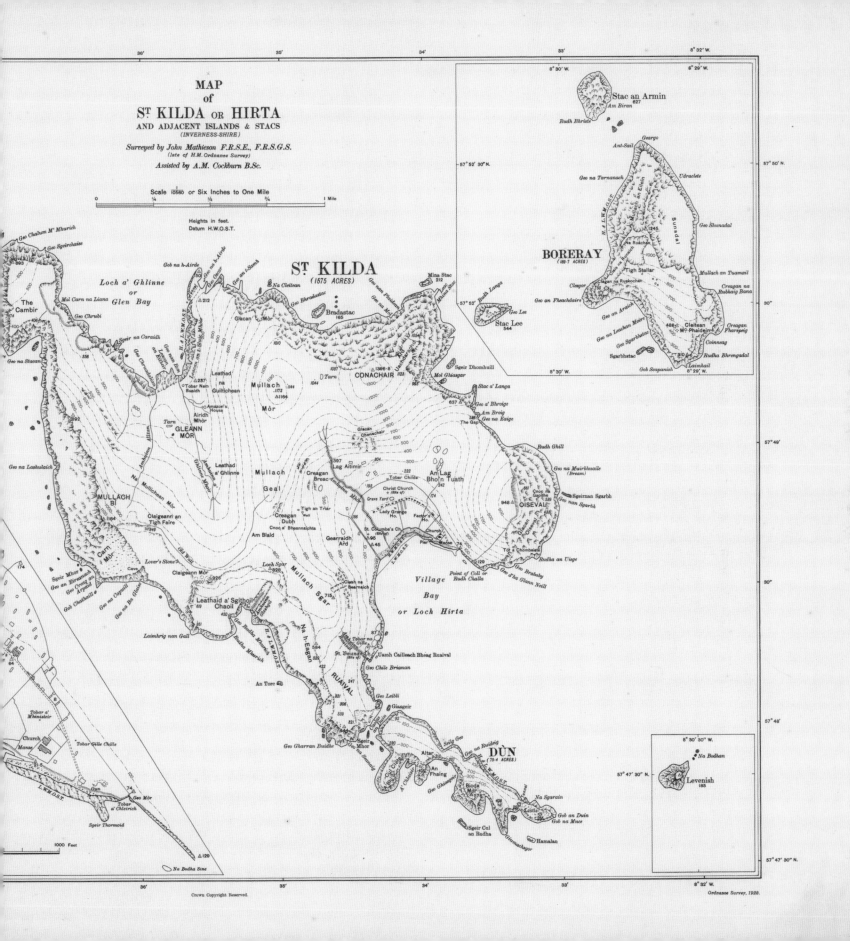

MAP
of
ST. KILDA OR HIRTA
AND ADJACENT ISLANDS & STACS
(INVERNESS-SHIRE)

Surveyed by John Mathieson F.R.S.E., F.R.S.G.S.
(late of H.M. Ordnance Survey)

Assisted by A.M. Cockburn B.Sc.

Scale 1/10560 or Six Inches to One Mile

0   ¼   ½   ¾   1 Mile

Heights in feet.
Datum H.W.O.S.T.

ST. KILDA
(1575 ACRES)

BORERAY
(189·7 ACRES)

Stac an Armin
627

DÙN
(79·4 ACRES)

Levenish
185

Crown Copyright Reserved.

Ordnance Survey, 1928.

TOO SMALL TO MAP? ROCKALL: LAST OUTPOST OF EMPIRE

Many Scottish islands have had military importance, and maps reveal this. In the west, most island and mainland castles reflect their strategic importance during the heyday of the Lords of the Isles in the fifteenth century and sixteenth-century chiefly resistance to royal authority. In the east, islands have at different times but for the same needs been turned over almost wholly to military requirements. Maps of islands in the Firth of Forth, for example, disclose military landscapes in miniature, laid out to counter threats from the east (fig. 7.17).

Scotland has always been at the forefront of changing geo-political priorities. This is apparent in the re-occupation of St Kilda by the military in 1957. As the Cold War between NATO and Soviet bloc countries intensified from the 1950s, modern military geographies of missile sites and early warning systems were established, and St Kilda, economically and cartographically marginal though it may have been, assumed a new centrality as a test bed for guided missiles in a world shaped by nuclear weaponry. Rocket ranges were established in the Outer Hebrides. Nowhere, however, assumed the significance of the smallest island to have such military importance – Rockall.

Rockall is tiny. It is an outcrop of rock, barely 63 feet of granite protruding above the North Atlantic about 290 miles from the Scottish mainland, and about 160 nautical miles west of St Kilda. Just like the uncertainly named and uncertainly located St Kilda group, Rockall – 'Rochol', 'Rokol', 'Rocol' as it was variously named – flickers into cartographic view at one time or another during the later sixteenth century on Dutch charts before becoming a constant feature in most Atlantic maps from the eighteenth century onwards.

Rockall became the object of more detailed attention in the early nineteenth century following the visit of Captain Basil Hall of the Royal Navy in July 1810. Hall landed on the outcrop and collected rock specimens. He did so partly to satisfy his curiosity and – odd though it may sound – to determine that Rockall was indeed an island. Hall later made clear what the issue was in a collection of his voyages and travels. The problem with Rockall, he recounted, was that it didn't look like an island at all, it looked like a ship: 'the top being covered with a coating as white as snow, from having been for ages the resting-place of myriads of sea-fowl, it is constantly mistaken for a vessel under all sail. We were deceived by it several times … even after we had been put on our guard and knew its place well.' Knowing that it was an island and placing it was only half the problem. The other was mapping it once placed. As Hall pointed out, 'The smallest point of a pencil could scarcely give it a place on any map which should not exaggerate its proportions to the rest of the islands in that stormy ocean.'

Here, encapsulated in the words of an adventurous nineteenth-century naval officer, is the cartographer's dilemma. Almost any representation of such a tiny feature on a map would be out of proportion to its real dimensions. How does one map a rock in something as big as the Atlantic? Not to map it would present a danger to safe navigation. But if it is mapped then its size on the map is out of proportion to its size in the world. The important thing to note is not the cartographer's dilemma but the different routes to its solution. Rockall's position as an island was regularly recorded on maps. Rockall was not itself mapped, at the scale of 1:100, until the 1970s (fig. 7.18).

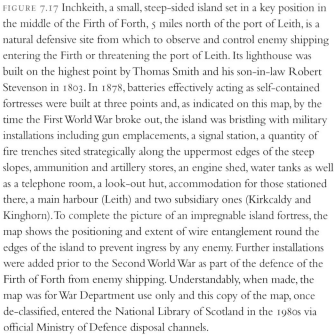

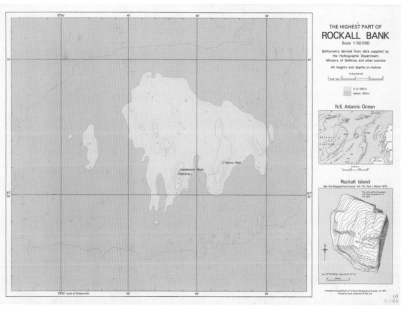

FIGURE 7.17 Inchkeith, a small, steep-sided island set in a key position in the middle of the Firth of Forth, 5 miles north of the port of Leith, is a natural defensive site from which to observe and control enemy shipping entering the Firth or threatening the port of Leith. Its lighthouse was built on the highest point by Thomas Smith and his son-in-law Robert Stevenson in 1803. In 1878, batteries effectively acting as self-contained fortresses were built at three points and, as indicated on this map, by the time the First World War broke out, the island was bristling with military installations including gun emplacements, a signal station, a quantity of fire trenches sited strategically along the uppermost edges of the steep slopes, ammunition and artillery stores, an engine shed, water tanks as well as a telephone room, a look-out hut, accommodation for those stationed there, a main harbour (Leith) and two subsidiary ones (Kirkcaldy and Kinghorn). To complete the picture of an impregnable island fortress, the map shows the positioning and extent of wire entanglement round the edges of the island to prevent ingress by any enemy. Further installations were added prior to the Second World War as part of the defence of the Firth of Forth from enemy shipping. Understandably, when made, the map was for War Department use only and this copy of the map, once de-classified, entered the National Library of Scotland in the 1980s via official Ministry of Defence disposal channels.
Source: War Department / Ordnance Survey, *Inchkeith (Kinghorn Ph.) Fifeshire. 1:2500* (surveyed 1911, printed 1914). Reproduced by permission of the Trustees of the National Library of Scotland.

FIGURE 7.18 *Source:* Royal Geographical Society, *The Highest Part of Rockall Bank. 1:50,000. Inset of Rockall Island 1:100* (1975). Copyright © Royal Geographical Society (with IBG).

By then, mapping Rockall was not only vital; it was a strategic necessity. It may be just a tiny outcrop, but in a nuclear age it was sufficiently close to Britain to be an object of concern: foreign military agents might use it as an automated listening post or observation post for the country's western defences. In September 1955, Rockall had been the object of a landing party of British sailors, who annexed the island to Britain (it formally became part of Inverness-shire in 1972). This 'island-grab' – consistent, of course, with a long history of island-grabbing geographies – was Britain's final imperial gesture: 'the last act of territorial annexation in the history of the British Empire'.

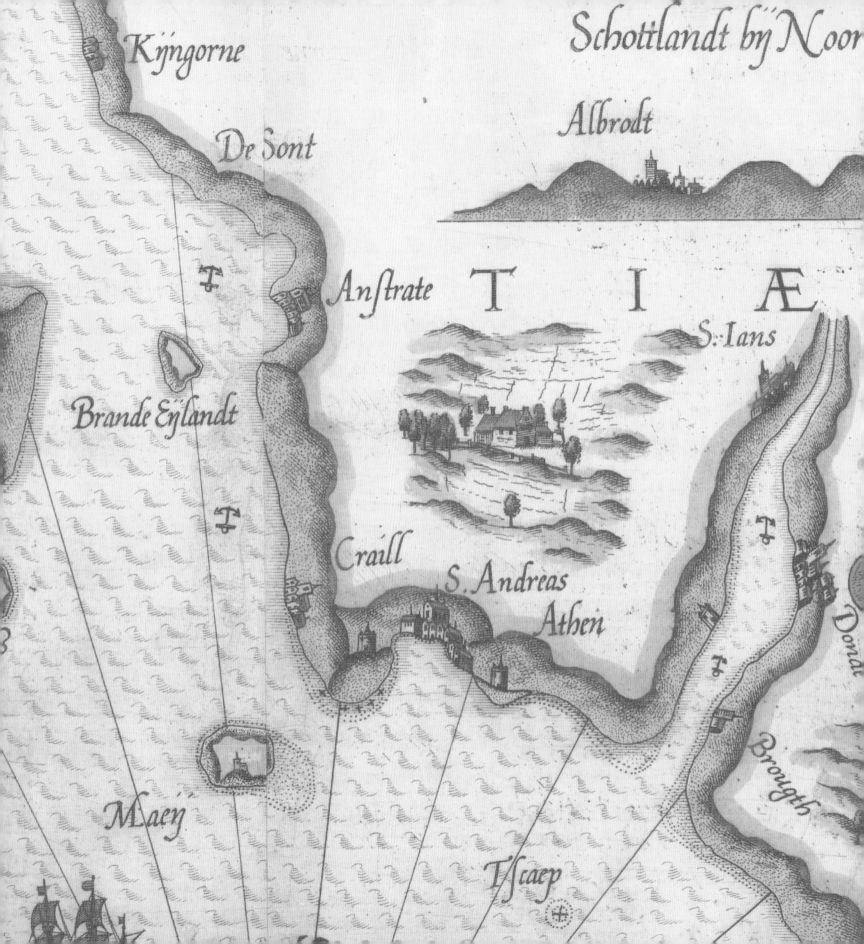

Kyngorne

De Sont

Anstrate

Brande Eylandt

Craill

Maey

Tscaep

Schottlandt by Noor

Albrodt

T I Æ

S: Ians

S. Andreas
Athen

Donat

Brougth

CHAPTER 8

SEAS AND WATERS

Why map the sea? For reasons of trade, safe navigation, exploration and to distinguish water from land in measuring the shape and extent of both. But we must also ask 'How should we map the sea'? For fuller answers, definitions are important. By long-standing cartographic convention, the term 'chart' and the act of producing such a thing – 'charting' – are used to refer to maps produced to facilitate sea and coastal navigation, and the processes of their making. The term 'hydrographic chart' is usually applied to maps of inshore coastal areas in contrast to 'nautical chart' or 'sea chart', which has wider connotations extending to sea navigation in general. Fuller answers depend also upon recognising that, no less than the land, the sea has long been the subject of political dispute. It is not simply a space or obstacle to be crossed by merchants and navigators and put to order by chart-makers. Marine cartography is distinctive, yet in its historical development and in its different forms it shares much with terrestrial and topographic mapping.

This chapter illustrates not just when Scotland's seas and waters came to be charted, but also how and why

Scottish map- and chart-makers played a major role in marine cartography. We look at Scotland on charts before c.1750 in relation to changing trends in European marine mapping; Murdoch Mackenzie's advances in charting in the eighteenth century, and how and why they were part of heightened interests in accuracy; the Admiralty surveys in the nineteenth century; the mapping of Scotland's lochs in the later nineteenth and early twentieth centuries; and the ways maps have been used over time to plot the content, not just the extent, of Scotland's seas.

For anyone trying to put Scotland to shape, from either land or sea, its indented and lengthy coastline presents a problem. As we saw in chapter 1 in John Cowley's extraordinary depiction produced in 1734, entitled '*A Display of the Coasting Lines of Six Several Maps of North Britain*' (fig. 1.2), different geographers and map-makers could not agree where the coast was. We should not be critical. Parts of the Scottish coast (notably south-west Lewis and the peninsulas of Skye) were not accurately charted until the mid-nineteenth century. With a total length of coastline (including its 800 or so islands) of over

10,000 kilometres (6,213 miles), an unpredictable climate, and, in places, a moving shoreline as processes of erosion and deposition act to change it almost daily, this is perhaps not surprising. We have to recognise, too, that for some people – Scots living in coastal localities, regularly navigating their local coastline or waterways – printed charts might not be necessary: the sea's tides and wind patterns, its currents, changing depths and offshore hazards are known through everyday experience. The seas are mapped in these people's memories: cartographic knowledge is not written but passed down orally. But, as we show with regard to the work of Murdoch Mackenzie in the mid-eighteenth century, paper charts could also replace such tacit knowledge, and this could have social consequences.

SCOTLAND ON CHARTS BEFORE *c.1750*

As far as is known, the use of charts in Europe was from classical times predated by written descriptions and sailing directions which centred upon the Mediterranean. It is thought that such written descriptions, known as *periplus* or *pilots*, were not accompanied by any form of chart: certainly none has survived. The Arabs created sea charts from around the tenth century, but an important development in European map history, the portolan chart, does not appear until the thirteenth century, again in Mediterranean context. Produced and decorated by hand, drawn usually on a single animal skin or vellum to better preserve them and their information content from the effects of salt water, portolan charts were produced principally in Majorca, Catalonia and Italian city-states such as Genoa.

Scotland starts to appear on portolan charts by the mid-fourteenth century but, as we have seen for other maps in this period (chapter 2), only marginally. These charts had their own symbolic language. All place and feature names were drawn in 'behind' the coastline, at right angles to it, leaving the coastal detail uncluttered for the navigator to follow. This convention was copied by later chart-makers, for Scotland and more generally (fig. 8.1). Such charts also included and used a system of compass roses from which were drawn rhumb lines, or lines of constant compass bearing, by which navigators could steer their course. That is why, as we have also seen, Mercator's projection of 1569 was significant as a development for seamen and as a moment in map history.

Some portolan charts were so richly decorated it is thought they never went to sea but remained on shore in the harbourmaster's care or in the counting houses of

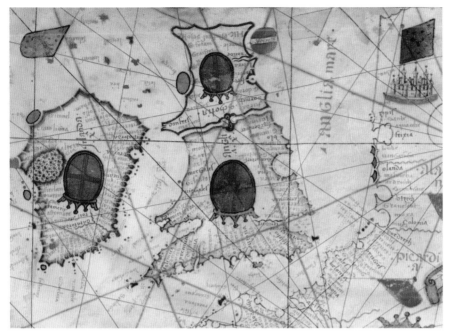

FIGURE 8.1 On this late portolan chart, Scotland appears at first sight to be portrayed as an island, though closer inspection of the place names and estuaries indicates that the seeming channel dividing Scotland from England is more likely to be an exaggeration of the width of the River Tweed (Tueda on the chart) in the east and the Solway Firth in the west. Place names are set at right angles to the coast in the typical portolan chart convention with important harbours indicated in red. Dundee (Donde) and the Firth of Forth (Fort) in the east, Dumfries (Donfres) in the west.
Source: Georgio Sideri (Calapoda), Portolan chart of the Mediterranean (1560). Reproduced by permission of the Trustees of the National Library of Scotland.

wealthy merchants. Even with the existence of portolan charts, books of written sailing directions known variously as 'rutters', 'routiers', 'waggoners' or 'pilot' books, unaccompanied at this period by charts, were the more common navigation tools. Following the invention and dissemination of movable-type printing, such printed sailing directions became more widely available: in addition to text arranged in a geographical progression round each bit of coastline, pilot books usually included small drawings, in profile, of significant coastal features to help minimize the mariner's exposure to danger. By the sixteenth century, with the burgeoning of navigation outside European waters and the need to record coastlines everywhere more accurately, sea charts were increasingly produced as separate entities and in larger numbers. As the world grew bigger, and as the centres of European map-making mirrored the rise of mercantile capitalism in north-west Europe, so Britain and Scotland moved from a position of marginality to a more central place on charts.

The earliest surviving charts showing the coastline of Scotland were not the work of Scots. The first known Scottish charting exercise took place in 1540 and involved a conspicuous display of royal authority in politically troubled waters. A fleet of twelve ships under the command of James V circumnavigated the northern and western coasts of Scotland, including the northern and western isles, in order, as we have noted (chapter 2), to know Scotland's shape and demonstrate the reach of kingly power. James V was accompanied by his pilot, Alexander Lindsay, who, as a result of the expedition, produced a detailed set of sailing directions, commonly known now as Lindsay's 'Rutter' (fig. 8.2). Interestingly, it has been conjectured that Leon Strozzi, Captain-General of the French fleet during the capture of St Andrews in 1547, made use of a copy of Lindsay's Rutter.

It is uncertain whether Lindsay produced any sea charts as a result of the voyage, but two small-scale manuscript charts of Scotland that appeared around 1580 are thought to have benefited from the information collected by Lindsay on that voyage. The compiler of one map is unknown; the other was the work of Nicolas de Nicolay, Sieur d'Arfeville and Cosmographer to the king of France (fig. 8.3). Nicolay's chart first appeared in published form

FIGURE 8.2 *Left.* Alexander Lindsay was the pilot on King James V of Scotland's voyage round the coast of Scotland, sailing from Leith north to Orkney via Aberdeen and the Moray Firth, then round the north coast to Skye and Lewis before returning south round the west coast and Kintyre. As a result of this he produced a rutter (a set of written sailing directions), at a time when there was a growing requirement for such sailing aids due to the increase in Scottish trade and with more and better ships plying these difficult waters. His rutter was originally written in Scots, but has not survived, although three English-text versions survive from the late sixteenth and early seventeenth centuries, as well as three variants of a French translation made in 1547. Of these six versions, only one was published (French text of 1583). A chart (fig. 8.3) by the Frenchman Nicolas de Nicolay, which accompanied three of the copies, was produced after the original rutter was completed, Nicolay having been loaned a copy by the Lord Admiral of England in 1546–47. *Source:* Alexander Lindsay, *A Rutter of the Scottish Seas* (*c.*1540 (early seventeenth-century copy)). Reproduced by permission of the Trustees of the National Library of Scotland.

FIGURE 8.3 *Opposite.* As a result of King James V of Scotland's two-month navigation of Scotland in 1540 his pilot, Alexander Lindsay, produced a pilot book containing sailing directions, one version of which was published in 1583 and accompanied by a chart of Scotland. The chart was produced by Nicolas de Nicolay, Geographer to King Henry II of France, and, according to Nicolay's own account, was drawn in 1540. For its time, it was a very accurate rendering of the coastline. It was still regarded as perhaps the most accurate representation of Scotland a century and a half later when John Adair made and published his own close copy of it in 1688 (fig. 2.11). *Source:* Nicolas de Nicolay, *Vraye & exacte description hydrographique des costes maritimes d'Escosse & des Isles Orchades Hebrides . . .* (1583). Reproduced by permission of the Trustees of the National Library of Scotland.

in 1583 as illustration to a French edition of Lindsay's Rutter. The chart shows an outline far superior in terms of its depiction of the north and west coasts of Scotland than any other contemporary maps or charts of the period, and this was to remain the case for many years.

Scotland featured on charts in other ways. The shift in the geography of European map and atlas making – from Mediterranean countries in the late medieval period to the mid-sixteenth century, thence to the Low Country centres of Antwerp and Amsterdam, before the rise to prominence of England, France and Germany in

the seventeenth and eighteenth centuries – is clearly evident in the story of charts. The first European sea atlas, *Spieghel der Zeevaerdt*, was produced in 1584 by a Dutch master pilot, Lucas Janszoon Waghenaer (from whom we get the term 'waggoner' to mean a chart or work of sailing directions), and contained charts of the east and south coasts of Great Britain as well as sailing directions. An English edition, *The Mariners Mirror*, was published in 1588. For the first time, comparatively large-scale charts also containing some topographical detail of areas inland from the coasts were available for mariners.

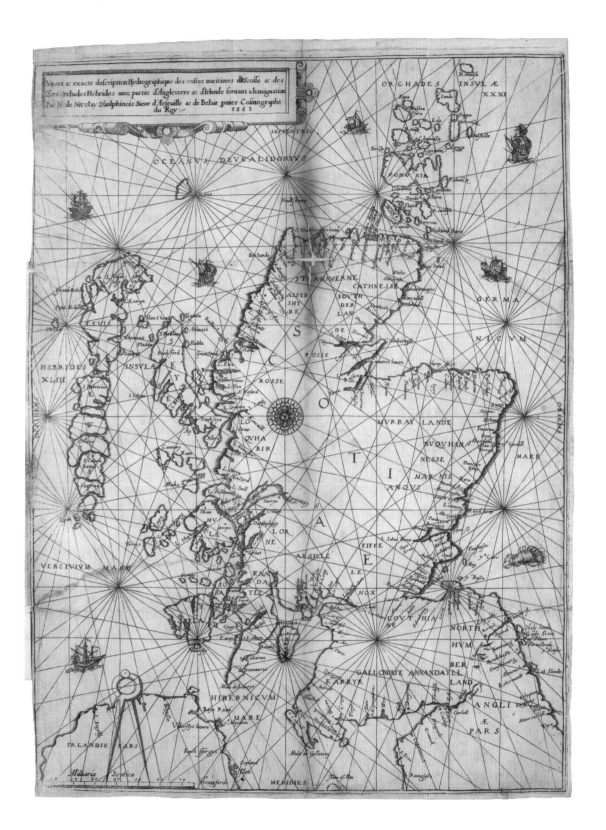

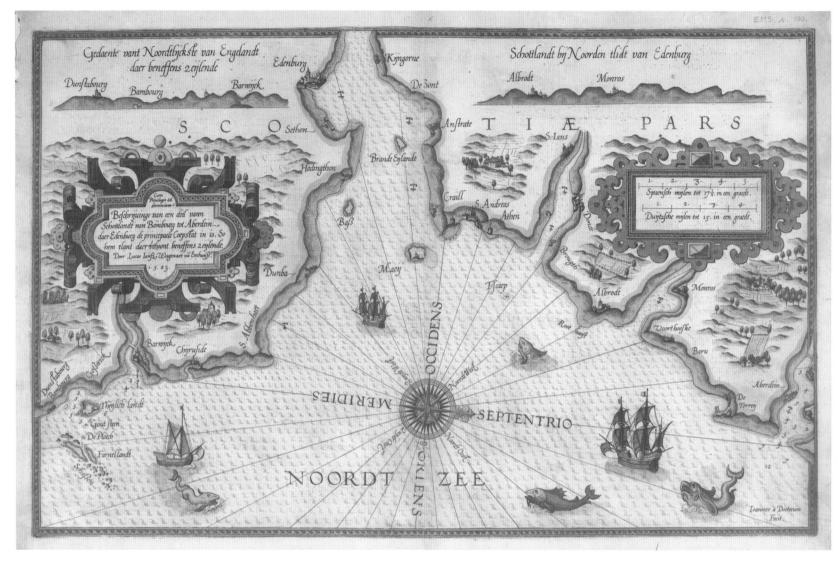

FIGURE 8.4 This map features in the first European printed pilot book to be illustrated by charts (1584). The Dutch compiler of this work, Lucas Janszoon Waghenaer, blends necessary navigational information with unrealised errors and some artistic licence. Drawn head-on as if viewed across the North Sea from the Low Countries, the unnamed Firth of Forth has Haddington (Hodingthon) and Edinburgh (rather than Leith) in erroneous coastal positions and a mysterious island – Brande Eylandt – located off Anstruther (Anstrate). The real mainland coastal settlement of Burntisland on the Fife coast lay some miles away up the Forth Estuary.
Source: Lucas Janszoon Waghenaer, *Beschrijvinge van een deel vann Schottlandt van Bambourg tot Aberdein . . .* (1583). Reproduced by permission of the Trustees of the National Library of Scotland.

Waghenaer included four separate but connected types of information: a bird's-eye view of the landscape inland as seen from an oblique angle close to the coast (rather like the view from an aeroplane coming in to land at a coastal airport); figures giving the depths of the water at various stages along the coastline and in navigable estuaries; scale drawings of significant physical features in the landscape; and a 3-D effect in rendering the coastal strip above the high water mark (figs. 8.4, 8.5). Scotland's east coast, its northern and western isles and the mainland west coast were also charted by other Dutch chart-

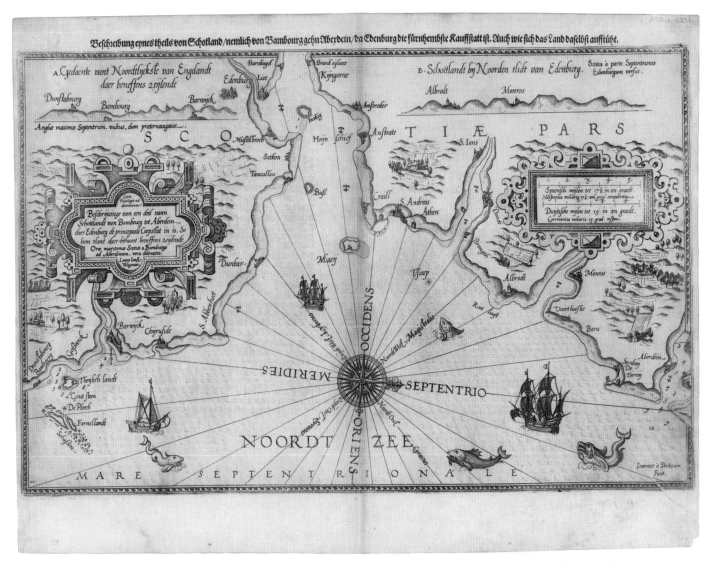

makers, notably by members of the Van Keulen family (figs. 8.6, 8.7). The contrast in relative accuracy between the better-known east coast and the less known north and western coasts is, however, often marked in such Low Country charts (figs. 8.8, 8.9).

Not until the seventeenth century did a Scots-born east-coast mariner, John Marr from Dundee, produce a chart of the east coast of Scotland from Berwick on Tweed to Buchan Ness, although, in part, given where the centre of map publishing technology then lay, this was jointly produced with Gerard Van Keulen and

FIGURE 8.5 By 1590, Waghenaer, made aware of his mistakes, perhaps as a result of reports of costly losses of ships and lives, has correctly substituted Leith for Edinburgh, added Edinburgh's river – the Water of Leith – has removed Haddington (substituting Tantallon) and replaced his mysterious island with Inchkeith (Inskig) in the more-or-less correct position. Burntisland (Brand eylant) is now accorded its correct coastal location.
Source: Lucas Janszoon Waghenaer, *Beschrijvinge van een deel vann Schottlandt van Bambourg tot Aberdein . . .* (1589). Reproduced by permission of the Trustees of the National Library of Scotland.

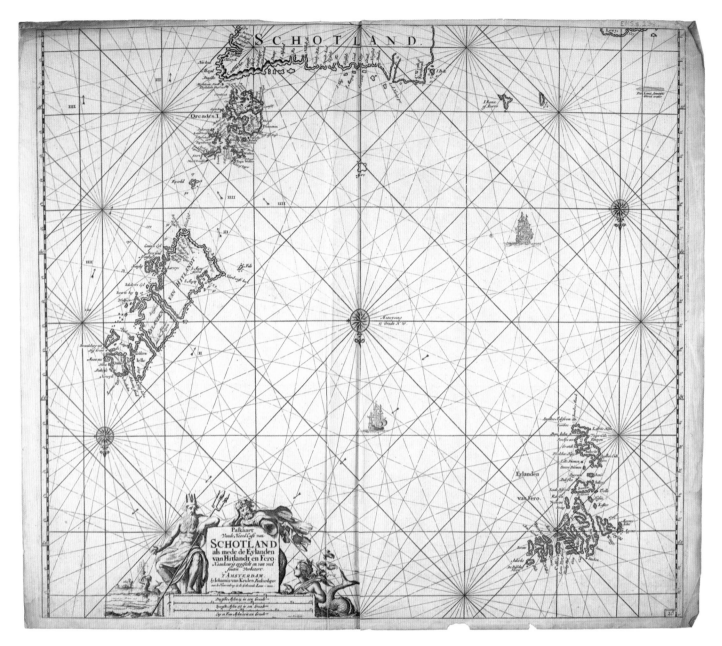

FIGURE 8.6 Not unusually for the period, this Dutch sea chart places south in the position more usually accorded to north, with the north coast of Scotland shown at the top, and includes the Faroe Islands, 300 kilometres to the north-west of mainland Scotland. Until 1380, the Faroes shared Norse rule with Orkney and Shetland, with the last two only annexed to the Scottish Crown in 1471. These three archipelagos also sat astride an important shipping lane from Scandinavia into the Atlantic and North America as well as being in rich fishing grounds – hence the placing of the ships on the chart both as decoration to fill empty gaps and to indicate that these waters were well known to mariners.

Source: Johannes van Keulen, *Paskaart Vande Noord Cust van Schotland als mede de eylanden van Hitlandt en Fero.* (c.1682). Reproduced by permission of the Trustees of the National Library of Scotland.

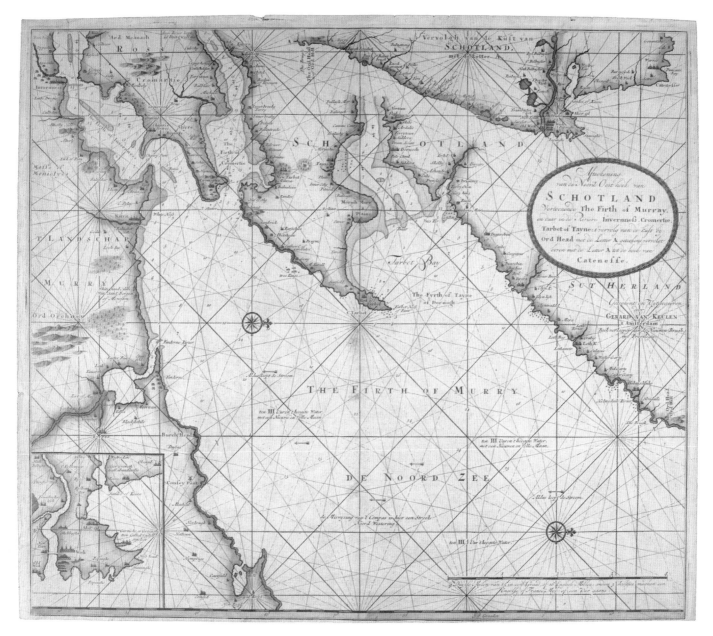

FIGURE 8.7 The chart-maker Gerard van Keulen, one of a dynasty of Dutch chart-makers, clearly thought he could best convey the intricate coastline of the Moray, Beauly, Cromarty and Dornoch Firths by realigning his chart with west at the top to represent the most usual directional travel into these waters from the coasts of mainland Europe. He included the north-eastern extension of the Caithness coast out of place in an empty space at the top of the sheet, with a small more detailed inset of the coast round Wick in the left-hand corner. His depiction of the large sandbar at the entrance to the Dornoch Firth, showing the

Firth's comparative shallowness, is in contrast to the greater depths shown by the soundings and absence of sandbars in the Cromarty Firth and illustrates the detailed knowledge of this stretch of coast that the Dutch had acquired through long familiarity.
Source: Gerard van Keulen, *Afteekening van de Noord Oost hoek van Schotland, vertoonende The Firth of Murray, en daar in de riviere Invernness, Cromertie, Tarbet of Tayne* (1734). Reproduced by permission of the Trustees of the National Library of Scotland.

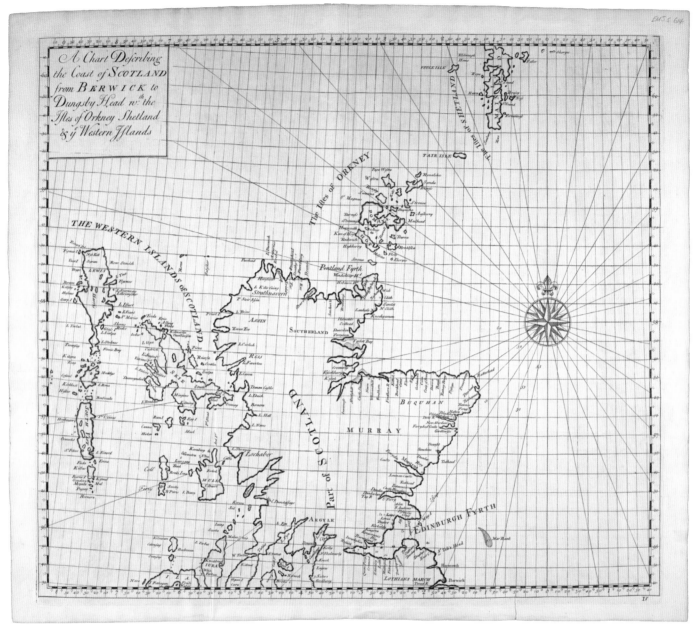

FIGURE 8.8 This chart appears (in terms of its depiction of the Western Isles and the north-west coast of Scotland) to be based closely on – and perhaps copied wholesale from – Martin Martin's map of the Western Isles of around 1695, which was itself produced by the Dutchman Herman Moll. The rest of the chart illustrates well its maker's dilemma in possessing different levels of knowledge – gained from different sources – of the outlines of the east and west coasts of Scotland, and making rather a mess of the outline in trying to fudge the issue. Place names are set at right angles to the coast in the manner of earlier portolan charts, to ensure the continuous line of the coast remained completely uncluttered for navigational use: even so, the chart remains more of a curiosity than a useful working chart.

Source: Anon., *A Chart Describing the Coast of Scotland from Berwick to Dungsby Head with the Isles of Orkney Shetland & ye Western Islands* (*c.*1700). Reproduced by permission of the Trustees of the National Library of Scotland.

FIGURE 8.9 Errors in the representation of the outline of Scotland's west coast and islands continued through the eighteenth century as shown on this manuscript chart of 1730 by a Lieutenant in the Royal Navy, Mark Tiddeman. Tiddeman includes some coastal castles but no anchorages and, according to the convention of the time, adds a plethora of crosses to indicate dangerous rocks, notably between the islands of Canna and Coll. The chart is dedicated to Admiral Sir Charles Wager, First Lord of the Admiralty from 1733.

Source: Mark Tiddeman, *To the Honorable Sr. Charles Wager, this Draught of Part of the Highlands of Scotland . . .* (1730). Reproduced by permission of the Trustees of the National Library of Scotland.

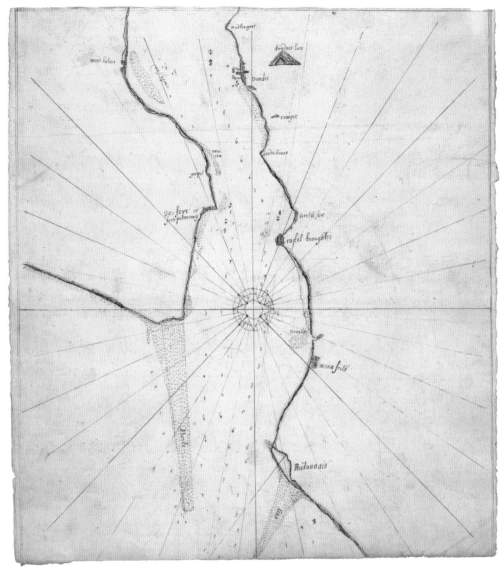

FIGURE 8.10 Charts 8.10 and 8.11 are closely related because of their common basis: the earlier chart of the Tay estuary in 1666 is almost certainly the work of John Marr, a chart maker, ship master and mariner based in Dundee, of which city he was also a burgess. Marr was also the author of an important pilot book, *Navigation in Coasting, or the Sea-man's Instructor: Containing Several Theoreticall and Practicall-parts of that Art: And Also, some Necessary Points of the Duty of a Carefull Sea-man . . .*, published in Aberdeen in 1683. This was the first Scottish-published pilot book. The second chart published in 1693 appeared in Captain Greenvile Collins's 'Great Britain's coasting-pilot', where Collins includes a small cartouche giving Marr his due as the surveyor and describes him as 'an injenious marriner of Dundee'.

Source: John Marr, A chart of the mouth of the Firth of Tay (*c.*1666). Reproduced by permission of the Trustees of the National Library of Scotland.

printed in Amsterdam in 1683 (fig. 8.10). Marr also drafted our earliest surviving chart of the Firth of Tay and wrote the only surviving pilot descriptions of Scotland's east coast in the eighteenth century. Greenvile Collins, the English hydrographer, was also mapping Scotland's east coast at this time as part of his *Great Britain's Coasting Pilot* (first published in 1693) (fig. 8.11). By the 1680s, John Adair was at work on his county mapping, in charting Scotland's eastern seas (fig. 8.12) and, later, charting the seas around the north and west coast and islands. By

then, however, charting the seas had assumed heightened political importance.

In his 1609 *Mare Liberum* (*The Free Sea*), the Dutch legal philosopher Hugo Grotius developed the idea of the open ocean, free to all nations. Others disputed this, the English philosopher John Selden proposing in his *Mare Clausum* (1635) that the sea, just like land-based territory, could and should be delimited. In his *De Dominio Maris* (1702), another Dutchman, Cornelius Bynkershoek, proposed as a workable compromise the

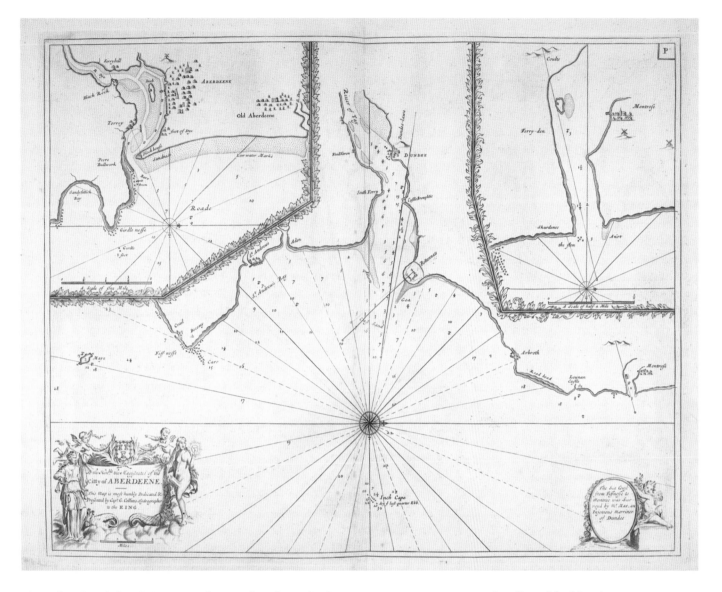

idea of national dominion over the seas but for only three miles – or, as he put it, within a cannon's shot from shore. The ideas of 'the freedom of the seas' and of 'territorial waters' are a product of this late seventeenth-century legal wrangling – which still continues as nations squabble over territorial rights to marine resources – but they gave charting a significance in later centuries that it had not had before. This issue may even help explain why, for example, John Adair was where he was when he was, charting for the Scottish Parliament.

FIGURE 8.11 *Source:* John Marr / Greenvile Collins, *The Sea Coast from Fiffnesse to Montros* (1693). Reproduced by permission of the Trustees of the National Library of Scotland.

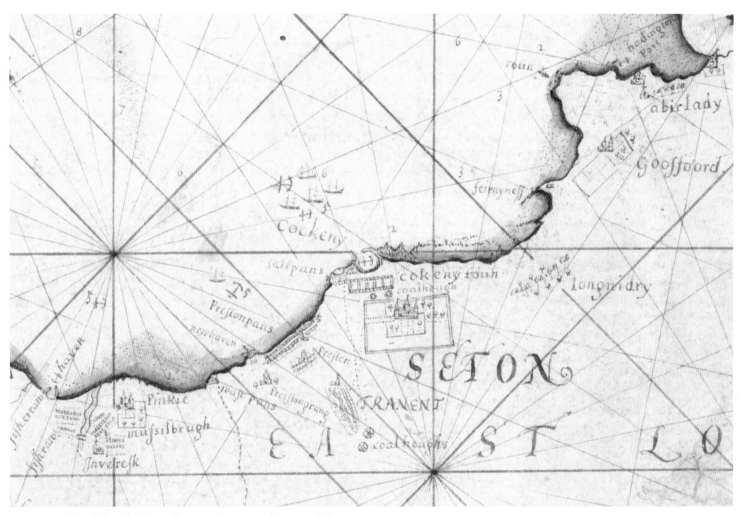

FIGURE 8.12 Although this sea chart was drawn up primarily to indicate safe passage into and along the Firth of Forth, together with the best anchorages and harbours, in this much enlarged detail from the chart, John Adair shows the concentration of important trading staples of the period in one small area of East Lothian – the extensive salt pans at Prestonpans and Cockenzie and the coal heughs (pits) behind Cockenzie and around Tranent. His drawing of ships at anchor nearby shows his recognition of the importance of this part of the Forth in trading terms.
Source: John Adair, *The Hydrographicall Mappe of Forth from the Entry to ye Quensferry* (1683). Reproduced by permission of the Trustees of the National Library of Scotland.

NEW ACCURACIES: MACKENZIE, DALRYMPLE AND THE ADMIRALTY SURVEYS

At much the same time as William Roy was engaged on the Military Survey of Scotland, another Scot, the Orcadian Murdoch Mackenzie, was undertaking a hydrographic survey of the coasts of Orkney and Lewis. Mackenzie owed the work to the patronage of two men: James Douglas, 14th Earl of Morton, who had succeeded to his estates, which included the Orkney Islands, in 1738; and Colin MacLaurin, professor of mathematics at the University of Edinburgh, who was greatly interested in the mathematics of mapping and taught the subject as part of his geography classes. In early 1743, Mackenzie appealed to the public to support his Orkney work via an Edinburgh newspaper, the *Caledonian Mercury*: all of this is evidence of private patronage and public recognition of the civic role of mapping and charting, but it points, too, to the often limited funds available to turn such schemes into reality.

But by July 1744, Mackenzie was ready: 'After long expectation of something more considerable I have at last received surveying instruments from the Admiralty'. And by August 1744, his survey of the Orkneys was under way. Mackenzie introduced new rigour and surveying techniques to charting around the coasts, including a first use of triangulation. This involved measuring a baseline – which was sometimes on the beach; once, in the winter months, on a frozen loch – and then taking readings to selected outstanding or prominent features. Men with poles 'and a cloath flying at the top of each' were used as sighting points: when the men were too few, beacons of stones and earth were erected 'upon some of the most conspicuous eminences up through the land'. This procedure, based on Admiralty instrumen-

tation, regularly repeated, allowed the calculation of distance and, with the taking of further readings from one feature to a new feature, produced a series of interlocking triangles by which coasts and seas could be accurately measured.

Mackenzie brought his northern charting and survey work together in *Orcades* (1750). By the standards of the time, this was a major advance (fig. 8.13); although, in fact, Mackenzie had intended fifteen maps of the Orkneys, he finished only five, and his survey of Lewis was put together much less well, almost as an afterthought. The Admiralty was nevertheless impressed enough with the result to commission him as a civilian surveyor from 1751 with a brief to do the west coast of Scotland, and, later, Ireland; his first ship was the 35-ton *Culloden*. In 1774, Mackenzie published his *Treatise on Maritim Surveying*, and, in 1776, again with the support of the Admiralty (then much concerned at America's naval intrusions into Britain's western seas), his *A Maritim Survey of Ireland and the West of Great Britain* (fig. 8.14). This included the taking of soundings to record water depths, had notes where cod and ling were to be found, and had small drawings of significant coastal features to help mariners relate better to the coastline. Mackenzie's methods and standards had a major impact on the later development of hydrographic charting by the Admiralty and raised standards of accuracy.

Imagine Mackenzie's surprise, then, when, in the early 1780s – years after the work had been done – he found himself and his mapping the object of fierce criticism in the newspapers. The author of the attack, James Anderson, an Aberdeenshire natural philosopher and principal

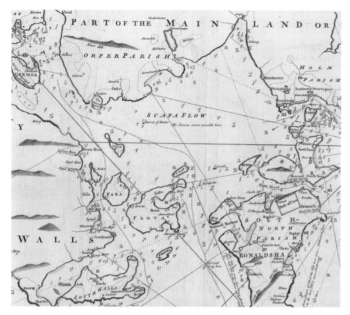

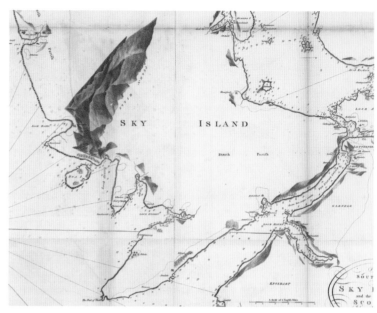

FIGURE 8.13 When Murdoch Mackenzie charted the huge natural harbour of Scapa Flow around 1750, this location did not have the resonance it would later acquire through the major naval activities there during the First and Second World Wars when it became the main naval base for the British Home Fleet. After the end of the First World War it saw the internment in 1919 of seventy-two German warships and their subsequent scuttling by those Germans remaining on board. During the Second World War it sheltered the Home Fleet again and saw the sinking of HMS *Royal Oak* by a German submarine. But, for Mackenzie, Scapa Flow was home; his family owned the property of Groundwater (on Mainland and shown on this extract) which looked south over Scapa Flow.

Source: Murdoch Mackenzie, 'The South Isles of Orkney', from *Orcades: Or, a Geographic and Hydrographic Survey of the Orkney and Lewis Islands, in Eight Maps* (1750). Reproduced by permission of the Trustees of the National Library of Scotland.

FIGURE 8.14 The interior of Mackenzie's chart remains relatively blank except for his dramatic representation of the Cuillins, mountains which, when free of cloud or mist, would have held the eye of all navigators in those waters. The depiction of the Inner Sound between Skye and mainland Scotland is peppered with soundings, particularly the narrows of Kyle Rhea, a key navigation channel as well as crossing point from Skye to mainland Scotland. Mackenzie includes the military installations of Bernera Barracks in Glenelg and Eilean Donan Castle. Both places would have acted as points of reference for sailors but were also a reminder of recent conflict in the Highlands.

Source: Murdoch Mackenzie, 'The South Part of Sky Island and the Adjacent Main of Scotland'. Plate XXV of Mackenzie's *A Maritim Survey of Ireland and the West of Great Britain* (1776). Reproduced by permission of the Trustees of the National Library of Scotland.

figure behind the production of the Enlightenment journal *The Bee, or Literary Weekly Intelligencer,* complained that Mackenzie's maps were far from accurate, that he, Anderson, had recently used them in the Hebrides and found them 'so erroneous' he could only suppose that 'they must have been sketched by the eye only, and that even in a hasty and superficial manner'. Mackenzie, naturally, refuted these charges. Between November 1784 and January 1785, the arguments flew back and forth. Mackenzie called upon his patrons in support and, of course, had the authority of the Admiralty to fall back upon.

More than that, he had the testimony of local sailors – despite the fact that, as they pointed out, they had every reason to dislike Mackenzie. His maps made tacit knowledge, and those who held it, redundant: as one

Hebridean sailor reported, 'they [Mackenzie's maps] have done prejudice to the pilots; for to my knowledge, many of them that used to be well employed and well paid, before your charts came out, are now obliged to stay at home idle, or enter before the mast, because masters through the Highlands, to the west of England and to Ireland, sail by your draughts without taking a pilot'. Accuracy always has a price.

In 1795, the British government established the Hydrographic Office. This was partly in response to the heightened levels of accuracy evident in Mackenzie's work – and in that of his charting nephew, Murdoch Mackenzie Junior – and partly mirrored their European counterparts: the French had established the Dépôt des Cartes et Plans de la Marine within their Navy Ministry in 1720, and the Spanish their Observatorio de la Armada in 1753. It was chiefly, however, because charting needed to be coordinated at a period of critical military and political importance given the war with France. For 1791 and Ordnance Survey, read 1795 and the Hydrographic Office: maps and charts were documents of and for the state; triangulation, measurement, trained personnel, institutional management were the means to produce them.

The first Hydrographer to the Admiralty was Alexander Dalrymple, born at Newhailes near Edinburgh in 1737. Dalrymple, Hydrographer to the East India Company before his Admiralty appointment in 1795, seems not to have been an easy man to like, or to employ: he fell out with the Royal Society over a voyage later led by James Cook, was dismissed from the East India Company in 1771 before being reinstated four years later, and was eventually dismissed, probably unfairly, by the Admiralty in 1808. But he set and certainly demanded high standards – often returning charts before printing if he thought they lacked detail or the author was not authoritative enough. With Mackenzie, he provided the foundations for Britain's modern marine charting.

Dalrymple's successors built upon his work by establishing surveying as an independent branch within the Royal Navy and, from the 1820s, Admiralty charts were made available for civil use. From the 1830s, the Admiralty engaged in a wholesale re-survey of the coastal waters of the British Isles. Scotland's seas were systematically charted as part of this 'Grand Survey of the British Isles' as it became known. By the mid-nineteenth century, the Hydrographic Department had produced some 255 charts of home waters. Charts were revised regularly to take into account changing estuarine forms in particular.

Admiralty surveys represent some of the most consistently produced high standard mapping anywhere in the world. Men like Captain, later Commandant, Henry Otter – who was fond of an early morning swim, naked, from the rocks near his home just west of Oban harbour – helped establish a comprehensive mapped record for Scotland's seas during the nineteenth century. Admiralty charts show dangers to shipping, such as wrecks and sandbanks, and also document notable relevant features, such as forts and other coastal defences (figs. 8.15, 8.16, 8.17). Unlike other charts or maps, which may not show north or which may not even be oriented with north to the 'top' of the mapped image, Admiralty survey charts use the Mercator projection as standard. Because the directions of the bearings on the chart are the same as the corresponding directions and angles in the real world – the map's bearings do correspond to reality – the Admiralty chart can be used to plot accurate directions and distances. Commercial chart-makers used these and other maps to cash in on the growing requirement for small-scale charts of well-used sea lanes.

FIGURE 8.15 Stranraer is depicted on this chart eight years before it became the base for the Admiralty's official mail and freight service to Northern Ireland. With its favoured position in the south-west corner of deeply sheltered Loch Ryan, and at a natural focal point on land, Stranraer had considerable advantages over nearby Portpatrick as a mail service port and blossomed accordingly from the mid-nineteenth century. The Admiralty's surveyors were more concerned, however, with the detailing of the waters and coastline of Loch Ryan than with giving much indication of Stranraer's increasingly important function as a significant shipbuilding centre and busy port with regular sailings to Glasgow and up the Clyde coast. *Source:* Hydrographic Office, *Loch Ryan.* Admiralty Chart 1403 (1841). Reproduced by permission of the Trustees of the National Library of Scotland.

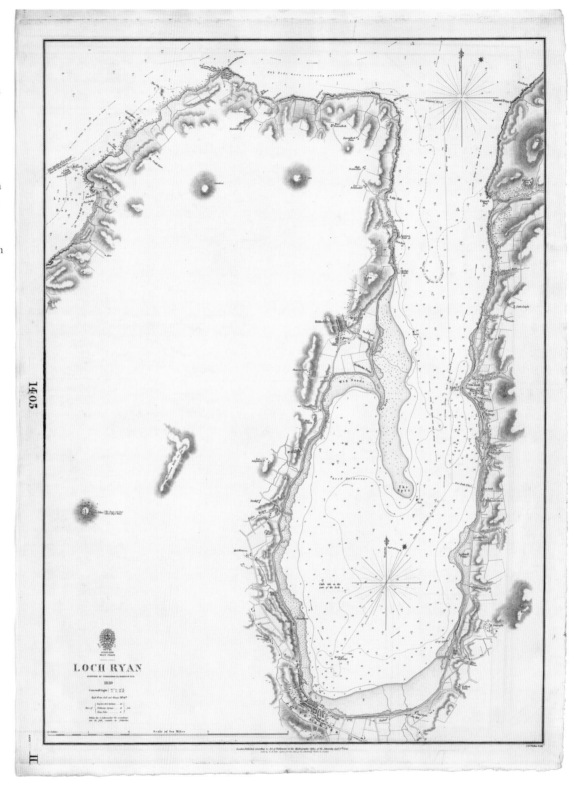

FIGURE 8.16 As well as giving detailed soundings to allow safe passage through the Sound of Islay, Admiralty surveyors of this period also incorporated in their chart any obvious topographic landmarks useful for pilots to steer by − not least the three Paps of Jura. They also included these in beautiful line drawings which frequently embellished Admiralty charts of this period, again as an aid to navigation.
Source: Hydrographic Office, *Sound of Islay*. Admiralty Chart 2481 (1856). Reproduced by permission of the Trustees of the National Library of Scotland.

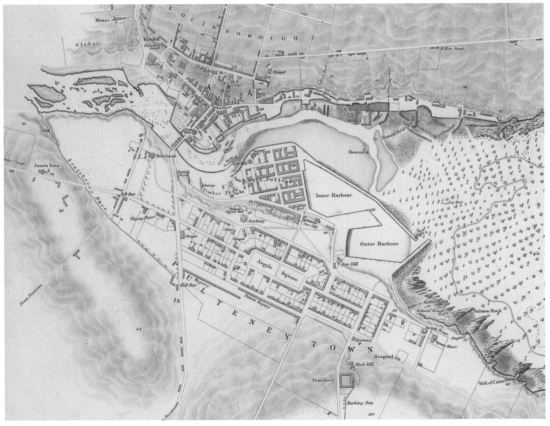

FIGURE 8.17 Not only does this detailed Admiralty chart give the soundings necessary for boats seeking to dock safely in Wick's outer and inner harbours, it also incorporates useful topographic data. Often such topographic detail shown on mid-nineteenth-century Admiralty charts fills an important information gap: in this case, Ordnance Survey had yet to produce detailed maps of Wick at large scales (1:1,056 or 60 inches to 1 mile in 1872) and (1:2,500 or 25 inches to 1 mile in 1877). Some of the Admiralty's topographic information here was important to sailors, such as the Custom House, Agents House, Ropery and Steamer's Signal Staff building, but there is much shown of more general interest, including Thomas Telford's planned settlements of Upper and Lower Pulteneytown, begun in 1786 for the British Fisheries Society.
Source: Hydrographic Office, *The Port and Vicinity of Wick*. Admiralty Chart 2170 (1839 (1857)). Reproduced by permission of the Trustees of the National Library of Scotland.

TAKING SOUNDINGS: LOCHS AND INLAND WATERS

As Scotland's seas were brought to cartographic order during the nineteenth century, attention turned to Scotland's many lochs. Some work was undertaken by the Hydrographic Department to measure the depths of several Scottish freshwater lochs, including Lochs Lomond, Tay, Awe and Katrine during the 1860s and 1870s. This work was partly motivated by a desire to find out how much water was contained in lochs such as Loch Katrine, given plans to supply Glasgow with water from the loch. In fact, the beginnings of such 'loch mapping' – using that term loosely to mean mapping both the extent of inland water bodies, and, more importantly, their depth – dates from the early eighteenth century when Joseph Avery, who was working with General Wade, undertook some mapping of the lochs of the Great Glen with a view to determining their depth. Systematic loch mapping dates from the last few years of the nineteenth century, and tended to focus on charting their depth since, by then, land-based county and other mapping had determined lochs' extent.

There were also scientific reasons behind the mapping of Scotland's lochs from this time: lakes and inland waters were becoming the focus of scientific study (limnology), and bathymetry (measuring the depth of water) was a major part of the by-then established marine sciences (oceanography).

Scotland's Bathymetrical Survey was undertaken between 1897 and 1909, although further loch sounding work has been undertaken since then. The idea for it was proposed by the Scot, Sir John Murray, who made his name as a leading marine scientist on the *Challenger* voyage of 1872–76: this, in its sea-based calculations and in its numerous post-voyage publications, effectively established oceanography as a science. With others, Murray recognised the value of the systematic study of Scotland's freshwater lochs – although, in part, his motivation for measuring loch depth lay in wanting to know the extent of Scotland's glaciation as well as how the biology of the waters varied with temperature and depth. Distinguished scientist as he certainly was, Murray could not convince the established mapping agencies to do the work: the Admiralty saw its work as based on the seas and so declined to help; Ordnance Survey declined because its focus was dry land.

Murray began his 'self-imposed task', as he put it, with a friend, Fred Pullar, in 1897, slowly establishing procedures both for loch sounding and, with the Bartholomew firm in Edinburgh, for the mapped representation of the work (fig. 8.18). Here, too, accuracy came at a price: Pullar was drowned in an accident in 1901, and Murray considered halting the scheme, but was persuaded to continue by Fred Pullar's father, who contributed £10,000 in support of the work. The recording work of the Bathymetric Survey came to an end in 1906.

Scotland's loch mapping is a particular illustration of the conjunctions between science and mapping that we explore in more depth in chapter 10. It is remarkable work, but hardly what we might think of as 'big science', and, for various reasons, it did not cover all of Scotland's lochs. Some of the little lochs, as Murray pointed out, 'are remotely situated among the hills, and could only be reached by cycling and walking', and so the machine which read the depths was designed to be 'lashed to a bicycle or carried in the hand'. On numerous occasions, Murray and others had the support of Mr William Fraser, 'cyclist boatman' as he was termed. Even then, rowing

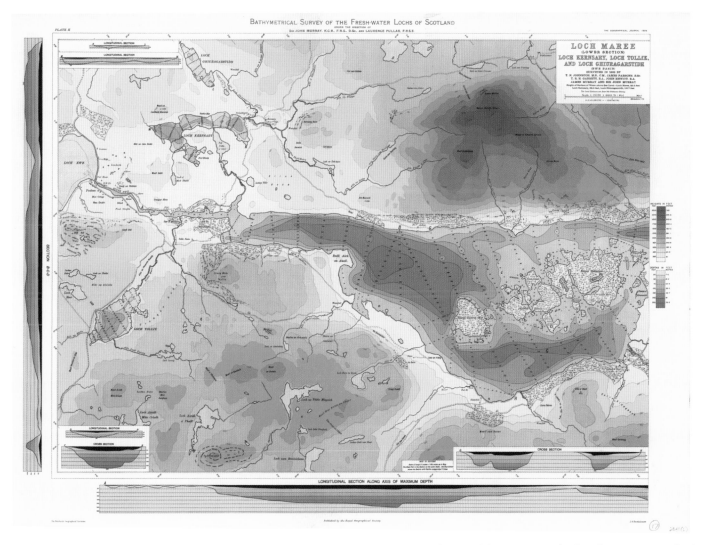

FIGURE 8.18 Production of charts was not exclusively related to the sea coast; here we see a bathymetric chart of lower Loch Maree in Ross and Cromarty, a freshwater loch. The chart illustrates well the pleasing Bartholomew layer-colouring developed for showing relief above and below water level. With contour lines on land at 200 foot intervals up to 1,000 feet and thereafter at 250 foot intervals, a flavour of the lie of the land is given (land contours taken from Ordnance Survey mapping) but these are of secondary importance here to the depiction of the sub-surface water levels with contour intervals of 25 foot down to 100 foot depth and thereafter at 50 foot intervals. Although the contour intervals chosen for land and for sub-surface water levels differ markedly, this does not jar on the eye of the viewer nor hinder acceptance or interpretation of the way in which the terrain is displayed. *Source:* Sir John Murray and Laurence Pullar, 'Loch Maree (lower section)', surveyed 1902 from *Bathymetrical Survey of the Fresh-water Lochs of Scotland* (1897–1909). Reproduced by permission of the Trustees of the National Library of Scotland.

boats were not always available during the fishing and shooting seasons: estate work took priority over loch mapping. Nevertheless, the work was of a high standard. The degree of accuracy achieved has been corroborated by more modern survey work, and Ordnance Survey, despite declining to be involved from the outset, has made use of information from these charts for its submarine contours shown on the 1:10,560 (6 inches to 1 mile) and for its smaller-scale topographic mapping.

THE CONTENTS OF THE SEAS

The charting of Scotland's seas and waters thus reflects many of the features we discuss elsewhere in this book – the value of maps as instruments (for safe navigation, defence and the state's political information), the chronology of institutional support for mapping (1791 on land, 1795 for the seas) and the ways Scots and others gave the nation shape when drawing its waters – as did Adair, Mackenzie, Dalrymple, Murray and Pullar, and others.

Scotland's charting in these ways can be read as a history and a geography, designed, like terrestrial mapping, to know the extent of the nation. Yet, as with much of the country's land mapping, charting has also been concerned with the nation's content, that is, with the economic resources in Scotland's seas. The fact that local commerce – and thus the wealth of a nation – could depend upon safe navigation was not lost on Dumfries Town Council when it commissioned a chart of the Solway Firth in the 1740s (fig. 8.19).

Elsewhere and at other times, Scotland's marine resources lay unrealised because, although local fisher folk might know where fish were to be found, such knowledge was not systematically known, and was not written down in map form. John Knox knew this well, for example, when he compiled his 1782 *Commercial Map of Scotland* in an attempt to map the nation's resources but also, and more vitally, to indicate where the lack of infrastructure hindered economic development. To the north and west, the problem lay with geography: the 'numerous channels' were full of different species of fish but awkward to navigate; in the Shetlands (fig. 8.20), the problem was the Dutch, whose shipping fleets combed the seas so thor-

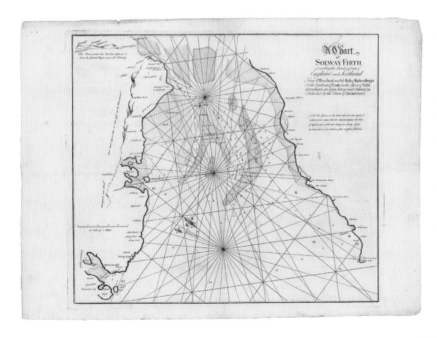

FIGURE 8.19 The safeguarding of the passage of boats up major estuaries with the intention of improving and extending trade was another reason for the production of charts. In this mid-eighteenth-century example for the Solway Firth, Dumfries Town Council Minutes give intriguing details of the original survey work and ensuing production of this chart, which was published by the town itself. The chosen surveyor, Thomas Winter, was initially approached to survey the channel banks at the mouth of the River Nith and to provide a necessary buoy there to aid safe navigation – all for £30 and the provision of a suitable boat from which to work. Having accomplished this, Winter was then asked to extend his work by making a survey of the Solway itself. This took him two months and nine days, for which work he was paid £9 10s per month for the survey work and a further £56 16s 8d for the chart and the fixing of a buoy. The chart was not a financial success. By 1745, only twenty-seven copies had been sold out of the 300 printed.
Source: Thomas Winter, *Chart of Solway Firth Describing the Banks & Coasts of England and Scotland* . . . (1744). Reproduced by permission of the Trustees of the National Library of Scotland.

FIGURE 8.20 *Below. Source:* John Knox,
A Commercial Map of Scotland (1782).
Reproduced by permission of the Trustees
of the National Library of Scotland.

FIGURE 8.21 *Right.* In charting Scotland's sea
coast, the activities which take place around it
also generated maps. Ole Theodor Olsen FRGS,
compass adjustor, nautical instrument maker,
chart and nautical bookseller of Grimsby,
Lincolnshire, produced this remarkable atlas in
1883. It details in a series of individual plates the
distribution of each fish species associated with
the then rich fishing grounds round the British
Isles. These include plates of such well-known
species as herring, haddock, hake, whitebait and
mackerel, but also of lesser-known species such as
ling, garfish, smelt, coalfish and shad. Other plates
include a map of the North Sea Bottom and of
the fishing grounds worked by trawlers, liners
and drifters. A picture is given of where each fish
type was caught in abundance, as well as their
spawning localities.
Source: O. T. Olsen, Haddock plate from *The
Piscatorial Atlas of the North Sea, English Channel
and St George's Channels* (1883). Reproduced by
permission of the Trustees of the National
Library of Scotland.

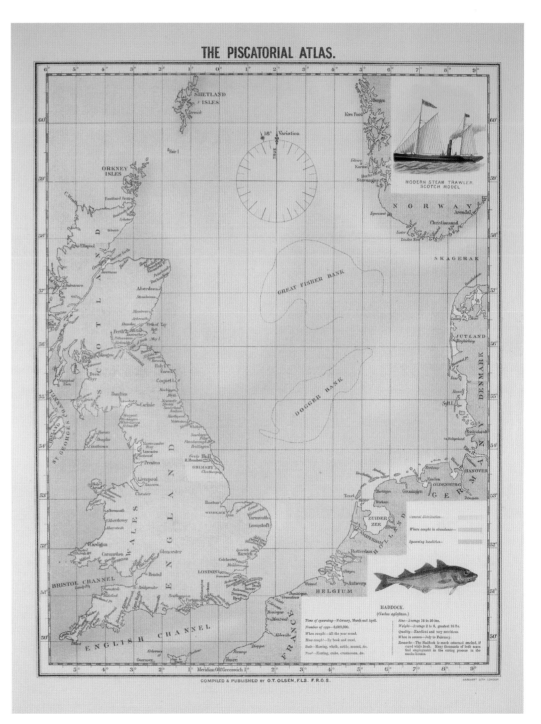

FIGURE 8.22 The importance of the growth of the North Sea oil and gas industry in the latter half of the twentieth century not only had a major impact on Scottish offshore and inshore waters, but also generated maps necessary to the planning and understanding of this key industry. This map shows the initial licence areas in 1965. Ten years later the first oil and gas came ashore in the UK from the Argyle and Forties fields. The subsequent development of Aberdeen (often quoted as the 'Oil Capital of Europe'), Orkney and Shetland with their terminals at Flotta and Sullom Voe, and sundry other Scottish spin-offs has seen the North Sea become the centre of one of the world's major energy industries, with Scotland playing a full part in this. *Source:* British Petroleum, *BP Map showing United Kingdom North Sea Oil and Gas Licence Areas* (1965). Reproduced with permission from BP plc.

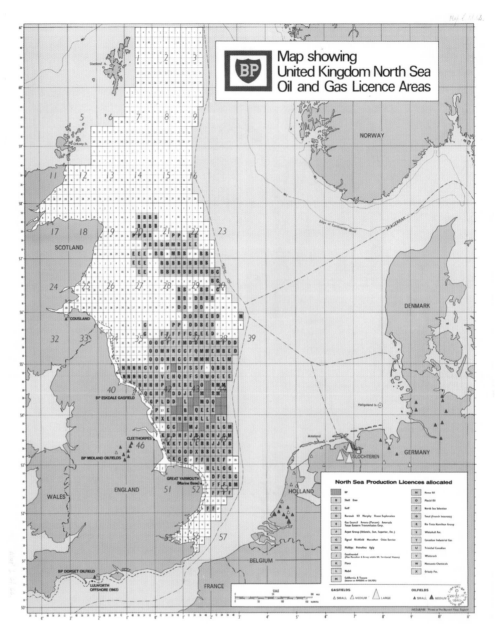

oughly hardly a single herring could be found by the Scots. Maps have been used as a basis to locate fish, or at least to plot fishing grounds (fig. 8.21). Olsen's *Piscatorial Atlas* (1883) is an indication not only of the development of a particular form of map and book history, the atlas. It is also, in being based on the testimony of skippers and fishermen, a good example of how maps in the mind could be translated into maps on the page. Maps of the sea can give a firm impression of clear property lines and so become involved in debates about national territory and national economies (fig. 8.22) even when the sea itself has no such fixed political or commercial affiliation. And maps can show, too, how we need to manage our seas and waters to keep them clean (fig. 8.23).

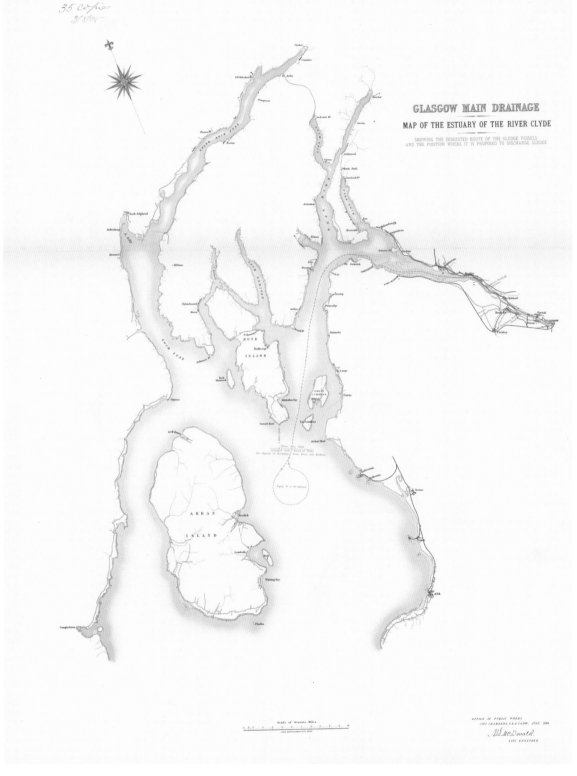

FIGURE 8.23 Another less-known aspect of the charting of Scotland's coastal features is exemplified here. Over a hundred years ago, the problem of sludge disposal occupied the minds of Glasgow's civic leaders. The City Engineer, N. S. McDonald, therefore arranged a 3 mile limit with the Board of Trade for the deposit of dredgings from the River Clyde and its harbours. The outfall position further down the Firth is clearly documented on this map and was at a depth of some 70–90 fathoms. The map was produced and printed by John Bartholomew & Co.; the company's archive records that only 75 copies of this map were printed. It was not a widely publicised matter!

Source: N. S. McDonald, *Glasgow Main Drainage: Map of the Estuary of the River Clyde showing the Suggested Route of the Sludge Vessels and the Position where it is Proposed to Discharge Sludge* (1898). Reproduced by permission of the Trustees of the National Library of Scotland.

STERLING

CHAPTER 9

TRAVEL AND COMMUNICATIONS

Maps showing travel routes and lines of communication – maps of roads, railways or bus routes – are very familiar objects. Modern society is highly mobile, and maps of different types cater for and direct such movement. Such maps need not be printed or electronic. Our mental maps of travel – what we hold in our heads as 'maps' to move between places – and our ways of visualising the world through maps are, of course, conditioned by present-day circumstances. In turn, modern maps determine patterns of movement: think of in-car navigation systems which may select the quickest route (time) as opposed to the shortest (distance). More than other sorts of maps perhaps, and certainly more than other information sources, maps to do with travel direct human mobility and make up the commonest form of maps today.

Yet using a map to find our way is a recent phenomenon. Until the twentieth century, the vast majority of people did not travel far. Before the eighteenth century, the few people who did travel rarely used maps to help them find their way. With the possible exception of sea charts, early maps were not created or used as route finders. The travel map thus has a particular history as a map type. More than that, such maps can help illuminate how conceptions of travel have changed over time, and how the requirements of movement over space gave rise to a certain sort of document about travel.

Travel maps indicate how perceptions of distance and accessibility radically altered with new modes of transport. They indicate the slow but growing awareness, particularly from the later seventeenth century in Europe, of the importance of a spatial or geographical perspective for travellers – thinking about a journey graphically rather than as an ordered list of places. Once represented graphically, journeys could be represented in terms of time as well as linear distance, or travel could be shown as a line of movement such that ancillary detail to the 'side' did not matter (and so need not be mapped). Travel maps thus provide a more deliberately partial view of the world than most other maps. This is not just because of their obvious focus on transport routes to the exclusion of other features, but is also due to the different purposes behind the mapping: to encourage construction of a transport link in the first place, to reassure investors of its financial viability, to promote travel by that means rather than another, and so on. Travel mapping as a genre clearly aims at different audiences – army officers, manufacturers, government planners and tourists might all have need of a travel map, but different types for different purposes.

Scotland's maps and mapping history offer a good example to illustrate these matters: there is, for Scotland, a long history of travel and a much shorter history of travel maps. There are routeways across Scotland today which date from every period in its history: routes made by pre-Celtic ancestors, converging on barrows, brochs and cairns; Roman roads, constructed with massive solidity, boldly driven by invaders across the southern and eastern parts of Scotland; roads created by pilgrims and drovers; roads made by military engineers in the eighteenth century; roads made by turnpike trusts, or resulting from acts of enclosure; coaching roads and Parliamentary roads. More recently, canals, railways (above and below ground), cycle routes, motorways and air travel often either follow or complement existing lines of communication.

If most maps in the past were not made for travel, who travelled Scotland's routeways, and how did they find their way? The conveyance of a verbal message or a letter on government or military business involved single riders, or relays of riders. The transport of more bulky or heavy goods, such as wool, hides or timber, involved trains of pack animals, wagons and carts, under the guidance of a merchant or his assistants. These people did not use maps for travel because they relied instead upon an array of oral and written information that can be loosely described under the term 'itinerary'. Written itineraries served their purpose well (and still do today: think, for example, of the short written accompaniments to maps of hill walks or town trails).

So why did people turn to maps for travel? Part of the answer lies in the differing purposes of journeys and the growing need to provide for more than a linear itinerary and to allow a degree of choice between alternative routes. Partly, too, travel maps reflect a growing variety in types of traveller and in the different technical bases to travel: remembered and time-worn routes through the hills, for example, might need to be written down, not just held in the head, if that route was to be developed; railway construction required new maps of a country since steep topography had to be overcome. And people turned to maps for travel because of the importance of maps as portable documents allowing a view of the land – that overhead perspective which provides a rationale for mapping as a whole – and a depiction of where places and features stand in relation to one another.

EARLY WAY-FINDING

The evidence of routeways is clear on some early maps of Scotland. This evidence is complemented by some later maps which incorporate evidence of earlier routeways. We know, for example, from twelfth-century monastic and other charters that there was by then a network of communication in Scotland. Very often these charters describe routes that have left their imprint on later maps, particularly through the course of parish boundaries. Routes of considerable antiquity also appear on maps, such as the Wheel Causeway used by Edward I in 1296 to cross the Cheviots (which appears on Tennant's map of Roxburghshire in 1840) (fig. 9.1 [A]), or trade ways such as the herring road from Dunbar to Lauder (which is shown on Roy's Military Survey of the early 1750s as the 'Muir Road'). The medieval road from Soutra to Melrose (known later as the 'Girthgate', and which appears on Armstrong's map of the Lothians of 1773) (fig. 9.1 [B]) may be prehistoric in origin, the

[A]

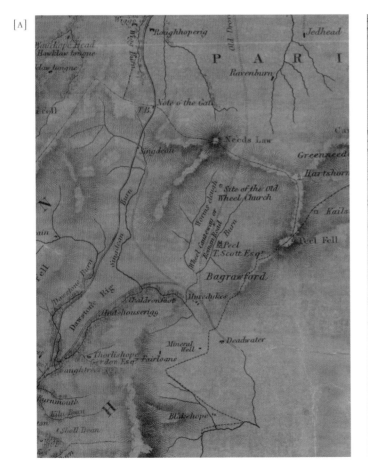

[B]

FIGURE 9.1 [A] *Source:* N. Tennant, *Map of the County of Roxburgh* (1840). Reproduced by permission of the Trustees of the National Library of Scotland.

FIGURE 9.1 [B] *Source:* Andrew and Mostyn Armstrong, *Map of the Three Lothians* (1773). Reproduced by permission of the Trustees of the National Library of Scotland.

FIGURE 9.3 Although figurative, Pont's distinctive outline of Ben Loyal in Sutherland can also locate his point of observation of the mountain on the ground. The position of the crowned An Caisteal (the castle or the fort) summit, only appears in this form at a particular place on the shore of Loch Loyal to the east: in Pont's time there was a small settlement here on the route north to Tongue.
Source: Timothy Pont, Representation of Ben Loyal, from Pont 1 (1583–1614). Reproduced by permission of the Trustees of the National Library of Scotland.

FIGURE 9.2 The barrier of the Mounth was enshrined in administrative documents and in statute. The fact that the Causey Mounth is the only clearly shown 'road' on a Pont map is significant in itself, as this was one of very few routeways that had been lined as a 'causey', or bedding of stones. One of the earliest records of it is in a charter of 1384 by John Crab of Kincorth, granting money for the maintenance of the bridge of Dee and Causey Mounth, but the route had probably been in use long before then. The Causey Mounth was of vital importance to Aberdeen and its communications and trade with the south, and before Pont's time three-quarters of the mile of causey had been built over the moss to the south of Aberdeen.
Source: Timothy Pont, Detail of Causey Mounth, from Pont 11 (*c.*1583–1614). Reproduced by permission of the Trustees of the National Library of Scotland.

Roman line of communication following an already-established route. The Minchmoor road from Peebles to Yarrow, which was used as a drove road and is named as such on John Thomson's 1824 map of Selkirkshire, was in use in the thirteenth century as part of the road between Kelso Abbey and its lands at Lesmahagow.

Timothy Pont's maps of Scotland allow inferences rather more than stated certainties regarding routeways and roads (fig. 9.2). This is because his maps are richer in related information – the location of entrances to burghs, for example, bridges, written notes on roads, and Pont's own itineraries – than they are as unequivocal sources for established routes of travel. If the evidence of the Pont and Gordon manuscript maps is combined with that of the Blaeu printed maps to provide national coverage, 294 bridges are shown for Scotland as a whole. Roads do not feature as much. This emphasis on bridges is to be expected. The main investment in communications prior to the eighteenth century was in bridge building. The distribution of bridges suggests that they were built for local convenience. Nevertheless, Pont's texts record the Rad-na-Pheny or 'way of wane wheills' – later known as 'Comyn's Road' – from Ruthven to Blair Atholl, which probably dates to the thirteenth century. We can also use his maps to determine which route Pont himself used: his view of Ben Loyal in Sutherland, for example, can be clearly located to a point by Loch Loyal to the east on a recorded routeway from the south towards Tongue (fig. 9.3).

Printed travel maps date from the 1670s. National maps for this purpose (fig. 9.4) were accompanied by county-based maps: the Reverend Robert Edward in his *Angusia* map of 1678 provides the first mapped depiction of routeways in Angus. And John Adair has left us a picture of at least the major routeways and bridges on his county maps. Other important graphical depictions of routeways also survive from this time: the Earl of Panmure, a patron for Edward's map, also helped finance the first known depiction of the 'leading lights' to guide the entry of ships into the Tay shown on John Marr's chart of the 1680s (fig. 8.10).

These endeavours closely followed developments elsewhere, and a Scot led the way. The earliest road atlas of England and Wales, *Britannia*, was published in 1675 by John Ogilby, who was born in Kirriemuir in 1600. It might seem strange for a person such as Ogilby to have made the advances in map-making that he did in *Britannia*: he was earlier involved in the theatre as a court dancer and actor in masques. In organising the civic displays and pageants in 1661 to celebrate the restoration of King Charles II, Ogilby effectively promoted geography as a form of street theatre, secured Royal patronage and established the basis by which he could make his name, make money and publish books and maps. (Ogilby held the title 'Master of the King's Imprimeries' (the King's Printer) as well as that of 'His Majesty's Cosmographer and Geographic Printer'.) He moved, moreover, in London's social world of emergent science and political influence (peers and friends included Robert Hooke and John Aubrey) and in an age – as we have seen for Adair, Martin and Sibbald – when new geographical information was reckoned vital to the prosperity of the nation.

Britannia was based on original survey and stimulated a new interest in depicting roads on maps (fig. 9.5). With its 200 pages of text and 100 strip maps, it illustrated 7,500 miles of roads in England and Wales. It was probably never an easy travelling companion – it weighed over 7 kilograms – but it was hugely influential, for its style, for its basis in new work and because it spawned a whole generation of similar maps, notably reduced-size pocket editions, throughout the eighteenth century. These were neither always original nor up-to-date, but they were popular because they were cheap and convenient (fig. 9.6). Other elements of Ogilby's *Britannia* – the importance of original survey and its depiction of routes at the scale of 1 inch to the mile – influenced county and Ordnance Survey maps.

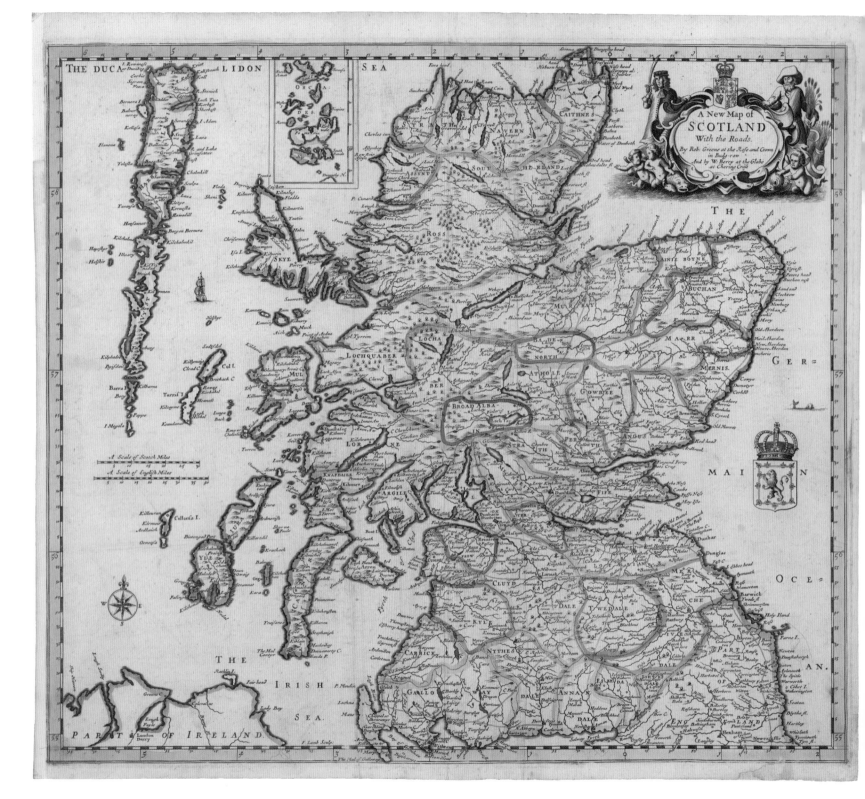

THE DUCALIDON SEA

ORCADES

A New Map of
SCOTLAND
With the Roads.
By Rob: Greene at the Rose and Crown
in Budg-row
And by W. Berry at the Globe
at Chering Cross

THE

GER=

MAIN

OCE=

A Scale of Scotch Miles
A Scale of English Miles

CAITHNES

STRATH

NAVERN

SUTHERLAND

ASSYNT

ROSS

SKYE

MURRAY

BUCHAN

MARR

MERNIS

LOCHABER

LOCHQUABER

ATHOLE

NORTH

BROAD ALBA

GOWRIE

MUL

LORNE

FERNE

PERTH

ANGUS

STRATH

ARGILE

FIFE

KNAFDAILE

Barra I.

CLUYD

LODEN

TWEDALE

MERCHE

CARRICK

NYTHESDALE

PART

KYLE

OF

GALLOWAY

ANNANDALE

DALE

ENGLAND

AN.

THE
IRISH
SEA

PARTE OF IRELAND

F. Lamb Sculp.

The Mull of Galloway

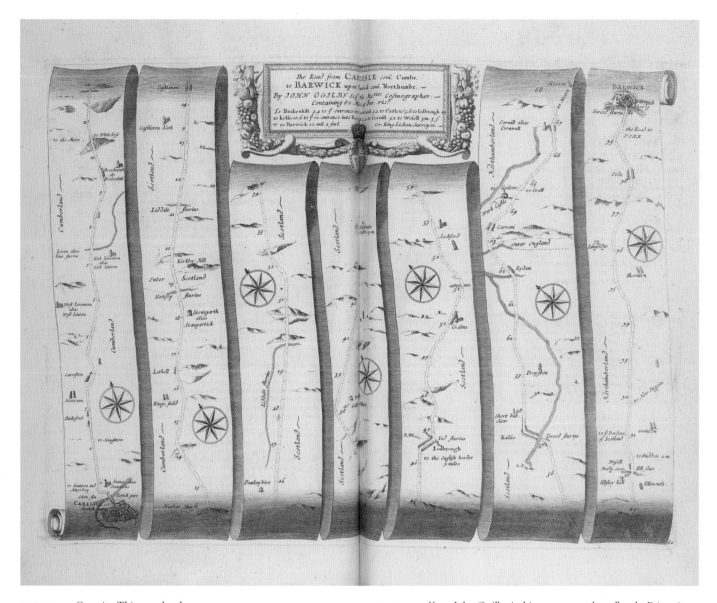

FIGURE 9.4 *Opposite*. This map by the London map seller Robert Greene is credited with being Scotland's earliest road map.
Source: Robert Greene, *A New Map of Scotland with the Roads* (1679). Reproduced by permission of the Trustees of the National Library of Scotland.

FIGURE 9.5 *Above*. John Ogilby in his monumental roadbook, *Britannia*, indicates on the title page that he is concerned only with the depiction of roads in England and Wales. However, a closer look at the road from Carlisle to Berwick-upon-Tweed reveals he was required to include a part of Scotland in order to portray the 55-mile stretch of road from Scotsdyke, 2 miles north of Longtown, up Liddesdale, across to Bonchester Bridge and on through Jedburgh and Kelso to re-cross the national border back into England near Coldstream.
Source: John Ogilby, 'The Road from Carlisle . . . to Barwick [sic] upon Tweed . . .', Plate 62 from *Britannia, Volume the First: Or, an Illustration of the Kingdom of England and Dominion of Wales . . .* (1675). Reproduced by permission of the Trustees of the National Library of Scotland.

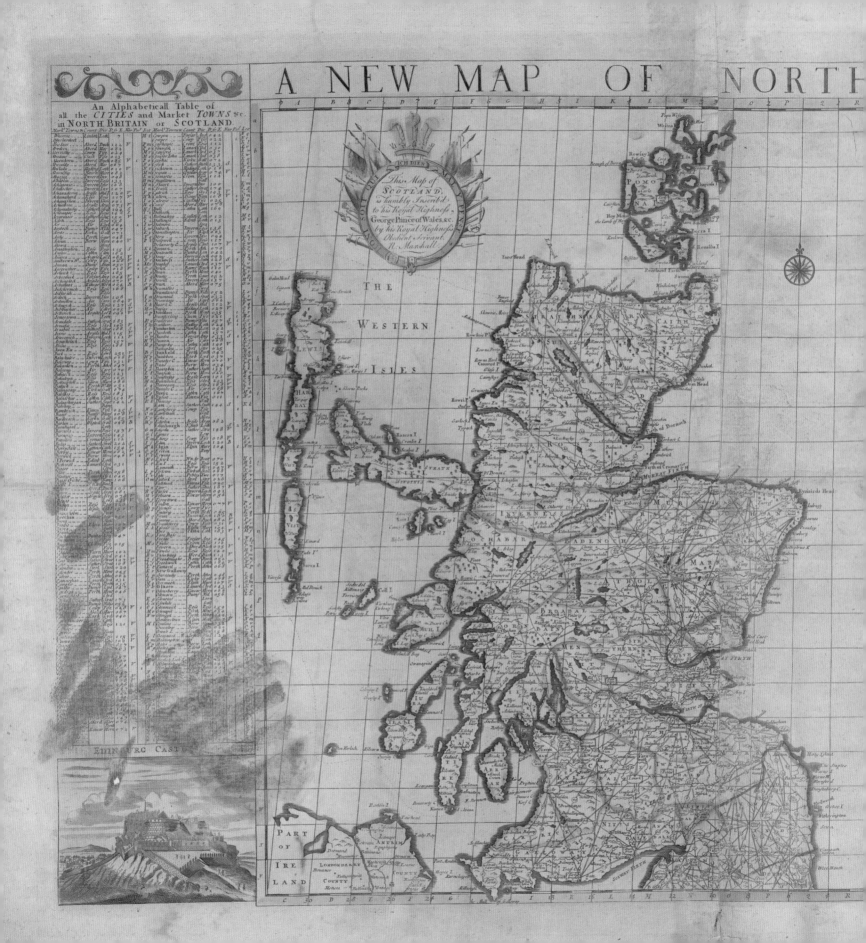

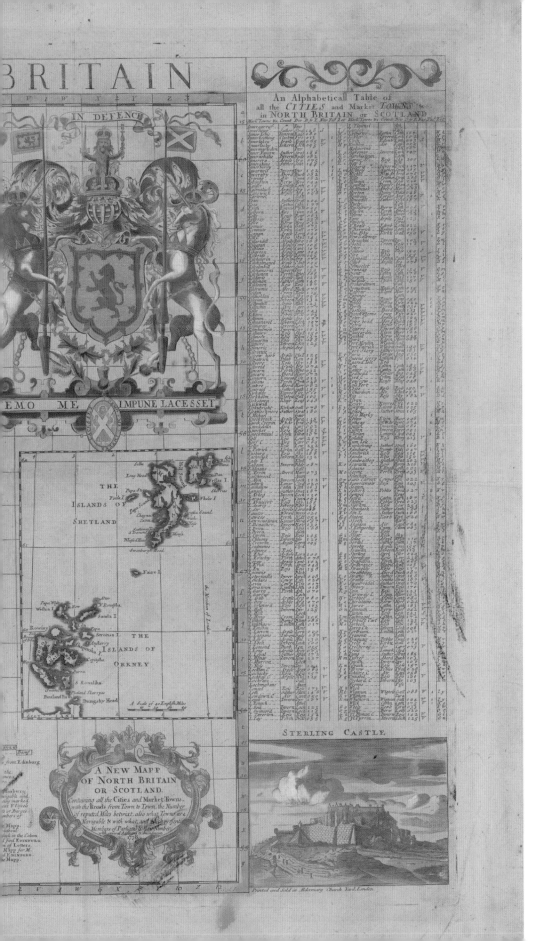

FIGURE 9.6 Sutton Nicholls' map, which was probably influenced by John Adams' 'distance line' maps of the 1670s for England and Wales, is the earliest 'distance line' map of Scotland. The map information is derived largely from Herman Moll's maps of Scotland, and in turn from the surveys of John Adair, so it was hardly up to date. Nor did it aim to include any detailed information on the roads themselves. 'Distance line' maps such as this were popular, however, as route planners in the itinerary tradition, and had practical and commercial applications as indicators of distance to markets.

Source: Sutton Nicholls, *A New Mapp of North Britain or Scotland (c.*1710). Reproduced by permission of the Trustees of the National Library of Scotland.

EIGHTEENTH-CENTURY ADVANCES

Although Scotland's military roads are often taken to be the work of Hanoverian engineers, there were important military motives behind early road building prior to the eighteenth century. The early postal network was lent impetus by the wars with England's Edward IV in the 1480s, for example, and by the Rough Wooing in the 1540s (see chapter 4). In the 1640s, conflicts in Cromwellian Ireland led to the upgrading of the road from Edinburgh to Portpatrick via Blackburn, Hamilton, Ayr, Girvan and Ballantrae.

Nevertheless, the eighteenth century witnessed considerable expansion in Scotland's road network. From 1725 until his departure from Scotland in 1740, General George Wade, Commander-in-Chief for North Britain, was responsible for planning the construction of about 250 miles of roads. Wade's protégé as Inspector of Roads, Major William Caulfeild, oversaw the construction of over three times this distance, some 830 miles of roads, before 1767 (fig. 9.7). Military road building – and the related maps by engineers to show them – was a priority after the 1745 Rebellion. As peace broke out, however, military expenditure on roads declined from the mid-eighteenth century, with responsibility for roads devolving to local landowners and county administrations.

From the late eighteenth century, the steady expansion of roads across Scotland is evident in travel maps, which appeared in ever greater numbers (fig. 9.8). The first Turnpike Trust was established in Midlothian in 1714, but the Turnpike Acts (which set up local tolls to secure funding for road building) were not applied in

FIGURE 9.7 Through its attractive use of colour and line style, this manuscript military map of Glen Shee clearly distinguishes the 'Made roads' and 'Roads still to be made' as well as the 'Dry Stone Walls' and 'Back Drains'. In pre-tarmacadam days, one of the major challenges of road maintenance in the Highlands was trying to prevent the surface (of rammed stones) being washed away. Effective drains were therefore important. The Glen Shee road was a key routeway from Perth and Blairgowrie to Braemar on Deeside. Maps such as these also reveal the emerging military colour scheme and styles in representing terrain and military topography (see chapter 4). With its attractive cartouche and finished appearance, maps such as these were of value in demonstrating progress to the Board of Ordnance in London and for justifying the major expenditure on roads.
Source: John Archer, *A Survey of the Road made by the Detachmt. of Genl. Guise's Regt. in Brae Marr, beginning where Genl. Blakeney's Left off . . . Continued to the Spittle of Glen-Shee* (1749). Reproduced by permission of the Trustees of the National Library of Scotland.

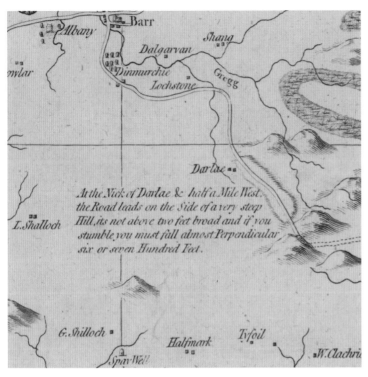

Within the map: *At the Nick of Darlae & half a Mile West, the Road leads on the Side of a very steep Hill, its not above two feet broad and if you stumble you must fall almost Perpendicular, six or seven Hundred Feet.*

FIGURE 9.8 This note from Andrew and Mostyn Armstrong's *A New Map of Ayr Shire* (1775), is a reminder of how dangerous travel could be, and how poor roads were, even in the Lowlands – this detail is from Carrick in Ayrshire.
Source: Andrew and Mostyn Armstrong, *A New Map of Ayr Shire* (1775). Reproduced by permission of the Trustees of the National Library of Scotland.

force until the later eighteenth and early nineteenth centuries. Between 1750 and 1844, some 350 local Turnpike Acts were passed in Scotland, and these led to rapid developments in the road network, especially in the more densely populated parts of the country. One of the most distinctive travel maps of the period was produced by the Aberdonian surveyor George Taylor and his Edinburgh counterpart, Andrew Skinner, in 1776 (fig. 9.9): although based on Ogilby's format, this is the Enlightenment's road atlas. From 1813, all proposals submitted to Parliament for new roads had to be accompanied by plans. And, as the government regulated its surveyors, so enterprising individuals turned to travel maps to guide the curious tourist (fig. 9.10).

In the Highlands by the late eighteenth century, new roads were increasingly seen as a means of stimulating economic growth and stemming emigration (fig. 9.11). The Commissioners for the Annexed Forfeited Estates encouraged road building as a means of pacifying and improving the Highlands. Through the work of the British Fisheries Society, new roads were surveyed by George Brown in the 1790s across Sutherland, Caithness, Ross-shire and Inverness-shire. From 1803 to 1821, the Parliamentary Commission for Highland Roads and Bridges was responsible for constructing 920 miles of roads and 1,117 bridges. As well as commissioning Aaron Arrowsmith's landmark topographical map of Scotland of 1807 (figs. 1.16, 1.17), each of the Commission's progress reports to Parliament carried maps, showing roads completed or under contract in red, and those under construction in green (fig. 9.12). Their work continued until 1862.

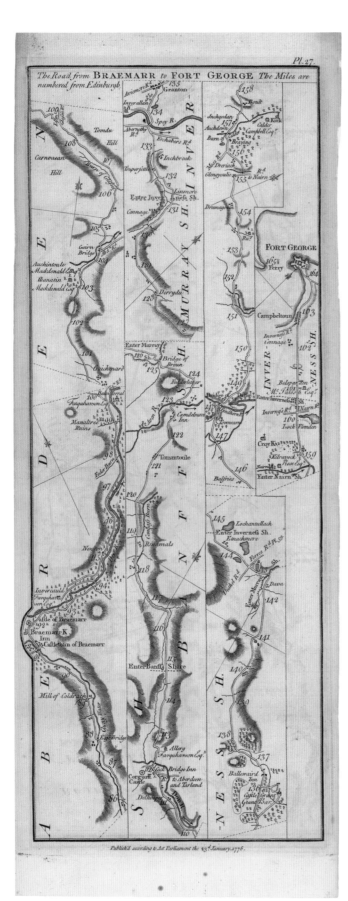

FIGURE 9.9 *Left*. The surveyors George Taylor and
Andrew Skinner were responsible for Scotland's first road
atlas in 1776, including sixty-one plates of roads shown in
strips. Although financed by subscription, a fact which is
evident in their flattery of local landowners and gentry
on the map, the publication was not successful in its day.
In 1778, 1,457 copies remained unsold, a reflection both
of the relatively small number of travellers then in
Scotland, and their limited need for detailed road
mapping. The map is now immensely useful for the
historian of routeways.
Source: George Taylor and Andrew Skinner, 'The Road
from Braemarr [sic] to Fort George', Plate 27, from Taylor
and Skinner's *Survey and Maps of the Roads of North
Britain, or Scotland* (1776). Reproduced by permission of
the Trustees of the National Library of Scotland.

*J. Ainslie will think himself much obliged
to the Commissioners for any New Roads or other
Gentlemen who will transmit to him an account
of such Roads with the Names of the several
Towns thereon and their distances from each other
which shall be Inserted and if desired he will
send them an Impression of the Plate to Satisfy
them of his care*

FIGURE 9.10 *Opposite and detail above*. John Ainslie was
one of Scotland's greatest map-makers. His impressive
1789 *Map of Scotland*, engraved in a series of angles and
astronomical observations, was the standard map of the
country for two decades. Ainslie also drafted smaller maps
such as this to cater for the new breed of 'romantic'
travellers to Scotland then arriving in numbers. Residents
also had use of such maps: the poet Robert Burns,
writing to his friend Peter Hill on 2 April 1789 to ask
him to forward certain books, wrote, 'I'll expect along
with the trunk my Ainslie's Map of Scotland'.
Source: John Ainslie, *Ainslies Travelling Map of Scotland,
shewing the Distances from one Stage to Another* (1789).
Reproduced by permission of the Trustees of the
National Library of Scotland.

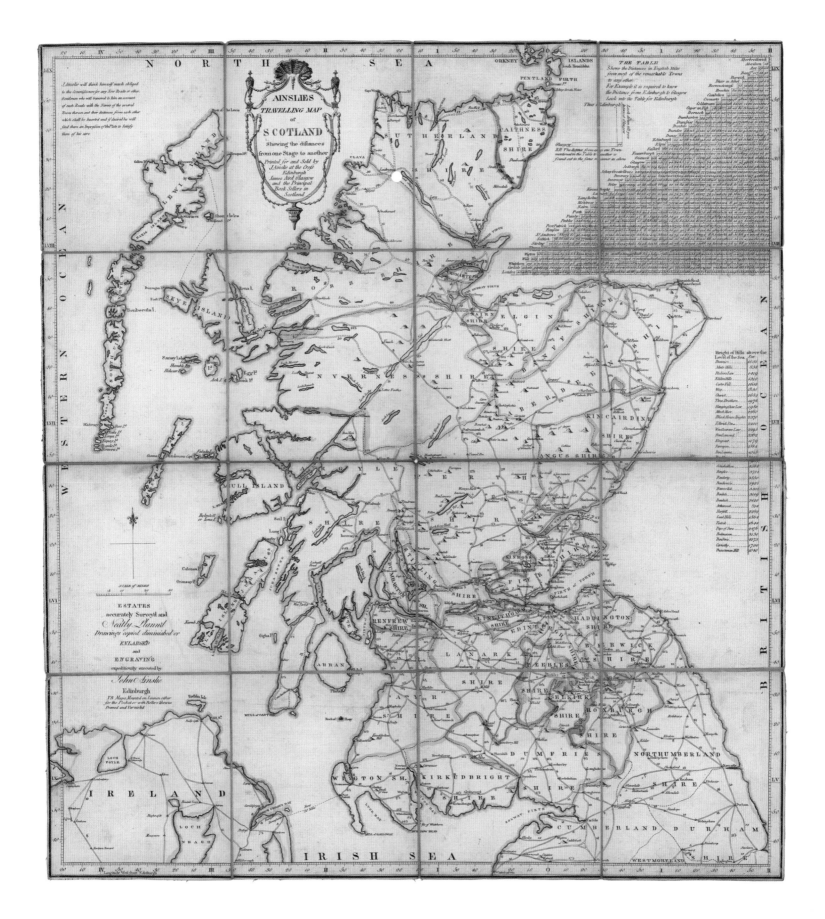

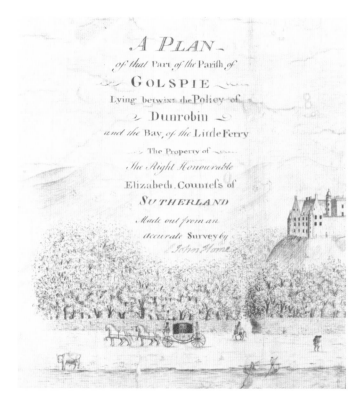

FIGURE 9.11 *Left.* The manuscript cartouche with its ferryman, travellers on foot, on horseback and in a stagecoach, set against the backdrop of Dunrobin Castle, nicely captures multiple means of travel in the 1770s. *Source:* John Home, *A Plan of that Part of the Parish of Golspie Lying betwixt the Policy of Dunrobin and the Bay of the Little Ferry the Property of the Right Honourable Elizabeth, Countess of Sutherland (c.1772).* Reproduced by permission of the Countess of Sutherland.

FIGURE 9.12 *Below.* The Parliamentary Commission for Highland Roads and Bridges' reports to Parliament carried maps to show updated progress in their work, using a topographic base by Aaron Arrowsmith, reduced from his much more detailed 1807 map of Scotland. This particular map, from the Commission's Fifth Report in 1811, shows several new roads (in green) under construction in Sutherland and Caithness, as well as a considerable network further south (in red) already built since 1803. The yellow lines are military roads, already in existence.
Source: Aaron Arrowsmith, *Map of Scotland from Original Materials obtained by the Parliamentary Commissioners for Highland Roads and Bridges: and exhibiting the Roads and Bridges Made, Constructed for, or under Construction* (1811). Reproduced by permission of the Trustees of the National Library of Scotland.

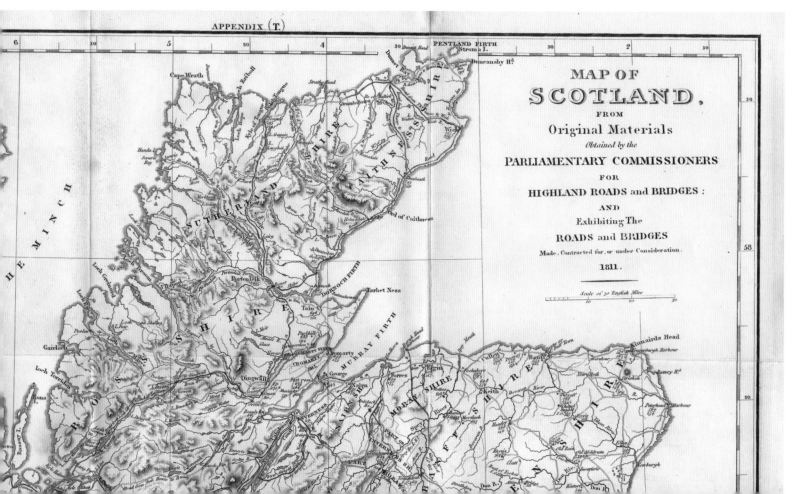

NEW MAPS, NEW MARKETS: NINETEENTH-CENTURY DEVELOPMENTS

In Scotland, as elsewhere, there was a rapid expansion in transportation cartography in the nineteenth century. This reflects developments in the technologies of travel. The spread of the canal network from the 1760s and of railways from the 1820s required new maps – often in large quantities (fig. 9.13). The work of civil engineers, then as now, is intimately cartographic, and, for all these and other engineering proposals, maps were required to plan work and to stimulate commercial interest and support, particularly in order to raise capital from potential shareholders. Maps were required to obtain Parliamentary assent through a private act, and as work progressed, or plans changed, maps were required to reassure those involved, purchase the land, locate the routes and demonstrate future importance.

Several of the most famous map-makers and engineers worked on travel projects in Scotland – on road, canal, railway, harbour and lighthouse work – including John Smeaton, John Ainslie, James Watt, John Rennie, Joseph Huddart, Robert Whitworth, Thomas Telford, Murdo Downie, Joseph Mitchell and the Stevenson family (figs. 9.14, 9.15, 9.16, 9.17, 9.18). Many more proposals were put forward than were ever developed, especially during the years of railway 'mania' in the 1840s, with the result that a variety of hypothetical and imaginary schemes survive on maps, triumphs of optimism and confidence to facilitate communication, including Scotland's own Victorian 'Celtic Sea Tunnel' (fig. 9.19).

In acknowledging this growth in travel maps, we must not neglect broader changes in map publishing and map consumption. The rise in literacy and education in association with newspapers and new printing technologies – particularly lithography and steel engraving – allowed massive print runs at relatively low costs and so encouraged map production and use. Maps became a feature of public life. More detailed maps for planning and engineering were used to produce more portable travel and road maps, often at smaller scales. For touring, trade, government, science, and in the schoolroom, maps of roads and routes appeared in different guises. Sheet maps showing transportation routes were published in a variety of bound formats and appeared in an ever-wider printed array – in journals, scientific transactions, tourist guides, geography books, advertisements and directories.

FIGURE 9.13 This extract from a map covering a wide area of Central Lanarkshire exemplifies the close connections between mining, heavy industry and rail links in this part of Scotland in the late nineteenth century. It also illustrates how important mining was to this area at this time: in 1871, there were 22,663 coal miners in Lanarkshire, 63% of all miners in Scotland. The map shows coal and ironstone mines as circular symbols, with existing and proposed railways as continuous and dashed lines respectively. The red lines are those of the Caledonian Railway Company – all the black lines were private goods lines. Most usefully, the map also serves as a cadastral map, showing the names of all the lease holders of mineral rights. Nearly all other features of the landscape are erased. Over the next three decades, coal output across Scotland trebled, and the landscape of this area was irreversibly changed through mining and related heavy industries.

Source: Anon., Map of Central Lanarkshire, showing coal and ironstone mines, lease holders to mineral rights and existing and proposed railways including mineral lines (1872).

Reproduced by permission of the Trustees of the National Library of Scotland.

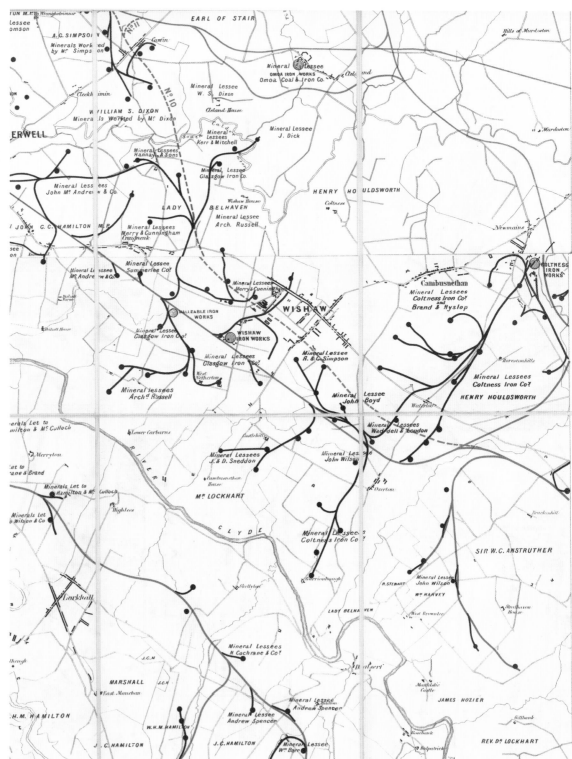

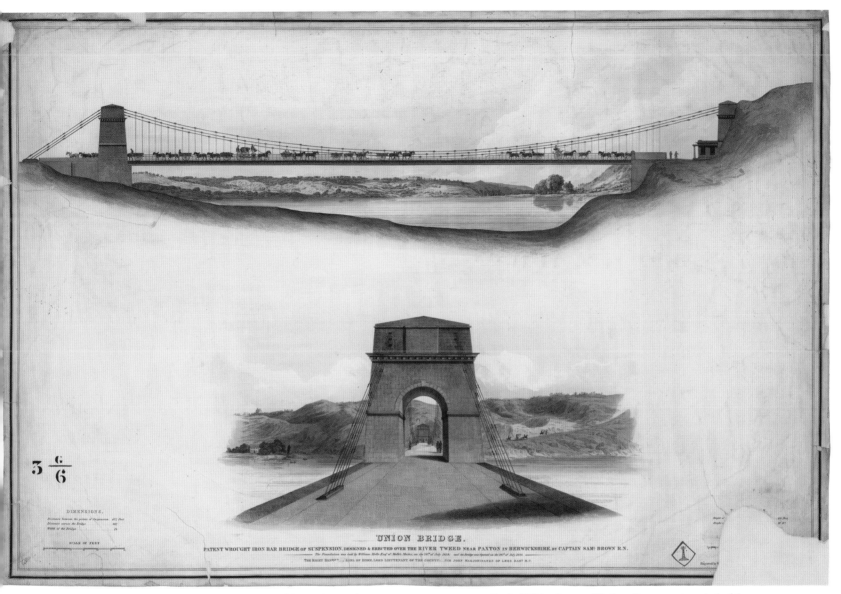

$3\frac{6}{6}$

DIMENSIONS.

UNION BRIDGE.

PATENT WROUGHT IRON BAR BRIDGE OF SUSPENSION, DESIGNED & ERECTED OVER THE RIVER TWEED NEAR PAXTON IN BERWICKSHIRE, BY CAPTAIN SAM! BROWN R.N.

FIGURE 9.14 This stunning profile and view of the Union Bridge near Paxton in Berwickshire is from the NLS Stevenson Archive. The Union Bridge was designed by Captain Samuel Brown of the Royal Navy, following revisions by John Rennie. When it opened in July 1820, uniting Scotland with England across the River Tweed, it was the longest wrought-iron suspension bridge in the world, with a span of 137 metres (449 feet), and the first vehicular bridge of its type in Britain. *Source:* [W. H. Lizars], View of the Union Bridge, Paxton, Berwickshire ([1820]). Reproduced by permission of the Trustees of the National Library of Scotland.

FIGURE 9.15 *Overleaf.* This scheme of Robert Stevenson is typical of the many railway plans proposed but not constructed. As gradients and the terrain were so important, the plan and profile were of a standard form, the latter, as in this case, also allowing the underlying rocks to be shown. Characteristically, the plan also names those landowners from whom land would need to be purchased. The eventual railway between Brechin and Montrose took a more southerly route. *Source:* Robert Stevenson, *Reduced Survey & Section of a Line of Railway from the Port of Montrose to the Borough of Brechin . . .* (1825). Reproduced by permission of the Trustees of the National Library of Scotland.

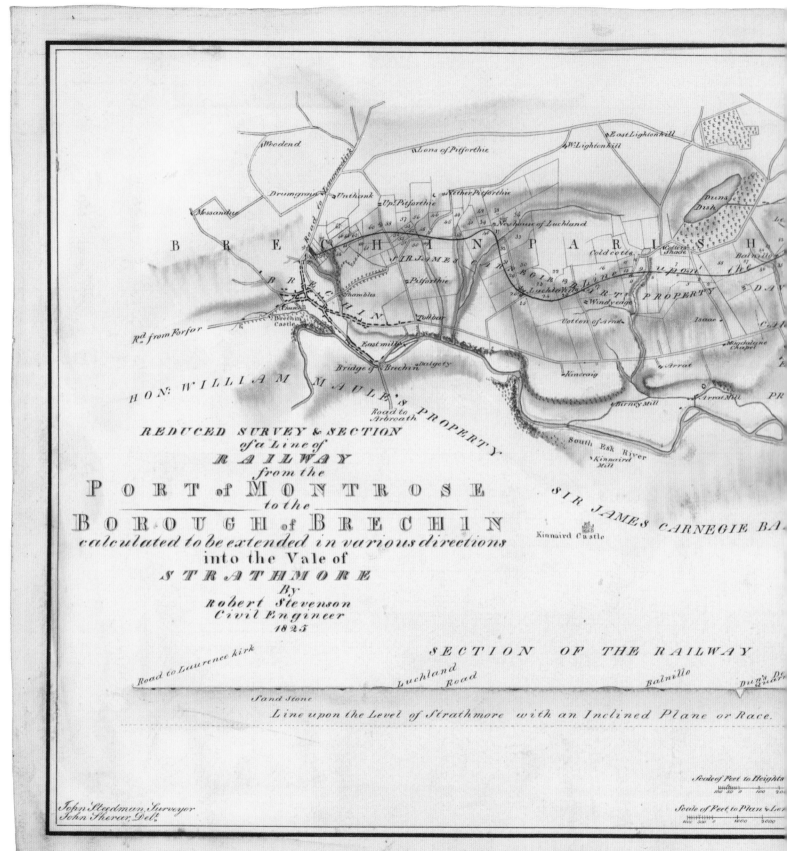

Woodend · Lons of Pitforthie · East Lightonhill · Wt Lightonhill

Drumgray · Unthank · Upr Pitforthie · Nether Pitforthie · Duns Dish

Road to Menmuirkirk

Messandue

B R E C H I N   P A R I S H

SIR JAMES CARNOIR LINE UPON the DAV...

Cold cotts · Balnillo

PROPERTY

B R E C H I N · Pitforthie · Nr house of Luchland

Church · Brechin Castle · Shambles · Luchie Wells · Windyeage

Cotton of Arrat · Isaac

Rd from Forfar · Tollbar · Magdalene Chapel

East mills

Bridge of Brechin · Dalgety · Kincraig · Arrat

HON: WILLIAM MAULE'S PROPERTY · Birney Mill · Arrat Mill · PR...

Road to Arbroath · SIR JAMES CARNEGIE BA...

South Esk River · Kinnaird Mill

REDUCED SURVEY & SECTION
of a Line of
RAILWAY
from the
PORT of MONTROSE
to the
BOROUGH of BRECHIN
calculated to be extended in various directions
into the Vale of
STRATHMORE
By
Robert Stevenson
Civil Engineer
1825

Kinnaird Castle

SECTION   OF   THE   RAILWAY

Road to Laurence kirk · Luchland Road · Balnillo · Dun's De... Grea...

Sand Stone

Line upon the Level of Strathmore with an Inclined Plane or Race.

John Steedman, Surveyor
John Sherer, Delt.

Scale of Feet to Heights
100 50 0 100 200

Scale of Feet to Plan & Len...
1000 500 0 1000 2000

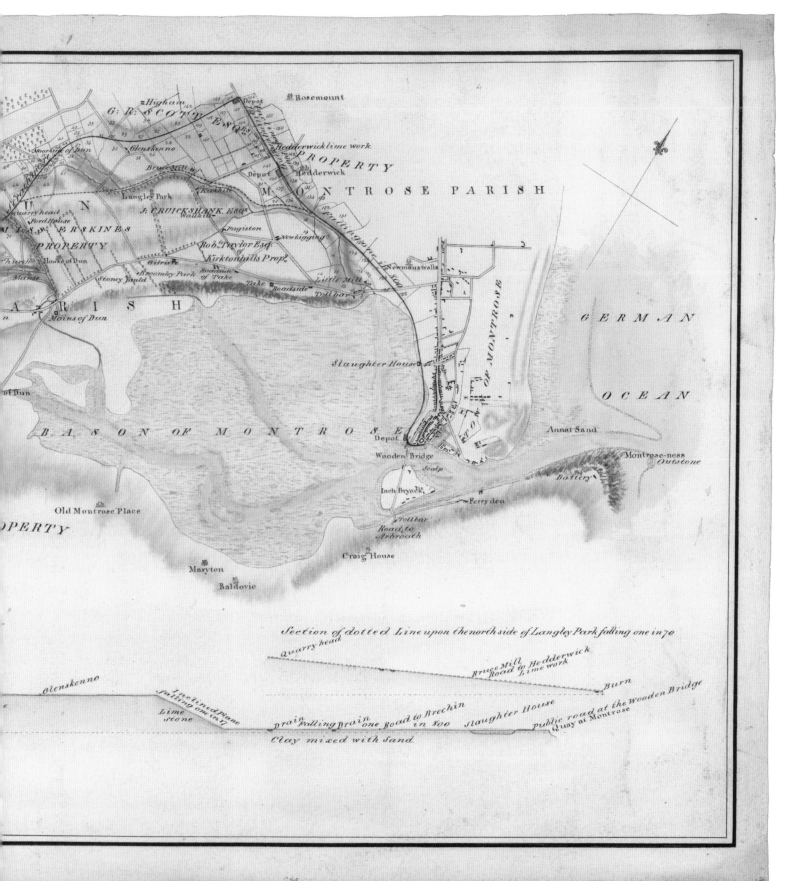

Rosemount

Higham

G: R: SCOTT E. SQ.

Glenskenno

Hedderwick lime work.

Bruce Mill

Depot

Hedderwick

PROPERTY

M

MONTROSE PARISH

Langley Park

Kirkhill

N

J: CRUICKSHANK. ESQ.

Wodhill

Quarry head

Ford House

Pugiston

ERSKINES

PROPERTY

Newbigging

Rob.t Taylor Esq.r

Oitrik

Kirktonhills Prop.r

Newmanswalls

Church

House of Dun

Broomley Park

Roadside

Manse

Stoney fauld

of Take

Take

Roadside

Little Mill

Toll bar

P A R I S H

Mains of Dun

GERMAN

Slaughter House

OF MONTROSE

of Dun

OCEAN

B A S O N   O F   M O N T R O S E

Annat Sand

Depot

Wooden Bridge

Montrose-ness

Scalp

Outstone

Old Montrose Place

Inch Bryock

Battery

Ferry den

OPERTY

Tollbar

Road to

Arbroath

Craig House

Maryton

Baldovie

Section of dotted Line upon the north side of Langley Park falling one in 70

Quarry head

Bruce Mill

Road to Hedderwick

Lime work

Glenskenno

Burn

Inclined plane

falling one in 11

Lime

stone

drain

Falling Drain

one

Road to Brechin

in 800

Slaughter House

public road at the Wooden Bridge

Quay at Montrose

Clay mixed with Sand.

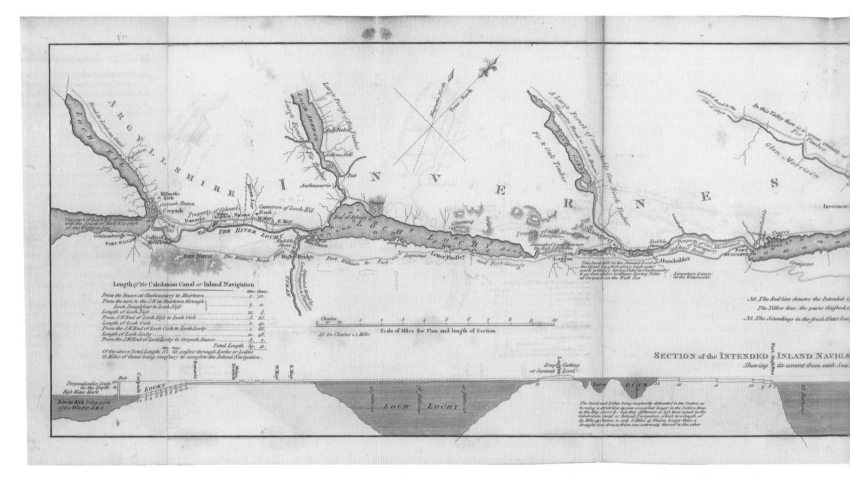

FIGURE 9.16 The Caledonian Canal, the most ambitious and magnificent of Scotland's canals, was constructed during the Napoleonic Wars to allow ships to avoid the dangers of the Pentland Firth and attacks by French privateers. Thomas Telford, the canal's main engineer, originally estimated the canal could be completed in seven years at a cost of £350,000. In the end, the canal cost double this amount and took three times as long to open and for only limited use. As well as having to overcome difficulties of terrain and climate, there were problems in retaining labourers and disputes with landowners in the Great Glen. Cameron of Lochiel and MacDonnell of Glengarry objected strongly to the canal; the latter in one case drove the workmen away with physical force. Some £50,000 was paid out to acquire land, and pay compensation for loss of privacy and disruption to fisheries. Each year Telford was required to report to the House of Commons on progress towards completing the canal. This engraved map of the area, based on existing maps and surveys by Murdo Downie, was marked up to show progress: red to show the intended canal, yellow to show the sections finished or in hand.

Source: Thomas Telford and John Downie, *General Map of the Intended Caledonian Canal or Inland Navigation, from the Eastern to the Western Sea, by Inverness and Fort William. By Messrs Telford & Downie.* Reproduced by permission of the Trustees of the National Library of Scotland.

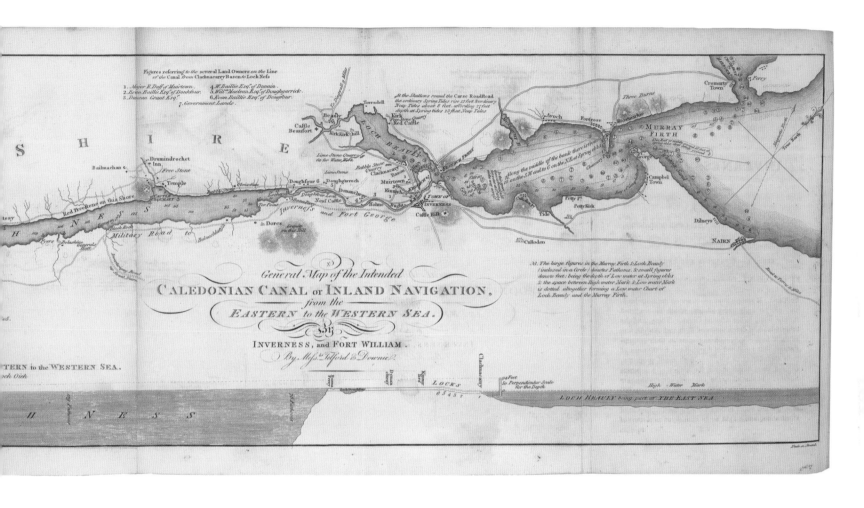

General Map of the Intended
CALEDONIAN CANAL or INLAND NAVIGATION,
from the
EASTERN to the WESTERN SEA.

INVERNESS, and FORT WILLIAM.

By Messrs Telford & Downie.

Figures referring to the several Land Owners on the Line
of the Canal from Clachnacarry Bason to Loch Nefs

1. Major R. Duff of Muirtown.
2. Evan Baillie Esqr of Donkfour.
3. Duncan Grant Esqr.
4. W.m Baillie Esqr of Dunain.
5. Will.m Maclean Esqr of Doughgarrick.
6. Evan Baillie Esqr of Doughfour.
7. Government Lands.

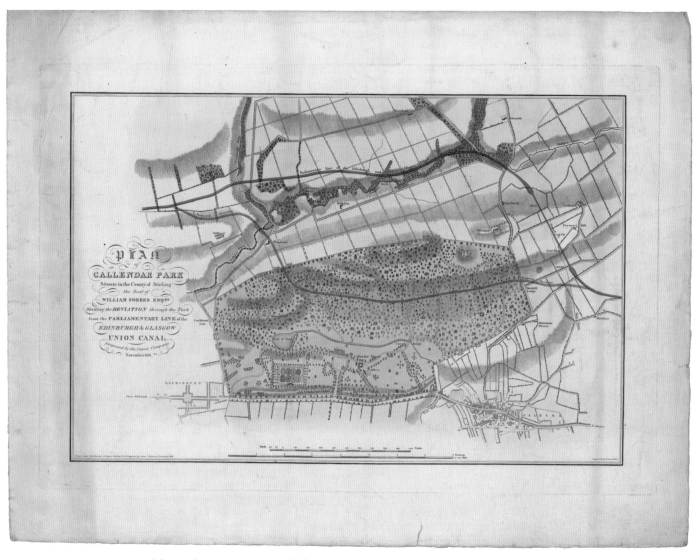

FIGURE 9.17 Maps were essential for canal construction, not only for planning the best route in relation to the complexities of geology, terrain, water supply and engineering, but also for planning deviations from the route to appease landowners. Following decades of wrangling, and many surveys to find the best route, work began on the Edinburgh and Glasgow Union Canal in 1818. Hugh Baird's 32-mile route followed the contours of the land to achieve a lockless route, albeit by constructing sixty-two bridges, five minor and three major aqueducts. There were, however, other difficulties. William Forbes, owner of the Callander Estate, forced the canal company to take a more difficult line than that approved in the Parliamentary Bill, and to build a tunnel so that the views from his estate would not be marred by canal traffic.

Source: James Jardine and James Anderson, *Plan of Callendar Park Situate in the County of Stirling the Seat of William Forbes . . . shewing the Deviation through the Park from the Parliamentary Line of the Edinburgh & Glasgow Union Canal Proposed by the Canal Company* (1818). Reproduced by permission of the Trustees of the National Library of Scotland.

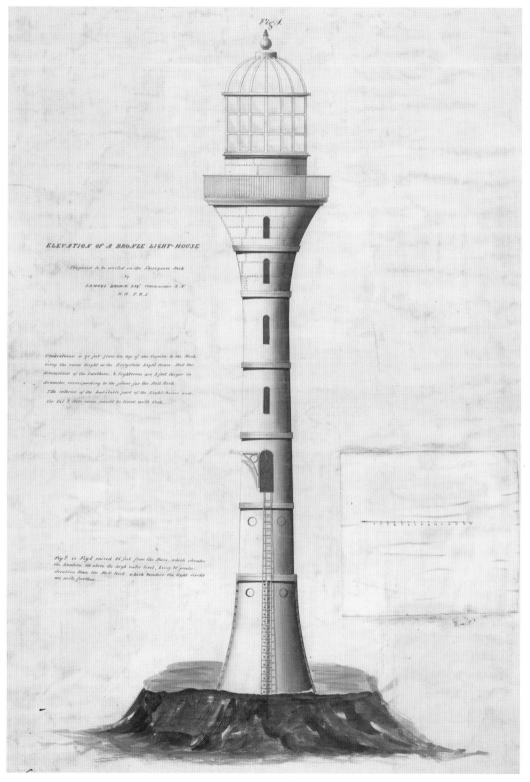

ELEVATION OF A BRONZE LIGHT-HOUSE

FIGURE 9.18 Situated on jagged rocks 12 miles west of Tiree, the Skerryvore Lighthouse is one of the most isolated in Scottish waters. Its construction involved considerable engineering skill. Robert Louis Stevenson, nephew of its engineer, Alan Stevenson, hailed it as 'the noblest of all extant deep-sea lights'. Captain, later Sir, Samuel Brown, originally suggested a tower of cast iron or bronze, and the engineering profile shown here shows this, as well as the plan for the stone construction eventually decided upon. Following the plan used for the Bell Rock Lighthouse, a barrack was erected for workmen on the rock, with accommodation and a signal station at Hynish on Tiree. The original barrack building was washed away in 1838 and a new stronger barrack was erected in 1839. A giant pit to hold the foundations was completed by 1840, and the Duke of Argyll, who had allowed quarries to be opened on his estates for the lighthouse stone, laid the foundation stone. Each stone was carefully cut on Tiree – no variation greater than 1/8th of an inch was allowed – and all 4,300 tons of stone were transported to the rock by steamer. When complete in 1842, the tower was 137 feet high, and cost £93,803, nearly double the original estimates. For the Northern Lighthouse Board and for the Stevensons, however, this was a resounding achievement that added considerably to the safety of local shipping and for navigation between the south west of Scotland and the Americas.
Source: Alan Stevenson / Samuel Brown, *Elevation of a Bronze Light-House Proposed to be Erected on the Skerryvore Rock* [1836]. Reproduced by permission of the Trustees of the National Library of Scotland.

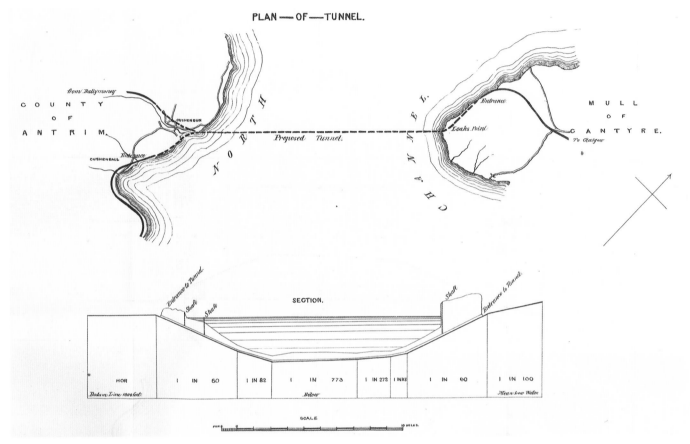

PLAN — OF — TUNNEL.

SECTION.

FIGURE 9.19 This exemplar of Victorian optimism and engineering confidence was one of the earliest proposals to link Scotland to Ireland by a rail tunnel, with an outline map and profile of the route and a 16-page report on the attendant benefits. Encouraged by railways rapidly extending across both countries, and recent practical test borings for proposed tunnels under the Thames and the English Channel, the proposed tunnel appeared quite modest compared with the projected giant causeway between Tor Head in Antrim and the Mull of Kintyre that had recently been presented to the House of Commons. This was the shortest route between the countries – the tunnel would have extended 14 miles under water – but it was also the deepest (as the profile finds difficult to disguise). The route proposed required at least 112 miles of new track to be laid through relatively hilly terrain in Scotland to link with the railway at Helensburgh. Careful consideration was given to drainage and ventilation shafts, the lining of the tunnel with brick and sandstone, and the need for an extra rail to accommodate the different gauges between the countries. Had the tunnel been built, the journey time from Belfast to Glasgow would have been halved from nine to four and a half hours, 'leaving out of the question' [as the report noted] 'the absence of sea sickness and its accompanying horrors'. With coal and iron ores regions that could be made more profitable, and expanding manufacturing and trade in both countries, a number of benefits – economic, political and pseudo-racial – were envisaged: 'The distinction of races has been ever a curse to Ireland; and no surer method exists for the complete amalgamation of the Saxon and Celt in the Briton, than easy and constant intercourse between the three countries.' Such a railway-led union would in turn 'tend to the consolidation of empire, so greatly desired by all lovers of order and prosperity'. The combined cost was estimated to be £4.25 million pounds.

Source: L. Livingston Macassey and William Scott, *Report on Proposed Railway Tunnel between Scotland and Ireland* (1868?). Reproduced by permission of the Trustees of the National Library of Scotland.

MAPS FOR MODERNITY, SPEED AND DAILY LIFE

In their development and infrastructure, cities particularly show the impact of changing technologies of travel. Following the Tramways Act of 1870, rails were first laid along a public highway, and 1872 saw the first horse-drawn trams in Glasgow, with electrification following in 1898 (fig. 9.20). Underground, the Glasgow District Subway – a six and a half mile circular railway – was first opened in 1896. Overground, railways symbolised modernity and helped unite the nation geographically (fig. 9.21). The development of the first pneumatic tyre in the 1880s and new cycle designs made cycling pleasant and affordable from the 1890s. The first motor car to reach Scotland arrived at Leith in 1895; an Act of Parliament the following year permitted such vehicles to travel at faster than walking pace without a man ahead with a red flag. Above the ground, the first scheduled air services in Scotland started in 1933 (fig. 9.22). If it was about anything, modernity in twentieth-century Scotland was about speed. Travel times to work were reduced, and so cities could expand: like the telephone and telegraphy, trains and trams collapsed distance. Bikes, cars and buses afforded quicker routes to work, as, for some, they facilitated an escape to the country (see chapter 11).

Map-makers were quick to respond to these developments, not only by plotting the construction and development of the transport infrastructure, but also in the promotion and use of these new ways of getting around. Several Scottish firms – Bartholomew, Adam & Charles Black, Gall & Inglis and W. & A. K. Johnston – became famous internationally as much for their travel maps as for their other work. Through their efforts, Scotland has a rich legacy of cycling maps, bus maps, tramway maps, motoring maps, aeronautical charts, and combinations of all of these for the general tourist and traveller.

Maps of travel and communication have a history, but they are also vital tools for revealing history in other ways. Scotland's physical geography has often created barriers to accessibility, and the integration of places into a national space and a modern mobile and globalised society has not been straightforward. Maps now help travellers get to their destination: but this was never maps' original purpose. Maps for travel provide a window into how travel, distance and transport were seen in the past, and therefore illustrate fundamental changes in the ways in which space and distance have been conceived over time. Scotland, more or less, is now the same size as it was when Pont was at work, even recognising that in the seventeenth century numerous geographers and map-makers could not agree on its shape (fig. 1.2). But in travel maps we can see that Scotland has become smaller over time. Travel closes space down. Travel maps, at least some of them, eliminate space altogether and work on time distance.

In travel maps we can see at a glance what was practical and possible – and occasionally what was ever only imagined (fig. 9.19) – concerning the movement of people and resources. Given the vital place of mobility in modernity, it is no surprise that routeways and lines of communication are the most prominent feature on nearly all cartographic representations of Scotland and its regions, in electronic and paper forms. Scottish map-makers and users before the last quarter of the seventeenth century would have found this very odd.

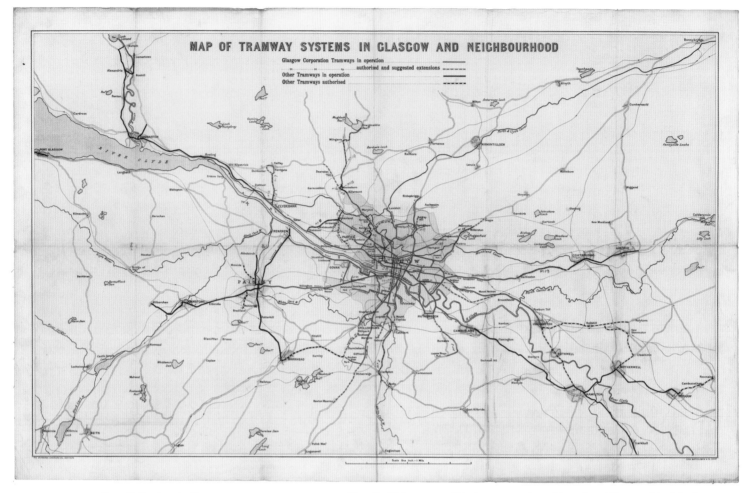

FIGURE 9.20 *Above.* Following the Tramways Act of 1870, which allowed rails to be laid along public highways, horse-drawn tram routes expanded rapidly in Scotland's main cities. In Edinburgh, cable tramcars began to replace these, although horses were still used to pull tramcars until 1907. Glasgow's municipal tramways were the first to use electric power, with 2.5 miles of horse tramway electrified in 1898. This map shows the routes in 1908. The network subsequently extended to a total of 134 miles, with 1,200 tramcars, and ran until 1962, the last of any town or city in Scotland. *Source:* Glasgow Corporation Tramways, *Map of Tramway Systems in Glasgow and Neighbourhood* (1908). Reproduced by permission of the Trustees of the National Library of Scotland.

FIGURE 9.21 *Opposite.* This poster strikingly captures the pride and confidence of the North British Railway at the height of its prosperity and influence, which was also during the time of massive expansion of its Waverley Station headquarters from 1892 to 1900, when it became the second largest station in Britain. Following the opening of the Forth Rail Bridge in 1890, competition with the Caledonian Railway witnessed the fastest-ever journey times between London and Aberdeen, averaging more than 60 miles per hour over 523 miles (a record not broken until the 1970s). The map also shows the newly completed West Highland Line to Fort William (in 1894), and the dashed lines show proposed railways – from Carrbridge to Inverness (opened in 1898), and from Banavie to Mallaig (completed in 1901). Whilst masquerading as an accurate railway map of Scotland, the map in fact shows just the North British Railway routes and those of its allies, including the Highland Railway and Great North of Scotland Railway, along with a host of connecting steamer and coach routes. The lines of the Caledonian Railway, the main rival to the North British, appear in thin, barely visible dark lines. Bartholomew also printed extensive posters, maps and publicity for the Caledonian Railway, showing an equally partial view of the network. Bartholomew were also major beneficiaries of railway company rivalry and its need for colourful promotional cartography. *Source:* John Bartholomew & Co., *North British Railway and its Communications* (1897). Reproduced by permission of the Trustees of the National Library of Scotland.

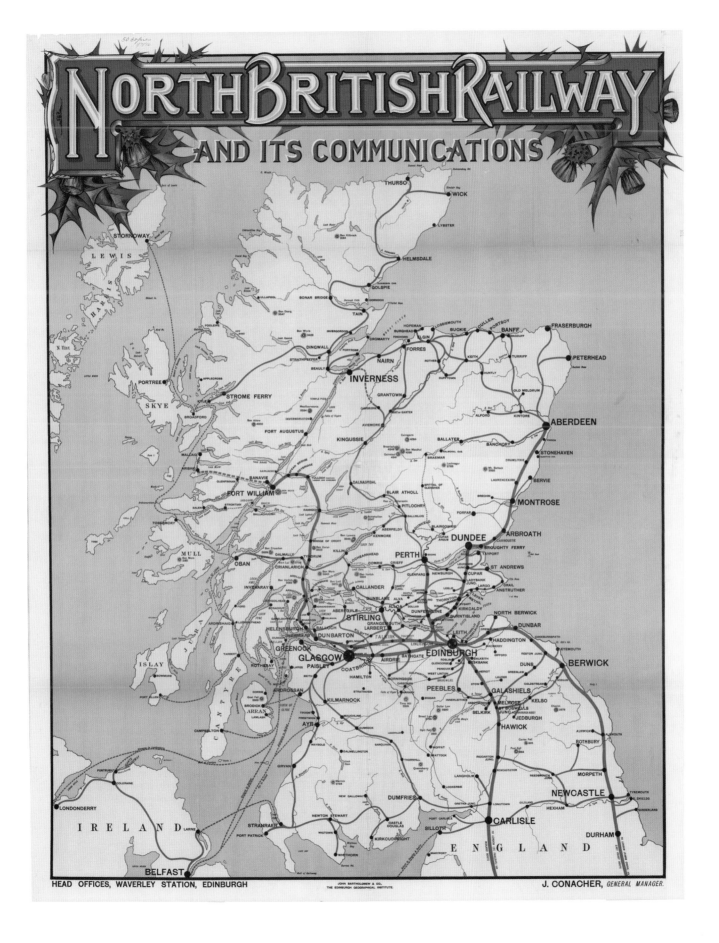

NORTH BRITISH RAILWAY
AND ITS COMMUNICATIONS

HEAD OFFICES, WAVERLEY STATION, EDINBURGH

JOHN BARTHOLOMEW & CO.
THE EDINBURGH GEOGRAPHICAL INSTITUTE.

J. CONACHER, GENERAL MANAGER.

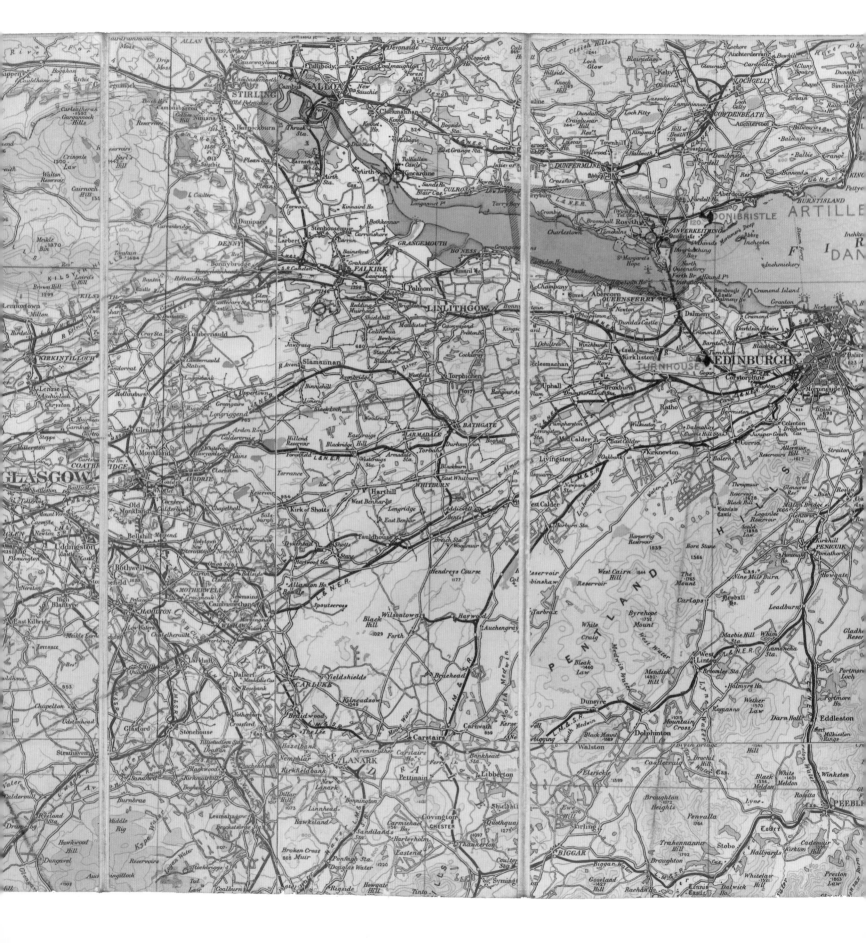

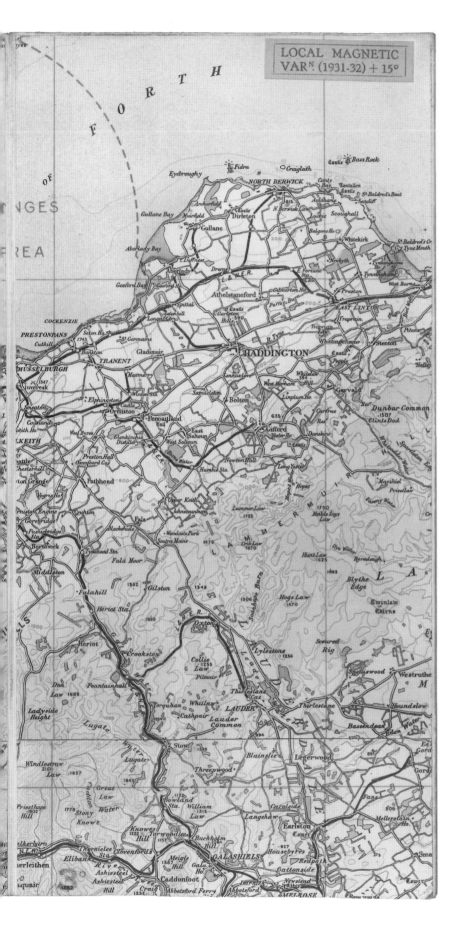

FIGURE 9.22 The earliest maps for aviation purposes were simply topographical maps with an overprint of information for air navigation. Commercial publishers of motoring maps were often able to adapt their existing material to this new market, as shown here. Ordnance Survey quarter inch to the mile maps were selected 'as the most suitable for flying', over which were printed symbols in red for aerodromes and landing grounds, as well as hazards to avoid, such as high wireless masts. Forbidden areas for flying (as shown here for the Rosyth area) were also indicated, as well as danger areas such as the artillery ranges further east in the Firth of Forth. The map was coated in 'Celanese dope' so that routes could be drawn on and then wiped clean, whilst meridians and details of local magnetic variation were also added to assist with cockpit navigation. It was not until the 1960s that air charts were designed specifically for air navigation and to global specifications, through the civilian International Civil Aviation Authority, and the military family of aeronautical charts: Operational Navigation Charts (ONCs), Tactical Pilotage Charts (TPCs) and Joint Operation Graphics (JOGs). *Source:* Automobile Association, *Automobile Association General Flying Map: England, Scotland and Wales, Sheet 9* (1928). Reproduced by permission of the Trustees of the National Library of Scotland.

CHAPTER 10

MAPPING SCIENCE

In Edinburgh in 1834 Sir Roderick Impey Murchison was greatly agitated about maps. Addressing the meeting of the British Association for the Advancement of Science (BAAS), Murchison – a leading geographer and geologist born at Tarradale House in Easter Ross in 1792, and in later years a distinguished advocate for British science – complained at length about the state of Scotland's scientific mapping. Scotland, railed Murchison, 'stood almost alone in Europe as a Kingdom without a map'. In terms of its mapping, the country 'was in a disgraceful condition in respect to geography'.

Murchison's views should not be taken literally: the evidence presented elsewhere in this book proves that. His intemperate remarks were directed at two specific targets: at the lack of an accurate and up-to-date geological map of Scotland, and at the still slow and interrupted progress of Ordnance Survey's mapping of the country, which had begun in 1819 but which had been interrupted since about 1823. The Survey's slowness was due in part to lack of agreement over what scales were best to use in the scientific work of the Survey, and partly

because the Survey was concentrating on England and Wales to the neglect of Scotland. Larger scales would, in time, mean that a closer and fuller view could be taken – as we have seen for the Survey's work in towns from the 1850s. But such accuracy demanded time, and time meant money. Some people even argued in this 'battle of the scales' that the countryside could be mapped at smaller scale since it contained less, and so coverage and accuracy was less important. But, for Murchison and others, completeness of view was important. And, as Murchison and his fellow scientists understood, mapping and science went hand in hand: specifically, as an aid to such things as navigation, commerce and agriculture; generally, because mapping was (or should be) itself a science as well as being part of what science did.

Murchison's remarks were apt given what else was happening in the world of natural knowledge at that time. His presence at the Edinburgh meeting of the BAAS is significant: the association had been founded in 1831 to promote science, and public understanding of it, throughout Britain. In the 1830s, the term 'science', and more especially the term 'scientist', were first assuming their current importance as a specialised disciplinary subject and a professional and institutionalised practitioner of that subject (and doing so, in part, because of the work of the BAAS). In the 1830s, the term 'cartography' was coined to describe the science of map-making. Given changes in publishing with the advent of lithographic reproduction – also in the 1830s – mapping and science could reach new and popular audiences as well as serve specialist needs. We have seen something of the results of this in the work of John Thomson and John Wood in the 1830s and in the rise of firms such as W. & A. K. Johnston and Bartholomew and Sons. As Murchison appreciated, mapping had great potential as a powerful form of representation in science. But, for it to work properly, mapping had to be done scientifically and systematically.

This chapter illustrates how Scotland, Scottish mapping and Scottish men of science figured centrally in the development of science through mapping, and in the development of mapping as a science from the nineteenth century. Our story begins not with Murchison in Edinburgh in 1834 but on a hill in Perthshire sixty years earlier.

MAKING A MOLEHILL OUT OF A MOUNTAIN: THE 'SCHIEHALLION EXPERIMENT', 1774–1776

One of the major questions which concerned early eighteenth-century natural philosophers and others studying the physical dimensions of the known world is simply put: 'What was the shape of the earth?' It is a question which mattered greatly at that time, not least because the two opposing theoretical explanations being advanced broadly followed national lines. To followers of the English philosopher Isaac Newton, advocate of the universal theory of gravitation, the earth was pumpkin shaped, flattened at the poles. But, for followers of the French philosopher Descartes, who argued with Newton about the effects of gravitation – what Descartes called 'vortices' – the result was otherwise: the earth was melon shaped, extended at its poles, flattened at its equator. Expeditions in the 1730s to South America and to Lapland – one as near to the equator as possible, the other as far north as possible – to measure the linear distance of one degree of latitude in time proved Newton correct: the earth is squashed at its poles; in technical terms, it is an oblate spheroid.

The 'shape-of-the-earth' debate helped set in train what we now know as the science of geodesy or geophysics, the science of the earth's structure. William Roy, the leading figure in the Military Survey between 1747 and 1756 (see chapter 4), was much taken up with geodetic questions in the 1780s, as was Ordnance Survey following its foundation in 1791. In the early 1770s, these concerns brought several of Britain's leading natural philosophers, including Nevil Maskelyne, the Astronomer Royal, to Schiehallion in Breadalbane in central Perthshire, to help address related questions about the density of the earth. Using mountains as sites of measurement was an important way of testing Newton's universal theory of gravitation: deflections of a pendulum from the vertical could, it was argued, be used to detect the gravitational attraction of a mountain. From this, its density and volume could be measured and, from those, the density and volume of the whole earth could be determined. Such mountain measurements during the French-led South American 'shape-of-the-earth' expedition in the later 1730s had proved inconclusive.

In 1772, plans were set in train to re-do the Newtonian experiments nearer home, and Schiehallion was selected as the best mountain for the purpose because of its wedge-like shape. With no other mountains nearby, there was likely to be little or no gravitational influence to interfere with the results. And so, at various times between 1774 and 1776, Maskelyne, accompanied by the mathematician and surveyor Charles Hutton and others, lived and worked on Schiehallion and conducted measurements on the north-east and south-west sides of the mountain. Mountain work was not easy: they were hampered by poor weather, by professors from Edinburgh keen to see their work (and keener still to see their state-of-the-art measuring instruments) and by a fire which destroyed one of the observing-measuring platforms (and which cost Neil Gow, the renowned Highland fiddler, his own prized instrument).

The Schiehallion experiment of 1774–76 helped confirm Newton's laws of gravitation, but it did something more besides. For Charles Hutton, the numerical recordings of magnetic declination, and particularly of the hundreds of surveying and triangulation observations, made greater sense if readings of the same value were connected by means of a line, from which one could glimpse the shape of the land overall and, importantly,

infer a value for any point along that line, even although that point had not been measured. Hutton spelled out these ideas and his calculations in a paper to the Royal Society, and presented a map which showed Schiehallion, 'Maskelyne's Mountain' as it has become known, as a molehill, framed by its observatory sites (fig. 10.1). We now know his workings and this idea as the 'contour line', a line connecting points of equal height above mean sea level or, in general cartographic terms, the 'isoline'.

It is not quite true to say that Hutton invented the contour line and that Schiehallion, Scotland's cartographic laboratory, was its only test site: French mathematicians and map-makers had come to much the same idea a few years earlier, and the English philosopher Edmond Halley had developed a similar idea for ocean currents at the start of the eighteenth century. But, in British and Scottish context, Schiehallion and Hutton put the contour on the map. In wider context, these experiments and measurements in central Perthshire – at much the same time and for much the same reason as Mackenzie's Hebridean maritime work– helped establish a new symbolic language for mapping and heightened recognition of mapping as a form of science.

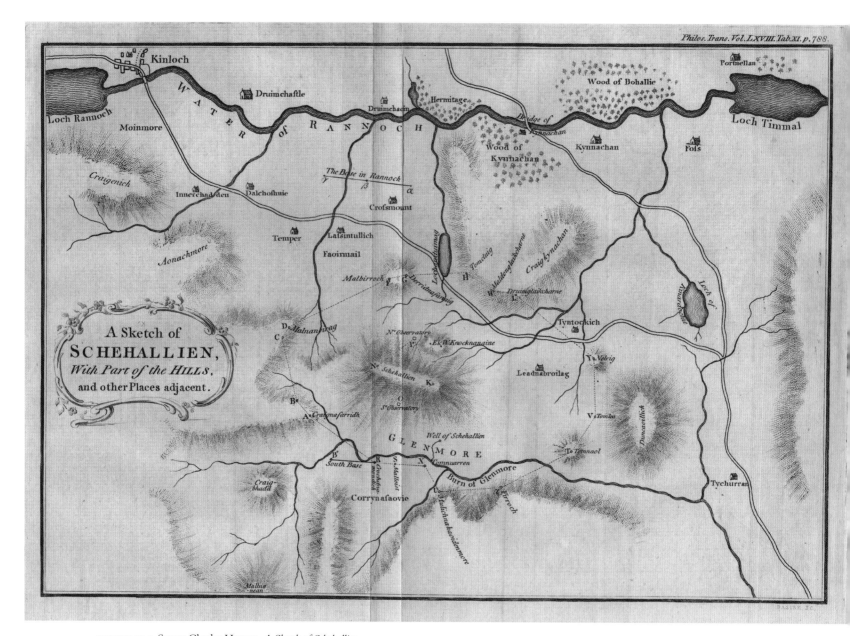

Philos. Trans. Vol. LXVIII. Tab. XI. p. 788.

FIGURE 10.1 *Source:* Charles Hutton, *A Sketch of Schehallien,
With Part of the Hills, and other Places Adjacent* (1778).
Reproduced by permission of the Trustees of the National
Library of Scotland.

SCIENCE, VISUAL REPRESENTATION AND THE LANGUAGE OF MAPPING AFTER *c*.1830

Just like mapping, the word 'science' was commonplace before the nineteenth century, but, also like mapping, it did not have a single definition. Three meanings were in use. The first was science as knowledge, understanding gained through enquiry, as opposed to belief or opinion. The second was science as a branch or order of knowledge in the sense of a recognised department of learning: this more common meaning was often prefaced by a specific descriptor – 'geological' or 'botanical' for instance. The third meaning embraced not just a branch of study but its methods. As methods in science became increasingly mathematical in principle and law-based, so mapping became associated with measurement, both in terms of the accurate location of phenomena, and their accurate representation in terms of shape.

It is for these reasons to do with Enlightenment interest in the authority of reason, and in the importance of mathematics as the language of 'scientific' authority and reasoning, that we can trace from the early nineteenth century that strongly-held view that maps were accurate mirrors to the world, and that map history was the story of progressive technical betterment in how maps work to show the world. We have already illustrated in several contexts one common form of mapping, namely topographical maps, maps which record geographical information according to place and distance and the proportions of features on the world's surface, mainly physical features. Estate plans, maps of canals and maritime charts depended upon such notions of accuracy in their undertaking: the reputation of the map- and chart-makers likewise depended upon producing reliable and 'accurate' maps from 'first-hand survey'. But, before

1800, that other form of mapping now so familiar to us, namely the thematic map, would not have been common. The thematic map appears as part of the new language of science and the sciences.

In thematic mapping, the primary purpose is to show not the geographical or topographical features of a chosen part of the world, but to depict the distribution of selected phenomena. Thematic maps come in three general types: maps of the physical world, maps of human activities and maps of the social environment (showing the pattern of some quality or, to use a nineteenth-century term, 'moral statistics', in relation to administrative regions, for example). There are two specific forms of these general types: the choropleth map, which shows value or qualities by region; and the isopleth map, which shows trends over space by lines of equal value, but without reference to region. For an example of a choropleth map, see Bartholomew's isochronic map of Edinburgh (fig. 5.1). For an example of an isopleth map, see the map of temperature variations across Scotland (fig. 10.3). In a sense, all maps are thematic maps since no one map can adequately show all the information for the area it represents. But the term is usually used in relation to the visual display of phenomena in one or other of these two forms. Maps of this type are particularly associated with the rise of science and with the need for visual authority in scientific representation. Like the graph and the bar chart with which they are associated as a form of what commentators called 'statistical graphics', thematic maps present, as a sort of visual shorthand, mathematical and statistically based patterns over space (fig. 10.2).

Take the commonplace weather map as an example

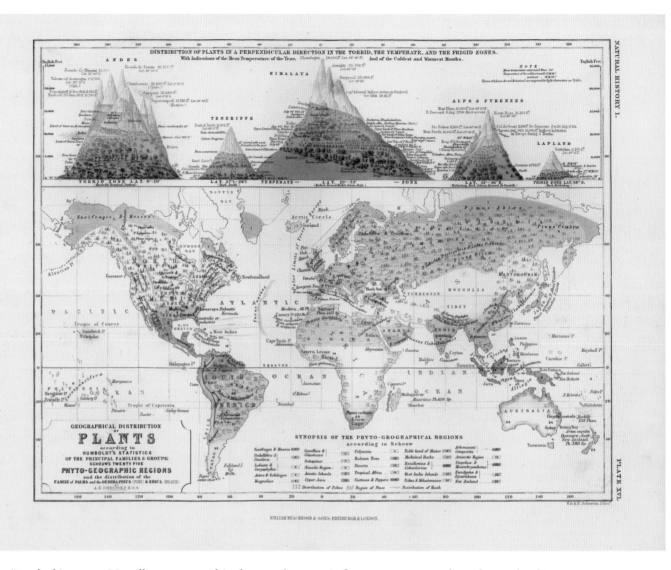

FIGURE 10.2 This depiction of the association between altitude, plants and geographical distribution illustrates beautifully the nature and style of 'statistical graphics' – a shorthand language of scientific visual representation in use from the 1830s. The 'Outlines of botanical geography' is from the *Physical Atlas* produced by the Scottish cartographer, geographer and natural scientist A. Keith Johnston in 1848. *Source:* Alexander Keith Johnston, 'Geographical Distribution of Plants' from *The Physical Atlas* (1848). Reproduced by permission of the Trustees of the National Library of Scotland.

of a thematic (isopleth) map. Usually, topographical details are absent, or given only in outline as, say, a nation's coastline. What is given is a mix of lines and symbols. The lines – of rainfall or of atmospheric pressure – suggest a value or amount over space (see fig. 10.3). Symbols – of wind direction, temperature, the nature of the weather 'front' as it moves west–east, for example – are substitutes for mathematical evidence gleaned from instruments in the field, or possibly from human observers. The thematic weather map is a statistical abstraction. The lines are drawn from a few data points: we are invited, as map readers, to infer a common value along the line even though not all points along the drawn line have been measured. Often, the data are time-specific: what may be more interesting are the processes operating over time to produce the situation at that given mapped moment. And the lines here have the effect of suggesting sharp 'edges' or boundaries to the recorded values when trends may be more important. Nevertheless, such maps are especially valuable tools for those sciences which derive their authority from fieldwork.

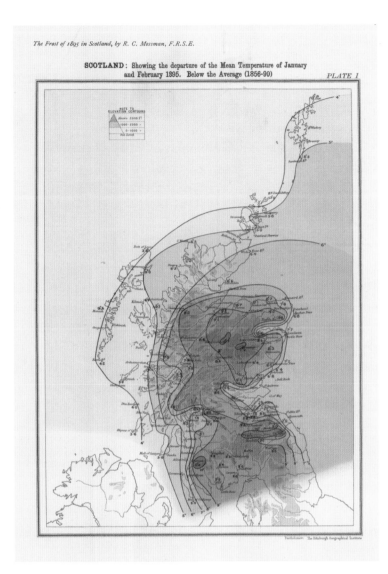

The Frost of 1895 in Scotland, by R. C. Mossman, F.R.S.E.

SCOTLAND: Showing the departure of the Mean Temperature of January and February 1895. Below the Average (1856-90)   *PLATE I*

FIGURE 10.3 Cold Scotland. This map shows the variations in temperature during the extreme frost of early 1895, in relation to average temperatures for the months of January and February over the period 1856–90: Braemar, the upper Tweed Valley and Pinmore in Ayrshire stand out – over 11° colder in 1895 than the seasonal norm.
Source: Robert Cockburn Mossman, Sheet with two maps, one entitled *Scotland: Showing the Departure of the Mean Temperature of January and February 1895 Below the Average (1856–90)* (1895). Reproduced by permission of the Trustees of the National Library of Scotland.

MAPPING THE UNSEEN: SCOTLAND'S GEOLOGICAL LANDSCAPES

More than most maps, maps of the world underground are built on trust. They invite the map reader to take for granted that lines on the map 'speak' to unseen truth: to what, in reality, is only inferred. This is nowhere more evident than in the science of geology.

The printed geological mapping of Scotland begins in 1804 with a map of Dumfriesshire by William Crawford in which 'the Mineralogy, or Internal Structure' of the county was revealed in order to locate mineral workings and coal mines. The terms in the title are not accidental: the first reflects the many eighteenth-century 'mineralogical maps', precursors to geological maps; the second hints at what geological maps do in providing 'internal' maps of unseen geographies. Overall, such maps were documents of potential, indicating what might be found below the ground and made use of for economic benefit.

Scotland was a key testing ground in these respects. Geological mapping went hand-in-hand with the emergence of a visual language in the earth sciences and with the work of Ordnance Survey. From a few such maps in the first two decades of the nineteenth century, Scotland beneath the surface was increasingly 'revealed' in maps from the 1830s and 1840s (fig. 10.4). One important figure in this respect was Guernsey-born John MacCulloch, who undertook geological surveys in Scotland for Ordnance Survey between 1814 and 1821, and, effectively on his own, surveyed throughout the period 1809–32. MacCulloch's motives were economic and utilitarian – initially a physician, he had begun geological work in the hope of finding limestone suitable for medical

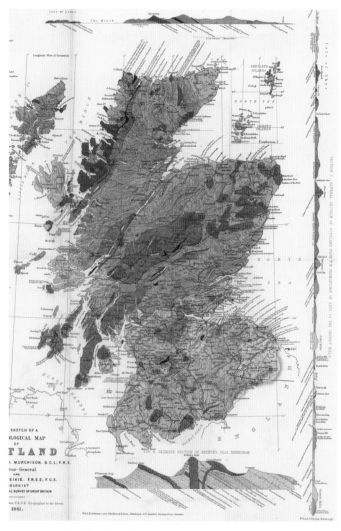

FIGURE 10.4 Scotland's bedrock revealed: in this map, the compilers, Roderick Impey Murchison and Archibald Geikie, advertise not only their new map and the geological knowledge it contains, but also their social status within the Geological Survey. Note, too, that the map was constructed by that leading Scottish man of science, A. Keith Johnston, 'Geographer to the Queen'.
Source: Roderick Impey Murchison and Archibald Geikie, *First Sketch of a New Geological Map of Scotland . . . Constructed by A. Keith Johnston* (1861). Reproduced by permission of the Trustees of the National Library of Scotland.

compounds – and linked to the national scientific enquiries of Ordnance Survey.

Following the establishment of the Ordnance Geological Survey in 1835, individual endeavours were increasingly replaced by organised institutional mapping. Murchison was much involved in this work (his arguments in 1834 had helped establish the geological branch). Professional geologists and geographers turned to the map and to other forms of statistical representation as their stock in trade. And as down-to-earth scientists, government or otherwise, mapped what could – and importantly what could not – be seen of Scotland, they disclosed not just the country's many coal and mineral deposits but also a country with some of the most complex geology in Britain, in the north and west Highlands especially, and some of the oldest rocks in the world (fig. 10.5).

Nature's complexity does not easily transfer to paper. The detail of these surface geographies (fig. 10.6), and of topography beneath the surface, required the use of a graphical cartographic language of sections and folds, and, importantly, of colour and symbol to signify different rock ages (fig. 10.7). Boundary lines on such maps suggest clear distinctions seldom encountered in the field (fig. 10.8). And, because they show what, commonly, cannot be seen, geological maps perhaps more than other thematic maps in science require faith from map readers and users in what is, after all, map evidence based more upon inference than upon direct observation.

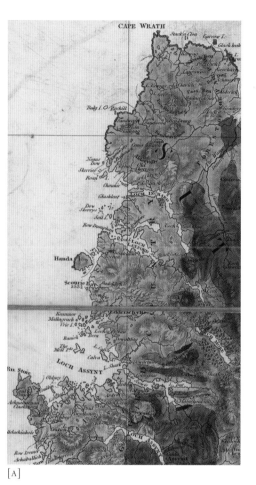

[A]

[B]

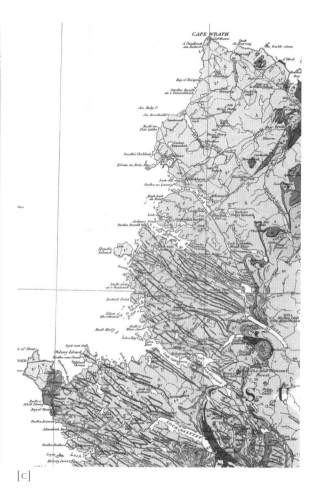

[C]

FIGURE 10.5 Mapping deep time and an ancient 'Scotland'. Geological maps can be used to compare change in our understanding of the structures and processes that have, literally, shaped Scotland as Scotland. Here, insets from three maps show the changing subterranean landscape of the north-west Highlands, one of the most ancient, challenging and complex geological areas in Britain.

FIGURE 10.5 [A] *Source:* John MacCulloch, *A Geological Map of Scotland* (1840). Reproduced by permission of the Trustees of the National Library of Scotland.

FIGURE 10.5 [B] *Source:* J. Nicol, *Geological Map of Scotland* [1846]. Reproduced by permission of the Trustees of the National Library of Scotland.

FIGURE 10.5 [C] *Source:* Benjamin Peach and John Horne, 'Geological map of the North West Highlands of Scotland' from *The Geological Structure of the North-West Highlands of Scotland* (1907). Reproduced by permission of the Trustees of the National Library of Scotland.

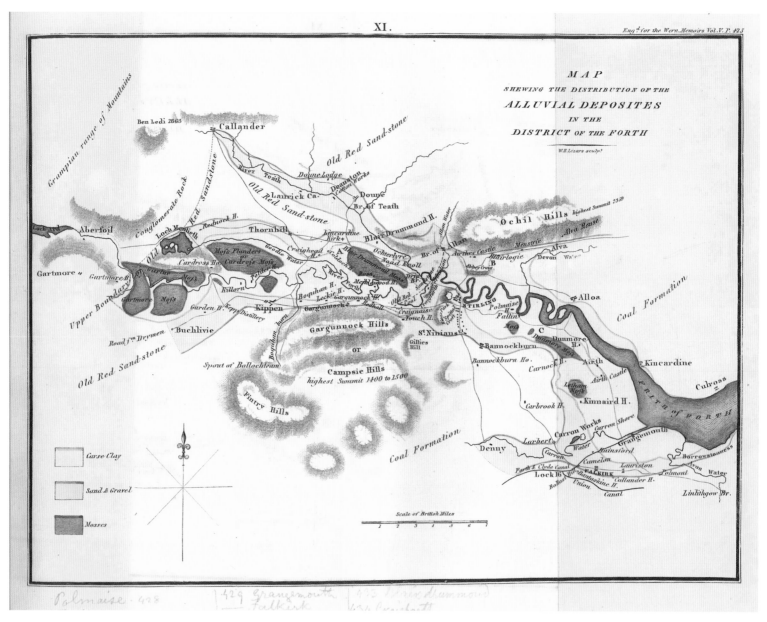

FIGURE 10.6 *Above.* An early example of maps being used to chart the distribution of surface geology – here, alluvial deposits in the Forth Valley. Such maps provided vital clues in the determination of different soil types – and thus agricultural productivity – and in the development in the 1830s and 1840s of modern glacial theory.

Source: Alexander Blackadder, 'Map shewing the distribution of the alluvial deposites in the district of the Forth', from 'On the superficial strata of the Forth District', *Memoirs of the Wernerian Natural History Society* 5 (1826), 424–39. Reproduced by permission of the Trustees of the National Library of Scotland.

FIGURE 10.7 *Opposite.* Map production and the earth sciences: the shading of the rocks of different type and age, here beneath Ardrossan and Saltcoats on a map of about 1869 (surveyed in 1856), was done by hand, using coloured wash. This attention to detail in the use of colour added visual impact to scientific mapping, but was time consuming and expensive.

Source: Geological Survey of Scotland, Six-Inch to the Mile, Ayrshire Sheet X (ca. 1871). Reproduced by permission of the Trustees of the National Library of Scotland.

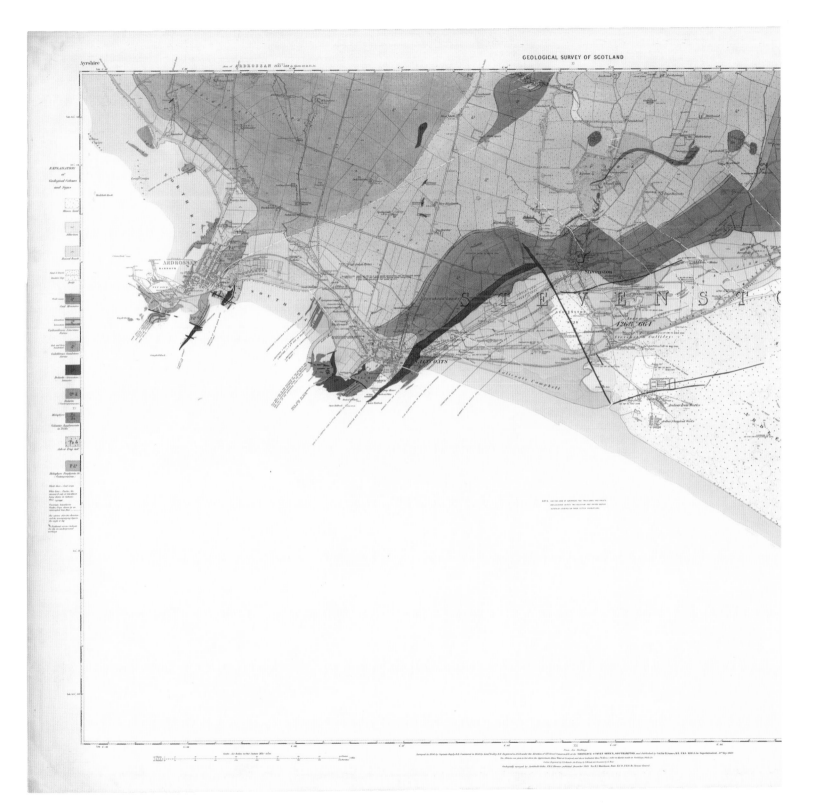

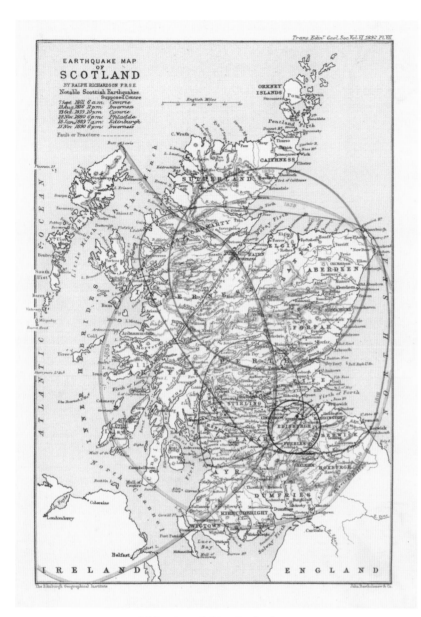

FIGURE 10.8 Mapping a shaking Scotland: the map, first compiled in March 1892, shows the area over which earthquakes were felt in nineteenth-century Scotland, from that of 7 September 1801, which was centred on Comrie, to that of 6.00 p.m. on 15 November 1890, centred on Inverness. *Source:* Ralph Richardson, *Earthquake Map of Scotland* (1892). Reproduced by permission of the Trustees of the National Library of Scotland.

MAPPING FOR THE UNSEEING AND FOR A DIFFERENT WORLD

One of the trends that we have documented and illustrated in a variety of ways in this book is the emergence of new markets for mapping from the 1830s. These new markets were linked with changes in the technology of map production, with public interest and, of course, with the rise of science. In this last sense, market growth was also a story of market specialisation. And one of the areas for specialist development was in mapping for the blind.

In Scotland, maps for the blind appear from the 1830s because society in general was by then aware of the power of maps to visualise social relationships – that is, it was understood that the significance of the connections between social and political processes could be demonstrated by plotting their distribution, by presenting moral statistics 'geo-graphically'. In Scotland's cities and amongst her educational and religious communities, men saw maps and mapping as part of their philanthropic concern to improve the lives of the less fortunate. Thomas Chalmers, for example, the influential churchman who led the Free Church of Scotland in its split from the Established Church in 1843, was much exercised by such questions, as was the leading Glasgow social statistician James Cleland. How could anyone administer to the poor, these men argued, if you knew nothing of their numbers, of where they lived, how they lived? Mapping was a means of realising the scale of social problems, of visualising society itself.

One such leading figure was James Gall, an Edinburgh minister who in 1858 founded the Carrubers Close Mission in Edinburgh's Old Town to aid in evangelising the city's destitute children. But Gall had other interests: author of what now seem odd books about the possibil-

FIGURE 10.9 The idea of maps for those with visual impairment may seem initially a strange concept, but 'feeling' the topography or street pattern through the fingers from some form of raised relief map was, and remains, a meaningful substitute for those unable to see. By incorporating a special form of raised relief, the geography of Scotland, its shape and situation of its towns, could make sense to those without sight. Edinburgh became an important centre in the nineteenth century for the development of educational aids for the visually impaired, largely and significantly through the interest and enthusiasm of James Gall, founder of the Edinburgh School for the Blind.
Source: Gall & Inglis, 'Map of Scotland' from *Geography of Scotland for the Use of the Blind* (1851). Reproduced by permission of the Trustees of the National Library of Scotland.

ity of life on other planets, he was also an amateur astronomer and mapper of the heavens and he promoted mapping for the blind, arguing that maps for the blind would help their integration into society. Maps made of a combination of Braille printing and twine for lines of communication, argued Gall, could show the blind how to 'read' the city. Others built on Gall's work. Thomas Haig, for instance, 'Superintendent and Teacher of the Edinburgh School for Blind Children' as he described himself in 1851, published *Geography of Scotland for the Use of the Blind* in 1851, including in it a map, by Gall and his partner Inglis, with raised borders for the county bound-

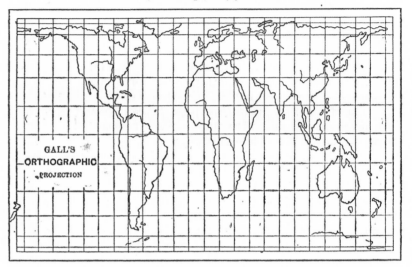

GALL'S ORTHOGRAPHIC PROJECTION.

EQUAL AREA.   PERFECT.

For Physical Maps, chiefly Statistical.

FIGURE 10.10 This map, entitled 'Gall's Orthographic Projection', was used as part of Gall's argument for a different projection which might, in its use of equal area, be 'greatly superior to Mercator's'.
Source: James Gall, *Gall's Orthographic Projection* from 'Use of cylindrical projections for geographical, astronomical, and scientific purposes', *Scottish Geographical Magazine* 1 (1885), 119–23, map on page 121.
Source: James Gall, Gall's *Orthographic Projection* (1885). Reproduced by permission of the Trustees of the National Library of Scotland.

aries and main features to accompany the Braille text (fig. 10.9).

James Gall has a perhaps greater claim to fame in map history. As someone who observed the heavens with a view to their study and mapping – like his Edinburgh counterpart Alexander Jamieson, for example, who published a *Celestial Atlas* in 1822 – Gall faced the same problem as Mercator had three centuries before (see chapter 2), but astronomically rather than terrestrially. How could one project celestial geographies, with stars and planets at different distances from the earthly observer, onto a flat piece of paper so as to map the heavens? Building in part upon the work of the Swiss mathematician Johann Lambert, Gall devised a map projection that, unlike Mercator's, which was based around equal or true shape, was based on the principles of equal area. And, like Murchison two decades before, Gall used a meeting of the British Association, in Glasgow in 1855, to promote his ideas for what he saw as a more truly representative and scientific form of cartography.

The mathematical details of Gall's 'Stereographic',

'Isographic' and 'Orthographic' projections (fig. 10.10) need not concern us so much as the intentions behind them and their longer-run history. Gall wanted to improve upon Mercator's projection and to have everyone benefit from these ideas: 'I make no pretensions' [to any copyright], he remarked; 'every person is welcome to use them'. Because of the currency of Mercator's projection, however, Gall's map ideas were not taken up until much later. In the late 1960s and early 1970s, they were adopted and adapted by a German historian, Arno Peters, in order to promote a world map based on the premise that map area should be true to countries' area in reality. Such a map, Peters reasoned, better suited the representation of countries which were, in other projections and politically speaking, marginalised by Europe and shown out of proportion to it. Numerous aid agencies have adopted this Gall–Peters projection. All maps are political, but James Gall cannot have foreseen the longer-run impact of his thinking about mapping as a form of science and as a campaigning graphic against global injustice and cartographic misrepresentation.

MAPPING SURFACE ASSOCIATIONS

In some forms of scientific work, such as botanical mapping, the aim is to understand 'plant associations' or 'plant assemblages': the distribution of species in relation to altitude, for example, or underlying geology or soil type (see fig. 10.2). As a form of mapping and of scientific method, botanical mapping has its origins in late eighteenth- and early nineteenth-century France and has a high point in the work of German cartographers in the mid-nineteenth century. Soil maps for many Scottish counties feature as part of the concerns of the Board of Agriculture in its many *General Views of the County of . . .*, books which used such mapping as part of plans to describe and improve the agrarian economy of Britain from the early nineteenth century.

In Scotland, systematic botanical mapping came later, developing in the 1890s under the direction of Dundee-based scientists Robert and William Smith and their successor, Marcel Hardy (fig. 10.11). Their work was scientifically and cartographically innovative, for its roots in fieldwork, in disclosing local, regional and national distribution patterns and because it was published, in Edinburgh, by the leading map publishing firm of Bartholomew. Others echoed their work in developing scientific maps of Scotland's nature (fig. 10.12), and in using maps as records of synthesis in plotting changes over time (fig. 10.13).

The scientific mapping in Scotland of agricultural land use and of industrial activity at a national scale is mainly a feature of the twentieth century, although, as we have shown, there is a rich record of earlier estate plans documenting the rural scene and of maps and plans of mines and mineral workings. An important milestone in Scotland's mapped history in this regard – as it was for Britain as a whole – was the work of the Land Utilisation Survey in the 1930s (fig. 10.14; see also fig. 6.16). This was undertaken by school pupils, teachers and some university students, working to produce maps – field by field, parish by parish, county by county – whose value now is as a record of an agricultural landscape before the many changes prompted by the Second World War.

Such land-use maps are the visual and scientific equivalent of planning documents. Whether of the countryside, towns or industrial activity, they afford a picture at a moment, and so may be used to help engineer future and different geographies. New town plans, developers' marketing of proposed housing or entrepreneurs planning a golf course in an area of scientific importance – other examples might be cited – all use the map as a form of evidence, a silent yet authoritative witness. The map is a scientific document (for so it is taken to be) and so – it is commonly assumed – it must be 'true'.

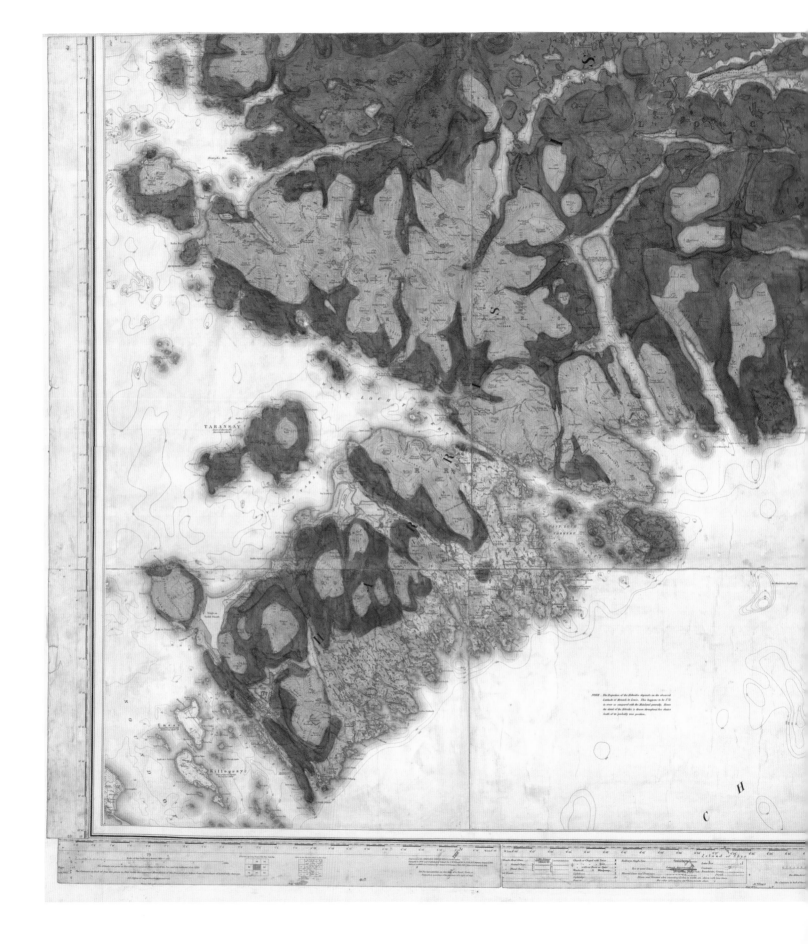

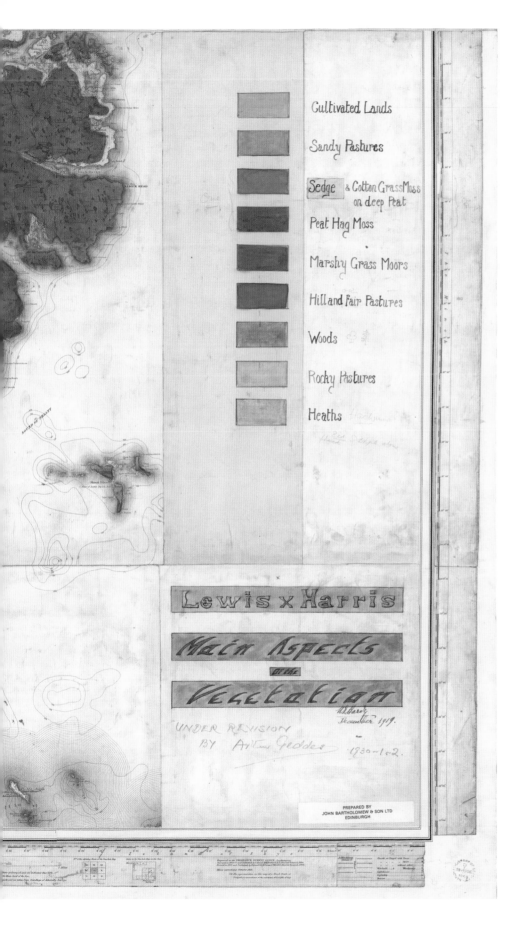

Cultivated Lands

Sandy Pastures

Sedge & Cotton Grass Moss on deep Peat

Peat Hag Moss

Marshy Grass Moors

Hill and Fair Pastures

Woods

Rocky Pastures

Heaths

Lewis x Harris

Main Aspects

of the

Vegetation

M. Hardy December 1919.

UNDER REVISION BY Arthur Geddes 1930-1932.

PREPARED BY
JOHN BARTHOLOMEW & SON LTD
EDINBURGH

FIGURE 10.11 This unfinished, hand-coloured map was principally undertaken by the botanist Marcel Hardy as part of his reconnaissance botanical survey of Scotland, begun *c.*1906. It was later added to, between 1930 and 1932, by the Scottish geographer Dr Arthur Geddes. The underlying maps on which the data were added were Ordnance Survey 1 inch to the mile sheets.
Source: Arthur Geddes and Marcel Hardy, *Lewis and Harris: Main Aspects of the Vegetation* (1919). Reproduced by permission of the Trustees of the National Library of Scotland.

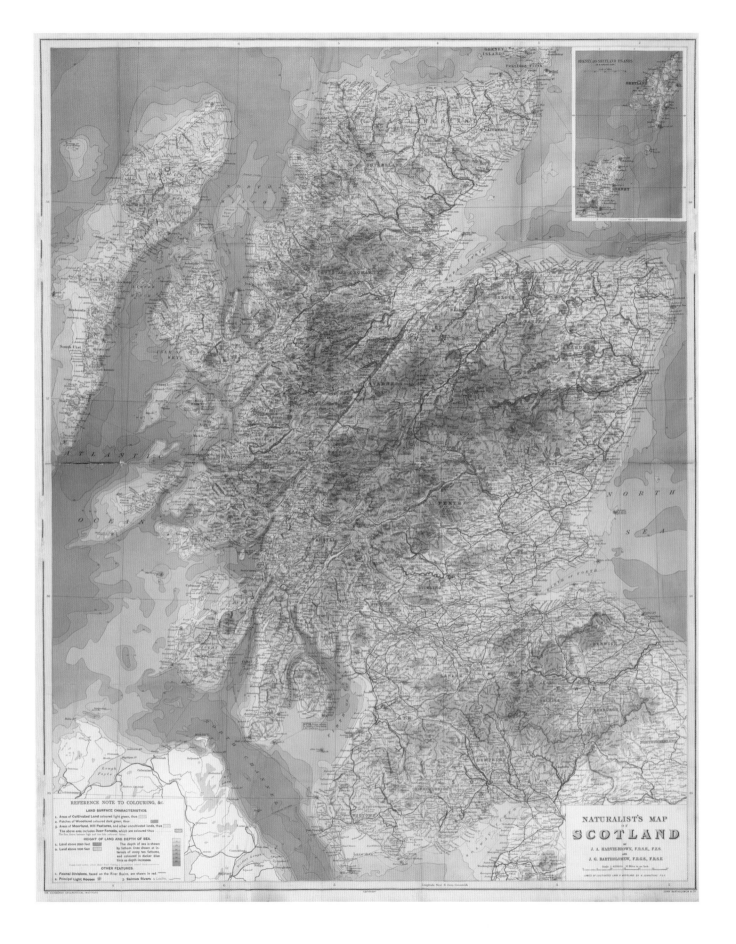

NATURALIST'S MAP
OF
SCOTLAND
BY
J. A. HARVIE-BROWN, F.R.S.E., F.E.S.
AND
J. G. BARTHOLOMEW, F.R.G.S., F.R.S.E.

REFERENCE NOTE TO COLOURING, &c.

LAND SURFACE CHARACTERISTICS.

1. Areas of Cultivated Land coloured light green, thus
2. Patches of Woodland coloured dark green, thus
3. Areas of Moorland, Hill Pastures, and other uncultivated lands, thus
   The above area includes Deer Forests, which are coloured thus

HEIGHT OF LAND AND DEPTH OF SEA.

1. Land above 2000 feet
2. Land above 1000 feet

The depth of sea is shown by fathom lines drawn at intervals of every ten fathoms, and coloured in darker blue tints as depth increases.

OTHER FEATURES.

1. Faunal Divisions, based on the River Basins, are shown in red.
2. Principal Light Houses
3. Salmon Rivers & Lochs.

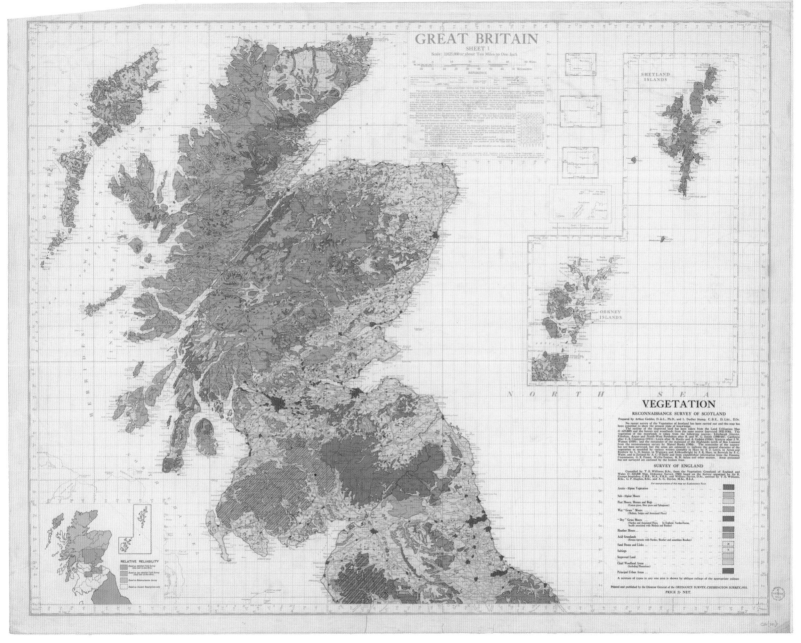

FIGURE 10.12 *Opposite. Naturalist's Map of Scotland* (1893) was jointly compiled by the leading Scottish naturalist, John Harvie-Brown, and the leading Scottish map publisher, John George Bartholomew. The association in maps between the distribution of animals and river basins as natural territorial divisions first appears in eighteenth-century French mapping. *Source:* John Harvie-Brown and J. G. Bartholomew, *Naturalist's Map of Scotland* (1893). Reproduced by permission of the Trustees of the National Library of Scotland.

FIGURE 10.13 *Above.* The presumed certainty of the different vegetation types is belied by the fact that this map is a synthesis of data from 1904, 1906 and 1939. *Source:* Arthur Geddes and Lawrence Dudley Stamp Ordnance Survey. *Great Britain, Ten Miles to One Inch (1:625,000). Sheet 1. Vegetation. Reconnaissance Survey of Scotland* (1953). Reproduced by permission of the Trustees of the National Library of Scotland.

FIGURE 10.14 Nationally, the Highlands–Lowlands distinction and, regionally, the many upland–lowland distinctions in land use stand out clearly in this *Land Utilisation Map*, undertaken in the 1930s from data chiefly derived by school-children under the direction of Professor L. Dudley Stamp.
Source: Lawrence Dudley Stamp, Land Utilisation Survey of Great Britain. 1:63,360, Scotland, Sheet 57 – *Forfar and Dundee* [1941]. Reproduced by permission of the Trustees of the National Library of Scotland.

MAPPING SCIENTIFIC PROCESSES

Maps permit a geographical diagnosis metaphorically as well as practically. This is true in relation to their use in modern medicine, for example, where neuroscientists talk of 'mapping the brain', or in astronomy, whose practitioners like Gall, Jamieson and others long sought 'to chart' the heavens. In using maps and mapping in this way, scientists and others seek insight into the causes of a distribution – the 'why' and 'how', not just the 'what' and 'where'.

Understood in such ways, and for the reasons we have seen, maps became tools for exploring the well-being of nations. Maps of 'ignorance' (as they were known) were drawn up of mid-nineteenth-century England and Wales which mapped by administrative region the proportion of the adult population who could sign their name in the marriage register. Maps allowed medical officers of health and civic officials to plot individual instances of disease (fig. 10.15), police authorities to locate criminal acts (fig. 5.16), and by association look, then as now, for 'hot spots' of such activity. Ecclesiastical authorities and well-intended churchmen could know where religious attendance was low and so take redemptive action. Scientific mapping has long been a form of social statistics and civic scrutiny.

Maps thus afford a form of powerful association in scientific work. But they do not themselves disclose causation, or the effects over time of a pattern revealed at one instant. Weather maps are more informative if produced and read in sequence, for example, rather than as single pictures of dynamic changes in atmospheric circulation. Land-use patterns do not change dramatically at parish or county boundaries. Maps that show the value or distribution of categories of a phenomenon in relation to an administrative unit – population density or voting patterns by enumeration district, for instance – are usually averages: the extremes in the values might be more significant. Natural phenomena seldom mirror on the ground – or on the wing – the neat lines of the mapmaker (figs. 10.16, 10.17). In thematic maps, neat lines have a tendency to produce clear boundaries when no such demarcation may be possible (fig. 10.18).

Maps have a status as scientific documents and are commonly used in the sciences as a form of authoritative representation. But because maps in and of science are always documents of compromise – between what has been selected to be shown and the scale at which it is to be shown – they need to be used with caution. Choropleth maps can be particularly easily manipulated through the grouping of data, colour and the units chosen to present the same results in different ways.

Science is not a neutral objective activity. Neither is mapping. We should perhaps be especially cautious in this respect given the increased prevalence of digital mapping, and in hand-held mobile devices, where the scientific evidence is assumed to be without contradiction or to be relevant for all time periods. The electronic mapping of flood hazard potential by the Scottish Environmental Protection Agency, for example, in its development of the Indicative River and Coastal Flood Map represents a real advance in public accessibility to mapping and as a precautionary planning device for public authorities. But it cannot be used as a safeguard against all local conditions, or extreme events, or to map quite when and where rising waters might break a river's banks. In science, as in other domains, maps are commonplace, vital yet limited.

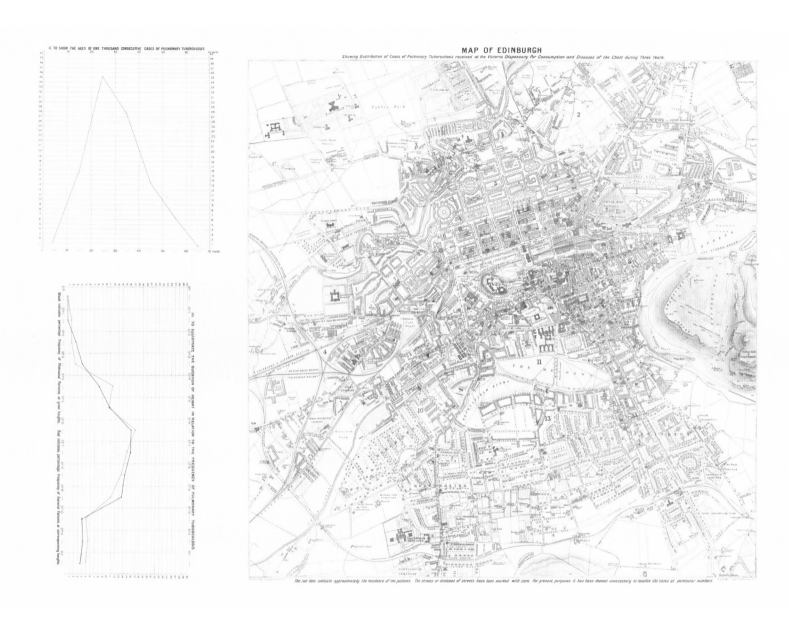

FIGURE 10.15 The association between geography and disease is revealed
in this map of 1892, showing the patterns of pulmonary tuberculosis
cases referred to Edinburgh Victoria Dispensary, 1889–92. Lung disease
is more prevalent amongst residents of 'Old Town' Edinburgh.
Source: Bartholomew / Oliver & Boyd, *Map of Edinburgh showing
Distribution of Cases of Pulmonary Tuberculosis Received at the Victoria
Dispensary for Consumption and Diseases of the Chest during Three Years*
(1892). Reproduced by permission of the Trustees of the National
Library of Scotland.

FIGURE 10.16 Mapping moving distributions – bird map 1: this map of
1879 shows the spread across south-central Scotland of the capercaillie
(*Tetrao urogallus*) following its re-introduction at Taymouth in 1838–39.
The spread between 1838 and 1879 can also be traced from the faint blue
concentric circles (to the east of Kirriemuir, for example) and the located
dates (for example, near Cortachy, 1862).
Source: Bartholomew, *Map to Illustrate Extension of range of the Capercaillie in
Scotland since its Restoration at Taymouth in 1837–1838* (1879). Reproduced
by permission of the Trustees of the National Library of Scotland.

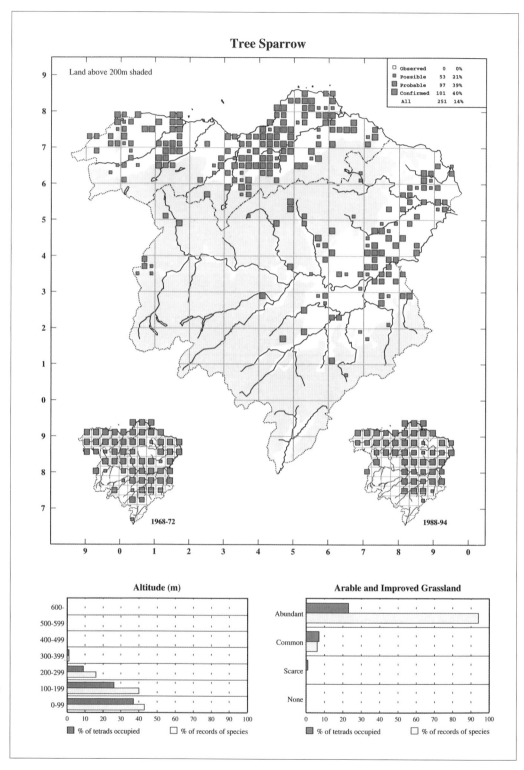

Tree Sparrow

Land above 200m shaded

		Observed	0	0%
		Possible	53	21%
		Probable	97	39%
		Confirmed	101	40%
		All	251	14%

1968-72

1988-94

Altitude (m)

600-
500-599
400-499
300-399
200-299
100-199
0-99

0 10 20 30 40 50 60 70 80 90 100

■ % of tetrads occupied   □ % of records of species

Arable and Improved Grassland

Abundant

Common

Scarce

None

0 10 20 30 40 50 60 70 80 90 100

■ % of tetrads occupied   □ % of records of species

FIGURE 10.17 Mapping declining distributions –
bird map 2: this map showing sightings of the
tree sparrow (*Passer montanus*) reveals regional
clustering within south and south-east Scotland
and a decline overall since the late 1960s, the
result of changes in farming practice.
Source: R. Murray / Scottish Ornithologists'
Club, 'Map showing sightings of the tree sparrow
(*Passer montanus*)', p. 293, from *The Breeding Birds
of South-east Scotland: A Tetrad Atlas 1988–1994*
(1998). Reproduced by permission of the
Scottish Ornithologists' Club.

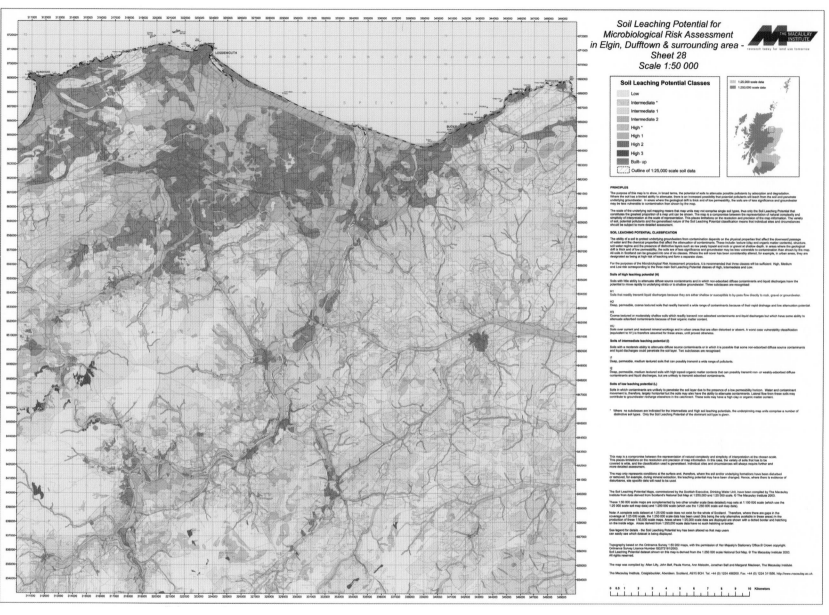

FIGURE 10.18 Mapping natural processes: this detail is part of maps produced
in 2005 detailing the soil leaching potential for microbiological risk assessment –
attempts to locate and classify the future potential for soils to act as a barrier to
pollutants entering the groundwater system. As its compilers recognise, the map
is a visual compromise between the representation of natural complexity and the
scale chosen.

Source: Macaulay Land Use Research Institute, *Soil Leaching Potential for Microbiological Risk Assessment in Elgin, Dufftown & surrounding area. 1:50,000. Sheet 28.*
(2005). Reproduced by permission of the Macaulay Land Use Research Institute.

253

I R E L A

Lough
Foyle

Londonderry

SHINTY.

Longitude West from Greenwich

CHAPTER 11

OPEN SPACES – RECREATION AND LEISURE

Scotland is a natural playground. It is endowed with a rich diversity of landscapes, ranging from extensive and varied mountain and moorland topography, deeply indented glens, wide straths, broad firths and a lengthy and intricate coastline with numerous islands. Scotland's geography is also one of large stretches of coastal flats, an abundance of rivers, superb beaches and machair, particularly off its northern and western coasts. This embarrassment of geographical riches provides a backdrop of open spaces for recreation and leisure on which many outdoor pursuits have developed. Some of these pursuits – golf, for instance, deer stalking, curling, shinty and highland games – have an identifiable resonance throughout the world as being somehow distinctively Scottish, not just part of Scotland's culture and history but integral to them, woven into the fabric of Scottish life and identity. And so they are.

Yet many questions underlying recreation, leisure and Scotland's open spaces – questions to do with the cultural values placed on outdoor nature, with the significance of wild mountain scenery as visually pleasing and a recre-

ational arena free for all to access and use, with nature's spaces as important socially, economically and scientifically – are not constant and unchanging facts. They have been 'invented' in a variety of ways, culturally manufactured as elements of Scotland's history and geography. Before the late eighteenth century, for example, mountainous landscapes, in Scotland and elsewhere, were not regarded as 'scenery', but as ruins, wilderness, as indications of moral sloth, as the home of barbarians and primitive cultures. Particularly for the Highlands but not only there, the cultural invention of certain icons to do with leisure and recreation has denied other historical and cultural processes. 'Open' spaces for hunting and shooting in the nineteenth century appeared because working farms were cleared; certain places and features – the Trossachs, Loch Ness, Glencoe to name but a few – carry the cultural and symbolic value they do because of important historical associations: with Sir Walter Scott's novels; with monsters real or not; with massacres, betrayal and mountain gloom.

A glance at the ways recreational activities are portrayed on maps in modern society will distinguish several features. Maps are commonly drawn up at the planning stage for such activities by architects, chartered surveyors, civil engineers or designers and later developed into blueprints from which the site is created, developed or amended. Maps, paper or electronic, are used to show how the recreation or leisure pursuit is part of the total topographical and social information portrayed: there is, after all, no reason not to show such features. Maps for locating and planning sports facilities, maps taken into the outdoors as we walk and climb – either the Ordnance Survey Landranger or Explorer series – maps of rivers and fishing grounds, of ski slopes, and many others – are now so common in relation to our leisure pursuits that we are in danger of assuming them to have been always present.

Looked at historically, maps were not a major part of these social matters. Maps of and for leisure do not, in general, appear before the mid- to later nineteenth century for the simple reason that leisure, as a widely available social phenomenon, was not common before then. Holidays, time for recreation, Saturdays and Sundays off work (usually half a day off work on a Saturday), regulated days free from paid labour: these are, for most Scots, Victorian inventions. They were consequent upon the development of factory-based systems of production, a growing working-class political voice, the emergence of the 'public holiday' and, of course, an available transport infrastructure to get one to the seaside or the mountainside, if only for a short time. That is not to say that the history of maps and mapping does not connect with the social history of leisure and questions of access to Scotland's open spaces. As we have shown throughout the book, maps are social documents and, in this context as in many others, study of them can help illuminate how ideas that we take for granted about recreation and leisure were produced in certain ways and for particular reasons.

MAPS FOR THE ANTIQUARIAN AND THE ROMANTIC TRAVELLER

Timothy Pont included written comments about the presence of fish and the abundance of game for hunting on some of his late-sixteenth-century manuscript maps (see fig. 3.9 for example). But these remarks should be seen as pointers to survival and the daily diet more than as statements of possible leisure activities: if they were anyone's 'recreation', it was for the well-to-do in society.

Maps for individual leisured travellers to Scotland's and Britain's open spaces – the early scientific observer, for instance, on the lookout for exposures of rocks, or travel writers keen to produce narratives of their journey – appear in books and learned periodicals by the end of the eighteenth century. Such maps often followed the tour or exploration in question rather more than they directed it: that is, the map appeared as result of the traveller's itinerary, rather than as an in-the-hand practical guide to it. They are not common for Scotland before the early nineteenth century for the simple reason that the Scottish landscape, especially in the Highlands, was not popular as a venue before then, and because leisure and recreation were the pursuit of the wealthy few: maps for such a purpose did not yet have a mass market.

Four main trends may be identified in what we can think of as the recreational 'discovery' of Scotland. The first was the representation (from the early eighteenth century) of the country (and the Highlands in particular) as a place of natural and cultural curiosity (this is exactly what motivated Martin Martin's correspondents in the Royal Society as they urged him towards St Kilda: chapter 7). The second was the philosophical view, from the later eighteenth century, that Scotland's upland scenery was sublime, that it could provoke emotions of awe and wonder, even of terror, at the sweeping mountain topography, the signs of God's handiwork and nature's almost boundless magnificence. The third trend which we may identify was the 'vulgar tourism' of the later nineteenth century (where, as we have seen, railways were especially important). Lastly, the mass tourism of the twentieth century and later was evident in a variety of ways and rooted in questions of access (understanding that term to mean both different forms of transport and permission to walk in, climb over and run across others' property). In later years, access to Scotland's open spaces has been accompanied by a renewed sensitivity to the precious qualities in nature and by recognition of the need to manage recreation lest wild places and nature as a whole be sullied.

Evidence for these trends is clear. Take as one illustration Captain Edmund Burt, a military engineer at work in the early eighteenth-century Highlands. In his *Letters from the North of Scotland* written in the 1720s but not published until 1754, Burt made his distaste for the whole Highland landscape very plain: this was scenery [Burt wrote] of 'monstrous Excrescences' and drab colours, 'a dismal gloomy Brown drawing on a dirty Purple'. But by the later eighteenth century, men like Thomas Pennant and others had toured the Highlands and much of Lowland Scotland as natural and social observers, pointing not just to the merits of the scenery and the charm of the people but to the future prospects for the nation (fig. 11.1).

In the wake of Culloden, the Highlands became safe to visit, and the Highland way of life became an object of antiquarian interest to Samuel Johnson and many others like him (Johnson took with him a copy of Martin Martin's Hebridean travels as a guide to his own travels). Artists such as Jacob More, Alexander Nasmyth and, in later decades, J. M. W. Turner, Horatio MacCulloch and Edwin Landseer amongst others, portrayed Scotland, especially Highland Scotland, as a land of castles, majestic mountains and, if not wholly empty glens, then glens populated by stylised lone figures clad in tartan, parodies of a defeated clan system, servants to their own landscape. Burt's 'dirty Purple' became instead associated with hillsides of bonny heather, mountain magnificence and majesty. The visit of King George IV to Edinburgh in 1822, a royal 'plaided panorama' that was stage-managed by Sir Walter Scott and David Stewart of Garth, helped link Scottishness, tartanry and monarchy as never before. Queen Victoria's love for the Highlands further developed the links between Scottishness, Highlandness and 'Balmorality'.

Where the mapping of clan lands had once been associated with a real military threat (see chapter 4), clan maps appeared as icons of a society seemingly neatly ordered by territory but which was, in reality, then in its death throes (fig. 11.2). Scotland was put on the map of culture in these ways — put on the tourist trail, so to speak. But, before the 1820s and 1830s, maps of Scotland did not document these cultural changes in attitude because, in truth, they could not. The market did not exist. Maps served those other functions we have documented here. Tourist maps had no place in the absence of tourists. Scotland's open spaces existed but were not yet the nation's playground.

In some urban mapping and occasionally on some county maps of Scotland, where scale and space permitted, references to such things as curling ponds, bowling greens, golf links and open green spaces speak of different cultures of leisure and recreation (figs. 11.3, 11.4). It would have been surprising, of course, had such things not appeared. These features, like everything else selected,

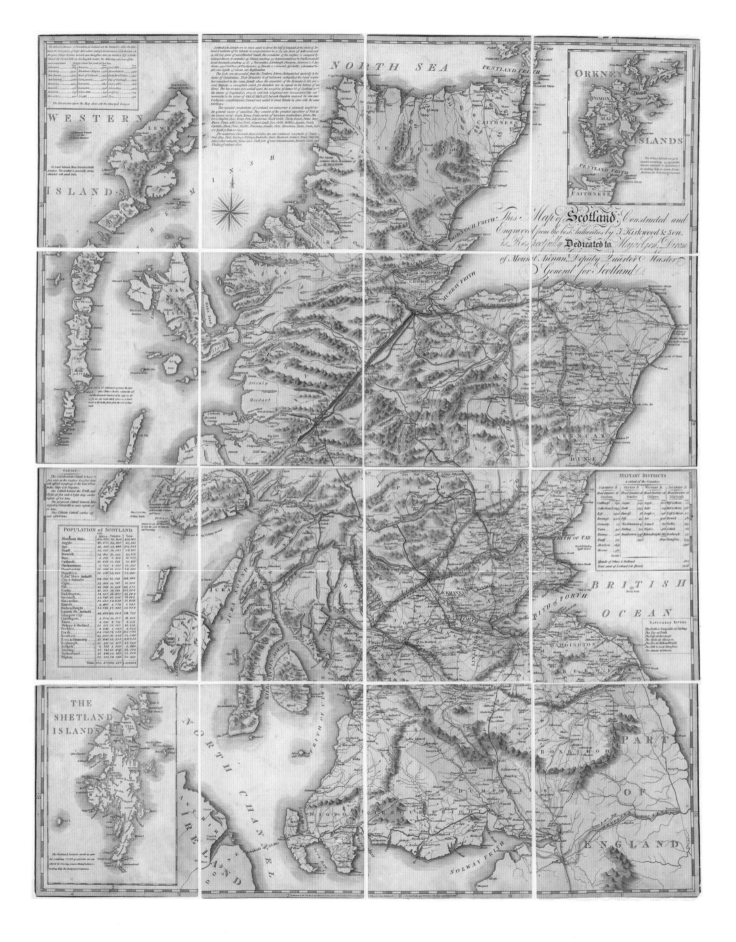

FIGURE 11.1 *Opposite*. Respectfully dedicated to Major General Dirom, Deputy Quarter Master General for Scotland, whose father had been Provost of Banff, this encyclopaedic map is described on its cover as a 'Travelling Map' and contains a huge amount of textual information on Scotland for the interested traveller. Although in no sense a tourist map at this period, it lists Scotland's extent, history, principal mountains, navigable rivers, 1811 Census population figures by county, projected and existing railways and canals, as well as its major products. The Highland Line (historic line of separation between the Highlands and Lowlands) is drawn in, as well as the Highland Road and Bridge District, and the Highland Distillery Line (the area north and west of which paid a lower duty on spirits produced). Reference is made to Scotland possessing 'the greatest repository of fish in the known world' and to the weather in Lewis and Harris as 'generally stormy attended with much rain'. It also reminds the traveller there is 'no land between these islands [Outer Hebrides] & North America'. It is a superb and concise geographical exposition of Scotland in one small map. *Source:* James Kirkwood & Son, *This Map of Scotland, Constructed and Engraved from the Best Authorities . . .* (1810 [1811]). Reproduced by permission of the Trustees of the National Library of Scotland.

FIGURE 11.2 *Left*. Coinciding with the visit of King George IV to Edinburgh in 1822, this map is an attempt to delimit the clan territories behind the Highland Line. Each is differentiated in colour, though not all clans feature. Partial reference too is made to lands no longer viewed as a particular clan's territory, as for instance 'anciently MacLeods' over part of Assynt and 'Anciently Macdonald' over Ardnamurchan and the south shore of Loch Shiel. While the large swathe of Campbell territory is all coloured pale yellow, the clan name itself is not shown. Perhaps the map-maker felt such a major clan's territory was self-evident. *Source:* W. H. Lizars, *Map of the Highlands of Scotland Denoting the Districts or Counties Inhabited by the Highland Clans* (1822). Reproduced by permission of the Trustees of the National Library of Scotland.

FIGURE 11.3 Nineteenth-century Royalty's recreational facilities are shown here in the form of the bowling green at the rear of Holyrood Palace, together with the extensive gardens available for the pleasure of the then monarch, George III, and his Court. It was not until 1822 that his successor, George IV, paid a first visit to Edinburgh. *Source:* William Bell, *Plan of the Regality of Canongate Comprising the Liberties of Pleasance, North Leith, Coal-hill and Citidal thereof* (1813). Reproduced by permission of the Trustees of the National Library of Scotland.

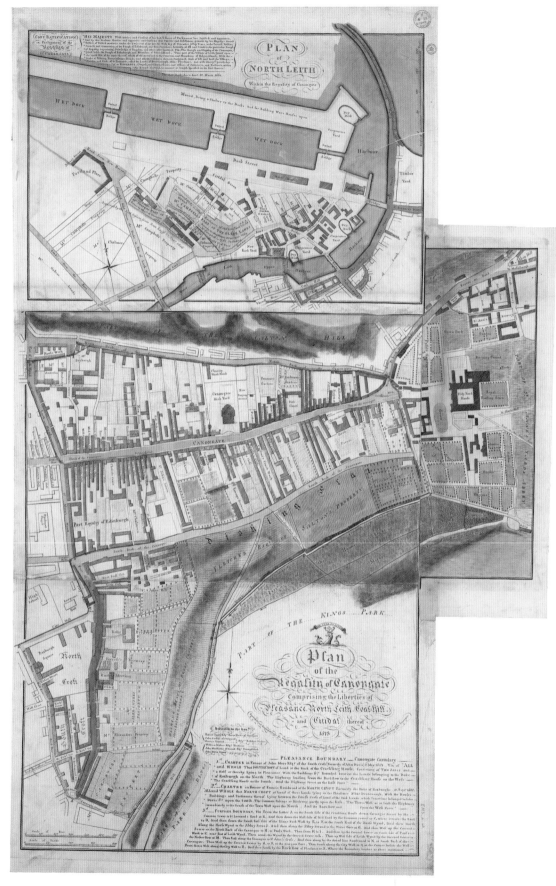

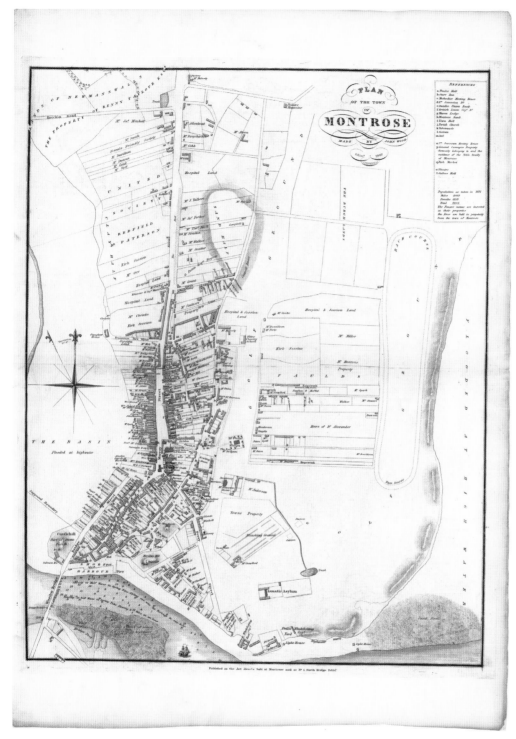

FIGURE 11.4 As part of his survey of towns in Scotland between 1818 and 1846, John Wood collected detailed information not only of the street layout and buildings of a town but also of the principal industries, landowners and proprietors, as well as other interesting information. Some of this was added to the map in textual form as a block of notes or key, while other details were fitted in between the linear features on the map. Despite restrictions on the space available – and hence the amount of information he could squeeze in without making the map over busy – Wood was intent on portraying as full a picture as possible of the town. The long strip of links ground near the coast were used, as he indicates, for the playing of golf, as a race course, and included a bowling green.
Source: John Wood, *Plan of the Town of Montrose* (1822). Reproduced by permission of the Trustees of the National Library of Scotland.

were all grist to the cartographer's mill. And as Ordnance Survey began production of its large-scale Scottish town plans, recreational features such as bowling greens and curling ponds were regularly depicted. By the mid–nineteenth century, however, maps – often in combination with other visual imagery – were beginning to market the nation as a whole, and particular places, as a tourist commodity.

SCOTLAND THE BRAND

The sense in which maps and images in combination have portrayed the nation as a recreational space is clear in Tallis's map of 1851 (fig. 11.5). Certain vignettes – the playing of shinty against a Highland backdrop, and the depiction of locations associated with Sir Walter Scott – are here used to illustrate the possibilities for recreation and leisure, either actively in the outdoors, or at a more pedestrian pace in the streets of the capital.

The association between map-making, place marketing and recreational activity was particularly clear by the early twentieth century, partly because changes in affordable transport allowed more people to have access to the countryside than before (see chapter 9), partly from a conscious decision on the part of map companies to portray an almost iconic, even an imagined, Scotland in maps and related publicity, and because Scots and visitors to the country now had the means to take advantage of leisure time. At the turn of the twentieth century with the growth in tourism, the rapid development of seaside and inland resorts and the invention of the bicycle and the motor car, markets were created for new map products to cater for those persons now able and willing to explore the countryside, or even their local environment, at weekends and for longer holidays (fig. 11.6). Touring and the tourist took on new prominence.

Scottish map-makers were to the fore here in catering for what became a mass demand, and a plethora of maps emanated from such Scottish publishing houses as Bartholomew (fig. 11.7), Gall & Inglis (fig. 11.8) and W. & A. K. Johnston (fig. 11.9). These and other map-making firms, together with local authorities, heritage and special interest groups, and other bodies (public and private), as well as Ordnance Survey, competed for this growing market both with individual products and series mapping such as the Bartholomew Half-inch Series and the Gall & Inglis Graded Road Maps. From the 1920s, Ordnance Survey used artists to design special covers for their folded tourist map series of such popular tourist areas as the Cairngorms, Burns Country, Rothesay and the Firth of Clyde, the Trossachs, Scott's Country and Deeside (figs. 11.10, 11.11). Bartholomew also began to use professional artists at this time to design a number of colourful map advertisements, particularly geared to the motorist (fig. 11.12). From this period onwards, maps were central to Scotland's marketing of itself. Today's tourist maps are produced for historic castle trails, long-distance footpaths and so on.

FIGURE 11.5 *Opposite.* Published in 1851 by John Tallis & Co. in *The Illustrated Atlas and Modern History of the World: Geographical, Political, Commercial & Statistical*, this beautifully decorated map attempts to personify in its borders those facets of Scotland best known to the mid-nineteenth century public. Six fine vignettes of Scottish scenes, including the playing of shinty and three men stalking a deer, fill open spaces outwith the actual map of Scotland. The delicate fretwork border includes the Scottish regalia and other symbols of 'Scottishness', not least the ubiquitous thistle. *Source:* John Tallis, 'Scotland' (1851). Reproduced by permission of the Trustees of the National Library of Scotland.

SCOTLAND

EDINBURGH.

BRIG OF DOON & BURNS MONUMENT.

SCOTT'S MONUMENT.

DEER STALKING.

SHINTY.

HOLYROOD HOUSE.

J. & F. TALLIS, LONDON, EDINBURGH & DUBLIN.

FIGURE 11.6 *Below.* This display of covers shows the typical tourist and travelling maps produced in the last quarter of the nineteenth century and the first quarter of the twentieth century by such Scottish publishing houses as Bartholomew and Gall & Inglis.
Source: A selection of map covers (1926). Reproduced by permission of the Trustees of the National Library of Scotland.

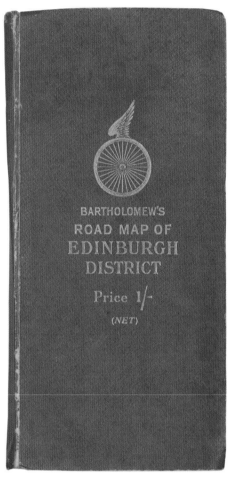

FIGURE 11.7 *Above. Source:* Bartholomew, *Bartholomew's Road Map of Edinburgh District* (1898). Reproduced by permission of the Trustees of the National Library of Scotland.

FIGURE 11.8 *Right. Source:* Gall & Inglis, *Tourists' Map of Loch Lomond and the Trossachs* (*c.*1915). Reproduced by permission of the Trustees of the National Library of Scotland.

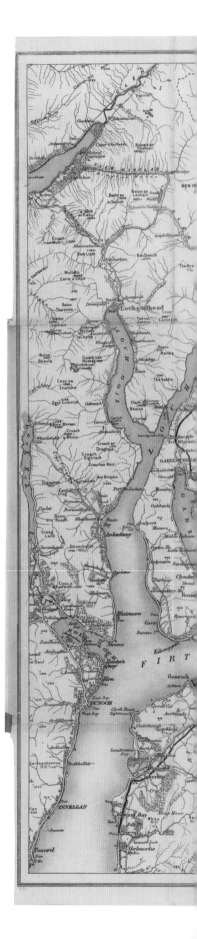

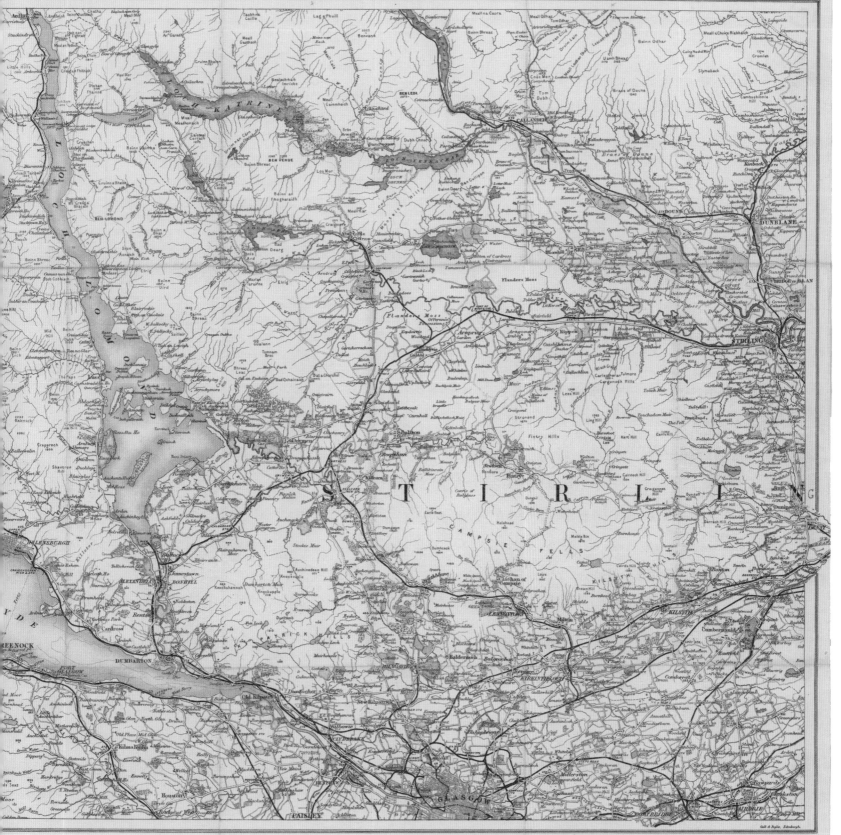

Gall & Inglis, Edinburgh.

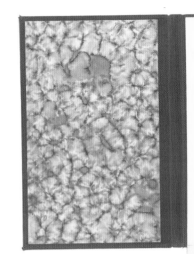

FIGURE 11.9 Constructed and printed by the map-makers W. & A. K. Johnston in Edinburgh, this unusual map was published in Glasgow by McCorquodale & Co. The idea of using maps to 'sell' a new sporting venture is used to the full here in promoting the brand new resort of Gleneagles, sited largely in what had been a wilderness of glacial sand and gravel deposits left behind after the Ice Age. The venture – the idea of Donald Matheson, General Manager of the former Caledonian Railway – consisted of two new golf courses (the King's and the Queen's) a luxury hotel to accommodate tourists and golfers, and a new railway station to allow direct access. The hotel was introduced to the public as a 'Riviera in the Highlands' and Gleneagles was duly marketed – as shown on the map – as being at the geographical heart of Scotland. The opening Gala took place on 7 June 1924, though the King's Course opened in 1919, the same year as the new railway station. The addition of tiny vignettes of interesting places in Scotland for tourists to visit such as Inveraray Castle, Brig O' Doun and Sir Walter Scott's home, Abbots-ford, adds to the attractiveness for the potential tourist. The stress on the good railway connections, including from the Continent, all help to 'sell' the map and Gleneagles as a resort.

Source: W. & A. K. Johnston, *The Heart of Scotland – Gleneagles* (c. 1925). Reproduced by permission of the Trustees of the National Library of Scotland.

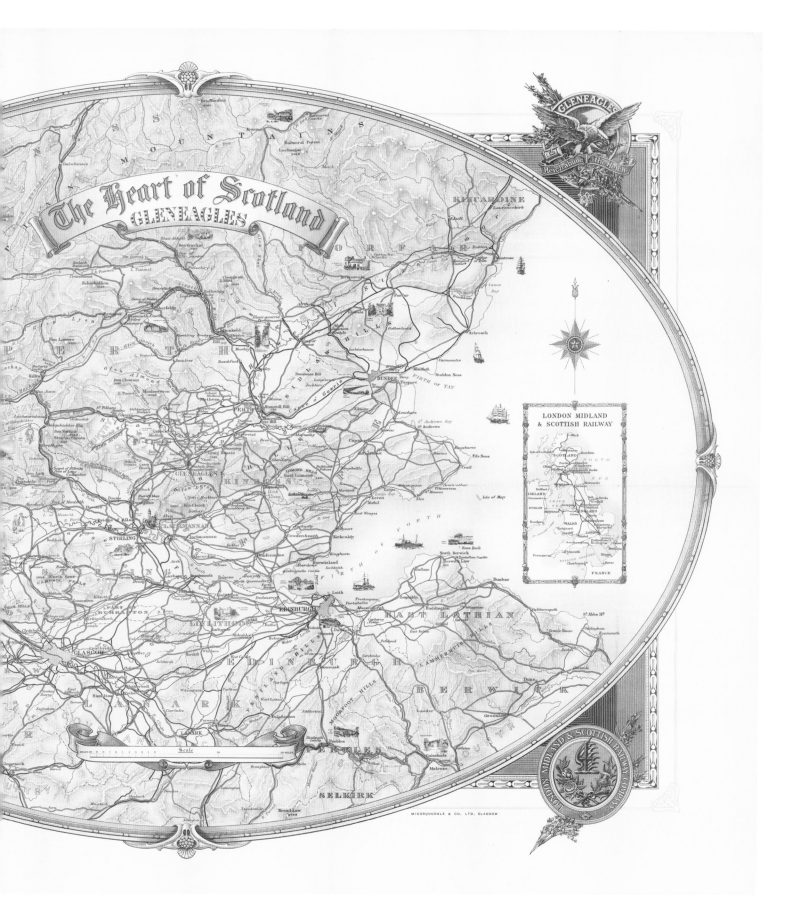

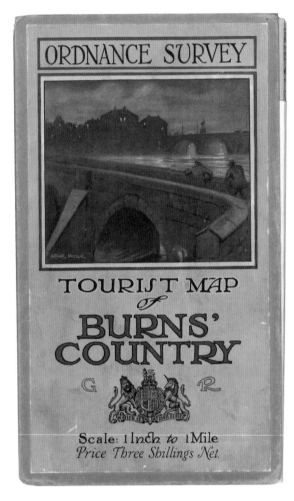 

FIGURE 11.10 Tempting the potential map buyer or traveller to purchase a map through the message of 'pick me up, look at me because I'm attractive' was what Ordnance Survey wanted to convey in the early 1920s through the use of well-designed and interesting map covers. Both examples set out to give a flavour of the region depicted on the map and were delivered in a folded, compact form for ready carriage in the new motor car or on a bicycle while touring Scotland. These covers were the work of Ordnance Survey's amateur artist assistant Arthur Palmer, who also had a separate, more mainstream, full-time job as a photo-writer with Ordnance Survey. Palmer's dramatic painting of the iconic Auld Brig at Ayr seems more suited to the cover of a detective novel, but his choice of subject is linked cleverly to the map title, 'Burns Country', through Robert Burns's poem, 'The Brigs o' Ayr', well known to the travelling public at that time. The melodramatic result might indeed persuade the passerby to purchase the map and visit Ayr. Palmer's painting of the railway and ferry terminals, the harbour and sea front of the burgeoning resort of Oban, capital of the West Highlands, is in contrast much brighter, even though portrayed in dominantly brown shades. Without words, it epitomises Oban for the tourist: the railway, which reached Oban in 1880 and by way of which many would travel from Glasgow and central Scotland; the ferry terminal from which they could take steamer trips to explore the Inner and Outer Hebrides; and the seafront and beach where they might take the air.

Source: Arthur Palmer / Ordnance Survey, covers of Ordnance Survey tourist maps – Burns Country (1921) and Oban (1920). Reproduced by permission of the Trustees of the National Library of Scotland.

FIGURE 11.11 Pictorial maps, where icons and imagery overshadow the topography, have graphic similarities to medieval maps with their overt religious and political messages (see figs. 2.3 and 2.6). By the twentieth century, they became popular promotional tools – particularly by corporations for marketing purposes – employing skilled artists and illustrators to create a pleasing aesthetic, and carrying similarly potent promotional messages. Charles Pratt was an oil company director, and his 'High Test' motor fuel was popular in the inter-war period, promoted on a range of merchandise, including maps. Pratt's *High Test Plan of Scotland* was published by the Anglo-American Oil Company (which became British Petroleum in 1954), and attractively transforms Scotland into a paradise for leisure and recreation.

Source: A. E. Wilson, *Pratt's High Test Plan of Scotland: A Curious yet Authentic Plan setting forth the Principal Highways and Romantic Places of the Country* (1931). Reproduced by permission of the Trustees of the National Library of Scotland.

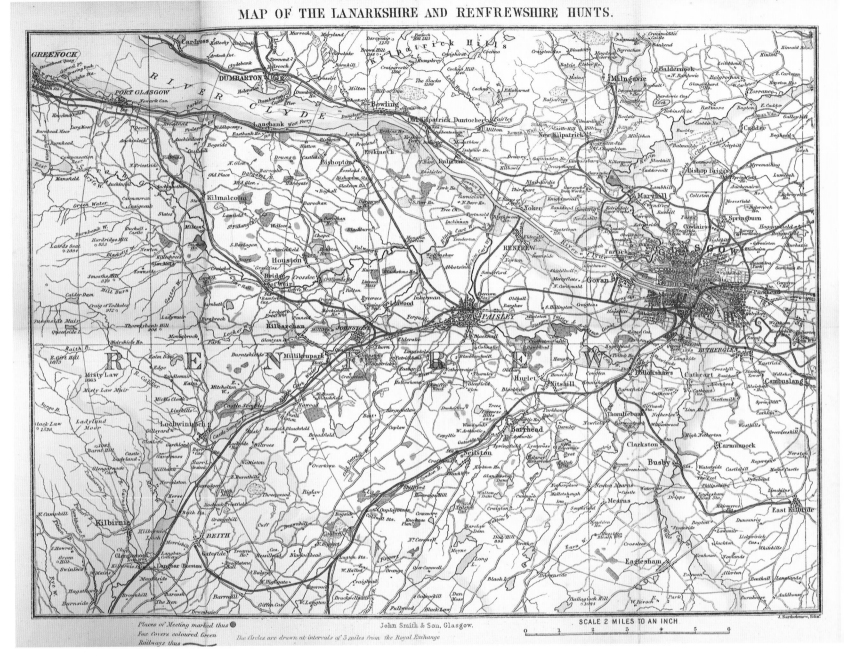

MAP OF THE LANARKSHIRE AND RENFREWSHIRE HUNTS.

John Smith & Son, Glasgow.

Places of Meeting marked thus ●
Fox Covers coloured Green
Railways thus

The Circles are drawn at intervals of 3 miles from the Royal Exchange

SCALE 2 MILES TO AN INCH

FIGURE 11.12 The popularity of hunting as a sport in the mid- to late-nineteenth century led to the publication of a number of maps of particular hunts in Great Britain, including a few in Scotland. Printed by Bartholomew but published and distributed by John Smith's (Scotland's oldest bookselling retailer in Glasgow, founded in 1751), this late-nineteenth-century recreational map of the hunts to the west and south of Glasgow defines the hunt Meets with red dots, shows the fox coverts in green and the distances from Glasgow in 3-mile circles.

Source: Bartholomew, *Map of the Lanarkshire and Renfrewshire Hunts* (1875). Reproduced by permission of the Trustees of the National Library of Scotland.

270

A SPORTING NATION

As the market for recreation specialised, suitably specialised maps were produced in response. Each pursuit, recreation and leisure activity has acquired – or usually requires – its particular territory or pitch. Some pursuits, such as golf, horse racing or football, have long had a presence in Scotland and so have evolved through time into an ordered activity requiring a set-aside space, specifically and individually tailored for that pursuit at a particular location. Of course, many sports and leisure activities can be undertaken or played only where there is a suitable designated space. Yet others, such as orienteering and mountaineering, work well only in the great outdoors and so have prompted particular types of maps and map-using skills.

Scotland's modern geography and cartography shows in several ways the impact of the advance of recreation and leisure. For some sports, of course, the arena is nature: maps point the way, but all that is needed is care, a compass, suitable clothing and good weather. In sports such as deer stalking and grouse shooting, no specialist maps may be necessary: Ordnance Survey maps of one type or another will suffice. Other sports, such as orienteering or fell walking, rely on such sources as Ordnance Survey for the background information and data, but adjust and add their own data as required. Yet others increasingly rely on mapping and satellite imagery generated on websites by search engines such as Google.

The geography of the country – and of the countryside in particular – has been transformed, much of it in recent memory. Landscapes have been modified, managed and even artificially contrived to create open spaces suitable for sporting pursuits (stocking shooting estates, for example). Golf links and courses, ski runs, car rallying tracks, forest parks and theme parks all need redesigned landscapes, which may have to fit within a working agricultural landscape, or incorporate the management of protected natural wildscapes or rare species.

These are everyday concerns for twenty-first-century Scotland, but they have historic expression. Maps appeared in the mid-nineteenth century for specialist sports like hunting, and even for particular hunts, as in Bartholomew's *Map of the Lanarkshire and Renfrewshire Hunts* (fig. 11.12), published in 1875, or for a particular county such as a *Hunting Map of Ayrshire*, published in Glasgow in 1862. Horse racing, supported strongly by royalty (and an especial favourite of King Edward VII), led to the publishing of *The Race Courses Atlas of Britain and Ireland* in 1903 (fig. 11.14). In the 1930s a series of fishermen's maps was produced covering the Spey, the Tweed, the Dee and the Tay (fig. 11.15). For golf, such maps may show merely the course or links (fig. 11.16); but today these maps also need to indicate the boundaries, access points, car parking facilities and the location of key requirements such as public conveniences and eating places in relation to the site.

In the later twentieth century, a number of smaller specialist map-making companies, geared particularly to the leisured public, for example Harvey Maps, located in Doune, and Stirling Surveys, based in Stirling, have embraced the need to produce special maps of particular areas of geographical interest or for an individual sport. These companies have produced maps for mountain climbing, orienteering (fig. 11.17), cycling (fig. 11.18), long-distance walking, nature trails, national parks and, linking with such official bodies as the British Geological Survey, the British Mountaineering Council and

FIGURE 11.13 *Right.* Bartholomew was one of several cartographic firms keen to capitalise on the commercial opportunities associated with new forms of recreational travel. The dramatic expansion of the automobile market, with its associated infrastructure and publications, allowed good opportunities for advertising, and other promotional artwork commissioned by the firm. Through their attractive style, rich colours, and broader imagery, these promotional items encapsulate something of a spirit of optimism and pleasure during this early era of British motoring.
Source: Bartholomew *Bartholomew's Maps – the Wise Motorist's Guide* (*c.* 1930s). Reproduced by permission of the Trustees of the National Library of Scotland.

FIGURE 11.14 *Below.* This racecourse atlas, appearing 'under the gracious patronage of His Majesty the King [Edward VII] and His Royal Highness the Prince of Wales', contained maps of all the existing racecourses in Great Britain and Ireland (its author proudly asserting it was the first to do this) and incorporated in each a brief description of the course, as well as showing any gradient changes and an indication of the underlying subsoil or geology. A number of the racecourses depicted in the atlas have not survived, and Eglinton, better known as Bogside, by Irvine, Ayrshire, is now abandoned though a few vestiges of the grandstand and hurdles can still be seen on the ground.
Source: F. H. Bayles, 'Eglington Hunt' from *The Race Courses Atlas of Great Britain and Ireland* (1903). Reproduced by permission of the Trustees of the National Library of Scotland.

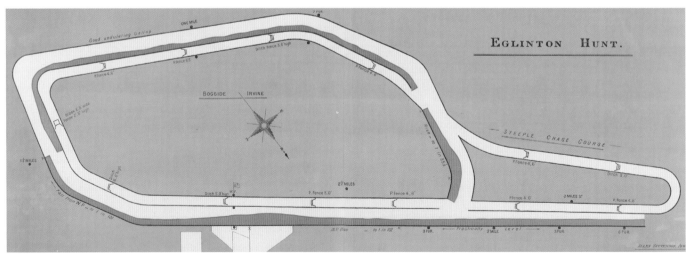

National Parks authorities, have made an even wider range of mapping available for exploring and utilising Scotland's open spaces. In maps for tourism, recreation and leisure, Scotland markets itself as a wholly healthy country (it does not map its geographies of inner-city deprivation, 'hot-spots' of cancer-related mortality or areas prone to flooding) and as a national space whose history — its castles, battlefields and sites of interest — can easily be reached through its compact geography (fig. 11.19). Maps of and for recreation are amongst the most heavily selective forms of cartography and create very particular ways of seeing often far removed from those of residents or workers in the same place.

Many maps of recreational and leisure facilities are customised and ephemeral, sometimes with little attention paid to what might be thought of as standard cartographic conventions, or apparently not owing anything to official topographic maps such as those produced by Ordnance Survey. The prevalence of recreation and leisure has prompted not so much a modern cartographic revolution as a shift in emphasis towards graphic designers rather than cartographers. Product and production are highly market and place specific. In numerous cases, perhaps because of the criteria of content selection and because so much 'real' Scotland is omitted, maps may not be used — or even read — properly. If Scotland's countryside and open space is found not to correspond with the patterns of lines signifying contours, rough terrain or no right of way, or if stylised distances and map selections do not caution about the nature of Scotland's nature, there can be fatal consequences.

It is almost impossible to 'get away from it all' without creating or looking at a map or plan in connection with Scotland's open spaces. But the very ubiquity of such maps — and the fact that we each carry maps of places in our heads as well as in our rucksacks — should not blind us to the fact that maps for recreation and leisure are a recent part of Scotland's map history.

FIGURE 11.15 *Overleaf*. Fishing has always been a very popular sport in Scotland and during the 1930s Maude Parker, RWA, produced a number of fishing maps including maps of the rivers Tweed, Spey, Dee and Tay. There was an obvious market for these, and her attractive drawings of these key Scottish salmon rivers detailed the salmon pools as well as local river features. We see here both her original artwork for the salmon pools on part of the River Spey and the final printed map by Bartholomew in 1933. Parker made changes on the manuscript version to the stretch of the Spey between Grantown and Ballindalloch Castle, and a note in pencil indicates that a reduction in scale to half was necessary for the printed version.

FIGURE 11.15 [A] *Source:* Maude Parker, 'Fisherman's map of salmon pools on part of the River Spey' — original MS artwork (*c.*1933). Copyright © Published with permission of HarperCollins Publishers.

FIGURE 11.15 [B] *Source:* Maude Parker, *Fisherman's Map of Salmon Pools on Part of the River Spey* — printed map (1933). Reproduced by permission of the Trustees of the National Library of Scotland.

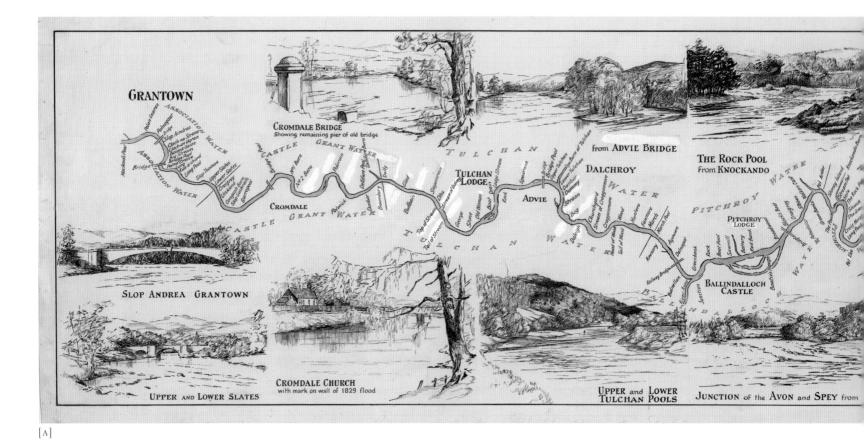

[A]

GRANTOWN

CROMDALE BRIDGE
Showing remaining pier of old bridge

from ADVIE BRIDGE

THE ROCK POOL
From KNOCKANDO

TULCHAN
LODGE

DALCHROY

ADVIE

PITCHROY

PITCHROY
LODGE

BALLINDALLOCH
CASTLE

CROMDALE

SLOP ANDREA GRANTOWN

CROMDALE CHURCH
with mark on wall of 1829 flood

UPPER AND LOWER SLATES

UPPER and LOWER
TULCHAN POOLS

JUNCTION of the AVON and SPEY from

[B]

GRANTOWN

CROMDALE BRIDGE
Showing remaining pier of old bridge

from ADVIE BRIDGE

THE ROCK POOL
From KNOCKANDO

TULCHAN
LODGE

DALCHROY

ADVIE

PITCHROY

PITCHROY
LODGE

BALLINDALLOCH
CASTLE

CROMDALE

SLOP ANDREA GRANTOWN

CROMDALE CHURCH
with mark on wall of 1829 flood

UPPER AND LOWER SLATES

UPPER and LOWER
TULCHAN POOLS

JUNCTION of the AVON and SPEY from

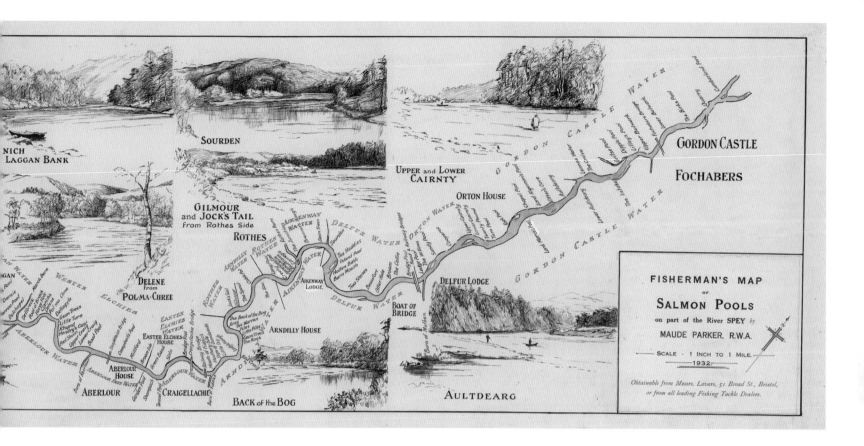

FISHERMAN'S MAP
of
SALMON POOLS
on part of the River SPEY by
MAUDE PARKER, R.W.A.

SCALE - 1 INCH TO 1 MILE.
1932.

Obtainable from Messrs. Lavars, 51 Broad St., Bristol,
or from all leading Fishing Tackle Dealers.

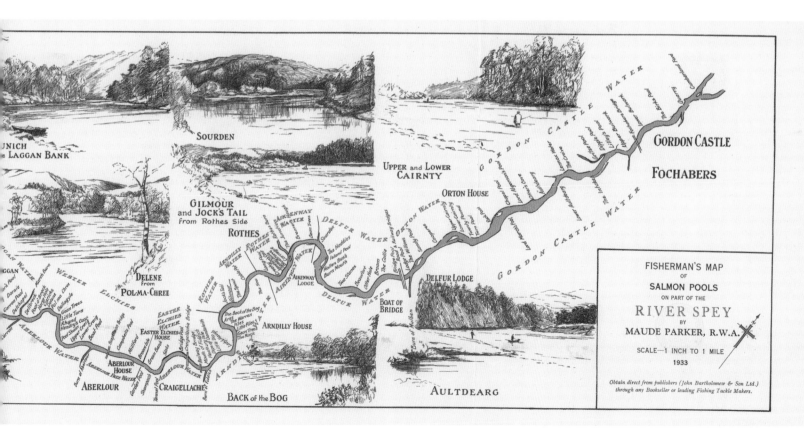

FISHERMAN'S MAP
OF
SALMON POOLS
ON PART OF THE
RIVER SPEY
BY
MAUDE PARKER, R.W.A.

SCALE—1 INCH TO 1 MILE
1933

Obtain direct from publishers (John Bartholomew & Son Ltd.)
through any Bookseller or leading Fishing Tackle Makers.

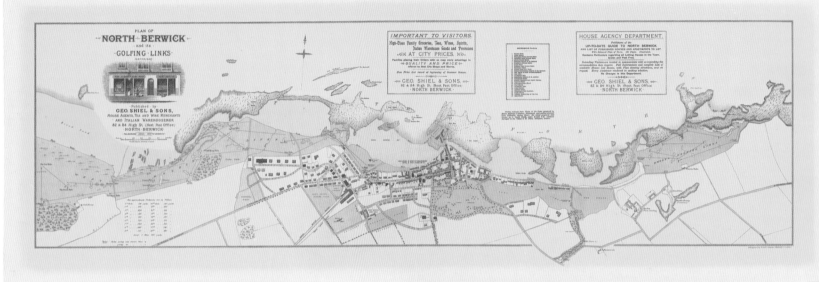

FIGURE 11.16 *Above*. Golf, another popular pastime in Scotland and with a long history, has seen the publication of innumerable books, as well as maps of individual golf courses and atlases containing multiple plans. Plans of the local links also appeared in tourist guides, particularly in the earlier twentieth century. This attractive plan of the golfing links at North Berwick on the East Lothian coast shows two courses set out on the links, one on each side of the town and harbour. It was printed by the well-known Edinburgh map-makers W. & A. K. Johnston. The smaller course on the East Links was a nine-hole course only. Attractive insets advertising some of the local shops and tourist facilities are placed to each side of the plan to entice the would-be golfer and tourist to visit the resort of North Berwick.
Source: J. Gould Smith, *Plan of North Berwick and its Golfing Links*. Reproduced by permission of East Lothian Libraries.

FIGURE 11.17 *Right*. An example of an early orienteering map of an area in the Trossachs produced by Harvey Maps, based in Doune, central Scotland. Using map scales usually between 1:5,000 and 1:15,000, such maps were aligned to magnetic north rather than true north because of the use of magnetic compasses by orienteers. Orienteering events take place in both rural and urban environments and test navigational skills over a course between set points. With a well-developed use of colouring to distinguish open land (yellow) from forest (white or green) and water (blue), and with further sub-categories in varying shades, a subtle and very detailed form of land-use map is produced.
Source: Harvey Maps, *Achray North; Achray South* (1983). Copyright © Harvey Map Services Ltd.

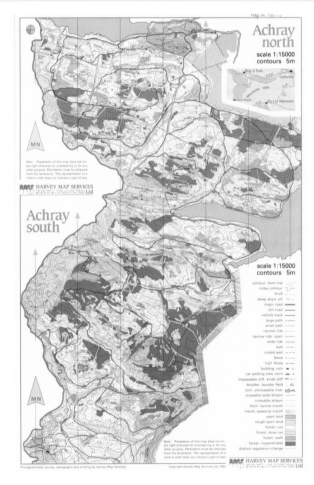

276

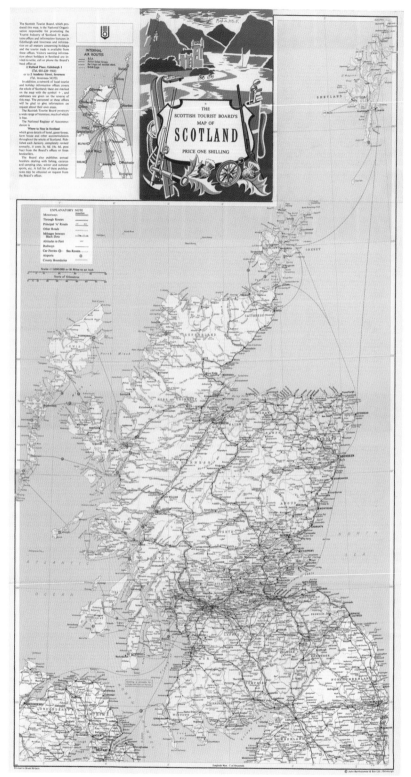

FIGURE 11.18 *Above.* A Scotsman, Kirkpatrick Macmillan, born in Nithsdale at Keir, some 15 miles north-north-west of Dumfries, is credited with the invention of the rear-wheel-driven pedal cycle around 1840, although it was not until after 1888, with the invention of the pneumatic bicycle tyre, that bicycling as a mode of transport, and a sport, took off as an everyday pursuit for the public at large. A hundred years later, further impetus was given to bicycle use as a means of transport, and particularly as a leisure pursuit, with the development of lightweight mountain bikes suitable for rough terrain, and the promotion of cycling as a healthful form of exercise. This impetus was followed by the production of specialist cycling maps, giving not only suggested cycle tours along minor roads and off-road trails but also information about places of interest en route. Covering a circular tour of some 250 miles through the eastern Scottish Borders and taking in the towns of Duns, Eyemouth, Kelso, Hawick and Melrose, this official route map and guide, made of a durable waterproof paper, was published by Stirling Surveys, a specialist in this field of mapping. The company used out of copyright Ordnance Survey mapping of the 1926–45 period as a basis for the map, updating it with its own field surveys and showing the relief through easy-to-read gradient tints.
Source: Stirling Surveys, *Borderloop: The Scottish Borders Cycle Tour. Official Route Map and Guide* (2008). Reproduced by permission of Stirling Surveys.

FIGURE 11.19 *Right. Source:* Scottish Tourist Board, *The Scottish Tourist Board's Map of Scotland* (1970). Reproduced by permission of VisitScotland.

BOWMORE ★ DISTILLERY
ISLAY

W & J MUTTER, BOWMORE DISTILLERY, ISLAY.

OFFICES, 41 ANN ST (CITY.) GLASGOW.

CHAPTER 12

POPULAR CULTURE

'The map is dead.' 'Long live maps.' These sentences are not the paradox they may appear. In the pre-television and pre-computer age, it was said (with some justification) that maps were out of date in terms of their information content – by months or years rather than by hours or days – by the time they were published or became available for public sale. Until the later twentieth century there were no instantly generated maps capable of being updated within minutes if required and easy to get hold of through electronic means for mass consumption on a worldwide scale. Until the mid-nineteenth century, there was no mass market for maps. Before then, maps were used in various ways for the reasons we have already explored, but they were not widely available as public commodities in popular culture.

Things seem different now – but are they? In the twenty-first century, information presented in map form is now much more readily in the public domain and, in electronic format, is also much more rapidly being transformed through available technology, most often as a result of the almost ubiquitous ownership and use of the computer, the mobile phone and satellite navigation packages. The public is now simply more aware of maps. Websites featuring data in map form, the growing ability to interconnect and overlay these data and the almost universal use of dynamic online portals such as Google Earth and Google Maps with its sidekick Street View: each has helped bring about what, in terms of the map's place in popular culture, its presence as a form of public information, we might term a 'public revolution' in the way map information is placed in popular culture. Even so, much 'modern' Google mapping is often quite dated (several years old) and inconsistent in its quality.

Nevertheless, this is a revolution rooted in technical changes and the capacity to make maps available as popular, cheap, public documents. These technological changes are based on the ability to geo-locate all data, including satellite imagery, with the ability to zoom in at close range to almost any neighbourhood on earth and add an almost instant map overlay of the settlement and street names and other textual information if required. Satellite navigation in private and commercial vehicles and its application in leisure pursuits such as walking and climbing have further increased map consciousness. The presence of maps as 'apps', applications in hand-held devices, has served to make map reading – even, after a fashion, forms of map-making – a popular process undertaken by the public in places and in ways far removed from the techniques pursued in specialist premises in past ages.

The impact of these technological changes is both a new and general public map awareness, and recognition of the benefits for particular markets – in geographical teaching and education, for example, where the capacity for new forms of thinking about and working with maps is immense. To computer-literate generations, maps that can be almost instantly manipulated, created and read may be educational and fun to use at the same time.

While it is true that maps did not have a place in popular culture in the past in the ways they do now, the modern history of the map as a public and cultural document cannot be understood without recognising the social contours of its use in the past. Maps may not always have been popular and certainly were not always public artefacts, but they have long had a public presence and a diversity of forms and purposes as popular objects. And, in novels, poetry and in other forms of creative writing, the idea of the map – that mapping is a creative writing process and a powerful metaphor for finding one's place – is evident in a variety of ways. To appreciate maps as documents in popular culture, as a representative form of history that has its place in Scotland's history, we need to understand these different forms of 'map consciousness' and to stretch our imaginations over different sorts of 'mapness', over what a map is and how maps work in popular culture.

THE MAP-MINDED PUBLIC

In contrast to the almost universal access to and availability of map information today, ownership or access to maps in Scotland before the middle of the nineteenth century was mainly the preserve of the well-to-do or the military. The public at large had little understanding or appreciation of maps because they seldom encountered or required them. By the mid-eighteenth century, maps featured in the newspapers and public broadsheets of the day, and were more and more used as illustrations of the language and practices of science in the learned periodicals. Yet these and other forms of print in the public sphere were mainly available to, and read only by, the more educated classes. The better-off in their country seats or town houses had their own libraries where atlases, county maps and road books might feature, and such persons often demonstrated their social standing and their purchasing power by subscribing to a planned new map of their county or town, or to a world or Scottish atlas. Maps had status as well as utility.

From the later eighteenth century, travellers to Scotland might make use of the strip road books produced by map-maker–surveyors, such as George Taylor and Andrew Skinner's *Survey and Maps of the Roads of North Britain, or Scotland* (see fig. 9.9), their attention having been drawn through advertisements in newspapers or through booksellers. Pocket versions of similar road books could also be purchased, which gave an idea of what to find in the immediate vicinity, or were used to plan journeys further afield. The status and utility of maps were part of a growing public sphere. Map history in that regard is connected with book history and print history, mapping with printing, print with literacy, literacy with social change, societal change with education, with individual and national betterment.

We must be wary, however, of equating the ubiquity and utility of maps with a familiarity with maps, with how they worked or were put together. Large numbers of maps and plans produced by Scotland's many land surveyors from the mid-eighteenth century onwards detailed the changing landscapes and estates upon which agricultural labourers toiled (see, for example, figs. 6.9, 7.12 and 7.13). But the land labourers whose lives were transformed by the processes set in train by such maps may never have set eyes on them. In the nineteenth century, navvies working on canal building, on railway construction or in the urban building industry may have seen maps and plans in the hands of their overseers, but did not themselves read these maps. These were products for a specific purpose and not marketed for popular or mass consumption. Maps were not read by all in society. The power of the map as a paper landscape, actual or projected, did not have to be seen to be felt.

For yet others, however, the map was felt as it was seen. Maps in other forms were popular and private objects designed for domestic use and to instruct in things other than geographical knowledge or the layout of estates and roads (figs. 12.1, 12.2). Sampler maps were gendered objects, devices to promote women's skills in embroidery and manual dexterity, and were mainly used in domestic spaces not public ones. The particular purpose of such tactile maps is to be explained by reference to what was in the past held to be appropriate for women to do, for their capacities and place in society. Our more general point now is that it is dangerous to generalise about the place of maps in popular culture without paying attention to the different material forms taken by maps, the audiences using them and the technologies used to meet the different market demands. The

FIGURE 12.1 Sewing a sampler was a common requirement for young ladies in earlier centuries, and their mothers saw this as a means of acquiring facility with the needle as well as being educational in terms of selecting the theme and the text to be included. With large families the norm, and with the prospect of a fair number of daughters in each, the London-based map-makers Robert Laurie and James Whittle took advantage of this potentially lucrative market to produce a printed template in the form of a paper map of Scotland, adapted in terms of its information content to one suitable for embroidery. Such template maps endured hard handling and, once the embroidered map was complete, the paper map may have been seen as superfluous and therefore destroyed. Their survival is therefore rare.
Source: Robert Laurie and James Whittle, *A New Map of Scotland for Ladies Needle Work* (1797). Reproduced by permission of the Trustees of the National Library of Scotland.

FIGURE 12.2 Around 1800, Margaret Montgomery began working a sampler and, from the outlines of Scotland and its counties displayed on this, it does not seem to have been based on Laurie and Whittle's template map of 1797 (fig. 12.1). Her mother and governess no doubt hoped Margaret would learn something of the geography of Scotland through laboriously stitching in the names of its counties – in this case often shortened to fit the necessary geographical space on the sampler. Curiously, Margaret included only one town, Port Patrick [sic], then the main ferry point for travellers crossing to Ireland. This may indicate that Portpatrick was the nearest town to Margaret's home or perhaps that she began stitching in town names at the south-west corner and quickly shied away from adding more. It was not until the mid-nineteenth century, forty years after Margaret worked her sampler, that the coastline of Scotland and its islands was finally surveyed accurately. Margaret's rendering of Scotland therefore reflects the outline of Scotland as found on maps of her time, some parts of which appear wrong to those viewing her sampler today.
Source: Margaret Montgomery, *A Map of Scotland* (on linen, as a sampler) (*c.*1800). Reproduced by permission of the Trustees of the National Library of Scotland.

fact that there were caricature maps by the end of the eighteenth century, for example, tells us something about the image some people then had of Scotland and the power of maps as figurative national icons, symbols of a country, not documents of accuracy and geographical reality (fig. 12.3).

Until the mid-nineteenth century, paper maps and atlases were principally produced by the labour-intensive process of engraving onto a copper plate and then printing onto paper. But the invention of lithography in the late eighteenth century, and its application to map production in Scotland from the first quarter of the nineteenth century, revolutionised the speed and cost of such production. Here, too, was a 'revolutionary' technological shift of great social consequence, quite in keeping with our modern electronic revolution even if the effect was slower in being felt. The possibility of printing multiple copies of cheap maps from the 1830s was, in cartography, part of a 'print revolution'. Associated new technology for use in the paper-making industry and in the binding

FIGURE 12.3 A colourful, satirical, yet rather ugly caricature of Scotland. Robert Dighton, was well known as a painter of portraits and satirical drawings, as well as a popular actor at Sadler's Wells Theatre. Dighton also drafted similarly unflattering 'droll caricature maps' of England and Wales, as well as of Ireland, which were issued as a set, 'Geography Bewitched!' *Source:* Robert Dighton, *Geography Bewitched! or, a droll caricature map of Scotland* (1794). Reproduced by permission of the Trustees of the National Library of Scotland.

process greatly facilitated the production and publication of cheap atlases for dissemination to an increasingly literate, and map literate, public. Map-makers took full advantage of these technological advances to enhance sales, deliberately targeting their products at a wider social strata, especially the middle classes in the fast-growing towns and cities. The most obvious way to reach the literate and reading public was through advertisements in newspapers by surveyors and map-makers drawing the public's attention to their new county maps, for instance, and often inviting subscribers for their new product (fig. 12.4). As mapping became professionalised, so map-makers had to create a public for their wares. As Scotland came to know itself through national written surveys, maps were produced to accompany them (fig. 12.5).

Popular atlases are one reflection of this growing popularity of maps and the growth of specialist markets. The *Shilling Atlas*, the *Half-Crown Atlas* and the *Sixpenny Atlas*, from Edinburgh and Glasgow-based map publishers such as W. & A. K. Johnston, Gall & Inglis, Black-

FIGURE 12.4 Map consciousness and promotion could sometimes be furthered in unexpected ways and in a format which had little chance of survival. Here, on an example of the surviving thin paper folder in which a subscriber received his copies of the county maps comprising John Thomson's *Atlas of Scotland*, a list of the booksellers offering these maps for sale is revealed, allowing us to gain some idea of the distribution pattern for the sale of such maps. A subscriber's list also appeared on another of these same wrappers, giving an indication of those who had been persuaded to acquire this atlas and of where they lived. Note the comments by the harassed publisher on the dilatoriness of some surveyors in not returning their promised work on time.

Source: John Thomson, *Atlas of Scotland – Haddingtonshire*, paper wrapper (1820). Reproduced by permission of the Trustees of the National Library of Scotland.

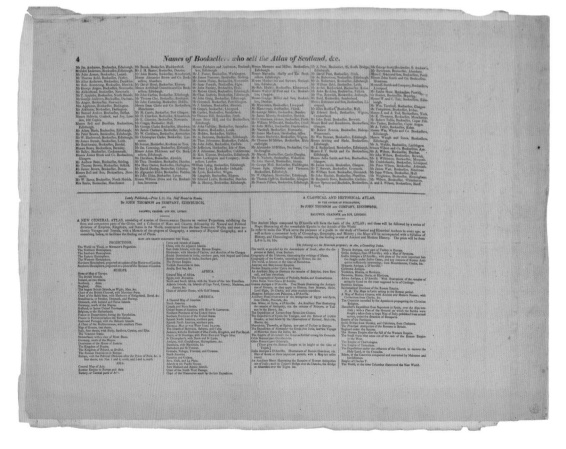

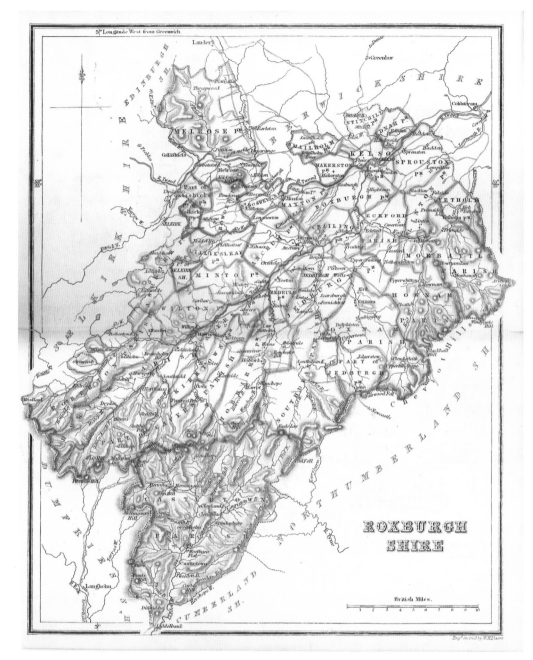

FIGURE 12.5 Compiled and engraved initially to accompany the written parish descriptions for the county of Roxburgh, which were contained in the third volume of *The New Statistical Account of Scotland* (1834–45), this map complemented the textual descriptions by showing the boundaries of the parishes described in the account and placing them in the context of the general topography of the county, as well as locating the main place names contained in each parish description. In this way, those members of the public reading this work became accustomed to the presence of maps complementing and enhancing the text. This pattern of text plus maps was a common component of gazetteers of the period. The publisher, William Blackwood & Sons, used the same maps in a separate atlas volume published in 1838, but without the parish texts. By the time of the second edition of this atlas in 1854, the growth of railways greatly facilitated and encouraged mass travel, and railway lines in existence were therefore added to some of these county maps. To cater for the growing need for more readily portable maps to slip in a pocket while travelling, these maps were also sold separately on a county basis for the benefit of the potential traveller not necessarily doing the 'grand tour'.

Source: W. H. Lizars, 'Roxburgh Shire', from *New Statistical Account of Scotland* (1834–45). Reproduced by permission of the Trustees of the National Library of Scotland.

wood's, Collins and Bartholomew, exemplify this output aimed at mass consumption. Globes, sometimes objects of status more than utility, were made for schools and colleges, not just for display in private drawing rooms. Educational aids such as large-sheet wall maps of the world and of its parts were produced and printed off in great number from the later nineteenth century. These products, and the evidence of even more specialist maps (figs. 12.6, 12.7, 12.8; see also fig. 10.9), point to an increased but varied public consciousness of the map and of its different capacities to amuse, educate and amend people's lives.

FIGURE 12.7 *Below.* Today's children play computer games and consequently may only occasionally resort to doing a jigsaw puzzle as a leisure pursuit. But in the 1890s, 'dissected maps', as they were known from the 1760s, were very popular with parents as gifts, not least for their instructive element – in this case a map of Scotland. The base map for this wooden jigsaw puzzle was a standard atlas plate used by the Edinburgh-based publisher, Gall & Inglis. Once the map was affixed to the wooden base, the whole was cut into sixty-three pieces and presented attractively in a wooden box with a decorated, varnished lid.

Source: W. & A. K. Johnston, *Superior Dissected Maps: Scotland* (1893). Reproduced by permission of the Trustees of the National Library of Scotland.

FIGURE 12.6 *Above.* Aimed at the cheaper and popular end of the burgeoning educational market for atlases, publishers were very conscious of the need to entice the would-be purchaser by using striking designs on the covers of such atlases.
Source: Various: W. & A. K. Johnston, Bartholomew, etc., covers of popular nineteenth-century Scottish-published atlases. Reproduced by permission of the Trustees of the National Library of Scotland.

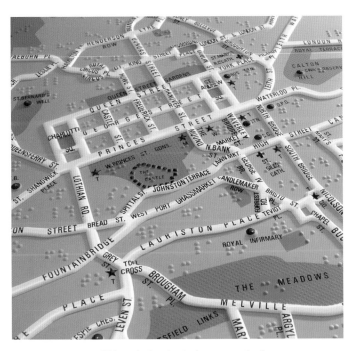

FIGURE 12.8 Although the aim is the same as in the nineteenth-century map of Scotland for the blind (fig. 10.9), this more recent 'tactile' map of Edinburgh allowed the visually impaired to feel – as a substitute for seeing – the shape and road pattern of central Edinburgh. The addition of vivid colouring was to help those with partial sight.
Source: D. Amor, *Central Edinburgh: A Guide to the Map of Central Edinburgh / Compiled and Written by D. Amor* (1978). Copyright © RNIB.

MAPS IN THE MIND

Maps are works of selective inscription. They function by writing things down and by leaving things out. If there is, as we have suggested, a history of map mindedness in popular culture, we must not neglect that parallel history of maps in the mind. Maps aid the literary imagination because they can help fix or place a narrative: in his *Life of Scott,* for example, John Gibson Lockhart, son-in-law of Sir Walter Scott, describes Sir Walter making use of maps in writing his novels: 'I remember observing him many times in the Advocates' Library poring over maps and gazetteers with care and anxiety.' Robert Louis Stevenson wrote *Treasure Island* around a map that has become one of the most famous images in literature. (The original manuscript map of Treasure Island was lost on its passage to Cassells, Stevenson's publisher, but Stevenson, through the help of John Bartholomew of the map-making firm, ensured another was substituted.) His narrative would have been much diminished without this map (fig. 12.9). Stevenson relied upon maps as elements of his narrative in other books too (fig. 12.10).

Maps work, in popular literature and in other ways, because they are powerful prompts to our imaginative geographies. Another great Scottish 'teller of tales', John Buchan, refers frequently to maps in his fictional works and several – for example, *The Island of Sheep, The Three Hostages, The Courts of the Morning* and *Prester John* – include maps, part-imaginative and part-'real' geography, as illustrations. In his final novel, *Sick Heart River,* Buchan describes the principal character, the lawyer Sir Edward Leithen, as having 'a passion for studying maps', something that almost certainly reflected Buchan's own fondness. In another of his novels, *A Prince of the Captivity,* Buchan, in describing one of the principal characters,

287

FIGURE 12.9 Maps are not necessarily confined to portraying the real world: they may also be a creation of the imagination, though that imagination may consciously or subconsciously have been influenced by a place or places in the real world. Such maps have a long history, including the famous examples of Lilliput and Utopia. But, in the case of Treasure Island, people in Shetland have argued that the outline of Treasure Island may not be a feat of complete imagination on the part of the author as it has a resemblance in outline to that of the real island of Unst. Such unconscious absorption of reality into the imagination may have occurred as a result of the young Robert Louis Stevenson accompanying his father in 1869 on a visit to the most northerly lighthouse in Scotland, Muckle Flugga (1857), off Unst's northern coast. Stevenson is known to have been fascinated by maps, and in his novel he describes the finding of the map of Treasure Island: 'The doctor opened the seals with great care, and there fell out the map of an island, with latitude and longitude, soundings, names of hills, and bays and inlets, and every particular that would be needed to bring a ship to a safe anchorage upon its shores.'

Source: Robert Louis Stevenson, *Treasure Island* (1883). Reproduced by permission of the Trustees of the National Library of Scotland.

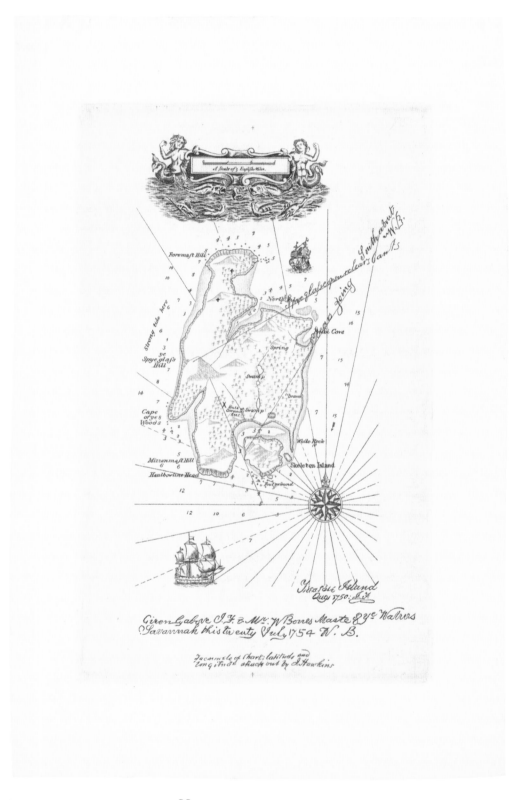

Adam Melfort, wrote, 'He had always had a passion for geography, and now, by much reading and poring over maps, he acquired an extensive book-knowledge of many countries.' Writers such as Buchan, Sir Walter Scott (for the Borders), Neil Gunn for the western Highlands, Lewis Grassic Gibbon for the Mearns, John Galt for Ayrshire, and many others past and present, succeed because they transmit a distinctly geographical 'feel' for landscape – allowing readers to place the narrative and to map scenes in their heads.

Novelists are not alone in this. 'Poets make the best topographers': Hoskins's claim in his *The Making of the English Landscape* has its parallels in Scotland's poetic cartography. The Dundonian poet W. N. Herbert who uses both Scots and English to present a view of Scotland as a land of contrasts begins his 'Mappamundi' with the line 'Eh've wurkt oot a poetic map of the warld'. Like the medieval mappamundi to which it refers, 'Scoatlan' hardly figures, featuring only with 'ither bits in Britain' (see fig. 2.2). In his 'Maps', Norman MacCaig wonderfully captures the power of the map's symbolic language, its unnerving graphic compression of the world: 'Planning a journey / is always a bit frightening – / all those contour lines on the hills: / that blue wriggle meaning a stream: / a small dot that turns out to be a city'. Sorley MacLean's Gaelic poetry evokes a sense of place, a looking back and a longing for landscapes long gone (see figs. 7.11, 7.13). Artists, too, can capture Scotland's topography in a striking map-like fashion (fig. 12.11); Gillies's Highland scene employs a 'bird's-eye' perspective and a colourful chorographic style which echoes Pont's work and other map styles from the sixteenth century (see chapters 2 and 3).

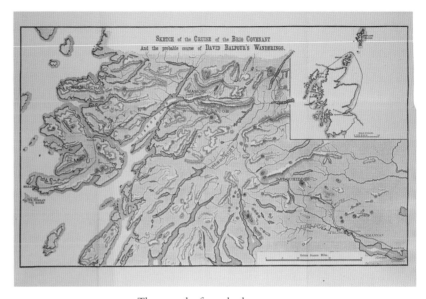

FIGURE 12.10 There can be few who have not read *Kidnapped*, Stevenson's rousing tale of David Balfour and Alan Breck, and followed every inch of David's journeyings. Yet many will have needed to consult a map to trace the supposed route of the brig *Covenant* and, subsequent to David's arrival on Erraid, wished to work out his likely path from Appin and through the wilds of Rannoch Moor on his tortuous way back to Edinburgh. Stevenson's publisher provided this route map to allow readers to identify more closely with the tale. *Source:* Robert Louis Stevenson, *Sketch of the Cruise of the Brig Covenant and the Probable Course of David Balfour's Wanderings* (1886). Reproduced by permission of the Trustees of the National Library of Scotland.

FIGURE 12.11 Art as map, map as art: this painting in 1937 of the small west Highland settlement of Achgarve, by the distinguished Scottish artist Sir William George Gillies, has all the qualities and visual impact of a map: there are parallels with estate mapping (see figs. 6.7, 7.12, 7.14) and, in the stylised picturing of the houses, with the chorographic style of Timothy Pont (see fig. 3.7).
Source: Sir William Gillies, *Achgarve* [Ross & Cromarty Division, Highland Region] (1937). Copyright © Royal Scottish Academy. Collection of Perth Museum and Art Gallery, Perth and Kinross Council, Scotland.

MAP MARKETING

With the swift technological advances in printing and the use of colour, maps were used extensively in popular culture from the late nineteenth century as marketing devices, even as symbols to stand for the nation as a whole (fig. 12.12). The map thus often stands for a thing beyond itself; it is more than the map. In Scotland maps feature on the labels of foods, on wine and whisky bottle labels and whisky packaging (fig. 12.13), and even on domestic items such as tablecloths, tea towels, paper napkins, plates and mugs. Ephemeral products – 'carte-facts' – though they are, they nonetheless form part of the social history of Scotland and can reveal changing trends and fashions in the use of maps for marketing and design purposes. The maps themselves may have been converted or adapted from a 'real' map or may be new creations by a designer specifically to suit the style, shape or content of the product to encourage its sale (fig. 12.14). Maps appeared as illustrations in books published in Scotland from the later sixteenth century, and in far greater numbers in later periods; they also feature on dust jackets, their basic function to complement, sometimes to sum up in graphic form, some of the descriptive topographical content of the book or to put the narrative into geographical context by tying it to a locality (figs. 12.15 and 12.16). Similarly, maps featured in stationery such as greetings cards, either as a miniaturised reproduction of an original earlier map or as the product of a designer's imagination. Maps on television and in the newspapers are familiar objects: but they are often highly selective, where the message is presented in the form of a map or map-like graphic but where cartographic conventions have been deliberately omitted in order to make a point.

There are, indeed, few areas where maps do not now feature in popular culture. Even in the past, maps had an important but never singular role in Scottish public consciousness. We cannot doubt that the twenty-first century has seen the greatest impact of maps on the public at large and that this is directly attributable to the electronic revolution. This modern ubiquity and the popular currency of electronic maps is but the latest chapter in the long history of maps in and of Scotland and would be a thing of wonder to map-using Scots and others in the past.

FIGURE 12.12 *Overleaf.* The idea of a recognisable map outline of a country or territory being altered to incorporate within it representation of a human form has a long history back to the sixteenth century. In this humorous mid nineteenth-century example, intended by the author (sheltering under the pseudonym of Aleph) to make geography – and maps – a more attractive and amusing educational subject for schoolchildren, he depicts Scotland as a piper. Attractively kitted out in kilt and jazzy checked socks, the piper also sports a wind-blown sporran against a background of red deer (shown geographically rather out of place!). Aleph also added a witty four-line jingle under the map. This is one of twelve maps published in the volume, all of which represent a country in Europe. *Source:* Aleph (William Harvey), Cartoon map of Scotland as a piper (1869). Reproduced by permission of the Trustees of the National Library of Scotland.

SCOTLAND.

A gallant piper, struggling through the bogs,
His wind bag broken, wearing his clay clogs;

Yet, strong of heart, a fitting emblem makes
For Scotland—land of heroes and of cakes.

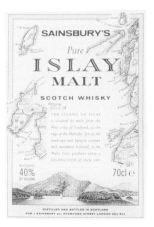

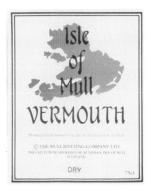

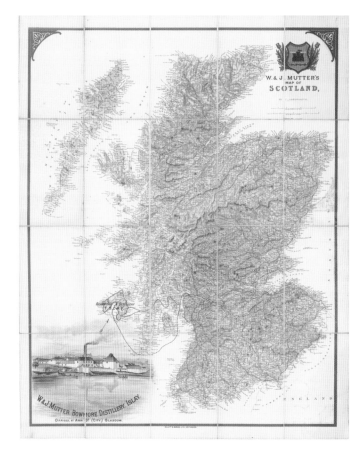

FIGURE 12.13 *Left*. Walking round a supermarket inspecting labels on foods and beverages often yields a few examples of maps being used in some form as packaging, for instance as whisky, cheese or wine labels. Their message is usually to stress the geographical context of the product and to catch the passing eye with the hope of increasing sales.
Source: National Library of Scotland, Scottish examples of whisky, beer, wine and vermouth labels incorporating maps (1991). Reproduced by permission of Margaret Wilkes.

FIGURE 12.14 *Above*. William and James Mutter, and later their sons, owned the Bowmore Distillery on Islay between 1837 and 1892. Using a base map produced by John Arrowsmith, they drew maximum attention to their product by commissioning their own map of Scotland to tie their product to its geographical location. In one corner of the map was placed an attractive view of their distillery. The Mutters, who were Glasgow merchants, greatly improved and expanded the distillery, shipping their product to the Glasgow warehouses in their own boat. Their entrepreneurial skills significantly raised the profile of Bowmore as a single malt whisky. It was truly put on the map.
Source: John Arrowsmith, *W. & J. Mutter's Map of Scotland* [1875?]. Reproduced by permission of the Trustees of the National Library of Scotland.

293

CENTRAL SCOTLAND

FIGURE 12.15 *Left.* After training under the distinguished Austrian panorama artist Professor Heinrich Berann, Dr Michael Wood of the University of Aberdeen compiled this panorama of central Scotland for the then Central Regional Council local authority. Its principal aim was to lure tourists to visit the region and on the verso of the map a printed text gives the principal tourist attractions, together with town plans of Stirling, Falkirk and Alloa. More recently this panorama has been re-published by Harvey Maps of Doune. The representation of a part of the Scottish central belt backed by the Highlands of Scotland, all viewed from a point south and above the Forth–Clyde corridor, presented a major cartographic challenge, not least in effecting an acceptable level of generalisation, shaping the complex topography to make the panorama credible to the viewer, and in gauging what the viewer's eye would accept in terms of the necessary degree of distortion.
Source: M. Wood / Clyde Surveys, *Central Scotland* (1982). Reproduced by permission of Dr Mike Wood.

FIGURE 12.16 *Above.* A book's dust jacket may attract or turn away potential purchasers, so its design is of considerable consequence to the book's saleability. Where a dust jacket features a map, this may be based on an original period map but include deliberate manipulation of that image for reasons of design or to provide historical accuracy. A good example of such manipulation is the cover of *The Unicorn Hunt*, a volume in the Edinburgh-based historical novelist Dorothy Dunnett's (1923–2001) eight-volume Niccolo saga set in the mid- to late fifteenth century. Lady Dunnett sought a contemporary fifteenth-century map of Edinburgh for the dust jacket: but no such plan survives. The earliest plan incorporating sufficient detail for her purpose was produced a century later around 1583 by Georg Braun and Franz Hogenberg and included in their *Civitates Orbis Terrarum* (see fig. 2.8). Four hundred years later, Lady Dunnett's designer therefore altered the costumes of the people in the foreground and the buildings in the town to the author's requirement so that they conformed to those of a century earlier.
Source: Dorthy Dunnett / Nicky Palin, Dust jacket for *The Unicorn Hunt*, based on Braun and Hogenberg's, *Edenburgum, Scotiae Metropolis* of 1583 (1993). Reproduced by permission of Penguin Books Ltd.

CHAPTER 13

MAPS AT WORK – WORKING WITH MAPS

Scotland is indefinable; it has no unity except upon the map.

ROBERT LOUIS STEVENSON

Scotland's mapped unity has been the work of Scots and non-Scots, of enterprising individuals working to different purpose and of institutions working to render the nation in standard cartographic ways. We have shown how Scotland's place on the map – how and why it came to be mapped in the ways it has been – echoes the experiences of other countries and must always be understood in relation to this wider context. This book has shown how Scotland has moved from a position of mapped marginality in early and medieval maps, and from being the subject of foreign map-makers, to a position in which, by the late sixteenth century, it was centrally placed on the map and had become the object of mapping by Scottish map-makers keen to know their nation – and to show their nation – by means of cartography. Scotland's slow move to unity on the map has involved different processes of map-making, and has produced a range of map types, but it has always been part of European and wider political and intellectual trends and of a concern to see maps as documents of national self-definition.

The connection between maps, mapping and those feelings of identity associated with this national shape – the powerful conjunction of that idea of 'Scotlandness' with the idea of 'mapness' – is a strong one. In an important sense, Scotland's unity, the geographical image that is held of the historical nation, is not something simply revealed by maps. It is, rather, the result of maps and of mapping processes which, as well as reflecting the 'real' geography and shape of the country, have powerfully determined the public's map consciousness of Scotland as a nation and as a national space. Scotland has a distinguished map history, the essential features of which we have illuminated and explained in this book. What we have also suggested is that the country's maps have acted to produce a distinctive form to Scotland at certain moments and in certain ways. Maps help shape nations – they produce and reinforce national identity and unity – just as much as nations make maps.

For many people today, of course, Scots and others, the idea of the nation and of national space as defined by the map is taken for granted: what can you trust if you cannot trust the map to be accurate and up-to-date, to depict the shape of a country, the location of places, the heights of hills, the routes of railways, and so on? And, today, many people's experience of maps is perhaps less with national dimensions and certainly much less with paper documents (which, as J. M. Barrie found, won't easily fold up 'convenient for the pocket' in any case) than it is with electronic maps for a specific purpose. Electronic maps of a city's streets or as route planners are easy to access, can be easily updated and don't have to fold up. The dimensions of the nation are not important in finding your way in a city or from one place to another. Maps serve and have served different purposes, and come in different forms to suit these needs. Scotland's maps, and its cultures of map using, have likewise evolved: away from private printed documents made and read by a few to an everyday utility managed on behalf of a mass public which, if it is not familiar in every detail with the making of maps and with the language of maps, is certainly aware of the commonplace nature of maps.

Scotland's map history spans two millennia and more. Its current dimensions are more diverse than in the past and its future features can only be guessed at. We have shown here how questions such as 'What is a map?', 'What does a map do?' 'How does a map work, and for whom?' have little meaning without reference to specific periods, types of map, their purposes and to social context. The history of the map in and of Scotland is a history of the processes of mapping and of map use, of the historical place of maps as social documents – whether they were printed and read in daily newspapers, used in court rooms or at sea, to teach stitching or to aid the unsighted. Scotland's map history is at once a combined history of map-making, of differences in map type and of the different purposes and uses for maps.

MODERNITY, TECHNOLOGY AND MAP HISTORY

Maps symbolise our world. Maps symbolise Scotland (figs. 1.5 and 12.12 for instance). With maps, we can hold bits of geographical space in our hands, pictures of Scotland or elsewhere. Today, the attractiveness of being able to click on a mouse pad or press on a button to instant effect with the ability to use electronic devices for access to information in graphic form is transforming our map consciousness. The attraction of being able to interact with large amounts of electronic data, to download and tailor it for one use or another, has brought about a modern revolution in how the map and the information contained in it is viewed, adopted and adapted. Technical advances have also aided research into maps and map history. The ability to zoom in closely to the map image and to see detail previously not noticed has added a new dimension to the study and the attraction of maps, amongst scholars and the general public.

For these reasons, the history of the map in Scotland and the history of mapping more generally is in one sense a history of technical achievement. It is, after all, a considerable skill to be able to reduce the world or any part of it to a piece of paper or computer screen and for the lines and symbols to be made to stand for nature's complexity in ways that different audiences can comprehend. But we must be wary of reading history backwards and of seeing this technical history as an inevitable narrative of progress. There have been, of course, several other such revolutions in the past: the shift from manuscript maps to printed maps, from copper-plate engraving to lithography, from lithography to digital printing, from paper printing at all to interactive electronic maps. Map history must also be seen from the point of view of the time, not judged from later perspectives.

In almost every case we have illustrated here, what was being dealt with was 'modern' when understood in its own time. There was nothing inevitable about the changes over time: developments occurred because earlier maps and map-makers were found wanting, their claims to accuracy false. New or later maps were not necessarily better maps. Not all maps had the same end in view. For Pont's maps as Robert and James Gordon and Joan Blaeu put a manuscript Scotland to printed form in the 1640s and 1650s; for John Adair as he worked around the coasts in the 1680s; for William Roy and his military surveyors; for Murdoch Mackenzie in the 1740s; for the staff of Ordnance Survey from the 1840s; or for Sir John Murray in the 1890s, the story is the same: what they were doing was modern mapping, mapping in and of their age and for the future. They were doing this because maps were not just useful things, they were different yet vital things – used in navigation, for trade, in representing scientific processes, for getting from A to B, for charting the depth of the sea, for mapping the shape and the contents of cities, for representing scientific patterns or in addressing contemporary social problems, and so on.

Map history can be read as a narrative over time – and there is no doubt that the shape and unity of Scotland as a nation has changed, that it became 'modern' between Ptolemy's outline of two millennia ago (a pre-Scotland 'Scotlandness') and, say, the image derived from satellite imagery (cf. figs. 2.1 and 1.1). But Scotland's map history, we have argued, is also a history of how maps and mapping should be understood in the past, in the context of their making, in relation to different ideas of utility and different experiences of technical change and other notions of 'modernity'.

The 'gap' between the map and the real world – the lack of complete correspondence which results from things being left out and other things being drawn in ways which distort the reality – is thus a conceptual and a technical matter and it is a matter of time. In earlier periods, the time delay in map information reaching its audience related mainly to the time required for the necessary editorial and technical stages to be effected. Pont's maps took years in the making, for example, and decades to be printed, and, even when they were printed, there was no English language edition of the result. The results of Roy's Military Survey were brought together quite quickly, but because it was held in the King's collection in London, hardly anyone knew of the work until Arrowsmith unearthed it and used it as the basis for his 'modern' map of 1807. Individual estate maps and county maps were produced more quickly: they had to be to be useful in settling property disputes and so on.

Unless drawn by hand and not intended for publication, maps were always subject to the constraints imposed by the artefacts and machinery available at the time of their production. The production and dissemination of maps, plans and charts in Scotland – everything that is embraced by the phrase 'working with maps' – was restricted by the time it took to draw the lines, etch the metal, colour the sheets, fold them, trim them and get them to market. We know more about this for later periods than for earlier centuries (see figs. 13.1–13.4), but the point still holds for the whole of Scotland's map history. This in turn has affected the dissemination of the map and, thus, its place and use in society. The more streamlined and sophisticated the production stages, the faster and greater the output of maps and map-related publications as well as the lower their costs to the public.

In this refined sense, different technologies act at different speeds to close the gap between the moment

FIGURE 13.1 Alexander Knox at Bartholomews in the 1950s, carrying out corrections on a copper plate. Copper-plate engraving was the standard method of reproducing multiple copies of maps, particularly from the sixteenth to the twentieth centuries. The process involved creating a map image in reverse, using sharp implements to scratch lines in the soft copper, then rolling the inked plate through a printing press. Even as newer printing methods, such as lithography, overtook it in importance during the nineteenth century, copper-plate engraving continued to be used in conjunction with lithography, especially for producing the highest-quality results with line work and text. Bartholomews' last copper-plate engraver, David Webster, retired in 1977.
Source: Bartholomew Drawing Office. Copyright © published with permission of HarperCollins Publishers.

FIGURE 13.2 Bobby Morrison at Bartholomews in the 1950s, preparing a deep-etch printing plate, used for lithographic printing. Lithography was based on the chemical separation of oil and water, whereby an image drawn in wax or other oily substance on a prepared flat surface attracted ink which was then transferred onto the printed paper sheet. Limestone was originally used from the early nineteenth century, later supplanted by zinc, glass plates, and plastic film from the 1950s. Lithography allowed much cheaper methods of reproducing maps in colour, although the most colourful, high-quality maps required considerable expertise and time to do well, with multiple tints and printing pulls, as well as very accurate registration of these pulls, to achieve the composite result.
Source: Bartholomew Printing Room. Copyright © published with permission of HarperCollins Publishers.

the map is begun or brought to print and the time of the action or state of a place which the map seeks to capture and illustrate. The story of Scotland's mapping from a technical point of view may be seen as one of multiple episodes of shift involving different technologies: manuscript to print (Pont to Blaeu); the organised use of instruments in the field (by Mackenzie in the Orkneys, Charles Hutton on Schiehallion, John Ainslie in county

FIGURE 13.3 The division of cartographic labour was often highly segregated along gender lines. At Bartholomews, the Drawing Office was very much an all-male preserve until the 1970s. This photograph from the 1950s shows, from the right: Derek Wilson, Tommy Cameron, Jack Milligan, Jimmy Galloway, David Webster, Alec Coventry, Alex Elder, and Willie Kerr or David Knowles.
Source: Bartholomew Drawing Room. Copyright © published with permission of HarperCollins Publishers.

FIGURE 13.4 This photograph of the Bartholomew Mounting Room or Bindery in the 1950s shows 'girls' (as they were always referred to) in practical work, including fixing covers. From the earliest records relating to staff and wages in the Bartholomew Archive from the 1880s, it is clear that women were allotted relatively menial and lower-paid functions, including colouring, folding and mounting, a position that remained unaltered until after the 1970s.
Source: Bartholomew, Mounting Room. Copyright © published with permission of HarperCollins Publishers.

mapping, Ordnance Survey staff throughout the later nineteenth century); developments in printing (Thomson's use of lithography); developments in colouring (military maps in the 1740s, Bartholomew's use of tinting in 1919); and the digital production of atlases in 1999, to highlight only a few. Scotland's map history is a story of different rates of change and a history of different technologies, not a straightforward chronology of betterment.

MAP HISTORY AND MAP USE

Scotland's maps, for all their variety, were always produced for a purpose. For Timothy Pont, Robert Sibbald and John Adair, Murdoch Mackenzie and William Roy, albeit at different times, mapping was about national self-knowledge. The maps they produced were not mass produced. There was then no map-buying public in terms we would recognise today. Their maps, together with other work in the seventeenth century (see fig. 1.2), and much more then than for later mapping projects, were influential in bringing unity to the shape of Scotland. Scotland's islands were not finally put accurately on the map until the nineteenth century. By that time, there was a map-buying public, and different sectors in society had different sorts of maps to hand: those in schools and universities, for example; the blind (see figs. 10.9, 12.8); games-playing children; sailors; tourists. For Pont, and perhaps for some of his later map-making counterparts, the ubiquity of maps in twenty-first century Scotland and their utility – to say nothing of their electronic production – would be baffling.

That is why, just as we have shown that map history is not a simple record of technical achievement and that notions of 'modernity' and 'accuracy' must always be used with reference to context, we urge caution in using terms like 'audience' and map 'users'. It is inappropriate to think of a strict 'readership' or audience for Pont's manuscript maps, although we can certainly do so for his printed maps in Blaeu's *Atlas Novus*. There were several users of Blaeu's works: Edinburgh students who were chastised by the university librarian for damaging the maps of Scotland in a copy of the atlas; diplomats who were given copies of Blaeu's work; other intending map-makers (such as Sir Robert Sibbald), keen to use others' maps

and claims about their inaccuracy and lack of utility as a basis for their own intellectual and material advance (see chapter 3). We have seen maps in specific contexts of use, actual and intended: in court and for royal scrutiny, for example, as monarchs surveyed their nation (see fig. 2.11); in wars as others surveyed that nation (figs. 4.1 and 4.16); in the aftermath of battle as symbolic representations of broken dreams (fig. 4.12); for ship's captains as they charted unknown waters (fig. 8.17); even for children as they learnt the shape and unity of the nation piece by piece (fig. 12.7). Such variety of usage points to the complexity of Scotland's map history and to the centrality of the map as a form of print culture in Scotland's cultural and social history.

We cannot really speak, then, of a map-using and map-reading Scottish public until, perhaps, the last years of the eighteenth century and, with more certainty and also a greater degree of specialisation of use within that public, from the second quarter of the nineteenth century. There were, of course, map users and map buyers before then. People were map minded: the Scottish Parliament from the 1680s and the Royal Society from the 1660s amongst them. Maps were present in newspapers from the 1740s. The growth in the number of estate maps from the 1760s, the fact that maps and atlases were advertised by subscription – recall that Murdoch Mackenzie sought public funding for his project via newspapers and that John Thomson went public in order to raise funds for his *Atlas* – indicate a map mindedness in the public, an awareness of maps as having functions and cultural value beyond their specialist purpose. There would not have been general public audiences for the maps of Ordnance Survey or of the Admiralty's work through its Hydrographic Department until later in the nineteenth century. By then, and throughout the twentieth century, the variety of maps available — for tourists, travellers, scientists and others — points to a culture of map use that is familiar to us today but which would have been alien to John Adair, or even to John Ainslie and John Thomson.

As audiences and users became variously specialised, so did maps. Thematic maps appear in numbers in Scotland — as elsewhere — from the 1830s and 1840s as illustrations of selected natural and social phenomena. Maps for school and in education appear in numbers from the later nineteenth century, in response to the work of the Royal Scottish Geographical Society, the activities of leading firms such as Bartholomew and W. & A. K. Johnston and the emergence of specialisation in science. Maps became the hallmark of certain subjects — geography, geology, botany to name a few — because these subjects were concerned with questions of distribution and location. But, for all their use in these specialist subjects, and their use by the temperance movement in the nineteenth century (fig. 5.15), the police (fig. 5.16), or by twenty-first-century soil scientists (fig. 10.18), maps do not themselves explicitly reveal the dynamic processes behind the patterns they disclose.

Scotland has no history and no geography without the map. Scotland does not exist in the mind — at least, not in any powerful sense of 'Scotlandness' — without the map. Before the mid-sixteenth century and in terms of maps used to illustrate particular conceptions of the world and of Mediterranean Europe as the then centre of the world, Scotland hardly figures at all. In terms of the use of maps for state purposes, for knowing the bounds and contents of the nation, Scotland was at the heart of such developments, certainly as they were employed in Europe, from the late sixteenth century, definitively so from 1654. By the seventeenth century, Scotland was one of the best-mapped countries in the world. In the Enlightenment and since then, Scotland has been put to order in the map: bounded on paper, mass produced, its dimensions increasingly well known, and well known to an increasingly large number of people. Making Scotland the nation has long been, and it has differently been, the work of maps, mapping and map-makers.

GUIDE TO FURTHER READING

CHAPTER I

More detailed general guides to Scotland's maps and map history come chiefly as bibliographical listings (each giving different amounts of discussion as to map content, context and particular map-makers). The fullest bibliographical record remains D. G. Moir (ed.), *The Early Maps of Scotland to 1850*, 2 volumes (Edinburgh: Royal Scottish Geographical Society, 1973 and 1983). Also useful is J. N. Moore, *The Historical Cartography of Scotland* (O'Dell Memorial Monograph No. 24: Aberdeen: University of Aberdeen, Department of Geography, 1991). I. H. Adams, *Descriptive Lists of Plans* [in the Scottish Record Office] 2 volumes (Edinburgh: HMSO, 1966–70) has still useful introductions to the nature and range of Scotland's estate mapping. A third volume appeared in 1970 and a fourth volume, by Ian H. Adams and Loretta Timperley, was published in 1988 by the then Scottish Record Office. The essays in M. Wood (ed.), *Cartography – The Way Ahead* (Norwich: Geo Books, 1987) were given as papers to a joint meeting in 1985 of the Royal Scottish Geographical Society and the British Cartographic Society and cover numerous facets of the cartography of Scotland, in historical and in thematic context. For other summary guides to Scotland's map history, see J. Stone, 'Maps and map-making', in M. Lynch (ed.), *The Oxford Companion to Scottish History* (Oxford: Oxford University Press, 2001), 405–7; and M. Wilkes, *The Scot and his Maps* (Motherwell: Scottish Library Association, 1991). Relevant work on particular items and periods is incorporated into the reading guides that follow with respect to individual chapters.

There is, in marked contrast, a much greater range and volume of material for the history of cartography as a whole. Summary histories of changing ideas of map history are provided by J. B. Harley, 'The map and the development of the history of cartography,' in J. B. Harley and D. Woodward (eds), *The History of Cartography. Volume 1: Cartography in Prehistoric, Ancient and Medieval Europe and the Mediterranean* (Chicago: University of Chicago Press, 1987), 1–42 (one of the best essays on the map as a social and political document), and by M. Edney, 'Cartography without "progress": reinterpreting the nature and historical development of mapmaking,' *Cartographica* 30 (1995), 54–68. The late Brian Harley had a significant impact in re-thinking the history of cartography (although not everyone agreed with his ideas): many of his influential essays are collected together in J. B. Harley, *The New Nature of Maps: Essays in the History of Cartography* (Baltimore: The Johns Hokins University Press, 2001).

The *History of Cartography* project being published by the University of Chicago Press is a multi-volume endeavour and represents perhaps the greatest single venture in the history of maps and mapping: volume 4, on the eighteenth century and the European Enlightenment, is in an advanced state of progress as we write this, and volumes 5 and 6, on the nineteenth century and twentieth century, respectively, are being planned and prepared.

For a recent and accessible book-length study of maps and map history in historical context, see J. R. Akerman and R. W. Karrow Jr (eds), *Maps: Finding Our Place in the World* (Chicago: University of Chicago Press, 2007). The introductory essay, by Bob Karrow, is engaging and informative, particularly in discussing the changing fashions of map history. Denis Cosgrove's essay on 'Mapping meaning', the introduction to his edited volume *Mappings* (London: Reaktion Books, 1999), is also worthwhile. Much less accessible, but rewarding of patient study for those interested in the theories behind map history, is C. Jacob, *The Sovereign Map: Theoretical Approaches throughout History* trans. T. Conley (Chicago: University of Chicago Press, 2006). C. Delano-Smith and R. J. P. Kain, *English Maps A History* (Toronto: University of Toronto Press,

1999) provides a similar, largely thematic treatment of that country's maps to the Scottish focus here.

By far the most important online source for Scotland's maps and map history is the website for the Map Division of the National Library of Scotland: http://maps.nls.uk/. To date, this invaluable electronic resource allows access to over 20,000 high-resolution and 'zoomable' images of Scotland's maps, together with commentary. Reference is made in following chapters to maps and texts relating to the different periods and themes embraced by this book. 'Charting the nation', a web-based resource which brought together over 3,500 images of maps of Scotland and related manuscript material for the period c.1550–c.1740 from a range of different map libraries and other repositories is also useful: http://www.chartingthenation.lib.ad.ac.uk/ Scotlandsplaces is a collaborative web portal, launched in 2009, allowing access to records and images of maps held by the Royal Commission on the Ancient and Historic Monuments of Scotland, the National Records of Scotland and the National Library of Scotland: http://www.scotlandsplaces.gov.uk

CHAPTER 2

For the best overview of the history of mapping in this long period, see the essays in J. B. Harley and D. Woodward (eds), *The History of Cartography. Volume 1: Cartography in Prehistoric, Ancient and Medieval Europe and the Mediterranean* (Chicago: University of Chicago Press, 1987). A useful summary of the principal men and main dates in Scotland's mapping before 1595 is to be found in D. G. Moir (ed.), *The Early Maps of Scotland to 1850*, Volume 1 (Edinburgh: Royal Scottish Geographical Society, 1973), 1–29, although Moir pays scant attention to the wider intellectual context.

On Ptolemy's map of Scotland and its background, see J. T. Tierney, 'Ptolemy's map of Scotland', *Journal of Hellenic Studies* 79 (1959), 132–48. On Lindsay's rutter, see I. H. Adams and G. Fortune (eds), *Alexander Lindsay: A Rutter of the Scottish Seas* (Edinburgh: National Museum of Scotland Monograph Number 44, 1980). Still useful are R. A. Skelton, 'Bishop Leslie's maps of Scotland, 1578', *Imago Mundi* 7 (1950), 103–6; and E. G. R. Taylor, 'French cosmographers and navigators in England and Scotland, 1542–1547', *Scottish Geographical Magazine* 46 (1930), 15–21.

On the connections between mapping, the Military Revolution and the art and practice of statecraft in early modern Europe, see G. Parker, *The Military Revolution 1500–1800: Military Innovation and the Rise of the West* (Cambridge: Cambridge University Press, 1996 edition) and D. Buisseret (ed.), *Monarchs, Ministers and Maps: The Emergence of Cartography as a Tool of Government in Early Modern Europe* (Chicago: University of Chicago Press, 1992). The life and map work of Gerard Mercator has received considerable attention. For an accessible discussion of the development of the Mercator Projection, and later moves away from it as a 'Eurocentric' form of mapping, see M. Monmonier, *Rhumb Lines and Map Wars: A Social History of the Mercator Projection* (Chicago: University of Chicago Press, 2004). Amongst the biographical treatments of Merca-

tor, see N. Crane, *Mercator: The Man who Mapped the Planet* (London: Weidenfeld and Nicolson, 2004) and A. Taylor, *The World of Gerard Mercator: The Mapmaker who Revolutionised Geography* (London: HarperCollins, 2004).

On maps, mapping and historians treating geography as part of Scottish national consciousness, in the late sixteenth century and later, see C. W. J. Withers, *Geography, Science and National Identity: Scotland since 1520* (Cambridge: Cambridge University Press, 2001). For a comparable study of mapping in early modern Britain, see B. Klein, *Maps and the Writing of Space in Early Modern England and Ireland* (Basingstoke: Palgrave, 2001).

CHAPTER 3

Timothy Pont's mapping and the production of the 1654 Blaeu *Atlas Novus* has been the subject of considerable study. The leading modern scholar of Pont's work is Dr Jeffrey Stone, and his findings are available in two accessible books: J. C. Stone, *The Pont Manuscript Maps of Scotland: Sixteenth-Century Origins of a Blaeu Atlas* (Tring: Map Collector Publications, 1989) and J. C. Stone, *Illustrated Maps of Scotland from Blaeu's Atlas Novus of the 17th Century* (London: Studio Editions, 1991). For a more recent chapter, see J. C. Stone, 'The Kingdom of Scotland: cartography in an age of confidence', in D. Woodward (ed.), *The History of Cartography. Volume 3: Cartography in the European Renaissance* (Chicago: University of Chicago Press, 2007), 1684–92.

In 1995, the National Library of Scotland (NLS) initiated 'Project Pont' to mark the 400th anniversary [in 1996] of the only dated Pont map. This five-year research project culminated in an edited volume whose essays discuss Pont's maps and their wider context: I. C. Cunningham (ed.), *The Nation Survey'd: Essays on Late Sixteenth Century Scotland as Depicted by Timothy Pont* (East Linton: Tuckwell Press in association with the National Library of Scotland, 2001). In July 2010, the importance of the Pont maps was further recognised by UNESCO who included them as amongst the first things in the UK 'Memory of the World' Register, a list of documentary items of major historical and cultural significance to the United Kingdom: see http://www.unesco.org/webworld/mdm/

The work of Joan Blaeu has also been the subject of much study. The NLS launched its Blaeu *Atlas* website in 2004 and published the first English-language translation of the Blaeu *Atlas* texts. The site contains a searchable facsimile of the *Atlas* together with indexes of place names and personal names and introductory and biographical essays: http://maps.nls.uk/atlas/blaeu. A set of seven papers marking the 350th anniversary of the publication of the Blaeu *Atlas* appeared under the title 'Look at Scotland and enjoy a feast for the eyes', in the *Scottish Geographical Journal* 121 (2005), 235–320. A printed facsimile edition of the 1654 *Atlas Novus*, with introductory essays, is also available: *The Blaeu Atlas of Scotland* (Edinburgh: Birlinn in association with the National Library of Scotland, 2006).

The role of geography in an emerging Scottish national identity in this period is discussed in M. Lynch, 'A nation born again? Scottish identity in the sixteenth and seventeenth centuries', in D. Broun, R. J. Finlay and M. Lynch (eds), *Image and Identity: The Making and Re-making of Scotland through the Ages* (Edinburgh: John Donald, 1998), 82–104. Chorography, geography and map-making in England is the subject of L. B. Cormack, *Charting an Empire: Geography at the English Universities, 1580–1620* (Chicago: University of Chicago Press, 1997). On John Adair's work and mapping at the end of the seventeenth century, see J. N. Moore, 'Scottish cartography in the later Stuart era, 1660–1714', *Scottish Tradition* 14 (1986–87), 28–44, and J. N. Moore, 'John Adair's contribution to the charting of the Scottish coasts: a re-assessment', *Imago Mundi* 52 (2000), 43–65. On Sibbald and Adair, see C. W. J. Withers, *Geography, Science and National Identity: Scotland since 1520* (Cambridge: Cambridge University Press, 2001), chapter 3.

CHAPTER 4

The Rough Wooing and related events is the subject of M. Merriman, *The Rough Wooings: Mary Queen of Scots, 1542–1551* (East Linton: Tuckwell Press, 2000). On map-making, military engineering and the Military Revolution in this period, see M. Merriman, 'Italian military engineers in Britain in the 1540s', in S. Tyacke (ed.), *English Map-Making, 1550–1650* (London: British Library, 1993), 57–67, and D. Buisseret, *The Mapmakers' Quest: Depicting New Worlds in Renaissance Europe* (Oxford: Oxford University Press, 2003), chapter 5. The connections between military engineers and hydrography (marine mapping) are explored in A. H. W. Robinson, *Marine Cartography in Britain* (Leicester: Leicester University Press, 1962), chapter 5.

The Cromwellian fortifications in Scotland are described in A. A. Tait, 'The Protectorate citadels of Scotland', *Architectural History* 8 (1965), 9–24. The wider military background of this period is discussed in C. Duffy, *Fire & Stone: The Science of Fortress Warfare, 1660–1880* (London: Greenhill, 1996). On the work of Lewis Petit, see C. Fleet, 'Lewis Petit and his plans of Scottish fortifications and towns, 1714–16', *Cartographic Journal* 44 (2007), 329–41. On the Board of Ordnance as a whole in Scotland, see C. J. Anderson, 'State imperatives: military mapping in Scotland, 1689–1770', *Scottish Geographical Journal* 125 (2009), 4–24. The general connections between mapping becoming militarised and the military becoming map minded in the eighteenth century are explored by M. Edney, 'British military education, mapmaking, and military 'map mindedness' in the later Enlightenment', *Cartographic Journal* 31 (1994), 14–20.

The Military Survey of Scotland has been the focus of much study. See, for example, D. G. Moir (ed.), *The Early Maps of Scotland to 1850*, Volume 1 (Edinburgh: Royal Scottish Geographical Society, 1973), 103–13; and R. A. Skelton, 'The Military Survey of Scotland 1747–1755', *Scottish Geographical Magazine* 83 (1967), 5–16. This was reprinted as R. A. Skelton, *The Military Survey of Scotland, 1747–1755* (Edinburgh: Royal Scottish Geographical Society, Special Publication Number 1, 1967). See also G. Whittington and A. J. S. Gibson, *The Military Survey of Scotland*

1747–1755: A Critique Historical Geography Research Series, Number 18 (Norwich: Geo Books, 1986). The best study of William Roy and the Military Survey is provided by Y. O'Donoghue, *William Roy 1726–1790: Pioneer of the Ordnance Survey* (London: British Library, 1977).

Roy's 'Great Map' is available as a facsimile edition: [W. Roy], *The Great Map: The Military Survey of Scotland, 1747–1755*; with introductory essays by Y. Hodson, C. Tabraham and C. W. J. Withers (Edinburgh: Birlinn in association with the National Library of Scotland, 2007). The map is available for consultation electronically via the Map Division of the National Library of Scotland: http://maps.nls.uk/roy/. This link has accompanying essays on the maps, their content, and on William Roy.

The Ordnance Survey as a whole is the subject of R. Hewitt, *Map of a Nation: A Biography of the Ordnance Survey* (London: Granta, 2010) and due credit is given there to Roy's important stimulus to the Survey and to its Enlightenment background. The work of Ordnance Survey in military mapping is discussed in two accessible histories of the Survey: W. A. Seymour, *A History of the Ordnance Survey* (Folkestone: Dawson, 1980) and R. Oliver, *Ordnance Survey Maps: A Concise Guide for Historians*, 2nd edn (London: Charles Close Society, 2005)

The Russian military mapping of other countries is engagingly dealt with by J. Davies, 'Uncle Joe knew where you lived – Part 1', *Sheetlines* 72 (April 2005); Part 2 in *Sheetlines* 73 (August 2005). Part 1 provides an overview of the history and scope of Soviet global mapping. Part 2 contains a detailed examination of the large-scale town plans and their sources of information. In a related piece, D. Watt, 'Soviet military mapping', *Sheetlines* 74 (December 2005), describes the history of the Russian Military Topographic Directorate (VTU) from 1812 to the present day.

CHAPTER 5

There is a huge literature on Scotland's urban history. Not all of it discusses the role of maps and mapping as part of that history. One article which discusses the growth of the town in the early modern period in relation to map evidence is N. P. Brooks and G. Whittington, 'Planning and growth in the medieval Scottish burgh: the example of St Andrews', *Transactions of the Institute of British Geographers* 2 (1977), 278–95. On Pont's urban Scotland, see P. Dennison, 'Timothy Pont's depiction of towns', in I. Cunningham (ed.), *The Nation Survey'd: Timothy Pont's Maps of Scotland* (East Linton: Tuckwell Press in association with the National Library of Scotland, 2001), 125–38.

Few individual cities have been the subject of separate map histories. For Edinburgh, two useful, if now dated, studies are: W. Cowan and H. R. G. Inglis, 'The early views and maps of Edinburgh', *Scottish Geographical Magazine* 35 (1919), 315–30; and a later revision and expansion by W. Cowan, *The Maps of Edinburgh, 1544–1929*, 2nd edn, revised by C. B. Boog Watson (Edinburgh: Edinburgh Public Libraries, 1932). For Glasgow, there is a full study by a modern map historian: J. Moore, *The Maps of Glasgow: A History and Cartobibliography to 1865* (Glasgow:

Glasgow University Library, 1996). For Perth, see J. Duncan, 'The early maps of Perth, 1715 to 1902', *Journal of the Perthshire Society of Natural Science* 18 (2010), 10–54.

The evidence that, in Enlightenment Scotland, urban audiences (including some in smaller towns and villages), were 'map minded', going to lecture classes on geography and map-making, buying maps and using them, and globes, as objects of utility and of domestic display, is discussed in C. W. J. Withers, *Geography, Science and National Identity: Scotland since 1520* (Cambridge: Cambridge University Press, 2001), chapter 4.

For studies of Dundee, Edinburgh and Glasgow which discuss the conditions of the city in the nineteenth century and use maps as part of their narratives, see, respectively, the essays in L. Miskell, C. A. Whatley and B. Harris (eds), *Victorian Dundee: Image and Realities* (East Linton: Tuckwell Press, 2000); R. Rodger, *The Transformation of Edinburgh: Land, Property and Trust in the Nineteenth Century* (Cambridge: Cambridge University Press, 2001); and the essays in W. H. Fraser and I. Maver (eds), *Glasgow, Volume II: 1830–1912* (Manchester: Manchester University Press, 1996).

One useful guide to the study of maps for urban history is provided by D. Smith, *Maps and Plans for the Local Historian and Collector* (London: Batsford, 1988), chapter 15. Many Scottish town plans and maps are available for online study via the Map Division of the National Library of Scotland: see http://maps.nls.uk/towns/ where maps of Scotland's towns and cities in the period 1580–1919 are listed alphabetically by place. There are also separate sections on the Great Reform Act plans (1832) and the Ordnance Survey large-scale town plans 1847–95.

CHAPTER 6

Extensive use has been made of map evidence by many of the geographers and historians studying Scotland's countryside. For one study illustrating the work of land surveyors in the eighteenth century, see I. H. Adams (ed.), *Papers on Peter May, Land Surveyor, 1749–1793* (Edinburgh: Constable for the Scottish History Society, 1979). On the maps of the Forfeited Annexed Estates, see V. Wills (ed.), *Reports on the Annexed Estates, 1755–1769* (Edinburgh: HMSO, 1973). John Thomson's *Atlas of Scotland* (1832) is available in a facsimile edition: [John Thomson], *The Atlas of Scotland: Containing Maps of Each County*, with Introductory Essays by C. W. J. Withers, C. Fleet and P. Williams (Edinburgh: Birlinn in association with the National Library of Scotland, 2008). The Assynt Survey in the 1770s is the subject of R. A. Adam (ed.), *John Home's Survey of Assynt* (Edinburgh: Constable for the Scottish History Society, 1960).

Modern studies which either make much use of map evidence, or explain the transformation of the countryside in more detail than is possible here, include T. M. Devine, *Clearance and Improvement: Land, Power and People in Scotland, 1700–1900* (Edinburgh: John Donald, 2006); E. Richards, *The Highland Clearances: People, Landlords and Rural Turmoil* (Edinburgh: Birlinn, 2008); R. Gibson, *The Scottish Countryside: Its Chang-*

ing Face, 1700–2000 (Edinburgh: John Donald in association with the National Archives of Scotland, 2007). Gibson's book is especially good on the map evidence, drawing as it does on the many estate plans and maps held by the National Records of Scotland. For a guide to the topographical, engineering and architectural plans held by the NRS (its 'Register House Plans'), go to http://www.nas.gov.uk/guides/plans.asp

The seventeenth-century quote on improvement is taken from I. Whyte, *Agriculture and Society in Seventeenth Century Scotland* (Edinburgh: John Donald, 1979), still the best study of 'pre-Improvement' Scottish rural society. On eighteenth-century improvement and mapping in Scotland, see C. W. J. Withers, 'Situating practical reason: geography, geometry and mapping in the Scottish Enlightenment', in C. W. J. Withers and P. Wood (eds), *Science and Medicine in the Scottish Enlightenment* (East Linton: Tuckwell Press, 2000), 54–78. On pre- and post-improvement Highland landscapes and surveying, see N. Wilkins (ed.), *Alexander Nimmo's Inverness Survey and Journal, 1806* (Dublin: Royal Irish Academy, 2011).

A valuable source for identifying who was at work as a land surveyor before the mid nineteenth century is S. Bendall (ed.), *Dictionary of Land Surveyors and Local Map-Makers of Great Britain and Ireland, 1530–1850*, 2nd edn (London: British Library, 1997). For a guide on estate maps in local history, see D. Smith, *Maps and Plans for the Local Historian and Collector* (London: Batsford, 1988), chapter 4.

On the 1930s Land Utilisation Survey, see L. D. Stamp (ed.), *The Land of Britain: The Report of the Land Utilisation Survey of Britain* (London: HMSO, 1937). The work of maps in Historic Land-Use Assessment in Scotland is discussed in L. Dyson-Bruce, P. Dixon, R. Hingley and J. Stevenson, *Historic Land-Use Assessment (HLA): Development and Potential of a Technique for Assessing Historic Land-Use Patterns* (Edinburgh: Historic Scotland, 1999). In addition to the National Library of Scotland and the National Records of Scotland, the Royal Commission on the Ancient and Historical Monuments for Scotland has a large holding of digital mapping: http://www.rcahms.gov.uk/map-collection.html

CHAPTER 7

The discussion of Pont's manuscript maps of South Uist is taken from J. C. Stone, 'Timothy Pont', in F. MacLeod (ed.), *Togail Tir Marking Time: The Map of the Western Isles* (Stornoway: Acair and An Lanntair Gallery, 1989), 13–22. This volume offers several essays on the mapping of the Western Isles between Pont's work and the mid nineteenth century. D. Rixson, *The Hebridean Traveller* (Edinburgh: Birlinn, 2004) discusses early maps and map-makers of the Western Isles before 1700. M. Harman, *An Isle called Hirte: History and Culture of the St Kildans to 1930* (Waternish: Maclean Press, 1997) discusses the early mapping of St Kilda (pages 18–37) with a detailed cartobibliography. For Orkney, J. Chester, *A History of Orkney Maps* (http://www.ronaldsay.plus.com/orkneymaps/index.htm) describes the mapping of Orkney from the mid sixteenth to the late nineteenth centuries, along with a cartometric analysis of the maps and their provenance. J. Irvine, *The Orkneys and Schetland in Blaeu's Atlas Novus, 1654* (Ashstead: J. M. Irvine, 2006) reproduces the Blaeu/Pont map, and the translated descriptions of Walter Stewart of Orkney and Shetland, and has useful explanatory footnotes. On Scotland's islands in general, see H. Haswell-Smith, *The Scottish Islands: A Comprehensive Guide to Every Scottish Island* (Edinburgh: Canongate, 2004).

There is a wide range of literature on social transformation and agrarian change on Scotland's islands, as there is for the Highlands and mainland as a whole. In addition to the single volumes by Devine and Richards that are mentioned above with reference to chapter 6, the earlier two-volume work by Eric Richards makes much mention of the clearances from different islands throughout the nineteenth century, especially: E. Richard, *A History of the Highland Clearances: Agrarian Transformation and the Evictions, 1746–1886* (London: Croom Helm, 1982) and *A History of the Highland Clearances: Volume 2, Emigration, Protest, Reasons* (London: Croom Helm, 1985). Two of the examples illustrated here – that of Bald's map of Harris, and the later map of Lewis – are discussed in more detail in J. B. Caird, 'Early 19th century estate plans', in F. Macleod (ed.), *Togail Tir Marking Time: The Map of the Western Isles* (Stornoway: Acair and An Lanntair Gallery, 1989), 49–78.

The connections between John Adair, Martin Martin and the Royal Society's interests in mapping the Hebrides are discussed in C. W. J. Withers, 'Reporting, mapping, trusting: practices of geographical knowledge in the late seventeenth century', *Isis* 90 (1999), 497–521. Martin Martin's *St Kilda* book of 1698 and his *Description* (1703) are both available in modern reprints with introductions: Martin Martin, *A Description of the Western Islands of Scotland, c.1695 – A Voyage to St Kilda* (Edinburgh: Birlinn, 1999).

Like St Kilda, the range of work on Rockall's history belies its small size. We have taken our discussion of its mapping, including the words of Captain Hall, from the following accounts: M. Christie, 'Rockall', *Scottish Geographical Magazine* 14 (1898), 393–415; G. S. Holland and R. A. Gardiner, 'The first map of Rockall', *Geographical Journal* 141 (1975), 94–8; and F. MacDonald, 'The last outpost of Empire: Rockall and the Cold War', *Journal of Historical Geography* 32 (2006), 627–47.

CHAPTER 8

A summary history of maritime surveying in Britain is offered by C. Terrell and H. Wallis, 'Maritime surveys', in H. Wallis (ed.), *Historians' Guide to Early British Maps* (London: Royal Historical Society, 1994), 66–9. M. Deacon, *Scientists and the Sea 1650–1900: A Study of Marine Science* (London: Academic Press, 1971) provides a still-useful outline history of that subject but without mention of either Murdoch MacKenzie or Alexander Dalrymple. Marine mapping as a genre of cartography is the subject of A. H. W. Robinson, *Marine Cartography in Britain* (Leicester: Leicester University Press, 1962). The emergence of thematic maps of ocean phenomena, such as currents and tides, is

discussed in A. H. W. Robinson, *Early Thematic Mapping in the History of Cartography* (Chicago: University of Chicago Press, 1982).

For a full discussion of the emergence and development of the portolan chart, see T. Campbell, 'Portolan charts from the late thirteenth century to 1500', in J. B. Harley and D. Woodward (eds), *The History of Cartography. Volume 1: Cartography in Prehistoric, Ancient and Medieval Europe and the Mediterranean* (Chicago: University of Chicago Press, 1987), 371–483.

Alexander Lindsay's Rutter and the Nicholay map of 1583 is discussed in D. Moir (ed.), *The Early Maps of Scotland to 1850*, Volume 1 (Edinburgh: Royal Scottish Geographical Society, 1973), 19–23. Adair's coastal mapping is the subject of J. N. Moore, 'John Adair's contribution to the charting of the Scottish coasts: a re-assessment', *Imago Mundi* 52 (2000), 43–65.

The example of Murdoch Mackenzie is based on D. C. F. Smith, 'The progress of the Orcades Survey, with biographical notes on Murdoch Mackenzie Senior (1712–1797)', *Annals of Science* 44 (1987), 277–88; D. C. F. Webster, 'A cartographic controversy: in defence of Murdoch Mackenzie', in F. Macleod (ed.), *Togail Tir Marking Time: The Map of the Western Isles* (Stornoway: Acair Ltd and An Lanntair Gallery, 1989), 33–42. Mackenzie receives brief attention (Alexander Dalrymple none) in E. J. Graham, *A Maritime History of Scotland 1650–1790* (East Linton: Tuckwell Press, 2002). Although it is outside the Scottish context, Alexander Dalrymple's hydrographic work in the Indian Ocean is a central feature in an engaging study: A. Cook, 'Surveying the seas: establishing the sea routes to the East Indies', in J. R. Akerman (ed.), *Cartographies of Travel and Navigation* (Chicago: University of Chicago Press, 2006), 69–96.

On the Admiralty chart and on the Admiralty's charting work, see G. S. Ritchie, *The Admiralty Chart: British Naval Hydrography in the Nineteenth Century* (Edinburgh: Pentland Press, 1995). A. Day, *The Admiralty Hydrographic Service, 1795–1919* (London: HMSO, 1967) is more focused on the institution within the Admiralty as a whole.

The work of the Bathymetrical Survey is discussed by J. Murray and L. Pullar, *Bathymetrical Survey of the Freshwater Lochs of Scotland*, 6 volumes. (Edinburgh: Challenger Office, 1910). For a much shorter summary, see R. Duck, 'The charting of Scotland's lochs', *Forth Naturalist and Historian* 13 (1990), 25–30; and the brief history and images incorporated in the National Library of Scotland's website: http://maps.nls/uk/bathymetric

CHAPTER 9

The importance of travel maps, and the relative lack of research on their different types despite their prevalence, is the subject of the essays in J. R. Akerman (ed.), *Cartographies of Travel and Navigation* (Chicago: University of Chicago Press, 2006). For Scotland, D. G. Moir (ed.), *The Early Maps of Scotland to 1850*, Volume 2 (Edinburgh: Royal Scottish Geographical Society, 1983) has a series of useful chapters on road maps, military roads and maps, canal plans and railway plans, on pages 27–122, but these are without reference to other work in Scottish history or to more recent work in map history.

John Ogilby's work, on *Britannia* and more widely, is discussed in C. W. J. Withers, *Geography, Science and National Identity: Scotland since 1520* (Cambridge: Cambridge University Press, 2001), 61–7. For a facsimile of the work and a discussion on Ogilby's life and his undertaking of *Britannia*, see J. B. Harley (ed.), *Britannia, London, 1675* (Amsterdam: Theatrum Orbis Terrarum, 1975). For all his importance in Scotland's map-making, John Ainslie still awaits detailed study: for an important beginning, see I. H. Adams, 'John Ainslie, map-maker', Unpublished manuscript in the National Library of Scotland Map Library, 1971 [1973].

The history of roads in Scotland has been documented in a series of studies by A. R. B. Haldane: *The Drove Roads of Scotland* (London: T. Nelson & Sons Ltd, 1952); *Three Centuries of the Scottish Posts* (Edinburgh: Edinburgh University Press, 1971); and *New Ways Through the Glens: Highland Road, Bridge and Canal Makers of the Early Nineteenth Century* (Newton Abbot: David and Charles, 1973). Many of the map-makers and the roads concerned feature in R. Gibson, *The Scottish Countryside: Its Changing Face, 1700–2000* (Edinburgh: John Donald in association with the National Archives of Scotland, 2007), particularly in chapters 13–16. For a regional study of the historical development of travel and communications that is sensitive to map evidence, and to lines of travel never mapped, see O. Silver, *The Roads of Fife* (Edinburgh: John Donald, 1987). The military roads of Scotland are the subject of W. Taylor, *The Military Roads in Scotland* (Newton Abbot: David and Charles, 1976).

A variety of works cover other forms of travel and communication, but do not always pay full and critical attention to map evidence as an historical and geographical source: see, for example, J. Lindsay, *The Canals of Scotland* (Newton Abbot: David & Charles, 1968); L. Paterson, *From Sea to Sea: A History of the Scottish Lowland and Highland Canals* (Glasgow: Neil Wilson Publishing, 2006); P. J. G. Ransom, *Iron Road: The Railway in Scotland* (Edinburgh: Birlinn, 2007); R. W. Munro, *Scottish Lighthouses* (Stornoway: Thule, 1979); T. Nicholson, *Wheels on the Road – Maps of Britain for the Cyclist and Motorist, 1870–1940* (Norwich: Geo Books, 1983).

CHAPTER 10

There is no single volume that covers the thematic mapping of science in Scotland. D. G. Moir (ed.), *The Early Maps of Scotland to 1850*, Volume 2 (Edinburgh: Royal Scottish Geographical Society, 1983) discusses thematic maps, with geological (pages 126–37) and agricultural maps (pages 123–5) the only scientific topics.

There is some attention to thematic maps in science in Part I, 'The history and purpose of Maps', by various authors, in H. Wallis (ed.), *Historians' Guide to Early British Maps* (London: Royal Historical Society, 1994), 1–91. Thematic maps are also the focus of A. H. Robinson, *Early Thematic Mapping in the History of Cartography* (Chicago: University of

Chicago Press, 1992). For an overview of the connections between mapping, moral statistics, statistical graphics and the rise of science, see M. Friendly and G. Palsky, 'Visualizing nature and society', in J. R. Akerman and R. W. Karrow Jr (eds), *Maps: Finding Our Place in the World* (Chicago: University of Chicago Press, 2007), 207–53.

On Ordnance Survey in nineteenth-century Scotland and for something about the 'Battle of the Scales', see the discussion of the first 6 inch to 1 mile series on the National Library of Scotland's website: http://maps.nls.uk/os/6inch/os_info1.html. There is some discussion of botanical and geological mapping in C. W. J. Withers, *Geography, Science and National Identity: Scotland since 1520* (Cambridge: Cambridge University Press, 2001), 211–15 (Murchison's testimony of 1834 is discussed on pages 158–9), and, in the same work, mention is made of the geographical imagination of men like Thomas Chalmers and James Cleland in the context of nineteenth-century urban philanthropy.

The importance of revised map projections is discussed by James Gall in his 'Use of cylindrical projections for geographical, astronomical, and scientific purposes', *Scottish Geographical Magazine* 1 (1885), 119–23. The longer-run history of the Lambert–Gall–Peters projections and the debates about the 'political correctness' of Peters' modification of Gall's work is discussed in M. Monmonier, *Rhumb Lines and Map Wars: A Social History of the Mercator Projection* (Chicago: University of Chicago Press, 2004).

The mapping of the north-west Highlands of Scotland is the subject of D. Oldroyd, *The Highlands Controversy: Constructing Geological Knowledge Through Fieldwork in Nineteenth-Century Britain* (Chicago: University of Chicago Press, 1990). On early plant mapping, see M. Hardy, 'Botanical Survey of Scotland', *Scottish Geographical Magazine* 22 (1906), 229–41.

The valuable work by the Scottish Environmental Protection Agency in development of flood maps and in its use of the Indicative River and Coastal Flood Map in particular may be consulted via http://www.sepa.org.uk/flooding/flood_map.aspx

CHAPTER 11

For all the ubiquity and variety of modern maps dealing in one way or another with the range of recreational and leisure pursuits in Scotland, and with access to the country's open spaces, there is a surprising dearth of scholarly literature on the topic. This is in contrast to the range of literature on the history of tourism, in Scotland and elsewhere, most of which pays little attention to the role of maps and mapping.

In terms of the history of tourism, recreation and leisure in Scotland – and, importantly, their account does give some attention to maps in promoting recreation – we have found useful J. Gold and M. Gold, *Imagining Scotland: Tradition, Representation and Promotion in Scottish Tourism since 1750* (Aldershot: Scolar Press, 1995). The visual development of Scotland as a 'space' which attracted people to explore the countryside is the subject of J. Holloway and L. Errington, *The Discovery of Scotland:*

The Appreciation of Scottish Scenery Through Two Centuries of Painting (Edinburgh: National Galleries of Scotland, 1978). But this otherwise excellent book pays virtually no attention to the role of maps as visual sources in this respect.

The history of the recreational traveller is addressed in T. C. Smout, 'Tours in the Scottish Highlands from the eighteenth to the twentieth centuries', *Northern Scotland* 5 (1983), 99–122 and it is from Smout's still-valuable paper that we note here the four phases in the chronology and type of Scottish recreation and access to its open spaces. On this topic, see also D. McArthur, 'Blasted heaths and hills of mist: the Highlands and Islands through travellers' eyes', *Scottish Affairs* 3 (1993), 23–31. The idea of 'Scotland the brand' is drawn from D. McCrone, A. Morris and R. Keily, *Scotland the Brand: The Making of Scottish Heritage* (Edinburgh: Edinburgh University Press, 1995) but this book missed the opportunity to connect map history to social history.

For a number of websites which show the development of particular firms' cartography for recreation and leisure, see: http://www.harveymaps.co.uk/; http://stirlingsurveys.co.uk/; http://digital.nls.uk/bartholomew; http://www.johnbartholomew.com/; http://www.bartholomewmaps.com/about.asp?pid=305

CHAPTER 12

The place of maps in popular culture and in the public domain is a central focus of the American geographer Mark Monmonier. Although most of his work draws on examples from North America, the points he makes about the popularity of maps, about the ways that maps distort geographical relationships, and, importantly, how the present ubiquity of maps may obscure their history, apply readily to Scotland. See, for example, Mark Monmonier, *How to Lie with Maps* (Chicago: University of Chicago Press, 1991); Mark Monmonier, *From Squaw Tit to Whorehouse Meadow: How Maps Name, Claim and Inflame* (Chicago: University of Chicago Press, 2007); Mark Monmonier, *No Dig, No Fly, No Go: How Maps Restrict and Control* (Chicago: University of Chicago Press, 2010). For an historical perspective on map consumption by the public, and the different forms of maps – in games, as domestic artefacts and so on – see D. Dillon, 'Consuming maps', in J. R. Akerman and R. W. Karrow (eds), *Maps: Finding Our Place in the World* (Chicago: University of Chicago Press, 2007), 289–343. Almost no work has been done on this topic for Scotland's mapping and its different cartographic products and markets.

The opening line of W. N. Herbert's 'Mappamundi' is taken from the poem of that name in D. O'Rourke, *Dream State: The New Scottish Poets* (Edinburgh: Polygon, 1994), 146. The extract from Norman MacCaig's poem 'Maps' is from E. McCaig (ed.), *The Poems of Norman MacCaig* (Edinburgh: Polygon, 2005), 483. For a preliminary attempt to draw connections, with maps, between Scotland's geography, languages and literatures, see C. W. J. Withers, '"The image of the land": Scotland's geography through her languages and literature', *Scottish Geographical Magazine* 100 (1984), 81–95.

In a sense, all maps are works of art (although not all art is cartographic). For an exploration of the map–art relationship in modern context, see K. Harmon (with essays by G. Clemans), *The Map as Art: Contemporary Artists Explore Cartography* (New York: Princeton Architectural Press, 2009).

CHAPTER 13

Almost by definition, there is no work yet available that looks at the future dimensions of Scotland's map history, any more than there is one that provides detailed biographical information for all of Scotland's map-makers in the past. The literature we have cited in relation to the previous chapters provides a thorough and further background to the history we have discussed here. A useful collection of essays, published in 2009 under the title 'Mapping and Meaning' to mark the centenary of The Royal Commission on the Ancient and Historical Monuments of Scotland (RCAHMS), looks at military mapping and battle maps in Scotland, at the mapping of the rural landscape in 1769 and in 2000, at the role of maps in Historic Landscape Assessment in Scotland and, in its final essay by Bruce Gittings, at the current, but rapidly changing, state of modern and digital mapping in Scotland: see *Scottish Geographical Journal* 125 (2009), 1–94. Gittings's essay is 'Reflections on forty years of geographical information in Scotland: standardisation, integration and representation', *Scottish Geographical Journal* 125 (2009), 78–94. The websites of those bodies in Scotland officially charged with holding, managing and publicising the study of maps – the Map Division of the National Library of Scotland, the National Records of Scotland and the Royal Commission on the Ancient and Historical Monuments of Scotland – have been referenced above. Each of these institutions holds many more paper maps and plans than are listed in their online catalogues and digital holdings.

INDEX